C000130276

# Castles in Italy

# Castles in Italy
## The Medieval Life of Noble Families

Text by Clemente Manenti
Photographs by Markus Bollen

With contributions by
Margit Bachfischer, Katrin Boskamp-Priever,
Hartmut Diekmann, Chiara Frugoni, Astrid B. Koberstein-Pes,
Eberhard König and Jochen Staebel

**KÖNEMANN**

# Contents

# Rome and the Church in the Middle Ages

# The Hinterland and the Great Dynasties

# The Coastal Region and the Islands

# Appendix

# Rome and the Church in the Middle Ages

# Castel Sant' Angelo

## Symbol of papal power

Perino del Vaga
(Pietro Bonaccorsi)
*Emperor Hadrian*, 1546/48
Fresco (detail)
Sala Paolina,
Castel Sant'Angelo, Rome

The Roman emperor Hadrian
(117–138 A.D.) himself
designed the mausoleum that
later became the Castel
Sant'Angelo, the scene of
major events in the history of
Rome for many centuries.

Right: A view of the Castel
Sant'Angelo and the Ponte
Sant'Angelo.

The bridge is adorned with
ten figures of angels by the
sculptor Gianlorenzo Bernini
(1598–1680).

Previous page:
A view of the Castel
Sant'Angelo from the Tiber,
also showing the Ponte
Sant'Angelo with
Bernini's sculptures.

### The emperor's mausoleum

The massive round structure that looms over the narrowest stretch of the Tiber is generally known as the Castel Sant'Angelo. Yet originally it was not a fort but the mausoleum of the Roman emperor Hadrian, who designed it himself. His model was the mausoleum of Augustus, built a century and a half earlier barely 200 yards away on the other bank of the river. Hadrian's mausoleum was begun in 123 A.D. and completed in 139, a year after the emperor's death. In accordance with his will, this was also the final resting place of all his imperial successors (up to Caracalla, died 217) and members of the imperial families. To link the mausoleum with the Campus Martius on the other bank of the Tiber, the emperor commissioned a new bridge, called the Pons Aelius. As it is now decorated with ten 17th-century Baroque angel statues by Gianlorenzo Bernini, the bridge is called Ponte degli Angeli (Angels' Bridge) or Ponte Sant'Angelo (Holy Angel's Bridge).

Publius Aelius Hadrianus was the best-educated emperor in the history of ancient Rome. He spoke several languages, had studied in Athens, and spent his life traveling far and wide through all parts of the Empire. Each of his journeys began and finished with a long stay in his preferred home, Athens.

### Square and circle

The mausoleum originally consisted of a square plinth with sides 283 feet (86.3 m) long. On this was set a cylindrical structure 210 feet (64 m) in diameter. An earthen mound planted with cypresses covered this, with a smallish circular or square building on top. The whole structure was covered with ivory-colored marble. At the four corners of

the plinth stood groups of statues, and further figures adorned the circular structure. At the very top was a bronze *quadriga*. The actual crypt of Hadrian was in the center of the mausoleum, linked by a gallery to the entrance on the Tiber side. Above the crypt were three large rooms, one on top of the other, to which a double flight of spiral ramps led. These rooms served as sepulchers for the emperor's successors. The interiors and the vault of the ramps were faced in marble. A perfect ventilation system and a system for collecting rainwater ensured an almost constant temperature and humidity in the interiors. The whole upper structure of the building was destroyed during the Middle Ages, so that we can only surmise at the original design. Moreover, only a few fragments survive of the friezes, decorations and sculptures, as of the statue of the emperor that once adorned the ancient mausoleum.

## Memorial *manqué*

Hadrian's mausoleum, which is unique among the large buildings of ancient Rome, was a focal point of the city's history for 1,500 years. As waves of violence broke successively over the former capital of the world, other monuments collapsed, were swept away or reduced to ruins as their stone was used for

other purposes. Hadrian's monument stood firm, and in due course became the true fortress of Rome. It was predestined for this task because of its central position between the city and the Vatican, the extraordinary robustness of its masonry and, indeed, its very design. Whereas the medieval fortifications and castles suddenly became obsolete with the deployment of long-range firearms, the cylindrical structure of the Castel Sant'Angelo, which by then formed part of the fortifications of the city, stood defiant against the cannonballs. But the mausoleum had another factor in its favor. It was right next to St. Peter's, the original building of which dated to Constantine's time. This proximity is the real reason why the pagan mausoleum became the symbol of the imperial legacy of the Catholic Church and the might of the popes.

Above: A model of the ancient mausoleum Museo della Civiltà Romana, Rome
A cylindrical structure was built on a square plinth, surmounted by an earthen mound planted with cypresses. At the top of the mound was a small square or round building.

Opposite:
The remains of the ancient Roman walls in the lower part of the Castel Sant'Angelo still display a number of blocks of the original facing. The upper part was redesigned in the Renaissance.

Right: Two ramps run in opposite directions from Hadrian's vault to the rooms above, which were intended as burial chambers for the emperor's successors. All the walls were originally clad in expensive marble facing.

### The last bulwark

Between 272 and 275 A.D., the emperor Aurelian began work on the last great structure of the Roman Empire, a new city wall to encircle the entire city. It was nearly 12 miles (19 km) long and contained almost 400 watchtowers. On the north-western side, the walls followed the left bank of the Tiber, broke off before the Pons Aelius, then continued along the river as far as the Isola Tiberina. The Porta Aurelia was built at the bridgehead, with the mausoleum on the bank opposite likewise fortified with walls. Thus Hadrian's mausoleum became a kind of outpost of the newly fortified walls. Nevertheless, the imposing construction of the Aurelian wall did not prove sufficient to preserve the city from the invasions and sackings of subsequent centuries. In the course of the 5th century, when Rome was still formally the capital of an empire, the city was besieged, conquered and sacked no fewer than three times: in 410 by Alaric's Visigoths, in 455 by Gaiseric's Vandals and in 472 by an army led by Ricimer. In 452, Attila was about to let his Huns loose on Rome when a delegation of Roman senators headed by Pope Leo I begged him to spare the city. Legend has it that the Hun commander had an attack of dizziness at the sight of the Cross. At any rate, he did abandon the attack. It is not known what function Hadrian's mausoleum served during the first sieges and sackings.

Barbarian invasions of Europe, mid-4th to late 5th centuries A.D.

During these ethnic migrations, many (mainly Germanic) tribes entered the Roman Empire. However, decades passed before they succeeded in threatening the imperial government of Rome.

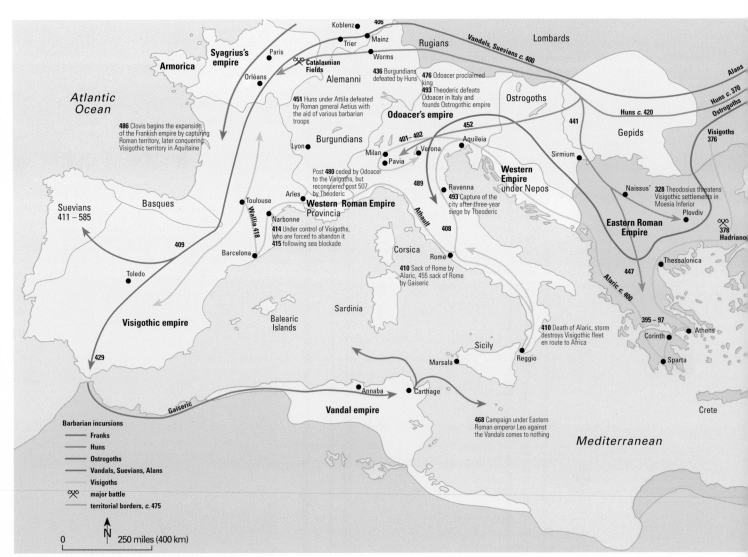

12

## Smashing statues

After the fall of the Roman empire in 476, the city of Rome enjoyed several decades of peace. Under the Ostrogothic empire of Theodoric (491–526), the mausoleum was used as a prison for the first time. Henceforth the Romans called it Theodoric's Prison. During this period, it must have remained unchanged externally. We can deduce this from the description by the Byzantine historian Procopius of Caesarea, who was in Italy as secretary to the great general Belisarius, commander of the Byzantine army during Constantinople's war with the Ostrogoths (536–553). Procopius said in 536: "The Emperor Hadrian's mausoleum lies outside the Porta Aurelia, a stone's throw from the walls. It is a magnificent building put together with ivory-colored blocks of marble placed on top of each other without mortar. The four sides are all the same length, being a stone's throw long. The height of the buildings rises above the walls surrounding it. On top float wonderful statues representing men and horses. They are carved out of the same Parian marble."

Only a year later, at the end of March 537, the statues described by Procopius no longer existed. The Ostrogoths had besieged the city, and on the 20th day stormed the walls. During the attack, the Byzantine defenders took refuge around the mausoleum and on Hadrian's bridge. When the Goths came and placed their slender ladders against the walls of the mausoleum, the Greeks smashed the statues and hurled the marble legs, arms and heads down on their attackers. They managed to kill some and put the rest to flight.

## The inundation

Later in the same Gothic war, which repeatedly turned Rome into a bloody battlefield, Belisarius ordered the destruction of the great aqueducts that supplied the baths and houses with water. He resorted to this step to prevent the Goths from smuggling their men through the walls of the city via the water conduits. When the aqueducts were severed, water

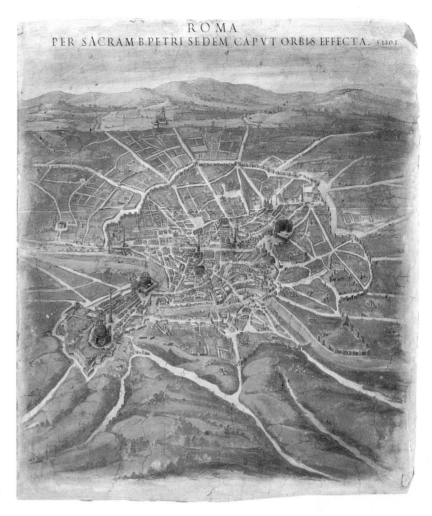

flowed unimpeded into the Campagna Romana, turning Rome into a swamp. Even at a later date, no one thought of closing the cracks and fissures. The capital that had once provided more than a million citizens with clear, clean water shrank to a motley collection of settlements housing no more than 40,000 residents. Towards the end of the 6th century, plague reached the city, which had already been weakened by two long sieges by the Lombards, famine and a catastrophic flood of the Tiber. In February 590, Pope Pelagius himself died of the disease.

Egnazio Danti
*Map of the City of Rome*,
1580–1583
Fresco
Musei Vaticani, Galleria delle Carte Geografiche, Rome

Some 1,000 years after the collapse of the Roman Empire, Renaissance Rome occupied only a small part of the city area within the Aurelian wall.

Joos van Gent
*Gregory the Great,*
1473/76
Oil on wood
Palazzo Ducale, Studiolo di
Federico Montefeltro,
Urbino

Pope Gregory the Great
(pre-540–604) came from an
ancient Roman patrician
family, and placed his
political skills and worldly
experience at the service of
the Church. He is considered
to be the real founder of the
Roman Catholic Church.
Tradition depicts this Church
Father as a hard-working,
tireless man who is supposed
to have devoted his limited
free time to his choir school.

Opposite:
Raffaello da Montelupo
*The Archangel Michael
Sheathing His Sword,* 1544
Marble
Castel Sant'Angelo, Rome

The 16th-century sculpture
was placed on top of the
Castel Sant'Angelo, in
accordance with Gregory's
apparition. As the stone
statue was too exposed to the
damaging effects of
weathering, it was replaced
two centuries later by a
bronze sculpture, and placed
in the *cour d'honneur*
(front court) of the castle.

## Gregory and the rainbow

Six months after the death of Pelagius II, the new pope, Gregory I, arranged a three-day procession. It was intended to evoke a sign from God and put an end to the epidemic. The whole city, including those suffering from the plague, took part in it. No sooner had the Pons Aelius come into view than the skies darkened, and over the mausoleum of Hadrian there appeared like a rainbow the radiant figure of an angel, sheathing its sword of flame. Some of the penitents recognized the Archangel Michael in the heavenly manifestation. On the very same evening, August 29, 590, the plague lifted, and the mausoleum of Hadrian was henceforth called the Castel Sant'Angelo.

The pontificate of Gregory the Great (590–604), thus launched with the wonderful apparition of the Archangel Michael, represented a turning point in the history of the city of Rome and the papacy. This was largely because of the extraordinary talents of the new pope. To the members of the patrician *gens anicia* into which Gregory was born, assuming and exercising civil power was a self-evident duty that passed from father to son. Thus Gregory, even before he decided to devote his life to the Church, had been prefect in Rome. Later he spent six years as Pope Pelagius's ambassador to the imperial court in Constantinople. When he returned to Rome in 585/86 as the pope's adviser, it was because he wanted to devote himself to a more contemplative life. His election as pope came thus as a great shock. "I have fallen into a deep sea, and the current carries me away," was his comment. According to legend, he sought to escape, and hid in a cave. Finally he bowed to his fate and accepted the election. The few Romans that still lived in the city trusted themselves blindly to Gregory's leadership, and political and religious power were fused into a formidable entity in his hands.

The various tragedies that had befallen the city may have drastically depopulated it, but they increased Church land holdings beyond measure. The richest Roman families had moved to Constantinople and left their immovable possessions to the Church. These Church *latifundia* stretched from Sicily to the Alps and from Corsica to Dalmatia. Gregory administered this property efficiently. He also collected as many relics of the apostles as he could, thus increasing their value by taking them out of circulation. It was also thanks to him that the bureaucratic tradition from the days of the Roman Empire was absorbed into the administration of the Church. The new possessions were used by the pope to establish a new entity – the Church/State.

Alas, the mighty legacy left by Gregory the Great proved too much for his successors.

## The Città Leonina

At the beginning of the 9th century Pope Leo III (795–816) drew up plans for a ring of walls around St. Peter's Church. The cornerstones of this system of walls were the Castel Sant'Angelo and its bridge. The construction of a new wall seemed necessary, since the whole Vatican hill, which had been unoccupied in Aurelian's time, lay outside the Aurelian boundary. In imperial Rome, the site where St. Peter's now stands had housed a garden, then Caligula's circus, where the first Christians had been thrown to the lions. The stones of the ruined circus were used to build the first church on that site.

The works for the new walls planned by Leo III started without delay, but construction soon had to be suspended. Disputes had broken out not only in the city but also in the Church, as not everyone appreciated the necessity for this expensive undertaking. It was argued that the pope lived in the Lateran palace, i.e. on the other side of the city, which lay within the Aurelian walls. Why then fortify the Vatican? To defend the bones of St. Peter? In the end the stone assembled for the

construction of the Vatican wall was stolen and used for private buildings.

Forty years later, in 846, Saracen pirates threatened the city; they had sailed up the Tiber from Ostia to Civitavecchia (then known as *Centumcellæ*), and had come overland from there. Hurried preparations were made for the defense of Rome, but the Saracens made straight for the Vatican and the church of St. Paul farther south, which also lay outside the walls. Both churches were ransacked, and the treasures and holy relics either stolen or smashed. After they had desecrated the churches, the Muslim pirates withdrew without taking any further interest in the city. Nothing like this had ever happened before. Goths, Vandals and Lombards may have been barbarians, but as Christians they feared the Cross. As a consequence of the Saracen escapade, the old pope, Sergius II, died of sorrow. His bones themselves became relics.

After his election in 847, his successor Leo IV resumed the old project of Leo III.

This time the wall was indeed constructed, and work continued uninterrupted from 848

*Prospect of Rome*, c. 1490
Saletta della città, Palazzo
Ducale, Mantua

In this late-15th-century view of the city, individual Roman monuments and houses can be identified, even if their position within the city's topography does not always correspond to reality. On the right, the Castel Sant'Angelo is clearly depicted with the Pons Aelius. On the left, the Aurelian wall runs in a great arc round the medieval city.

Egnazio Danti
*Map of Rome* (detail),
1580–1583
Fresco
Musei Vaticani, Galleria
delle Carte Geografiche,
Rome

The detail shows clearly the
Leonine city laid out by Pope
Leo IV and named for him. It
corresponds roughly to the
area of the modern
Vatican City.

until completion in 852. Saracens who had been taken prisoner by the pope's allies on the islands of the Tyrrhenian Sea were used as slave labor.

Leo's walls started at the Tiber and returned to it where the Castel Sant'Angelo continued the course of the Aurelian walls, encircling the whole Vatican hill. At least 44 watchtowers were included in the new protective ring. This was built of large blocks of tuff, with a horseshoe-shaped layout. Three tower-gate-ways, all quite close to the bridge, opened into the mausoleum, St. Peter's, and the church of Santo Spirito respectively. In its role as main entrance, the old mausoleum of Hadrian took on a new special function: it was the seam where the lines of the Leonine and Aurelian fortified walls on either side of the Tiber came together, linked by the bridge.

## Rome in Turmoil

Caspar Wittel (known in Italy as Gaspare Vanvitelli) *View of the Castel Sant'Angelo* (detail) Oil on canvas Musei Capitolini, Rome This famous *veduta* by Wittel (1655–1736) gives an accurate picture of the ancient mausoleum after the rebuilding and fortifications of the Renaissance.

Alas, the walls that Pope Leo IV constructed around the Vatican after the Saracen attacks in 846 did not offer sufficient protection against the repeated disasters that broke over the papacy, the Church and Rome at the end of the millennium and nourished the general conviction that the end of the world was nigh. Here is a brief summary of events.

### Marozia

A powerful Roman noblewoman called Marozia, widow of the city governor Alberich, has herself appointed senator, arrests Pope John X, locks him up in the Castel Sant'Angelo and has him smothered between two cushions. She then has one of her sons appointed pope in his place under the name of John XI. John XI then presides over the wedding of his mother to a certain Hugo of Provence, king of Italy – her third husband. Marozia's aim is to have her new spouse crowned emperor by her papal son, thereby herself becoming empress. But even while the wedding ceremony is being celebrated in the Castel Sant'Angelo, another of her sons, Alberich junior, attacks the fort with an armed band and arrests his brother and his mother. Hugo prudently manages to escape by abseiling down the wall, but Marozia remains a prisoner in the Castel for the rest of her life, while her son Pope John dies in confinement in the Lateran. This eventful family saga took place between 928 and 935.

### Thrice Otto, thrice Crescenzio

Act I: The scion of an old Roman family called Crescenzio, also known as *a caballo marmoreo* (of the Marble Horse), exploits the power vacuum following the death of Emperor Otto I in May 973 by having Pope Benedict VI arrested and confined in the Castel Sant'Angelo, where he throttles him with his own hands. Crescenzio gets one of his henchmen elected pope under the name of Boniface VII. Hardly has news of these events reached the ears of Otto I's heir, the young Otto II of Saxony, when he kits out an army and marches on Rome, in order to establish imperial order there again. Even before Otto's troops cross the Alps, Boniface VII leaves Crescenzio in the lurch and absconds to Constantinople with the Church's treasure. At this point Crescenzio also takes to his heels, abandons Rome for a monastery and becomes a monk.

Act 2: Ten years later Emperor Otto II falls ill and dies in Rome at the age of 28. The antipope, Boniface, returns from Constantinople, has the pro-imperial Pope John XIV arrested, locked up in the Castel Sant'Angelo and starved to death. In his turn, the son of Crescenzio *a caballo marmoreo* arrests antipope Boniface VII. The former favorite of his father is mutilated and chased through the city by a mob. Finally, his corpse is thrown at the feet of the equestrian statue of Emperor Marcus Aurelius.

Act 3: Scarcely waiting for his 15th birthday, Otto III assembles a large army and sets off for Italy to have himself crowned emperor. Otto is a blond youth of Graeco–Germanic descent, his mother the Byzantine princess Theophano. Otto's ambition is to unite East and West under his scepter. Arriving in Pavia in early 996, he is greeted with news of the death of Pope John XV, who was waiting to crown him in Rome.

Rome is in the hands of Giovanni Crescenzio, who exercises absolute power there. Otto has a new pope appointed in Pavia. He is a 23-year-old cousin called Bruno, who takes the name of Gregory V. He is the youngest pope ever and the first German-born pope. When the two cousins reach Rome, the city is peaceful. It appears to accept the new situation. After Otto has received the imperial crown from Bruno's hands, he sets off again over the Alps. Hardly is he out of sight when revolt breaks out. Crescenzio's soldiers occupy the Castel Sant'Angelo, and Gregory V is forced to take flight to Pavia. In early 997, Crescenzio appoints an antipope, a Greek from Calabria called Philagatus, who has already been a bishop in Piacenza and is supported by Constantinople. He enters office under the name of John XVI. The two popes excommunicate each other.

At the end of 997, Otto III once again arrives in Italy to restore order. He fetches his cousin from Pavia and they move on Rome together. They arrive there in February 998 at the head of a powerful army. While Crescenzio barricades himself in the Castel Sant'Angelo, Pope John XVI gallops off on horseback in the hope of catching the next ship to Greece. Unluckily for him, Otto's knights overtake him and capture him. They cut off his nose and tongue and put out his eyes, then put his papal robes back on and return him to the Lateran. After a trial, he is declared deposed and sentenced to life imprisonment. He is stripped once again, tied face down on the back of a donkey and trailed round the whole city. Meanwhile, the Castel Sant'Angelo is besieged, and finally stormed in April 998. Crescenzio is beheaded and his body thrown over the castle wall.

The horribly mutilated antipope John is transported to a German monastery in Fulda, where he dies 15 years later. Of all the actors in this drama, he is the one who survives longest.

This was then the state of the world, the Church and Rome on the eve of the millennium. In the meantime, a small church, *Sancti Angeli usque ad coelos*, had been erected at the highest point of the ancient mausoleum of Hadrian. It was dedicated to the Archangel Michael, in memory of the apparition that appeared to Pope Gregory I.

Giovanni Battista Piranesi
*View of the Castel Sant'Angelo*
from: *Vedute di Roma,* 1748
Etching, 4.15 × 5.55 cm
This *veduta* from the extensive architectural handbooks of Piranesi (1720–1778) shows a rarely seen rear view of the ruin of Hadrian's mausoleum.

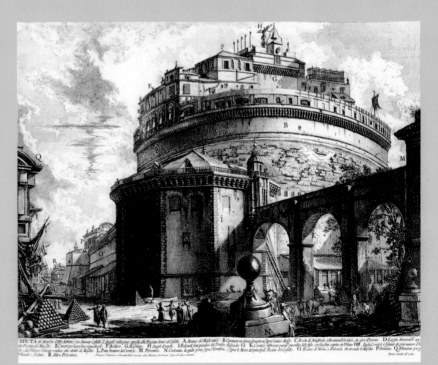

19

YTALIA

## The beginning of the second millennium

Over three centuries of the second millennium elapsed without any major changes to the old mausoleum of Hadrian. The patrician families who ruled the city, gradually acquiring greater influence, added a tower here, battlements there, and an arched gateway or two. The castle was controlled by successive popes, though its defensive function cannot have appeared compelling as long as they continued to live in the Lateran and did not retreat behind the Leonine walls.

Even during the two great conflicts between the papacy and the Empire between 1050 and 1250, the fortress only played a subordinate role. There was, however, a dramatic event in March 1084, as the conflict between Pope Gregory VII and the German emperor Henry IV was nearing an end. Threatened by the imperial army, Gregory VII had to seek refuge in the Castel Sant'Angelo. While he was there, the emperor occupied and ransacked the city. The Norman adventurer Robert Guiscard had rushed up from his possessions in southern Italy to save the pontiff. Setting fire to the city and sacrificing thousands of residents, he finally managed to liberate the pope from the Castel Sant'Angelo and carried him off to Salerno.

Finally, Pope Nicholas III, who belonged to the influential Roman Orsini family, in 1278 decided to move the papal residence from the Lateran to the Vatican. To this end, he started work on palaces near St. Peter's to house the papal government. However, it was only a century later (1367) that construction really got under way. The delay was due to the tendency of the papacy, following the election of a French pontiff in 1305, to abandon the Eternal City because of its dangers and move to Avignon, where a strong protector guaranteed the papal court both security and peace.

In the 1270s, the painter Cimabue visited Rome and painted a prospect of the city, which shows the Castel Sant'Angelo in side view. It is the only surviving depiction of the old mausoleum at the time, and it shows that large parts of the building were still clad in ancient marble.

## The Jubilee: cashing in on the faithful

In 1300, Pope Boniface VIII proclaimed the first Christian Jubilee year, the greatest commercial enterprise of the Middle Ages after the Crusades. Although pilgrimages to Rome had already reached impressive proportions at the end of the first millennium, the Jubilee year saw a massive increase in the numbers of the faithful arriving there. Apart from certain enemies of the pope, whom he excommunicated, Christians who made the pilgrimage to Rome that year, who subjected themselves to the prescribed penances and who followed a prescribed itinerary, were granted a plenary indulgence, or remission of their sins.

To give the Jubilee year a tradition that it did not have in reality, an old man was located in France who claimed to be over 100. He declared that he had made the pilgrimage to Rome as a child, in 1200. Following his example, various other living antiques came forward, all recalling the same event. This extraordinary news was proclaimed from pulpits all over Europe, undoubtedly making a huge contribution to the success of the Jubilee.

It was boom time for 14th-century Rome. Streams of money flowed into every corner of the city along with the pilgrims. One chronicler wrote that 30,000 people a day arrived and 30,000 departed. Over the year, more than two million pilgrims made the journey to Rome, said another. Giovanni Villani, a pilgrim from Florence, maintained that 200,000 people were added permanently to the city's population. In his report, he adds that the Romans who provided food and accommodation for them "all became rich." The crowds were so thick that many were trampled to death. To improve access, it was necessary to make a breach in the city wall. As we know from Dante (1265–1321), who was presumably also among the pilgrims, a thoroughly modern method was

Cimabue
*The Four Evangelists* (detail),
View of Rome, post 1277
Fresco
Chiesa Superiore, San
Francesco, Assisi

The detail from the famous fresco by Cimabue (c. 1240–post 1302) in the upper church of Assisi portrays buildings of Rome in the 13th century, including the dome of the Pantheon and the Castel Sant'Angelo. As such, it constitutes the sole authentic contemporary depiction of the mausoleum showing parts of the ancient marble facing.

invented of regulating the constant stream of people. Everyone heading for St. Peter's walked on one side of the bridge, while those returning used the other: "(...) just as the Romans, because of the great smother/ Of the Jubilee crowds, have thought of a good device/ For controlling the bridge, to make traffic smoother/ So that on one side all must have their eyes/ On the Castle, and go to St. Peter's; while all the throng/ On the other, towards the Mount moves contrariwise." (*Inferno*, Canto 18, 28–33, translated by Dorothy Sayers)

In the *Divine Comedy*, Dante banishes Boniface VIII to the Inferno, hurling the pontiff headlong into a well, among those who sell Church offices and trade in holy things. Nonetheless, his Roman contemporaries were thoroughly grateful for Boniface's declaration of the Jubilee year. Their elation turned to disappointment when the French pope Clement V moved his entire court to Avignon in 1309. Only the churches of the apostles Peter and Paul and the sacred relics were not moved to France. Thus Rome was abruptly shorn of everything that made it a Holy City and a New Jerusalem.

## Rome without popes

In the absence of the popes in the "Babylonian Captivity," Rome drew up its own communal laws. This step made the supreme pontiffs realize that they would lose the city and the whole of Italy forever if they remained in Avignon. The penultimate French pope, Urban V, therefore announced his return to Italy in 1367. After a long sea voyage he landed at Corneto (now Tarquinia), a few miles north of Rome, at the end of May. He made it a condition of his entry into the city that the keys of Castel Sant'Angelo be presented to him, and they were ceremoniously handed over by a delegation from Rome.

As the old papal palace in the Lateran had been destroyed in a fire seven years earlier, Urban V took up residence in the Vatican. Even then this was linked with the Castel

Anonymous
*Pope Boniface VIII Proclaims the Holy Year*, post 1300
Fresco
San Giovanni in Laterano, Rome

In the first Jubilee year proclaimed by Boniface VIII for 1300, more than two million people made the pilgrimage to Rome. Besides generating considerable revenues for the city, this also reinforced the position and importance of Rome.

Sant'Angelo by a bridge, the Passetto, which still stands. A covered walkway ensured a rapid and safe access from the palaces into the castle. However, Urban V's period in Rome remained thoroughly peaceful. Both the German and the Byzantine emperors used the opportunity to visit the pope. On November 24, 1370, Urban V suddenly departed again, however, saying only that "the Holy Spirit that brought me to Rome is taking me away again." He returned to Avignon, dying there on December 19.

## The return

The last in the series of French popes was Gregory XI. During his pontificate, the whole of Italy was seized by a violent anti-clerical mood. An anti-clerical league was set up under the leadership of the city of Florence, and it demanded that Rome abandon the papacy to its fate and place itself at the head of the league. The territories within the Church/State did indeed rebel, sending the papal governor packing. The papal response from Avignon in March 1376 was to excommunicate all of Florence. In September Gregory XI decided it was time to return to Rome. Like his predecessor he embarked on a ship in Marseilles, landing in Corneto on

Opposite:
A high-level, fortified walkway between the palaces of the Vatican and the Castel Sant'Angelo, the so-called *Passetto*, enabled the pope and cardinals to withdraw into the fortified castle in moments of danger. In 1277, Pope Nicholas III had the structure specially extended for this purpose.

23

The Well Court is at the back
of the Cortile dell'Angelo.
From here there was access
to the storerooms.

December 5. He had been preceded in his journey to Italy by 10,000 Breton and Gascon soldiers, who were considered the most fearsome warriors of the day. As a condition of his return, Gregory demanded the surrender of all bridges, towers, gates and fortresses, plus control of Trastevere and the Città Leonina. The Castel Sant'Angelo, still guarded by the French garrison of his predecessor, was already in his hands. On top of this, the pope demanded the civil authorities swear an oath of loyalty to him.

All the conditions were met, and Gregory solemnly entered Rome at the beginning of 1377. He immediately set about reconquering the newly independent papal territories. During the campaign, Breton soldiers butchered thousands of people in the city of Cesena.

### A tragic mistake

Pope Gregory died one year later. The conclave to elect a successor was one of the most turbulent in the history of the Church. The Roman people besieged the Vatican and demanded the election of an Italian pope. The cardinals, who were largely French, yielded to the pressure. They elected a man who, though he did not belong to the conclave, was believed to be susceptible to their control. He was a bishop from Naples, which was then ruled by a French dynasty. But in their haste, the cardinals chose the wrong man. The man they selected as a puppet, who became Pope Urban VI, turned out to have a rotten temper. The unexpected appointment shook him to the core, and at the very first consistory he roundly abused the cardinals who had elected him. For good measure, he announced that he wanted to change the composition of the college. In this pope, who had never worn the purple, the cardinals had chosen the most implacable enemy of their caste known to history. Urban VI appointed new cardinals only so he could persecute them later. To escape his fury, members of the conclave fled Rome. Some sought refuge in the Castel Sant'Angelo or at the Angevin court in

The structure was reduced to the foundations, and every trace of the classical friezes and the marble cladding that still existed at this date were lost.

## Restoration

Towards the end of the 14th century, during the reign of Boniface XI (1389–1404), the mausoleum half destroyed by the rage of the Roman mob was restored. The new pope was a member of the Neapolitan Tomacelli family. Boniface had been made a cardinal by Urban VI, and unlike many of his contemporaries had managed to weather the reign of the turbulent pope unscathed.

Boniface had the main cylindrical structure of the mausoleum repaired and then added a story. A ring was built on top with openings for cannons, and work was started on a new tower. The high-level walkway leading to the Vatican palaces was also repaired. Some of these works, carried out by the architect Niccolò Lamberti (1370–1451), are now unrecognizable because of later alterations. Major changes were also undertaken in the interior rooms. The radial structure of the mausoleum was turned into a series of windowless cells and large storage areas for provisions. At the same time, the first papal residence that was integrated into the Castel Sant'Angelo was built, though it was subsequently completely redesigned by Paul III (1534–1549). From Boniface onwards, the popes preferred to lived in the heart of the castle in times of unrest. Later residents were the secret archives and the Church treasury, the latter occupying the topmost of the three circular rooms of the ancient mausoleum.

Part of the income raised from the 1390 jubilee year was used to finance the work. In view of the success of the 1300 Jubilee further jubilee years were planned, only for every 33 rather than 100 years, in tribute to Jesus' age at his death. Urban VI had declared the 1390 Jubilee but he died a few weeks before it began.

His successor Boniface XI immediately confirmed the appointed jubilee dates, but

Naples. Finally, the cardinals met in Anagni and declared the election of Urban, which had been made under mob pressure, to be null and void. This plunged Rome into a conflict that resulted in the election of an antipope, a schism, and much loss of blood. The Church/State became the theater of a merciless war between the partisans of the Neapolitan pope and the Breton and Gascon mercenaries.

## In ruins again

The Castel Sant'Angelo had remained in the hands of the French military garrison, which had installed the latest military innovation – cannons, which had their baptism of fire when they destroyed whole sections of the Città Leonina. The deployment of this devilish weapon finally whipped the rage of the Romans to a peak. While a *condottiere* working for the pope was wiping out the Breton mercenaries stationed in the Church/State, the citizens of Rome added themselves to the troops besieging the Castel Sant'Angelo. Eventually their hunger became unbearable, and the French garrison surrendered the castle on April 29, 1378. Scarcely had the French withdrawn when popular rage was redirected at the time-honored mausoleum of the emperor Hadrian. The mob did not succeed in razing it to the ground as they intended, but they transformed it into a shapeless, disfigured lump.

FIRMITATEM COMMODAM VTILITATEM

made one critical change to the rules governing the jubilee system. To gain a plenary indulgence, it was no longer necessary to come to Rome in person. It was now enough to donate the expenses for travel and subsistence to the Church and add a lump sum as compensation for the penances not carried out. This had the dual advantage that the Church pocketed the whole sum in advance, and that the faithful were spared the discomfort and dangers of travel. Although they remained at home, they could still acquire a ticket to paradise. Only the Romans, who would get a raw deal from the system, were in uproar. In the event, the power of tradition and the enduring religious passion of Christians ensured a continuous stream of pilgrims in 1390 as in previous Jubilee years.

## The four Evangelists

With the popes undertaking numerous modifications and additions at the Castel Sant'Angelo from the beginning of the 15th century, each left traces of his transient presence. Thus three bastions were constructed northwest, northeast and southeast of the

The residential apartments installed in the Castel Sant'Angelo by Pope Paul III in the first half of the 16th century include a room named after the fresco of *Amor and Psyche*, seen here furnished as a bedroom.

Opposite:
The Sala Paolina, part of Pope Paul III's apartments, is lavishly decorated with frescoes and decoration by Perino del Vaga. In the middle of the composition is the painted statue of Emperor Hadrian, the founder of the mausoleum. This is the only place he is honored appropriately.

mausoleum at the behest of the humanist pope Nicholas V (1447–1455), who under his secular name, Tommaso Parentucelli, had founded the Vatican Library. Alexander VI (1492–1503), a Borgia, enlarged and strengthened these bastions. In addition, he constructed a fourth in the southwest corner, which meant the circular structure was now completely girt with fortifications. The bastions were given the names of the four Evangelists: Matthew, Mark, Luke and John. A large round tower, which initially served to guard the bridge but was later demolished, was also constructed. The number of prison cells was increased, and the Borgia pope took care to keep them constantly occupied. Alexander also built a huge cistern and extended the storerooms for provisions. These changes transformed the Castel Sant'Angelo into a perfect military defensive structure, and this is how it was described by contemporary writers. The only structure subsequently added in the second half of the Cinquecento was a pentangular ring of walls to protect the rectangular bastions. Overall, it gave the Castel Sant'Angelo the star-shaped ground plan that it still possesses. Thereafter, Alexander VI's successors could devote themselves to decorating the castle, which they did.

In the course of the 16th century, dozens of great artists worked at the Castel Sant'Angelo. Among them were Raffaello da Montelupo, who did a large marble statue of the Archangel St. Michael in 1544, depicting the moment where he sheaths his sword. This was erected at the highest point of the castle, in memory of the Gregorian apparition, where it remained for 200 years. Later it was replaced by the present bronze sculpture, a work by Pieter Antoon Verschaffelt, and Montelupo's angel has now been relegated to the Cortile d'Onore. The aedicule by Michelangelo, commissioned by the Medici pope Leo X, the son of Lorenzo the Magnificent, also faces onto this court. The beautifully curving loggia of Julius II, which looks over the Tiber and the bridge, was

designed by Giuliano da Sangallo. The magnificent apartments of Paul III, completed between 1542 and 1549, were designed by Antonio da Sangallo the Younger. The frescoes that decorate the rooms are the work of Florentine painter Perino del Vaga and his workshop. They include a picture of the emperor Hadrian, the only artistic tribute to the old master of the house, even if the resemblance is poor. By the end of the Cinquecento, the Castel Sant'Angelo was tricked out like a minor royal castle.

Pieter Antoon Verschaffelt
*Archangel Michael*, 1752
Bronze
Castel Sant'Angelo, Rome

The bronze angel replacing the 16th-century stone angel has been on top of the complex of buildings at Castel Sant'Angelo since the mid-18th century.

Opposite:
Michangelo
*Aedicule of the Chapel of Leo X*

The Chapel of Leo X flanks the Cortile dell'Angelo. It was commissioned by the Medici pope from Florence from his famous countryman Michelangelo (1475–1564).

# The Sack of Rome

Hans Burgkmair (1475–1531)
*Double Mercenary*
This woodcut shows a mercenary from the army that sacked Rome in 1527.

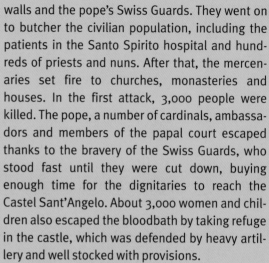

### Massacre and plunder

At dawn on Monday May 6, 1527, Charles V's 16,000-strong imperial army stormed the Leonine walls, broke into the Vatican City and slaughtered the Roman militia defending the walls and the pope's Swiss Guards. They went on to butcher the civilian population, including the patients in the Santo Spirito hospital and hundreds of priests and nuns. After that, the mercenaries set fire to churches, monasteries and houses. In the first attack, 3,000 people were killed. The pope, a number of cardinals, ambassadors and members of the papal court escaped thanks to the bravery of the Swiss Guards, who stood fast until they were cut down, buying enough time for the dignitaries to reach the Castel Sant'Angelo. About 3,000 women and children also escaped the bloodbath by taking refuge in the castle, which was defended by heavy artillery and well stocked with provisions.

On the afternoon of the same day, the emperor's German-Spanish mercenary army overran the Trastevere district, which like the Vatican was on the right bank of the river outside the Aurelian walls that protected the heart of ancient Rome. At sundown, before the defenders could blow up the bridge, the imperial troops crossed the Tiber by the Ponte Sisto and entered Rome itself.

By the evening the whole city was in the hands of the mercenary army. Thousands more corpses filled the streets. Churches and palaces were ransacked, women and children raped, libraries and archives burned, tombs of prelates and distinguished citizens desecrated and looted. The sack of Rome, the most tragic event in the long history of the city, lasted seven days and nights, and left a spectral city. After scouring the houses, the mercenaries set about searching the cesspits and drains, where they believed rich Romans had stashed their treasures. On May 17 the first signs of plague broke out among the German footsoldiers. The epidemic spread rapidly through the city, and finally even breached the massive walls of the Castel Sant'Angelo.

The news of the sack of Rome was greeted with horror throughout the civilized world. Rome is "not just the temple of Christian faith, the protector of noble souls, the home of the Muses

but also the mother of nations (...) This is not the destruction of a single city but of the world," was the judgment of contemporary observer Erasmus of Rotterdam.

## Pope and emperor

The sack of Rome was largely the result of a bizarre duel between two men – Emperor Charles V and Pope Clement VII. It was a punitive expedition by the secular ruler against the clerical, and one that even Charles agreed went badly wrong. Charles had signed up the most vicious desperadoes of the day as mercenaries for his army: Spanish peasants who had been defeated during the *comunero* uprising and the *Landsknechte* that had been on the losing side in the German peasant war. The emperor had recruited them

without having money to pay their wages. The mercenaries had mutinied against their own military leadership and rewarded themselves by ransacking Rome. Along with frustration and hunger, there was a third, "religious" motivation in the case of the *Landsknechte*: Rome was the city that Martin Luther had called the "new Babylon." This justified any kind of act of perversion and cruelty against its inhabitants. The "punishment" of the pope's city was an early manifestation of the religious wars that would afflict Europe for over 100 years.

Charles V was in Valladolid when he learned what had happened in Rome; he knew what the reaction of the civilized world would be.

In a letter to all the rulers of Europe, he expressed disapproval of what had occurred and

Matthäus Merian
*Sack of Rome, May 6, 1527.*
*German Mercenaries Mock the Pope by Imitating a Papal Procession*
Copper engraving, from Johann Ludwig Gottfried, *Historische Chronica,* Frankfurt, 1630

On May 6, 1527, all hell broke loose in Rome. Imperial mercenaries stormed the fortifications, and thousands were killed. The raping and looting continued for seven days and nights. After only a few days, plague broke out among the mercenaries. The sack of Rome aroused massive repugnance in the rest of civilized Europe.

commenced negotiations with the beleaguered pope in Castel Sant'Angelo. On June 5 there was a preliminary agreement, on the basis of which the pope formally undertook to pay a very high sum he did not have, and ceded six Italian cities as security. The garrison of the castle was replaced by *Landsknechte*, who kept the pope captive until he had paid the first installment. In addition, the pope lifted the edict of excommunication on the *Landsknechte* that he had pronounced. Although they were Lutheran, the German mercenaries were superstitious enough to feel uneasy at being excommunicated. Negotiations with the imprisoned pope lasted five more months, during which the pope commissioned Benvenuto Cellini to melt down old chalices, tabernacles and other sacred objects to meet the emperor's harsh terms. Then finally, on December 8, 1527, the news spread that the pope had escaped from Castel Sant'Angelo and had ridden off on horseback to Viterbo in disguise. The Romans concluded that Charles V and Clement VII had finally reached an agreement, and breathed a sigh of relief. The quarrel between the two adversaries had cost the city 30,000 lives and 13,600 houses.

## Clement VII the chameleon

Pope Clement VII, Giulio de' Medici from Florence, was the illegitimate son of Giuliano, the younger brother of Lorenzo the Magnificent. Giulio was born in 1478, a few months after the murder of his father, who had been stabbed in the forecourt of the church of Santa Maria del Fiore – an assassination which Lorenzo, also an intended target, only escaped by a hair's breadth. Giulio was brought up with his three male and four female cousins, the children of Lorenzo. He was 14 when his uncle Lorenzo died in 1492, the year of Columbus's first voyage to America. Soon after, Giulio was marked out for a Church career and joined the retinue of Cardinal Giovanni de' Medici, the most notable of his cousins. Giulio was 35 when Giovanni was elected pope as Leo X. One of the first measures taken by the new pope was to legalize Giulio's birth. He then conferred a cardinal's hat on him and appointed him archbishop of Florence, thus

transferring the "shadow government" of the city to him. Giulio had displayed political acumen from his youth. As a child in Florence, he had acquired the nickname "Bastard." This soon turned into "Chameleon."

When Leo X died in 1521, his cousin Giulio seemed a likely papal successor. Cardinal Giulio de' Medici himself suggested to the conclave the name of Hadrian of Utrecht, the old private tutor of Charles V. It was a move intended to checkmate the only rival he had to fear, because Hadrian was acceptable to the emperor and was financed by the Fuggers of Augsburg. Yet despite every expectation Hadrian was indeed elected. However, his pontificate lasted only a brief two years, and following his death Giulio de' Medici was finally elected pope on November 19, 1523. Four years later he found himself in the Castel Sant'Angelo, looking out from his terrace over the smoking ruins of the Holy City.

During the six months when Pope Clement VII was a prisoner of the emperor, the two men reached the following agreement: the pope would henceforth carry out the wishes of the emperor in all questions and everywhere in the world – except in Florence. In return, the emperor agreed to back the pope's ambitions in Florence. The pact was respected by both sides, and a kind of friendship developed from it.

Opposite:
The small bath commissioned by the second Medici pope, Clement VII, is lavishly adorned with plasterwork and frescoes attributed to Giovanni da Udine (1487–1535). Access to the bathroom is via a small flight of steps and linked with the papal chambers via a dressing room. The required water was heated in a room above the bath.

Giorgio Vasari
*Clement VII in Conversation with Charles V*, 1555–1562
Fresco
Palazzo Vecchio, Sala di Clemente VII, Florence

After the imprisonment of Clement VII, from which the pope had to buy his release, the two adversaries were reconciled. Respect, friendship and mutual assistance were henceforth to mark the relationship between pope and emperor.

## Expedition to Italy
Seb(astian) Schaertlin of Burtenbach (1496–1577)

Hans Burgkmair (1475–1531)
*Three 16th-Century Landsknecht Officers*

The imperial army involved in the sack of Rome consisted of two-thirds German *Landsknechte* and one-third Spanish peasant soldiers called *tercieros*. Among their officers was Sebastian Schaertlin of Burtenbach, shown on the left in the cartouche. He was personally present at the seizure of the pope.

On St. Martin's Day 1526, I went to Milan as captain in command of 40 troopers under Master Georg von Frundsberg, ready to relieve Master Kaspar von Frundsberg. He was sorely besieged in the City of Milan by soldiers of the French, Swiss, and the pope, and those of the Venetians. But when the enemy heard we were coming, he withdrew.

On the same expedition, Monsignore Johann de' Medici, the cousin of Pope Clement, had brought up 8,000 arquebusiers and many light cavalry against us on a dam in the Po in the margravate of Mantua. He wanted to stop us crossing in the morning. We therefore had exchanges from morning to midnight. Many good people on both sides were hit, and it was a hard, difficult withdrawal such as no one had imagined. The next day he came right up against us and wanted to attack us, but our side shot him with a falconet, of which he died. His men therefore withdrew. We spent this winter in the Piacentina mountains. In January 1527 we set off from Posto Novo near Piacenza, about 16,000 strong with troopers, curassiers, Spaniards and light cavalry. We marched with our colonel, the Duke of Bourbon, through the pope's territories. On the way we laid waste and burned everything around Bologna and elsewhere. On 6 May, we took Rome by storm, killed about 6,000 people in it and looted the whole city. We took everything we found in the churches and from the ground, we burned down a large part of the city (...) We tore up and smashed copisteries, registers, letters and cortisanals (archives).

The pope escaped into the Castel Sant'Angelo with guards, cardinals, bishops, Romans and other court people that had not been killed. We besieged him there for three weeks until hunger forced him to give up the Castel Sant'Angelo. Four of the German captains, of whom I was one, four of the Spanish captains, plus a person from Spain called Abbas de Naggera and a secretary were sent into the Castel Sant'Angelo to negotiate the surrender of the Castel Sant'Angelo on behalf of the Prince of Orange and the imperial counselors, which was carried out. We found Pope Clement together with twelve cardinals in a small room. We took him prisoner, and he had to sign the articles that the secretary read out. There was a great lamentation among them and they wept prodigiously. But we all became rich.

We had not held Rome for two months when about 5,000 of the troopers and members of the army died of the plague that broke out because of the dead bodies that had not been buried. In July, we left the city for the Marches (Ancona) because of the dying and to find better air. When the people of Narnia would not let us in nor give us food, even for money, I and another captain called Anton von Feldkirch were commanded to storm it. So we set about storming it with 2,000 troopers without shooting, with God's help conquered the town and the castle and killed over a thousand men and women. The women attacke us with weapons and hot water they poured down on us, causing great damage. We did well out of the city.

In September the same year we re-entered Rome and looted the city better this time, we found great treasures under the ground. We remained another six months in Rome (...)

# The Death of Pope Alexander VI

Francesco Guicciardini (1483–1540)

In his *History of Italy*, Guicciardini narrates events that took place from 1492 to 1533. Among these is his account of the strange case of Pope Alexander VI:

"But behold, when the pope was in highest hopes (how vain and deceitful are man's expectations), he was suddenly carried like one who is dead from the pleasure garden on the Vatican hill, as he was going to have supper in his palace; and the same thing happened not long after to his son. The pope died the next day, which was 18 August, and was carried into St. Peter's church. He was swollen and looked black and deformed, which were certain signs of poison being administered; but the Duke of Valence was younger and somewhat stronger, and immediately used the best medicaments against poison, and eventually escaped with his life after a prolonged serious illness. However it was quite certain that this mishap happened to them because of poison, and the general report is, it happened like this. The Duke of Valence (the son of the pope), who had also wanted to be present at this supper, had intended to poison Adrianum, the Cardinal of Cornet, in whose vineyard the supper was to take place; because it is well known that he and his father commonly used poison, not just against enemies for fear or revenge but also from shameful desire for their possessions (...). Thus the Duke of Valence wanted to do this again and had sent in advance some bottles of poisoned wine to the vineyard, and gave them to a servant who knew nothing of the matter, and ordered him not to give them to anyone; and lo the pope came that way unsuspecting before the supper and wanted a drink because it was very hot and he was thirsty. Meanwhile the things for the supper had not yet come from the papal palace, and as no other wine was there, the servant thought it would not be forbidden to give him the wine Valence had given him because it was so special, and so he poured out a glass for the old pope; as he was still drinking it, Valence came up and also drank some of the same wine. The whole city of Rome ran with incredible delight to St. Peter's Church to see the deceased pope's corpse, and no one could look enough at the great monster (who with immoderate ambition, pernicious perjuries and all kinds of heinous tyranny, casual promiscuity and unparalleled greed sold spiritual and secular things without discrimination and poisoned the whole world) as he lay dead there. Nonetheless, this pope had been from youth to his last day continuously fortunate and exalted and had received more than he wished at all times."

Pinturicchio (Bernardino di Betto) *Resurrection* (detail), Pope Alexander VI, 1492–1494 Fresco Appartamento Borgia, Vatican

Pope Alexander VI, the Borgia pope (1431–1503), is shown in majestic splendor and humble pose, though he was well known to contemporaries as violent, calculating and amoral.

# The Hinterland and the Great Dynasties

# San Leo
## The fortified rock

### The eagle's nest

San Leo perches atop a gigantic rock 2,090 ft (637 m) high and two miles (3 km) in circumference, with precipitous drops on all sides. The rock is an erratic boulder that was pushed to its present position by glacial action long before humans inhabited this part of the world. It balances precariously on a bed of clay that is sliding gradually towards the sea. A geological catastrophe is thus not merely probable; it's inevitable. The only question is when this will happen. For over 2,000 years the inhabitants of San Leo have been hoping that disaster will not strike during their lifetime.

A fortified site since the Roman period, San Leo is accessible via a road hewn into the rock

Previous double spread: The castle of the Guidi counts in Poppi dominates the hills above the Casentino Valley.

Left: San Leo, the castle of the Montefeltro dynasty, clings to the rock like an eagle's nest.

Below: Giorgio Vasari *The Medici Capture San Leo Castle,* 1555–1562, Fresco Palazzo Vecchio, Sala di Leone X, Florence

In his battle scenes Vasari celebrates the great victories of Florence over Pisa and Siena. He highlights the mighty defenses of San Leo, whose military architecture was long admired.

Opposite:
The interior of the huge rotunda in the crenellated south tower of the castle. The large windows were once tiny arrow slits.

by hand. In his *Divine Comedy* (1321), Dante compares the rock to the Mountain of Purgatory. San Leo was the native town of the mighty Montefeltro dynasty. They later moved to Urbino, where Duke Federico II di Montefeltro summoned several of the greatest artists and architects of the time to help him plan his "ideal city."

The Sienese Francesco di Giorgio Martini (1439–1502) was among them. He was entrusted with the prestigious task of rebuilding the old fortress of San Leo in 1479. The magnificent complex we see today is his work. Martini – a painter, sculptor and an architect – was also an expert on defense techniques against gunpowder-fired weapons. He had the old castle walls of San Leo encircled by a new ring of defenses. This consisted largely of an enormous rampart, the corners of which were guarded by huge round watchtowers scored with arrow slits. His contemporaries regarded San Leo as a gem of military architecture, admiring it also for its simplicity and elegance. This is how Giorgio Vasari (1511–1574) presents it in his famous fresco of the Battle of Anghiari in the Palazzo Vecchio in Florence.

Below: One of the two watchtowers on the mighty ramparts of San Leo. The fortifications of the castle were completely rebuilt in the 15th century by the Sienese architect Francesco di Giorgio Martini (1439–1502). In its day it was considered a brilliant achievement in military architecture.

## St. Francis of Assisi's Sermon

Above: The castle of San Leo, seen from the northwest. The curtain wall and towers encircling the oldest part of the fortress are the work of the Sienese Francesco di Giorgio Martini.

Below: San Leo's coat of arms. On the left is St. Francis giving his sermon, on the right the double eagle of the emperor.

On May 8, 1213, the castle of San Leo was brightly lit in celebration of the knighthood of a young member of the San Leo dynasty. Leading families from Tuscany and the Romagna had gathered at the castle. The festivities were well underway when Francis of Assisi unexpectedly appeared astride his donkey, accompanied by a Brother Leone. Passing the castle by chance, the monk had said to his companion: "Let us go to this celebration, for with God's help we will harvest spiritual fruits." Francis, "God's jester," was the man that all 13th-century society was talking about and a revered guest at banquets and functions.

On this particular occasion in San Leo, Francis preached to his followers under an ancient elm tree which is still standing (it was replanted in 1936). His sermon focused on the lines of an erotic rhyme, very popular in courtly society at the time, which begins: "Tanto è il bene ch'io m'aspetto/che ogni pena m'è diletto" (I expect so much happiness/that any pain shall delight me). Putting the rhyme into a religious context, Francis enlightened his audience on the benefits of a divine eroticism. Those present were so moved that Count Orlando Cattani from Chiusi della Verna promptly bequeathed to Francis the summit of his mountain. On top of this hill stands a rock similar to San Leo yet less perilously situated. Orlando's brother, the 16-year-old Duke Ugolino, decided that night to turn his back on the secular world and become a monk. When he later became a bishop, Ugolino paid for the completion of the La Verna monastery that had been started by the Franciscans.

# Cagliostro, The Reckless Clairvoyant

In 1791 the castle of San Leo had been in the possession of the Church for almost two centuries. On the night of April 20, after five days of rough traveling, a famous personality from Rome arrived at the fortress on horseback, escorted by a band of armed men. The 52-year-old was hauled from his horse and strapped to a basket which was then lowered down into the cell the locals called "del Tesoro." He was later moved to a dungeon known as "del Pozzetto" (the well), where the only light to penetrate the dark chamber was from a hole in the ceiling. The prisoner died here on August 21, 1795. His name was Giuseppe Balsamo, better known the world over as the Count of Cagliostro.

Cagliostro, a magician, seer, alchemist, healer, artist, counterfeiter and extremely skillful conjurer, was one of the most ingenious charlatans the Western world has known. He rose from the gutters of his native Palermo to the giddy heights of contemporary society. He was welcomed in salons across Europe, spoke six languages and counted Casanova and Cardinal de Rohan among his friends. It is even thought that he met Goethe, who wrote about the devious imposter in his novel *Der Grosse Coptha* (*The Great Coptha*). As founder of an order of freemasons based on Egyptian ritual, Cagliostro acquired followers all over the world. He visited the courts of England, France, Russia and Austria, where his counsel was sought and greatly valued.

In 1791, however, Cagliostro found himself a prisoner of the pope. While searching for a way to gain an audience with Pope Pius VI in Rome, he had walked straight into a trap. In mid-May 1789 at a meeting in the Villa Malta – at which the French ambassador, Cardinal de Bernis, was also present – Cagliostro allowed himself to be cajoled into performing some of his conjuring tricks. He then went on to predict the fall of the French monarchy, the storming of the Bastille and the lynching of Commandant Jourdan de Launay, whom Cagliostro knew personally. Two months later the Bastille was indeed attacked and de Launay's head impaled on a spike and paraded through the streets. Because

Previous page, top:
Friedrich Wilhelm Bollinger
*Count Alessandro of
Cagliostro (Giuseppe
Balsamo),* c. 1815
Stipple etching

Cagliostro (1743–1795) is
often regarded as one of the
most ingenious charlatans
and swindlers of all time. He
was a good friend of
Casanova, probably met
Goethe and also developed a
system of freemasonry based
on Egyptian ritual.

Previous page, bottom:
One of the underground
cells in the castle vaults
where Cagliostro was held
prisoner from 1791 until
his death.

Left: Pompeo Batoni
*Portrait of Pope Pius VI,*
1775/76
Oil on canvas, 138 × 99 cm
Galleria Sabauda, Turin

Pius VI (Giovanni Angelico
Braschi) was pope from 1775
to 1799 and the man who
had Cagliostro imprisoned in
San Leo castle. During his
papacy he witnessed the
turbulent events of the
French Revolution and the
Napoleonic Wars in Italy
firsthand. In 1798 the
Church-state was occupied
by Napoleon's troops, the
Roman Republic proclaimed
and the pope brought to
Valence as a prisoner, where
he arrived on July 14, the
anniversary of the storming
of the Bastille. He died six
weeks later.

Opposite, top:
Gioacchino Toma
*The Court of the Inquisition,*
1864
Oil on canvas, 99 × 131 cm
Collezione del Comune di
Napoli, Naples

An interrogation according
to the procedures of the
Inquisition.

Opposite, bottom:
The rock of San Leo in an
18th-century print. The rock
is seen from the north, the
pinnacle on the left pointing
towards Rimini and the
Adriatic Sea.

Cagliostro's dreadful prophecies turned out to be true, Cardinal de Bernis felt duty-bound to report back to the pope.

After Cagliostro had been arrested and taken to the Castel Sant' Angelo in Rome, he was interrogated 43 times according to the procedures of the Holy Inquisition. At the end of the trial he was given the death sentence, which was changed to imprisonment following a "special general pardon." In San Leo, Giuseppe Balsamo's powers deserted him and he lost his mind. The jailers heard the most violent curses and oaths echoing up from the "Pozzetto di Cagliostro."

To this very day, the thing that strikes the most fear into the hearts of San Leo's inhabitants is Cagliostro's prognosis that a natural catastrophe will wipe their rock from the face of the earth.

# Poppi
## The castle of the Guidi counts

View of Poppi.
The upper reaches of the Arno meander through the almost perfect oval of Poppi's valley floor. The castle's unusual shape, and the location of the town, enable Poppi Castle to be seen from both the slopes and peaks of the surrounding mountains which shelter the valley in a giant horseshoe.

Opposite:
The castle owes its excellent state of preservation to the fact that it has been inhabited since the mid-14th century.

### Fortress, palace and town hall

When you first see the castle in Poppi, the regional historical capital of the Casentino Valley, it's almost as if you have a piece of medieval Florence before you – an architectural remnant of the 13th or 14th century. You may be forgiven for thinking so; Poppi Castle is said to have been the model for the Palazzo Vecchio in Florence. Count Simone di Battifolle, a member of the powerful Guidi dynasty, had the fortress erected on the foundations of an ancient tower. Work started in 1274 and was continued by the count's son, Guido di Simone. According to Giorgio Vasari, in 1291 Guido entrusted architect Arnolfo di Cambio with further work on his fortified abode. Both Poppi Castle and the Palazzo Vecchio were originally conceived as fortresses, and modified in the Renaissance to afford their inhabitants greater comfort. The functional diversity of both edifices is still clearly visible.

Although no major alterations have been made to Poppi Castle since the middle of the 16th century, it remains in an excellent state of preservation, greatly distinguishing it from its contemporaries. This is due to the fact that the castle has been continuously inhabited since the beginning of the 14th century. The Guidi were superseded by governors elected by Florence, the *vicari*, who lived in Poppi for roughly three centuries. They were followed by administrators serving the Tuscan grand dukes of Habsburg-Lorraine. From 1861 to 1987 the town council of Poppi was based at the palace. The castle now houses a huge historical library which is used for exhibitions, meetings and various other cultural events.

1817 saw the only structural change to the castle. The tower, which was originally higher and surmounted by a pointed roof resting on corbels, was shortened by about 50 ft (15 m) to prevent it collapsing.

### In the paws of the Florentine lion

The facade of Poppi Castle faces a square called the Pratello ("little meadow"), which is lined with trees and the remains of a surrounding wall. This is where jousts and military parades once took place. The castle is reached by a bridge that spans a deep moat and leads up to a ravelin completing the inner curtain wall. In front of this stands a pillar supporting an enormous stone lion, his paw firmly resting on a coat of arms. The beast is Marzocco, the lion of Florence. He appears again in bas-relief above the castle entrance portal and at the foot of the stairs in the inner bailey. After Florence had gained control over the extensive feudal lands and estates of the Guidi after 1440, the Marzocco lions were erected as a symbol of Florentine dominance.

## Justice at the stone table

In the back corner of the inner courtyard squats the solid stone table at which the Guidi dispensed justice. The wall behind it is decorated with a fresco showing the Virgin Mary and various saints. The inner courtyard and stone staircase are extremely elegant; the stairs lead up on three sides, ending on the second floor. They rest on a caryatid depicting Simone da Battifolle, the castle's founder. At the top end of the stairs a pillar supports the overhanging roof.

Two sturdy oak galleries with Venetian-style ceilings run along the left wall. This is where the living quarters of the Guidi counts and later the Florentine governors were situated. The gallery on the first floor provides access to two large salons now occupied by the historic Biblioteca Rilliana. On the second floor there are more rooms and also the chapel adorned with 14th-century wall and ceiling frescoes attributed to Taddeo Gaddi.

After Dante Alighieri had been hounded out of Florence he took refuge with the Guidi counts on several occasions. They accommodated their guest not only in Poppi but also in

Above: A longitudinal section of the castle.

To the right is the outer watchtower, top left the chapel with the library below it. At the center of the plan is the courtyard, with the cistern right at the bottom.

Opposite: The inner courtyard of the castle.

On the right is the beautiful staircase in light stone, and on the left the wooden Renaissance galleries that provided access to the castle's living quarters.

the castles of Romena and Porciano. It was at Poppi that the poet penned the proud letter to the Florentines that resulted in his being exiled for the rest of his life in 1302.

## The Guidi, Florence and the gold florin

The Guidi are one of the great feudal families of Lombard origin in central Italy. The lands under their control were originally all in what is now the Romagna and covered an area from the Po to the Apennines. A deed of gift from 896 contains a list of their Romagnolian estates spread out between Ferrara, Imola, Faenza and Forlì. From the 10th century on, documents give details of further Tuscan terrain in the diocese of Pistoia. A contemporary chronicle written by a man generally known as Tolosano cites a wedding in 925 between a Count Teugrimo or Teudegrimo and a noblewoman called Englerata or Engelrade, daughter of the duke of Ravenna. According to the medieval chronicler the two met when Teugrimo, chasing after a hind and straying beyond his own hunting territory, suddenly found himself at the young lady's castle in Modigliana near Forlì. The wedding was held on the very same day. Their first son was called Guido, and the entire dynasty was named after him.

A few decades later a happy union was formed between Guido's son Teugrimo II and the fair Ghisla. The daughter of Margrave Ubaldo from Tuscany, her dowry included estates in the Casentino Valley. From one generation of Guidos and Teugrimos to the next, the counts' lands gradually expanded to include areas in Mugello, in the lower Arno Valley, in the Chianti region and in Val d'Elsa. The

Apennine regions in particular enabled the Guidi to establish control over the main roads linking northern Italy and the rest of Europe to Rome. The most important of these routes was the Via Francigena.

The domain of the Guidi counts continued to grow. The division of the family estate among Guido VII's four sons in the 13th century brought an abrupt end to their policy of expansion, however. The sons founded new branches of the family tree that became bitter rivals, often engaging in full-fledged feudal combat. Yet the family's greatest impediment proved to be not its internal bickering, but the growth and ambitions of the cities of Tuscany. Florence, especially, was on the verge of becoming a major center of trade and finance, one that was striving to guarantee its merchants and traders safe passage through northern Italy to new markets.

The dynasty's financial difficulties began immediately after the First Crusade, in which several members of the Guidi family had taken part. Through clever alliances formed during periods of regional conflict and skillful diplomatic handling in matters of the Church and the Empire, the Guidi were able to maintain a powerful grip on their position for a further two centuries. However, the Guidi were as unfamiliar with the ins and outs of the new economy as the other feudal families of the day. In an increasingly mercantile age they lived according to older sets of rules, as a contract dated 1169 in the Diplomatic Archives in Florence verifies. In this document the counts Guidi of Poppi pledge to defend the nearby abbey of Strumi and, in states of emergency, to offer military aid in exchange for

53

DE PERIN · OTTAVIANO · PETRI · IPORDO · DI · MICHELE · APDREA · DE SERTINIS · D · PILIPPO · SCHOLARI · RAFFAELLO · PERINI · GIOVANNI · DELLA

"two shoulders of pork, 25 cheeses of cow's milk and 25 new bowls" per year.

## Counterfeit money at the castle of Romena

Following a fire at the Borgo San Lorenzo in Mugello in 1281, the Florentines came across a large quantity of florins. Their shape, design and weight were perfect; upon closer examination, however, they were found to be made of a copper alloy and not gold. Forgeries! Extensive investigation finally revealed that the counterfeit coins had been minted at the castle of the Guidi in Romena. Under the threat of having their fortress besieged, they turned the counterfeiter over to the Florentines. The swindler in question was an Englishman called Mastro Adamo whom the Guidi had discovered in Brescia, where Adamo's skill in producing fake coins was legendary. He was sentenced without trial, tied to a cross and burned alive on the summit of the mountain that formed the border between Florence and the Casentino Valley. His body was left to rot for several months, torn apart by hungry birds and battered by the elements, as a grisly example to other would-be fraudsters.

Dante Alighieri elaborates on the sorry tale in Canto 30 of the *Inferno* (*Divine Comedy*). The ghost of the craftsman Mastro Adamo, first burned at the stake and then banished to Hell, vents his anger at the Guidi counts in Romena. His wrath is directed towards the clients who first commissioned him to work for them, then abandoned him and finally turned him over to the Florentines, who were eager for revenge.

As for Adamo's disloyal customers, a decade later the debts the Guidi had run up with a number of Florentine bankers prompted Florence to take several members of the family to court. The lack of disposable income became a larger and larger nightmare for the dynasty. In 1357 there was no alternative but for the Guidi to sell their Romena stronghold and its estates for 9,600 gold florins.

## The final mistake of the Guidi

The last domain in the possession of the Guidi counts was Poppi, with its wonderful castle at

A corner of the great hall of the castle, with terracottas by the della Robbia school. The room was used for government purposes and public functions. Today it is occupied by the local council, but also sees cultural events.

the center of the wide Casentino Valley. In view of the bitter experiences of their cousins in Romena, the Guidi of Poppi had engaged the services of a Jewish moneychanger and moneylender who worked within the castle walls. In the spring of 1440, however, Count Francesco Guidi di Battifolle, lord of Poppi, made a fatal mistake; he entered into an alliance with the Visconti of Milan who were at war with Florence. On June 29, 1440, the Florentines defeated the mercenary army of the Visconti in the Battle of Anghiari. They then proceeded to lay siege to the castle.

A month later, on July 29, Count Francesco Guidi was forced to accept a peace treaty 37 articles long, the wording of which has been preserved. Under its terms the count had to hand over all of his property, land, houses and castles to Florence. He was permitted to keep his movable assets. He was, however, forbidden

ever to return to the Casentino Valley or to come within ten miles of his former territories, although he was otherwise free to choose to live wherever he pleased, even in Florence. He could take with him his family, all those who were prepared to follow him and all his animals. The debts the count had incurred at Florentine banks were annulled and those at other banks paid off by Florence. Article 21 states that "the Jew who lives in the castle at Poppi with his bank and his family" and who exercised the art of moneychanging and moneylending there would be allowed to continue to operate in Poppi if he so desired after consultation with the new commissioners from Florence. Otherwise he was permitted to leave, with safe conduct guaranteed for himself and his family. In his *Istorie fiorentine*, Niccolò Machiavelli describes how Count Francesco, "unable to see any other possible solution, handed over all of his land and his rights to the Florentines and left, weeping, with his wife, children and effects, devastated that he had lost all the estates his forefathers had owned for 900 years."

Thus ended the rule of the Guidi. Count Francesco left his castle, with his wife, daughters, servants and 34 mules carrying

Above: The coat of arms of the Guidi counts.

Top: The castle of the Guidi counts in Romena.

What is now an impressive ruin was once a castle older and stronger than the fortress in Poppi.

Left: the entrance to the parade ground at the castle of Romena.

A double curtain wall with seven towers once protected the castle. Of all of the family's holdings, this was the one closest to the Florentine border.

ly's belongings in his entourage. The count opted for a life in Florence, later moving to Bologna and finally back to Florence, where he spent the rest of his days.

## Dante's letter to the Guidi counts

Dante Alighieri wrote the following letter to counts Oberto and Guido of Romena to express his condolences on the death of their uncle, Alessandro of Romena.

1. Your uncle, the Honorable Count Alessandro, who in recent days returned to the heavenly home whence his spirit first came, was my lord, and his memory will guide me as long as I am in this world; for his magnanimity, which is now amply rewarded above the stars with a worthy reward, brought him my spontaneous devotion these many years past. It was this virtue, united with all other virtues in him, that exalted his name above the merits of other Italian heroes. And what else did the hero's banners say but "The scourge that drives out vices have we displayed"? For outwardly he wore silver scourges upon a purple field, and within he manifested a spirit that banished vices in its love of the virtues. So lament then, lament indeed, O Tuscany's greatest line, that shone through such a man; lament, you friends and servants of his, whose hopes Death has now cruelly chastised. Among these lament also I, the poorest of them, driven from his homeland and innocently banished, who when I dwelt upon my miseries always soothed my cares in the hope of him.

2. But even the bitterness of the sorrow upon the loss of physical presence subsides and if we direct our gaze at the spirit that remains with us, the sweet light of comfort does indeed dawn. For he that honored the virtues here below is now honored by the virtues in heaven, and he that was the paladin of the Roman court in Tuscany shines upon the heavenly Jerusalem with the princes of the Blessed like a select orb of the immortal royal stronghold. I therefore urge upon you, my esteemed lords, my prayer and petition that you moderate your grief, and hold what you have lost in this world in memory as a paragon of your way of life so that in the future, as he has justly made you (being nearest to him by blood) heirs of his estate, you may take on the garb of his perfect principles.

3. Finally, however, I must also trust to your perceptive understanding that you may excuse my absence from the forthcoming sorrowful interment. In truth it is not carelessness nor ingratitude that hold me back, only the unexpected poverty that banishment has brought upon me. This implacable adversary it is that has robbed me of horses and weapons, thrust me into the cavern of her bondage and not ceased to cruelly detain with superior power one who seeks with all his might once more to arise.

Sandro Botticelli
*Dante Alighieri* (detail),
*c.* 1495
Oil on canvas, 54 × 57 cm
Private collection, Geneva

Dante Alighieri (1265–1321) came from a family of the Florentine petty nobility and was one of the foremost philosophers of his day. He participated in the political life of his city and held public office. His political views contradicted those of the rulers of Florence and he was banned from the city by the pope, on pain of death. In his years of exile (1303–1321) he was often a guest of the Guidi. His literary masterpiece is the *Divine Comedy*, which evolved between 1307 and 1321.

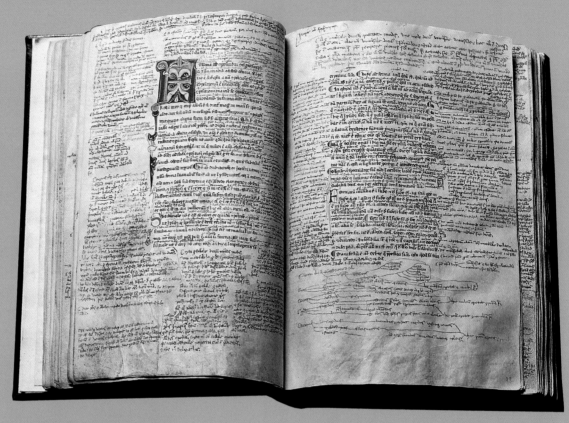

## The Secret of Illumination
Eberhard König

Quarto
Biblioteca Rilliana, Poppi

In the Middle Ages books
were either left untouched,
considered too precious to
handle, or used by countless
readers in many different
ways. These two pages
illustrate perfectly why the
main text only filled about a
quarter of the page; space
had to be left for the
numerous comments added
by avid students of the text
who considered it their right
to remark on the contents.
People wrote between the
lines and in the margins and
frequently expounded on the
observations already penned
in. Later editions often
incorporated these
annotations into the main
body of text.

Books in the Middle Ages were made by a very different process from that of today. Paper was not developed until the 13th century and it was not commonly used until the 15th century. Books were originally written on the skins of goats, sheep, kids or lambs. The Greeks on the coast of Asia Minor are said to have come up with the notion of writing on these specially treated animal skins a few centuries before the birth of Christ. Pergamum, at the northwestern tip of Turkey, had a library full of manuscripts inscribed on these skins, which we still call "parchment" after the famous town. The skin had to be specially tanned to produce fine white sheets of vellum, very different from ordinary leather, which were supple and soft yet still opaque; scribes could not have written cleanly on a transparent surface.

An enormous amount of animal hide was required to produce just one book. The entire skin of one animal was used in the making of the double leaf of a luxury Bible or a book of law in the largest size then common, simply called folio or "leaf."

Animal skin was also used for the book covers. Strong calf- or pigskin tanned by a very different process was stretched taut over thin wooden boards. Chains could be affixed to the binding if the book was to be kept in a library, and various types of clasp were used as decoration.

It would have been foolish to bind the book first and then start writing, for it was usually impossible to gauge exactly how long the work would be. The sheets were thus fixed to sloping desks one at a time. As the text was to be arranged in straight lines and not allowed to swim across the page at random, rows of letters in set blocks were needed. Pins were stuck into the edges of the leaf to guide the scribe in determining the line height, as pin holes found in uncut books testify. The lines were then inked in with a sharp stylus.

Ink was made from gallnuts, which are produced by wasps laying their eggs in the branches of oak trees, causing fat, tumorous bubbles of black liquid to be formed. This liquid is corrosive, so if the ink mixture was too concentrated it often burned holes in the parchment. Yet where parchment has remained intact the ink has proved to be more durable than many of the substances we now regard as "waterproof" or "permanent."

Quill pens made from the shafts of the feathers of large birds, particularly geese, were dipped into this ink and applied to the page. Those skilled in the use of the quill knew how to change swiftly from wide bars to delicate lines, producing exquisite calligraphic writing. The quills could only be used for a brief period before becoming blunt or splitting. Professional letterers thus always had a pot of spare quills to hand and also kept a sharp quill knife with them.

Black ink alone soon proved insufficient for writing purposes, however. Minium or lead oxide red, a byproduct of the processing of lead, could be used to produce red ink, ideal for underlining certain passages in the text or highlighting the information surrounding the main text. It was common practice to set what we would call titles or headings in wordy, consecutive lines executed in red ink. The main text endings were also often marked in red, with *incipit* used to denote the beginning and *explicit* the close of a passage, after the Latin words found at the start and end of most medieval texts.

The use of lead oxide red gave rise to two other expressions still used today, in slightly different contexts. *Rubrum* is the Latin name for "red" or an "entry in red" and "rubrics" are the words which help order texts. The Latin word for lead oxide red is *minium*; hence the delicate, beautiful ornamentation executed in this material is known as a "miniature."

Animal hide was expensive, and writing material thus rare. It is not surprising, then, that the creators of medieval books took great care to include as many words as possible in the space available. In a good medieval manuscript there are no paragraphs and absolutely no empty lines, except at the end of long passages. With their horror of leaving empty spaces (*horror vacui*), scribes crammed the ruled lines and blocks of text full of words.

So that they did not lose themselves in the impenetrable jungle of letters and characters, readers and writers alike devised two methods of marking their place. One of these was the bookmark, made of a material that did not damage the book, such as a piece of straw, a leaf or even a flower. In little-used books dating from the Middle Ages, some of these place markers can still be found. The problem with bookmarks, however, was that they often fell out, and this prompted illuminators to draw markers in the text itself. The important beginnings (or *initiae* in

*Luke the Painter at an Illuminator's Desk,* Lyon or Paris *c.* 1500 Illuminators' ink on parchment, leaf size 20.7 × 13.5 cm The Guémadeuc Book of Hours, fol. 8v Heribert Tenschert, Bibermühle

The young artist has a portable desk with him, equipped with drawers for the tools of his trade. He is depicted painting a portrait of the Queen of Heaven at the palace.

Le traif du soleil et de la lune
Chapistre premier·

E soleil selon ce
que dit le philo
soppte est loeil
du monde· la
iocundite de dieu· la beaute du
ciel· la mesure de temps· la
vertu et origine de toutte cho
se naissantte en terr· seul·
de planette· conducteur et

par faiteur de touttes les es
touttes· Et la lune come
dit monseigneur sainct
Ambroise en son liure inti
tule Exameron· est la be
aute de la nuit· mere et
ministre de toutte hunie
mesure de mois· Anne et
la mer· celle qui transmue
les airs· et est gouuernee
du soleil· Et pour ce quelle

Latin) of chapters were distinguished by large, conspicuous letters known as initials, decorated either just in red or in a range of bright colors. Early initials were drawn as branches or flowers, with tendrils curling into the margins to catch the eye of someone flicking quickly through the pages. In this approach to text layout, where very little was left blank, lie the roots of the miniature, an art form whose name is derived from the red minium ink. The striking initial bookmark heralds the beginning of the illuminated manuscript. Illustrations of animals were also used; in the early Middle Ages, between the 5th and the late 8th centuries, fish and birds in particular were popular forms of embellishment.

There were also other means of drawing the reader's attention to a particular passage in the text. Where it was considered necessary to point something out, a hand and finger signaling the point of interest were often sketched in the margin. Human figures were used to denote information pertaining to people. If an illness was being described, the human body was depicted. Illuminators also liked to portray the author as the pillar of authority on which a text rested. Today's title pages give the writer, title and date of a work, but in the Middle Ages books pictured someone writing, teaching or even seated on a majestic throne who presided over the text. This picture was seldom, if ever, of the actual author; as portraiture was virtually unheard of at the time, the writer's actual appearance went undocumented. The simple image of the author was often enhanced with scenes from his idealized working environment or with motifs from the book's subject matter.

Illumination had to be squeezed into the few spaces left blank in between the areas of text; blocks of varying size in the main body of text were reserved for the most important initial letters. The margins could be filled with illustrations. Leaving additional unfilled areas on the page for pictures was a rare occurrence; books made up of illustrations with little or no text were almost unheard of.

Although scribes were required to copy texts word for word, book illuminators were allowed to depict the author and the book content in

Left: Oderisio da Gubbio group
*Flight to Egypt* on a book leaf decorated with music and text, Bologna *c*. 1300
Illuminators' ink on parchment, 29.8 × 22 cm
Lectionary, fol. 14', Heribert Tenschert, Bibermühle

The illuminator's primary task was to stress the importance of the beginning of the text. Large initials were painted in gold leaf and ink which spread into the margin, here providing the artist with enough space to depict a scene from the life of Christ. The illumination is by one of the scribes of the school of Oderisio da Gubbio, the pope's scribe, who Dante mentions in the *Inferno*.

keeping with contemporary convention. Thus medieval manuscripts record interesting developments in social aspects such as clothing and housing and also through subtle changes in their illustrations .

One example of this centers on the Italian physician and astrologer Maino de Maineri. He studied in Paris, where from 1326 he was head of the medical faculty before being summoned to the court of the Visconti in Milan in 1346. He served here for 20 years. His main work, the *Dialogus creaturarum*, is a succession of dialogs in which he attempts to record the scientific knowledge of his era in an encyclopedic form. To give character to God's various creations he has the creatures speak to one another, with "protagonists" ranging from the sun and the moon to man and death engaging in verbal exchange. Yet the most beautiful copy of Maineri's book was produced much later, in a town far from where he worked. In 1482 an illuminator in Flemish Bruges painted Maino de Maineri writing his volume in a library almost devoid of books, noting down his ideas purely on the basis of his imagination and inspiration. The author sits enthroned on his chair with two

Opposite:
Old master from 1482
*Maino de' Maineri and the Dialogue of the Sun and the Moon*, Bruges 1482
Illuminators' ink on parchment, leaf size 37.5 × 26.5 cm
Gruuthuse copy, fol. 7r, Heribert Tenschert, Bibermühle

The author is sitting in an almost empty library in the main residential building of a medieval castle.
He is thinking about what he will have the sun say to the moon.

Sicilian or Salernitan
*Georgius Zothorus Zaparus
Fendulus at His Desk,* from:
*Liber Astrologiae,*
1225–1250
Book ink on parchment, leaf
size 27.5 × 19 cm
Ms. lat. 7330, fol. 1
Bibliothèque Nationale de
France, Paris

Authors could be
understood as rulers, as the
crown here indicate.

scribes huddled over their work in front of him, much smaller to indicate their lesser significance. Maineri voices his thoughts, which appear like a speech bubble in the window to his left, where the sun is talking to the moon in the first dialog.

Earlier authors were depicted with even greater honor than Maineri in the above example. A Sicilian illuminator during the reign of Emperor Frederick II in the early 13th century portrays the translator of an Arabic book on astrology, Georgius Zothorus Zaparus Fendulus, wearing a crown. The artist shows him holding his quill case with a small inkpot attached to it in his left hand, and working on a page of text with his right. Painstakingly written lines run across the page which is stretched taut on a writing desk. Even the emperor might pale into insignificance beside this majestic figure.

This miniature illustrates the awe with which people in the high Middle Ages regarded great thinkers and writers. However, when God himself appeared in a picture, humans of whatever status shrank humbly into the background. About 100 years before Fendulus, Oderiso of Monte Cassino, abbot of the famous abbey from 1099 until 1105, had himself portrayed in a prayer book, gazing up at the Mother of God on her throne. A mere mortal, he barely reaches the cushion the Virgin Mary is sitting on. The figures float across the empty parchment as if in space, a clear indication that this is the work of monastic illuminators rather than professional book artists. The prayerbook was produced at Monte Cassino, the lonely mountaintop where St. Benedict (*c.* 480–*c.* 560) had established a monastery centuries before. The raw materials for the book's manufacture were probably available on site. The monks tended the animals whose skins were turned into parchment and whose feathers were used as quills; they collected gallnuts from oak trees for the ink and possibly extracted some of the minerals they needed for color pigment themselves, preparing the verdigris for Mary's dress from copper. The blue was probably an import, most likely from Afghanistan, as the name ultramarine or "color from the other side of the sea" would suggest. The materials for the binding were also readily available at a large and well-managed monastery, from the clean-cut wooden boards to the leather covers to the metal clasps and fastenings.

For centuries the monks in the scriptoria worked to a strict discipline, training generation after generation of copyists, calligraphers, illuminators and miniaturists. The brothers were allowed to travel only with special permission,

revolves around their colleagues in the monasteries. For Dante, illumination had become an art practiced in the cities, with Paris its great metropolis.

Castles first obtained their books from the monasteries; by the 13th century universities and cities were giving the Benedictines some tough competition. In the early 1200s former monks and defrocked priests were among the first to make a living out of producing books, parchment and bindings and through writing and illumination. By the time printing was developed, the medium was dominated by the laity.

The era of printing naturally spelled the end of the illuminated manuscript. The first books printed in Italy came from the Benedictine abbey of Subiaco between 1464 and 1468. Prior to this date, all books had been laboriously created by the hands of scribes.

Left: Viennese illuminator *Castle with Attackers*, before 1439 (?)
Illuminators' ink on parchment, leaf size 37 × 30 cm
Book of warfare of King Abrecht II or Ladislaus Posthumus, fol. 9r, Heribert Tenschert, Bibermühle

Most illuminators restricted their work to the areas designated for text. Books of pictures were extremely rare. Miniatures served to instruct the reader. Castle archeologists in particular have a wealth of wonderful illustrations at their disposal in examples such as this one, part technical diagram, part cartoon, which shows a hostile army trying to force their way into a seemingly impenetrable stronghold.

which was rarely granted, meaning they had little contact with the outside world. Ancient traditions were easily upheld, with very few interested in following trends and fashions outside the monastery walls. The lives of the friars consisted of prayer and work, with many of their daily chores focusing on the various stages in the production of books, from tending their livestock to tanning the hides to writing and illumination.

Book production was far from being a monastic monopoly, however, and most of the monks' literary output had a strictly religious purpose. Scriptoria started to spring up in royal palaces and at universities, in which both calligraphy and book art were cultivated. In Dante's *Divine Comedy*, which is set in 1300 and which the author began writing in 1307, illuminators are no longer shrouded in monastic habits. In Canto 11 of Dante's *Inferno* the poet meets Oderisio da Gubbio (died 1299), the papal illuminator, among those who have been sent to purgatory to atone for their sin of pride. The late master pits his wits against those of one of his pupils, Franco Bolognese. Both are artists in a world of pride and careerism that no longer

Left: Luxury binding for the House of Visconti, between 1350 and 1401/02
Dark leather on wooden covers with brass corners, 30.5 × 22.5 cm
Lectionary, Heribert Tenschert, Bibermühle

Miniatures have been well preserved between the closed covers of medieval manuscripts. The bindings have not fared so well, however. Metal clasps and decorations were very popular, not least because they reflected the wealth and status of the owner. The metal got in the way, however, when several books were stored together on the same shelf. The bosses were thus often only preserved in private collections, while those in the major libraries were removed.

Far right: A room in the historic library at the castle of the Guidi counts in Poppi.

Right: The archives of the governors of Florence house over 5,000 bundles of civil and judicial documents from the Casentino region from between 1440 and 1735.

## Biblioteca Rilliana

Poppi Castle houses an enormous library of about 25,000 volumes. Over 500 of these are manuscripts, the oldest of which date from the 11th century. There is also a priceless collection of incunabula. The latter include valuable editions produced by the Venetian

printer Aldus Manutius. The library originates from the monastery of Camaldoli, founded in 1012 by the Benedictine monk Romuald of Ravenna in the Casentino Apennines. In the 15th century, Camaldoli was a major center of cultural activity and the seat of a philosophical academy. In the 19th century the Camaldoli library was enlarged with books contributed by Count Rilli-Orsini, from whom the present Biblioteca Rilliana gets its name.

# The Battle of Anghiari

Castello, and expansive fiefs, such as that of the Guidi counts. They were also traversed by major roads, enabling the new potentates to control communication between north and south.

Prior to the battle, Florence had ruled Pisa for over 30 years. Taking full advantage of this access to the sea, Florence had begun building its own fleet of ships. After acquiring the new Apennine regions the Florentines began to hope for a second maritime base on the Adriatic. Florence had originally been populated by people coming down from the mountains into the valley; now it looked as if the city could advance further to become a powerful seaport. This dream was never fulfilled, yet without the Battle of Anghiari Florence would never have become what it is today.

## The diplomatic game of the *condottieri*

The major event that fueled the Florentine dream of greatness came about by sheer coincidence. War had raged between Milan and Venice for many years, with the two sides fighting to gain control over the Po basin and the wealthy cities of Brescia, Cremona and Padua, all of them a long way from

Left: Bonifacio Bembo
*Francesco Sforza*, c. 1460
Oil on canvas
Pinacoteca di Brera, Milan

At the time of the Battle of Anghiari, Francesco Sforza commanded the allied army against the Visconti of Milan as a soldier of fortune. Ten years later Sforza was himself lord and master of the duchy of Milan.

Below: A political map showing the city-states in northern and central Italy in the 15th century.

The rulers of Florence wanted to create a state with one port on the Tyrrhenian Sea and another on the Adriatic.

## A minor uprising with major consequences

The Battle of Anghiari on June 29, 1440, was a milestone in the history of Florence and Tuscany. The consequences of the battle were in inverse proportion to the number of dead (one); on the day after the conflict Florence found itself master of two enormous stretches of the Apennines – the wide Casentino and the upper Tiber Valley, through which the upper reaches of the Arno and Tiber rivers flow. Through its expansion east-wards the state of Florence had suddenly meta-morphosed into a mighty regional power at the heart of the country. The geopolitical map of Italy as a whole was changed overnight. Having control over the sources of two "fateful" rivers was strongly symbolic and an excellent source of propaganda. The new territories included thriving cities, such as Borgo Sansepolcro and Città di

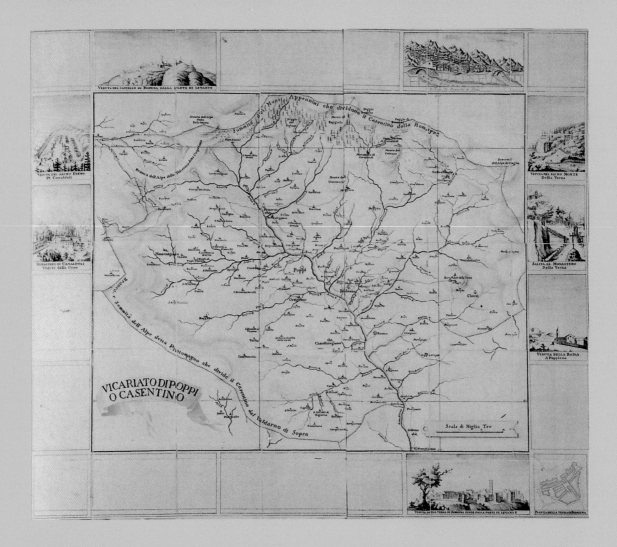

An old map of the Casentino.

After the Casentino fell to Florence in 1440 the region retained its boundaries. The area was under the direct administration of the governors of Florence.

Anghiari. The republic of Venice had formed a league with the pope and Florence in an attempt to curb the expansionist designs of the Visconti of Milan. The warring factions fought each other with armies of mercenaries drummed up by guerilla captains or *condottieri*. Niccolò Piccinino was fighting for the duchy of Milan, Francesco Sforza for the anti-Visconti alliance. As neither of the two *condottieri* were interested in settling their dispute on the battlefield, they both began to play a game of diplomacy based on the notion that the enemy of today could be the (paying) master of tomorrow – and vice versa. The armies of volunteers were like bands of nomads with no permanent territories of their own, ruled by a rudimentary brand of bureaucracy and an extremely sophisticated system of diplomacy. The greatest ambition of any *condottiere* was to obtain land of his own that he could turn into a small state with fixed boundaries. Here he would house his women and children and keep soldiers and farmers to protect and work the land. The *condottieri* thus preferred to fight their battles on the fringe, in places acting as buffer zones or "gray areas" with fluid borders. One of these weak spots was the eastern region of the Apennines between Tuscany and the Romagna. The area was riddled with local tyrants, with small towns having their own systems of self-government – and with large fiefs rapidly sinking into decline and disorder.

## The calm before the storm

Reacting to increasing pressure from the Venetians, in 1439 Francesco Sforza finally left the buffer zone of the Romagna, crossed the River Po and marched on Brescia, which for the previous three years had been besieged by

Leonardo da Vinci
*Study of a Head for the Battle of Anghiari*, c. 1503–1505
Silverpoint, black chalk and red ochre on paper,
19.1 × 18.8 cm (facsimile)
Gabinetto dei Disegni e delle Stampe, Galleria degli Uffizi, Florence

This head is a portrait of Niccolò Piccinino, *condottiere* to the Visconti. Sixty years after the historic event, the city of Florence commissioned Leonardo da Vinci to portray the Battle of Anghiari on the wall of the Sala dei Cinquecento in the Palazzo Vecchio. Some of the preliminary drawings and sketches have been preserved, but the fresco itself was never finished.

Milanese troops. Yet instead of meeting his aggressors face to face, Sforza's opposite number, Niccolò Piccinino, retreated to the eastern reaches of Tuscany, setting up camp in the upper Tiber Valley in Borgo Sansepolcro and Città di Castello. This move took the Florentines by surprise. Florence had joined the league but had expected only to take part in a diplomatic sideshow restricted to matters of authority and finance. Instead they found themselves on the brink of war. "We were convinced, and still are, that we could remain spectators (...) in this battle," Florence's ambassador Neri Capponi told the Venetian senators, thinly disguising his threat to terminate the alliance against Milan.

Realizing that it could have a real war on its hands, Florence maneuvered its provisional militia, reinforced with the pope's troops, to Anghiari, three miles (5 km) south of Sansepolcro. The two armies were at a standoff for several weeks without a single weapon clashing. An urgent dispatch addressed to Piccinino drastically changed the situation. His employer, Filippo Maria Visconti, ordered him to leave Tuscany and return to Lombardy post-haste; here *condottiere* Sforza had freed the city of Brescia from the siege and was now posing a serious threat to the entire duchy of Milan. Piccinino obeyed with a heavy heart. Spies behind enemy lines immediately informed the Florentines about both the defeat of the Milanese in Brescia and the order given to Piccinino to pack his bags. The danger now seemed to have passed for the Florentines. Once again they were relegated to being simple observers of war whose most strenuous task was to place bets as to its outcome. On the evening of June 28, 1440, both the Florentine and papal soldiers were given leave in Anghiari, where the wine flowed freely.

## The battle

On the morning of June 29, the commander of the Florentines, Micheletto Attendolo, noticed "great clouds of dust" collecting on the plain while taking his daily exercise on the battlements of Anghiari's city wall. What on earth was going on? Niccolò Machiavelli described the scene: "As soon as he realized it was the enemy, he called his men to arms. Great tumult broke out in the Florentine camp. Although the camps of armies such as these were always disorderly, here their carelessness was doubled by the fact that they had assumed the enemy to be far away and on the retreat rather than planning an attack. Thus all were unarmed, some of them here, the others there (…)."

And so it was. Piccinino, getting ready to leave, had decided to launch a surprise attack on the Florentines in order to teach them a quick lesson before heading north. Thanks to Attendolo's early morning workout, however, the Florentines were able to form ranks quickly to defend the hill at Anghiari. The lay of the land was also to their great advantage. For several hours the two armies fought over a small bridge which Piccinino's troops would have had to cross, with "the Florentines and then the enemy gaining control of the bridge. And although the two sets of troops were evenly matched in this battle, on both sides of the bridge the fighting was to Piccinino's disadvantage (…). But when the Florentines secured the bridge so that their army could advance to the road on the far side of it, the heavy attack and unfavorable

Tito di Santi (1536-1603)
*Niccolò Machiavelli*
Oil on canvas
Palazzo Vecchio, Florence

In his history of Florence the legendary political theorist and writer Niccolò Machiavelli (1469–1527) describes the Battle of Anghiari in absorbing detail.

terrain left Piccinino no time to have fresh troops advance so that the front lines muddled with the back, one pushing the other, until the entire army turned tail and all of them, without further ado, fled to the Borgo." Machiavelli closes his account of the clash with the following remark: "In this decisive defeat, in this battle which raged from the 20th to the 24th hour one single man died, not from a wound but from a fall, whereupon he was trampled to death by a horse."

The Florentines knew how to turn the situation to their advantage. They immediately seized control of all the towns and cities abandoned by Piccinino which had previously belonged to the pope or one of the local despots. They then laid siege to the towns and villages in the Casentino Valley and to Poppi Castle, putting an end to centuries of feudal rule under the Guidi counts, who had been careless enough to summon Piccinino to Tuscany. The victory at Anghiari also prompted a certain internal matter to be cleared up in Florence. The Florentine emigrant faction disbanded and their leader, Rinaldo degli Albizzi, decided to embark on a long pilgrimage to the Holy Land. On their return to Florence, the veterans of Anghiari were welcomed home as conquering heroes.

# Monteriggioni
## The crown of Siena

Far right: View of the walls of Monteriggioni.

The small fortified town was founded in 1214 by the republic of Siena near the border with the state of Florence and not far from two major medieval roads, the Via Cassia and the Via Francigena. The walls are 1,837 ft (560 m) long and encircle 138 houses and a church.

### A wall and 14 towers

Next to the gate facing towards Siena an inscription marks the commencement of building on the new fortified town: "In the month of March in the year of our Lord MCCXIII (...) with the aid of the payments and labor of the people of Siena." The Roman numerals stand for the year 1213, which according to the modern calendar is actually 1214. In medieval Siena and Florence, as with other Italian cities, the solar year began neither on the first of January nor on 25 December, the day Jesus was born. Instead a more logical principle was applied, with the start of the year calculated as March 25, nine months prior to the savior's birth. In the course of a normal pregnancy one could argue whether a fetus is a person in its own right from the time of its conception or not. In the case of Christ, however, this is not an issue. In Siena the first three months of the year were added on to the one before. Thus work started on Monteriggioni in March 1214.

Right: The stone inscription on the outer wall next to the southeast gate reminds us that the fortified town was built "with the aid of the payments and labor of the people of Siena."

70

## A ring of fire and water

Erecting a new walled town from scratch was a new concept in 13th-century Tuscany. Ancient Rome may have done so, but not the municipalities of the Middle Ages. They concentrated their energies on gaining control of existing castles and villages, fortifying them when a strategy of defense or expansion of the town was deemed necessary. After carefully surveying the area that bordered on Florentine terrain the members of the *comune* of Siena decided that the hill of Monteriggioni was the most suitable location for their new fortification. The clear view, elevated position and proximity to two major roads – the Cassia and the Francigena – were the criteria which helped the city fathers select this particular location.

Monteriggioni's air of artificiality, a town which has been conceived as a whole rather than allowed to evolve naturally, gives it an atmosphere both unreal and homely. Just 30 years ago, sheep still wandered through the streets and tourists were a rarity. The wall, 1,837 ft (560 m) long, is an almost perfect circle, punctuated by 14 square towers which jut out on both sides of the rampart. It is over 30 ft (about 10 m) high, with the towers almost twice this size. At the beginning of the 16th century, when guns were in common use, the towers were partly dismantled so that they were the same height as the wall. They were restored to their original height in the 1920s. An embankment and a moat with a drawbridge across it used to run round the outside of the wall. The moat has since been filled in and a ring road built on top of it. The stronghold was once encircled by a system of ditches filled with coal and pitch and camouflaged with leaves. These *carbonaie*, or charcoal stacks, could be set alight with burning arrows dipped in pitch and fired from a distance. The aim was to be enable to ensnare potential attackers between a ring of water and a ring of fire, where they were at the mercy of the town garrison.

## A city in miniature

Within the wall the architects built a city in miniature. The main street runs through the middle of town from southeast to northwest, linking the two town gates. The piazza, church and a fortified residential tower form the heart of the community.

By the end of the 13th century Monteriggioni had over 100 houses and about 300 inhabitants. Homes were built according to a plan which left a safe zone near the wall. The first people to acquire land and modestly priced

Monteriggioni is protected by 14 mural towers that dominate the town's skyline.

dwellings in Monteriggioni came from Siena. The majority of the permanent settlers, however, were families of farmers who had fields in the area or tilled the soil for the citizens of Siena. Many of the houses had their own vegetable patch, an inner courtyard and an oil press. Nobody was forced to move to the town; the authorities preferred to court prospective inhabitants with reduced taxes and other concessions. A town garrison numbering 100 in times of war was provided for the people of Monteriggioni, should they need it. Twenty of this number were crossbowmen hired from the market in Pisa, where the best professional marksmen of the day were to be found.

## The giants of Dante's *Inferno*

The Monteriggioni fortress soon aroused the covetousness and fired the imagination of its contemporaries. The sturdy structure was a thorn in the flesh of the Florentines in particular. As early as 1232, following a successful campaign against Siena, Florence dictated that Monteriggioni be destroyed as one of the conditions of the peace treaty. Not wanting to lose its *pièce de resistance*, Siena refused to accept the terms and continued to wage war against Florence – to its own detriment. In 1254 Florence managed to lay siege to Monteriggioni. Its attempt to storm the fortification and seize control failed, however. Florence then decided to try and take possession of the model stronghold instead of destroying it, thus playing the enemy at its

Seen from the air, Monteriggioni's regular structure and town plan is clearly recognizable. Enclosed by a defensive wall and mural towers the main street runs straight through the heart of town, linking the two gates and opening out onto the piazza in the middle.

Right: Philip Galle (after Johannes Stradanus, 1523–1605) *The Battle of Monteriggioni,* from *The History of the Medici*

In August 1554 Monteriggioni was captured by Florentine and Spanish troops following a brief siege. Siena finally capitulated in March 1555 after being besieged for over a year.

MONS REGONIS.

Iohan Stradanus inuentor.
Pils Galle fecit.

*Mons Regonis, oppidum, situ et manu munitum, magna tormentorum in quasatum,
praesidio metu percusso, à Caesarianis et Aethruscis superatur.*

Above: A 100 lire coin depicting the enclosing wall of Monteriggioni in the shape of a crown.

Opposite: The north-west town gate of Monteriggioni.

In the wake of the plague of 1348 the authorities drew up a strict code of conduct for its inhabitants in an effort to maintain a basic standard of hygiene and improve the living conditions of the community.

own game – a popular tactic in the Middle Ages. It had to wait 300 years to achieve this goal, however.

Dante Alighieri (1265–1321) greatly admired the "round enclosing wall flanked by towers" at the end of the 13th century. On the roads of his *Inferno* he espied a group of giants in the distance, standing in a circle, and mistook them for Monteriggioni. A second image inspired by Dante later become one of Italy's official icons and is still found on the 100 *lire* coin: a young girl wearing a crown of towers on her head.

## Capitulation

In 1554 war again broke out between Siena and Florence. On average this had happened around five times each century, but now things were to change. This was to be the final battle between the two Tuscan cities. With Florence backed by Spain and Siena by France, in the early days of January

Florentine and Spanish troops laid siege to their enemy. As Siena was to be gradually starved into submission, the aggressors began methodically cutting off the routes leading into the city. They destroyed the crops and burned the fields, and after eight months of siege turned their attention to Monteriggioni.

The mighty fortress was defended by a garrison of 100 men under the command of Captain Giannino Zeti. The latter, realizing he was fighting a losing battle, was prepared to negotiate as soon as the Florentines appeared on his doorstep. To provide the captain with an alibi, on August 28 the besieging army began an artillery attack. Zeti capitulated on August 29, but not before extracting various guarantees for himself and his men and securing his own future. When the news of the defeat reached Siena, it caused "so much sudden disgust, such a strong sense of ill, that everybody appeared to be half dead," one Sienese chronicler reported. From then on,

Siena's attempts to defend itself became feebler and feebler ("Monluc's List and the End of the Sienese Republic"). In order to justify the decision he had taken, Captain Zeti later published his version of events. On the evening before capitulating, he wrote, he had checked the water supply and found that "there was only enough water left for one day and this was so foul that it could not be drunk; indeed, one could not even bear to smell it." Also, he added, their entire stock of wine had been used up. Civilian officials also recorded that the water was bad and the town devoid of wine. Even the victors confirmed that when they marched into Monteriggioni there was neither wine nor vinegar to be found. Thus the Florentines, waiting for Siena to be starved into defeat, had instead vanquished Monteriggioni by thirst.

## The statute of Monteriggioni

In 1348 the population of Monteriggioni was halved by the bubonic plague, a fate that befell almost every city in Italy. In the aftermath of the epidemic the remaining inhabitants drew up a statute outlining a basic code of conduct for the community. From this we know that it was forbidden to wash your feet in a public fountain, to climb the walls without permission, to swear, to let your goat graze in your neighbor's garden, to sell meat from animals that had not been slaughtered within the town walls, to trade in wine that was not marked with the seal of the *comune* of Siena, to throw things onto your neighbor's roofs, to gamble or bet for money or wine, to call your next of kin a liar, matchmaker or whore, and to work on Sundays. These misdemeanors were all the more serious if they took place at night. It was a citizen's duty, on the other hand, to keep the area in front of his house clean, to carry out the guard duties required of him and to plant the occasional fruit or olive tree to evade "damage and disgrace." Even where such trivial matters were concerned, the proud fortress of Monteriggioni wanted to make sure that it was not dependent on the outside world.

The following text appears in the illustration in Gothic script:

Ainer vngrischen
Der ander rawschen
Der drit phamnischen ver
der viera darufth au der ster
Der funst reder chriechischen
der sechst haidnischen
Also her sich ir red verdiert
alt fi vor selter her gelert.
J n zwo vnd sibenczick zungen
also war in gelungen
Gesten siven ein maurmaister ver
der werdman ie ein anas ter
Wolt er stain er prahet im saut
wan im sein red war vnbechant
Da hiezen si den turn sten
vnd irsuingen an die erd sen
D ham maurer chom hin wider
also irlaib der turn sider
D ie sprach wil ich ew nennen
daz ir si mugt erchennen
V no wil auch si vescheiden
cew sprach vnder den haiden
Waz ain vnd sibenczick lerhant
vier al in der haiden lant.
D ie inden halent auch ainew
vnd auch nie dhainew
E braisch ist si genant.
wan si vor py dem ersten vant.
Da von so ist inir swar
daz gor vnser schepfer
Den christen hat newr zwelf seken
Di christenseichen solten leken
V no ist daz die zwelf zungen recht
lerent so sind si gotes chnecht.
D ie sechteut zung vlorn sint
die musten sein der hell chint
Al vm die pfaffen halent gesair
sur die ganczen warhait.

## Military Architecture: Protection and Prestige

Jochen Staebel

Illustration from *Les maçons et sculpteurs*, Viola Goldstream, Brepols 1992, ill. 59, Cod. Germ. 5, fol. 29 Bayerische Staatsbibliothek, Munich

When a tower was under construction the stones were hauled up to the top on ropes in baskets or giant pincers.

The development of military architecture in medieval Italy was not markedly different from the processes in motion north of the Alps. Many of northern Italy's fortified towns thus betray the influence of Germanic or Lombard buildings, with many of them understandably modeled on the well-known edifices of the late Romanesque.

*Castellum* or *castrum* are terms generally used to describe a fortified settlement which from the 11th or 12th century was usually enclosed by a stone wall. Inside the ramparts stood the fortified residence of the city potentate or local lord (*rocca castri*). These towns were popularly built according to a regular, fixed plan which imitated their Roman precursors; because of the irregular terrain on which they stood, the castles of northern Italy were, however, influenced by military models north of the Alps. The early history of the fortress in Italy is governed by the same conditions as those predominant in Charlemagne's empire, part of which Italy had become. Here, too, the feudal system acted as a catalyst in the construction of a great number of castles. The development of the *castri* in Italy in particular is inextricably linked to the rise of the local gentry, although geographical and local historical factors played their parts. A definite trend in the construction of territorial fortifications can be seen to have begun in the 10th century. The reasons for this sudden boom in castle construction at the dawn of the late Middle Ages related not only to the need for protection or a show of aggression towards neighboring feudal lords, however. Increasingly, socioeconomic factors had a role. From the late 11th century, as the feudal nobility grew in power, it desired ever more impressive strongholds to reflect its increasing stature. In the centuries that followed, the castle's role in defending the lives of its inhabitants and the local populace became overshadowed by its function of administering the lands and estates owned by the regional overlord.

The function of the medieval castle thus differed from that of earlier fortifications. For Celtic and Germanic tribes the "ringwork and refuge" were the basic components of complexes solely devoted to defense. An area of ground, usually quite large in size, was surrounded by a massive enclosure of blocks of stone or by earthen ramparts spiked with palisades. Often a system of wooden frames held together with nails (the Gallic wall) was inte-

Far right:
The fort at Otzenhausen
(Hunsrück, Germany),
c. 200 B.C.
Plan of the ramparts.
This fort is a typical example
of the "ringwork and refuge"
model with enclosing
earthworks (oppidum).

Below: Idealized plan of a
Roman castrum

grated into constructions such as these. It is in these early forts that we can recognize the basic structure of later fortresses and castles which had a second wall or curtain as an outer defense, ditches and palisades surrounding the outer bailey and an interior wall enclosing the inner bailey or inner ward.

A uniform military complex design evolved from the 2nd and 3rd centuries A.D. onwards: the Roman fort or permanent camp (castellum). This was usually square or rectangular, flanked by

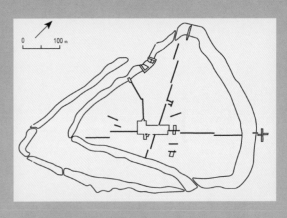

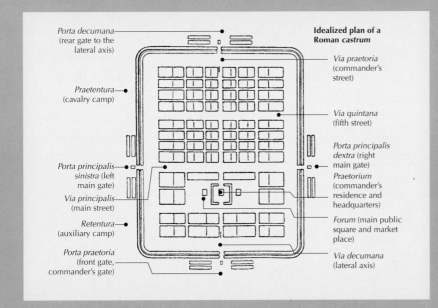

Idealized plan of a
Roman castrum

Porta decumana
(rear gate to the
lateral axis)

Praetentura
(cavalry camp)

Via praetoria
(commander's
street)

Via quintana
(fifth street)

Porta principalis
dextra (right
main gate)

Porta principalis
sinistra (left
main gate)

Via principalis
(main street)

Praetorium
(commander's
residence and
headquarters)

Retentura
(auxiliary camp)

Forum (main public
square and market
place)

Porta praetoria
(front gate,
commander's gate)

Via decumana
(lateral axis)

four corner towers, and housed the Roman legions, its primary purpose one of defense. Smaller outposts placed at fairly regular intervals secured the limes or Roman frontier. The larger field camp erected under the Roman emperors, the castrum, was normally square and surrounded by a wall with four rounded corners. A wide road (via decumana) cut across the camp horizontally, splitting it into a narrower front section (praetentura) and a wider rear section (retentura). A vertical main street (cardo) divided both areas into mirror-image halves. The most outstanding examples of Roman military architecture, and the ones that also marked its end, were the city wall around Rome, constructed by Emperor Aurelian from 272 A.D. onwards (the Aurelian Wall) and the mighty walls of Byzantium (Constantinople) from the 5th century.

The military architecture of the early Middle Ages is characterized by its use and re-use of existing sites from late antiquity (Castel Sant'Angelo); further development of these complexes or innovative adaptation of existing forms did not occur in this period. The fortified farms of the Franks and the imperial palaces of the Carolingians showed few if any special forms of defensive architecture. This lack of foresight was avenged in the 9th and 10th centuries when the Normans and Magyars ravaged Europe. In the wake of devastation people began rapidly garrisoning their towns, manor houses, churches and farms.

In the 10th century the forts and homes of the ruling aristocracy usually consisted of a wooden residential tower placed on top of a natural or man-made earth mound (motte) and enclosed by a ditch

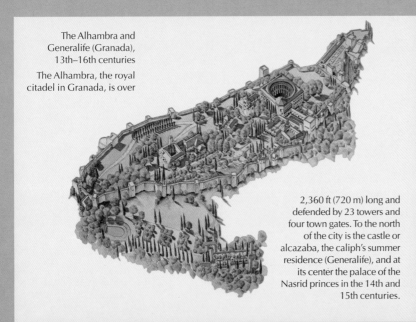

The Alhambra and
Generalife (Granada),
13th–16th centuries
The Alhambra, the royal
citadel in Granada, is over

2,360 ft (720 m) long and
defended by 23 towers and
four town gates. To the north
of the city is the castle or
alcazaba, the caliph's summer
residence (Generalife), and at
its center the palace of the
Nasrid princes in the 14th and
15th centuries.

and palisades. Beneath the ramparts of the motte was a fenced-in area (the bailey) to which the local populace could flee in times of danger.

The first stone castles were erected in about 1000. Largely because of changes in the socio-economic situation, the 11th and 12th centuries saw the evolution of the prototypical medieval fortress: what we still consider to be the "classic" castle. It is not possible to define *the* medieval castle per se, as there are many different types of castle known to us, each one distinguished by its topography, function, and the designs and demands of its builders. We shall thus limit our generalizations to a brief description of the basic sections of the medieval stronghold.

## Idealized plan of a medieval castle

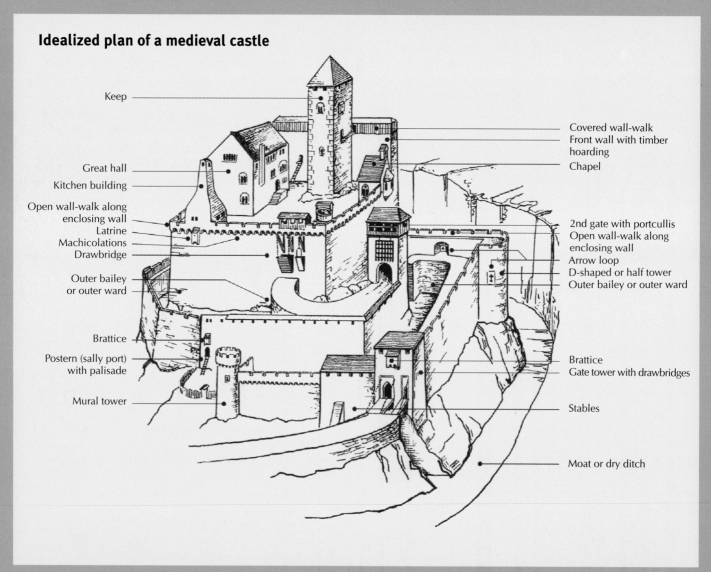

Keep

Covered wall-walk
Front wall with timber hoarding

Great hall

Chapel

Kitchen building

Open wall-walk along enclosing wall
Latrine
Machicolations
Drawbridge

2nd gate with portcullis
Open wall-walk along enclosing wall
Arrow loop
D-shaped or half tower
Outer bailey or outer ward

Outer bailey or outer ward

Brattice

Postern (sally port) with palisade

Brattice
Gate tower with drawbridges

Mural tower

Stables

Moat or dry ditch

An enclosing wall or *enceinte* surrounded the castle, with a dry ditch or moat in front of it. A smaller wall, called a *berm*, built between the *enceinte* and moat or a walled barbican acted as additional defensive areas. Palisades, or timber stakes rammed close together into the ground, were also often installed to deter intruders. An area of flat ground, the outer bailey, ran between the enclosing and outer walls. Mural towers jutted out from the *enceinte*, from which the castle garrison could bombard their attackers. Behind the rectangular, round or stepped merlons (the swallow-tail or forked merlon is typical of the Italian castles of the 12th and 13th centuries) running along the top of the wall were the battlements (wall-walk or *alure*); this was either a stone parapet or a timber hoarding. The only openings in the enclosing wall were slits which took on a variety of shapes to accommodate the weapons of the particular period; these included the simple firing slit or arrow slit, the gun loop or *oilette* and the cruciform embrasure or *balistraria* for the crossbow. Entrances to the castle were also defended by brattices resting on consoles; rows of these often found along the curtain wall are known as machicolations. Burning oil, water or pitch was poured through these holes down onto the enemy below. The castle gatehouse, the most vulnerable part of any stronghold, gradually developed into a fortification in its own right, equipped with a portcullis, drawbridge and flanking towers.

The inner ward within the outer curtain wall was dominated by the keep, the lowest level of which was often the dungeon. In France and England the keep or *donjon* was both a place of final refuge and one of residence. In the rest of Europe the living quarters consisted of the *palas* or *palatium*, the great hall, and the *caminata* or warming room, the area of the castle heated by a fireplace and often described as the ladies' chamber. The obligatory castle chapel was directly adjacent to the representative residential apartments. The only other buildings in the inner bailey were the service buildings and servants' quarters, and it also housed the castle well or cistern.

The isolated medieval fortress was not vastly different in plan to the fortified medieval town. The month of August in Duc de Berry's Book of Hours gives us a very accurate impression of the defensive nature of the royal 12th-century residence. In the foreground is the *castrum*, walled-in in 1020, containing the elements typical of the royal fortified palace of this period: the urban or lower castle or fortified gatehouse, the royal chapel and the royal monastery dedicated to the Virgin Mary. Outside the town walls, surrounded by a defensive curtain of its own, stands the majestic new castle from the early 12th century, built on an elevation and towering high above the town. The castle has a mighty *donjon*, the Tour-Guinette, and its own chapel of St. Laurent. This view of Étampes gives us a good

Above: Simone Martini
*Equestrian Portrait of Condottiere Guidoriccio da Fogliano*, 1330–1331
Fresco, 340 × 968 cm
Palazzo Pubblico, Sala del Mappamondo, Siena

Simone Martini's fresco for the west wall of the senior council chamber in the Palazzo Pubblico in Siena documents the capture of fortified Montemassi in 1328 under commander Guidoriccio. To the left is the fortress south of Siena, palisades erected by the siege army below it as noted in the city's chronicle; the camp of the Sienese army, equipped with siege engines and bearing the city's coat of arms, is on the bottom right.

Opposite, top:
*Building the Tower of Babel* (detail)
Illumination
The Bedford Book of Hours
Add. ms. 18850, fol. 17v
The British Library, London

This detail provides a wonderful illustration of the processes of medieval construction. Masons are depicted measuring enormous blocks of stone with a pair of compasses and a square, with others preparing the stone and mixing mortar. Their work is being closely observed by the man building the castle and his architect.

79

idea of just how important the medieval fortress was as a symbol of power. In this example, the political situation and architectural development of the period (during which the French king seems to have fallen behind his territorial neighbors with regard to military technology) called for the immediate erection of a new, state-of-the-art stronghold incorporating the latest technological standards, barely 100 years after the first royal residence and castle had been built.

The structural development of fortified places was greatly assisted by the information on architecture and defense gleaned from the Arabs during the crusades and the *Reconquista*. From as early as the 9th century Moorish models greatly influenced the fortified towns erected in Spain. These were made up of the *alcázar*, the fortified seat of government in the center of the city, and the *alcazaba*, the impenetrable, walled stronghold upon a hill or rock outside the town boundaries.

In Italy, the architectural development of the castle followed a different course from that of western and central Europe. The growing confidence of feudal lords and the struggles of many towns and cities for independence brought about a shift in power. The principal functions of

the fortifications of northern Italy, most of them erected on the outskirts of towns, such as the Castello Sforza in Milan and the Castello Estense in Ferrara, were to protect local rulers in the event of possible uprisings and unrest among the urban population and to highlight the power and prestige of the owners. New castles sprang up across the area, particularly as a result of the wars waged between individual autonomous towns; some had even played a strategic role since their founding in the 11th and 12th centuries as border posts monitoring the boundaries of the city states (Gavi for Genoa and Vicopisano for Pisa are two such examples).

The rise of the *comune* and of the *signorie* resulted in the construction of new types of castles out in the country from the late 13th century onwards. From this date a wide range of fortified settlements began to evolve, particularly in northern Italy, each with a particular function and structure, the consequence of architectural development and their increasing importance in political terms. The 14th and 15th centuries saw new castle-like complexes being erected in the centers of the cities themselves, among which we could count the representative

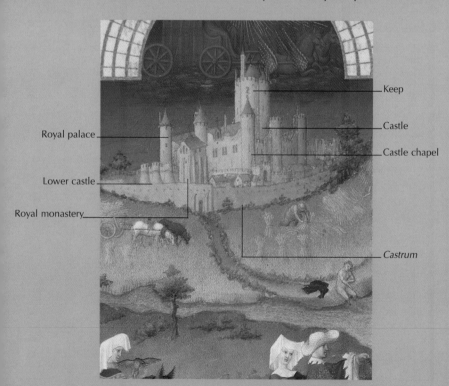

Below left:
Limbourg Brothers
Miniature from Duc Jean de Berry's Book of Hours
(*Les très riches heures*),
August, View of the City of Étampes, 1412–1415
Painting on parchment,
29 × 21 cm
Musée Condé, Chantilly

The month of August from the duke's Book of Hours provides us with a detailed view of the former Capetian residence of Étampes, showing all the elements of a fortified medieval town. In front of the castle with its mighty keep (Tour-Guinette) next to the castle chapel of St. Laurent from the early 12th century, rising up above the town outside the city walls, the miniaturist has painted the *castrum* with the lower castle, royal chapel and royal monastery of Notre Dame from the early 11th century.

Royal palace

Lower castle

Royal monastery

Keep

Castle

Castle chapel

Castrum

Illustration from *Les maçons et sculpteurs*, Nicola Goldstream, Brepols 1992, ill. 53
Illumination
Bildarchiv Preussischer Kulturbesitz, Berlin

Various primitive forms of scaffolding were used in building a tower. In this picture large stones are hauled up the tower interior using a block-and-tackle construction. Perhaps more interesting than this method of material handling, however, is the hierarchy which prevailed on site. We can tell how important the individual laborers were from how large they appear in the picture; the master builder, for example, is so huge that he appears to dwarf the rest of the elements in the scene.

Opposite, right:
*Construction of the Tower of Babel*
Miniature
Egerton 1894, fol. 5v
The British Library, London

Solid wood constructions made of rough, untreated timber were a much more secure means of transporting stone than ropes. The cost of the wood is often recorded in the builders' accounts.

public buildings of local government, such as the Palazzo Vecchio in Florence.

The decline of the medieval castle was precipitated by the perfection of firearms in the 15th century. Previously impregnable fortresses now found themselves unable to withstand bombardment by gunpowder-fired weapons. Major adjustments had to be made to render them safe again. Walls became thicker and lower so that projectiles had less surface area to impact upon. Italy pioneered the introduction of pentagonal corner bastions with two faces, two flanks and an inner opening to replace the round bastion. Regular polygonal forms were used, with the defenses encircling a fortification now mainly made up of bastions and curtain walls (a stretch of *enceinte* between two bastions). The keep was also replaced – by squat bastions and gun towers stocked with their own artillery.

The late 15th century and the 16th century marked a final flowering of military architecture.

The relentless advance of arms technology in the 17th century brought the construction of further forts to a gradual halt. Yet in populated areas away from the major cities and roads, the number of *castra* in Italy remained relatively high, particularly in Piedmont and Friuli. The castles here continued to function as strong-houses for the nobility or as the nuclei of areas of settlement whose populace was not dependent on a local lord. Existing castles such as these are today an impressive reminder of the great power and significance these buildings once held.

# Montalcino

## The pride of Siena

Right: View of Montalcino Castle from the south.

The castle crowns the highest point of the hill at the eastern end of the town. Construction began in 1361 when the town of Montalcino fell to Siena, losing its independent status. The fortress is the work of Sienese military architects Mino Foresi and Domenico di Feo, who were also responsible for the complete restoration of the enclosing wall, still intact today.

### Walls and a castle

Montalcino, an ancient town with Etruscan roots, perches atop a hill 1,860 ft (567 m) above sea level. The wall encircling the little town, interspersed with 13 towers and five gates, is over a mile (about 2 km) long. At the easternmost point of the town lies the highest point of the hill. This is crowned by a mighty fortress, the work of Sienese military architects Domenico di Feo and Mino Foresi. Construction on the castle began in 1361 when Montalcino was finally annexed by the republic of Siena and its inhabitants given Sienese citizenship. The ancient basilica of

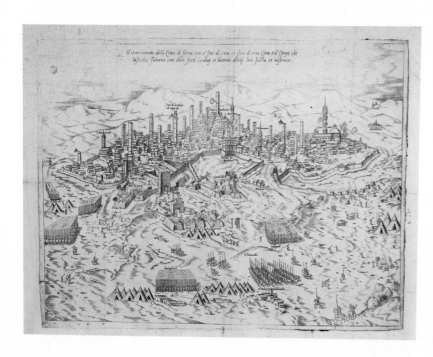

Above: *Siena During the Siege*, 16th-century print Cabinetto dei Disegni e delle Stampe, Galleria degli Uffizi, Florence

San Bartolomeo was torn down to make room for the new stronghold. All that was left standing of the church was the nave, which can still be seen in the inner ward. The fortification of the town, begun in the same

82

Above: Montalcino is 1,860 ft (567 m) above sea level. Like most Etruscan settlements, it was built on the top of a low hill.

year, also integrated much of what was already there, including parts of the 12th-century town wall which have been preserved to this day. The oldest sections of the wall also include the keep-like tower of San Martino and the San Giovanni watch-tower. The *glacis* outside the pentagonal castle wall was added in 1559 after Siena lost its status as a republic.

Right: Giorgio di Giovanni *L'assedio di Montalcino*, 1553
Plate from the Biccherna Archivio di Stato, Siena

The *Biccherna* was Siena's financial administration, headed by a magistrate who was nominated for six months at a time. When the incumbent's term of office came to an end, the documents amassed under his administration were bound, given an artistic frontispiece and archived. All of these covers, fashioned by Siena's best-known artists and dated between 1258 and 1659, have been preserved. The motif on the binding usually referred to the most significant event that had occurred during the magistrate's overlordship.

Montalcino is now famous worldwide for its wine, Brunello. The town still has roughly the same number of inhabitants as it did 800 years ago, when the populace numbered just over 6,000. Pope Pius II first proclaimed Montalcino a town in 1461. After Siena it was considered to be "the finest, the most densely populated and the most business-minded town" on Sienese territory. Even then its wines were highly regarded. The scholar Giovanni Antonio Pecci from Siena wrote: "as is generally known, the muscatels grown on this soil deserve great approval and should be served to great lords as delicate liqueurs." Montalcino's topography prevented the town from being extended, and it is still completely surrounded by its walls. Its unusual location has brought it both good fortune and bitter wars. For centuries the town was of great strategic importance; whoever held Montalcino also controlled the most important route to Rome, the Via Cassia, known in the Middle Ages as the Via Romana.

## The Battle of Montaperti

In the five centuries of war between Siena and Florence one of the chief objectives was to gain control of the Via Romana. For as long as possible the free *comune* of Montalcino tried to use the bitter conflict to its own best advantage. The town's usual plan of action was to revolt against neighboring Siena and forge an alliance with the more distant Florence. In 1255 Siena, Florence and other allied Tuscan towns signed a peace treaty that seemed destined to last. The main condition of the treaty was that the signatories vowed not to take in or offer help to citizens exiled from any of the other participating towns. In diplomatic terms this agreement was extremely sophisticated for its day, initiating a new form of legal culture in civil relations. Yet peace didn't last long. In 1260 Montalcino broke its pledge when it offered its hospitality and support to the Guelphs, who had been driven out of Siena. Their native city punished the rebel Montalcino by laying waste to the surrounding countryside and besieging the town. Florence replied in kind, destroying the fields around Siena and marching its army up to the city gates.

At first the Florentines seemed assured of victory over the Sienese. Yet once the initial chaos had abated the Sienese managed to break out of the city with their army and commenced battle. At a place called Montaperti near the torrential Arbia river the Sienese inflicted a crushing defeat on the Florentines. The Battle of Montaperti made history. Hostilities usually ended with a few dozen dead, and the number very seldom reached 100. But at Montaperti over 10,000 lost their lives, turning the River Arbia red with their blood, as Dante recorded a generation later. Montaperti heralded the dawning of an age of brutal massacres. For the first time craftsmen and merchants from Florence came face to face with craftsmen and merchants from Siena. Neither party showed mercy, hacking down anyone in their path.

The battle over, Siena unexpectedly found itself in a position of power over Florence. At a meeting of the Ghibelline cities of Tuscany in Empoli, the victorious army expressed its intention to wipe Florence off the face of the earth. Ghibelline exiles from Florence managed to prevent the bloody implementation of the plan. The Sienese then decided to at least raze Montalcino to the ground as an example to other would-be insurgents. The people of the doomed hill-town reacted immediately. One morning a group of about 400 pilgrims hobbled to the gates of Siena in single file, barefoot, with bowed heads and ropes around their necks, and begged the city governors for mercy. The gate was opened and the citizens of Montalcino entered, weeping and beating their chests, crying out for forgiveness. They were pardoned on the condition that they buried the 10,000 bodies that had been festering in the sun at Montaperti for days. The Montalcinians did so and from that day forward were Siena's most loyal allies.

The little church beneath the tower in the inner bailey.

The church nave is all that remains of the basilica of San Bartolomeo, which was taken down to make room for the castle.

## Monluc's List and the End of the Sienese Republic

ALTENPO          DETREMVOTI

Francesco di Giorgio Martini
*Plate from the Biccherna
Showing the City of Siena,*
Archivio di Stato, Siena

The top inscription reads: "At
the time of the earthquake."

The Roman proverb "O Francia o Spagna, purché se magna" (whether France or Spain, the main thing is we've got something to get our teeth into) originated in the 16th century. The people of Rome still use it to express their indifference to, and contempt for, politics. Yet those who best understood its true sentiment were perhaps the inhabitants of 16th-century Siena.

Florence laid siege to the Tuscan city of Siena on January 26, 1554. A growing power in the region, Florence was governed by the despotic son of an adventurer with the distinguished title of Cosimo I de' Medici. For centuries the republic of Siena had defied Florence's greedy attempts at expansion, clocking up a number of notable defeats. The siege promised to be a repeat of an all-too-familiar spectacle. Yet this time the outcome was very different. Cosimo, the duke of Florence, had the empire of Charles V behind him; the republic of Siena was backed by Henry II, king of France. Henry was married to Catherine de' Medici, who despite being queen of France had never ceased to consider herself a true Florentine. She also hated her cousin, Cosimo I de' Medici, with great passion.

Among the population of Siena were several Florentine exiles who called themselves republicans and who wanted to overthrow Cosimo. Their leader was Piero Strozzi, son and heir of a family of Florentine bankers whose wealth and power was second only to that of the Medici. Like Henry II, Strozzi's wife was also a Medici. The Strozzi were banished from Florence when Cosimo I seized power in 1537. Filippo Strozzi, Piero's father, placed himself at their helm, their strength barely diminished by expulsion, and made an attempt to defeat Cosimo I on the battlefield. He failed and was taken captive. Like the republicans of old before him (Brutus, Caesar's assassin, was the Strozzi contingent's role model), he committed suicide in prison.

On the tragic death of his father, Piero, the most promising of Filippo's four sons, fled to Catherine in Paris. Young, handsome, rich and educated, a skilled warrior, shrewd businessman and ally of the queen of France for good measure: Piero was a living nightmare, as far as Duke Cosimo I was concerned.

On January 7, 1554, Strozzi arrived in Siena, taking up residence at the palace of the Spannocchi family, then the most powerful bankers in town. For Florence, this was tantamount to open provocation. Less than three weeks later Siena found itself in the midst of a siege.

What had started out as a minor feud between Florentine financiers related by marriage now escalated into a full-scale war between major European powers. The Margrave di Marignano commanded a siege army of Florentine, Spanish, Bohemian and German troops. The military force of the besieged city consisted of the armed Sienese and professional mercenaries. The latter had been rounded up by Piero Strozzi, aided by the emigrant faction from Florence, their ranks swelled with French and Swiss soldiers sent by Catherine. The man in charge of the military was Blaise de Monluc, an adventurer from Gascony who was to become the progenitor of the literary heroes *The Three Musketeers*. Monluc was one of the first of the new age to write down his memoirs. In the third and fourth book of his *Commentaires* he describes the siege of Siena. The author was convinced that right from the outset the siege army intended to starve its opponents into submission. They had laid waste to the surrounding countryside, depopulated the area and forced the peasants to either flee to the city or move away. Four seasons passed. At the beginning of the second winter Siena's demise seemed imminent. Excerpts from Blaise de Monluc's report follow.

## January 1555: Monluc and the law of war

"We must set up shifts; your companies will rest for two nights and ours for one night. We shall also start reducing the bread ration to 14 ounces and yours to ten. We must remove all useless mouths from the city and delegate six people to draw up a list by tomorrow. In this way our provisions will last longer (...)

As everybody had somebody to protect, the [members of the council] could not pleasantly agree on those who shall be deemed useless. As a result they have unanimously appointed me their absolute dictator for the duration of one month. I named six commissioners entrusted with the drawing up of a list of the useless. I handed the list to a knight of St. John of Malta who was accompanied by 25 or 30 soldiers. Together they carried out the deportation over the following three days (...)

Know that the useless mouths did exceed the number of 4,400 and that of all the lamentable and desperate occurrences I have ever witnessed has none been like this (...) The weeping and despair continued for days. The unfortunate attempted to pass through the lines of the enemy army. They,

however, drove the Sienese back to the city so that they may be allowed to return. One hoped that the little bread remaining to us would be consumed the quicker for it or that people would show sympathy and an uprising would occur.

This all went on for eight days. The expelled fed themselves on nothing but grass. That is the law of war. One must be cruel to be able to resist the enemy. As we are committing so much evil, God must have great mercy upon us. Yet our own skin means more to us than our shirt. Do not fear to rid yourselves of the useless. Close your ears to their cries."

*Blaise de Monluc* from: *Episodes de sa vie* Bibliothèque Nationale de France, Paris

Monluc was elected dictator during the siege of Siena by Florence under the terms of the state of emergency. He passed laws on "useful and useless mouths."

## March 1555: Siena starves

"The month of March began and everything was lacking, for instance wine, of which there had not been a single drop in the entire city since the middle of February. We had eaten all the horses, all the donkeys, mules, cats and rats living in the town. Cats were sold for three or four *scudi* and a rat was worth one *scudo*. We lost inhabitants and soldiers who dropped dead while walking through the streets. People were dying without becoming ill. The physicians finally realized that this was due to the mallows we were eating; mallow is a plant which swells the stomach and hinders digestion without being nutritious. Along the city walls there was not a single blade of grass left. Everything had been eaten and we could not have gathered any more without having to pass outside and clash with the enemy (...) We dragged on in this condition until 8 April. We then lost all hope."

## The deportations

Documents show that there were actually five deportations of "useless mouths" from the city. In his memoirs Monluc summarizes events as one single episode.

In the first wave of expulsion at the end of the summer of 1554 the peasants and their families who had sought refuge in Siena at the beginning of the siege were hounded out of town. With them went the city's beggars and prostitutes. Most of the refugees were captured and strung up on the trees nearest the city walls. The besiegers wanted to terrify the Sienese and ensure that the evil stench of decomposing bodies polluted their streets and houses.

The second deportation, in October 1554, saw 250 children under ten chased from the orphanage of Santa Maria della Scala. French troops had confiscated the orphanage supplies. The Florentine alliance butchered the banished children just outside the city gates.

The third extradition in the early days of February 1555 again affected children, women and old people living alone, as well as many of the servants who had once worked for the rich families of Siena.

The fourth expulsion occurred during the carnival period. Again, 400 women and children were involved. At the same time tentative contact was made between the ambassadors to Cosimo I and the city of Siena with a view to negotiation. This time the Spanish and the Florentines were generous. They fed the deportees and took them to a convent. On the same day the commander of the siege army, the Margrave di Marignano, sent Monluc a fawn, four rabbits, four capons, white bread and wine.

The last group of people to be driven out of Siena again numbered several hundred. They had been deemed "useless" in the fourth week of March. They were again seized by enemy troops who cut off their noses and ears and sent them back to the city walls, streaming with blood.

*List of the "Useless"* (right) *and the "Useful"* (left) *Mouths*
Archivio di Stato, Siena

During the siege of Siena the first to be expelled were peasants and their families who had sought refuge within the city walls at the outset of the siege. Later 250 children under the age of 10 were banished, followed by two further groups of deportees.

## April 1555: capitulation

On April 17, 1555, the terms of capitulation were drawn up by the ambassadors of Siena and the representatives of Cosimo I. Siena was to put itself under the protection of the emperor of its own free will. Cosimo in turn pledged to defend Siena's independence. This meant that Siena avoided directly capitulating to Florence and the French were not forced to submit to the Spanish.

On April 21, the French, headed by Blaise de Monluc, pulled out of Siena with full military honors. Several hundred citizens followed, among them members of the great families of Piccolomini, Tolomei, Spannocchi and Bandini. They carried the standards of the republic of Siena and traveled to Montalcino where they met up with Piero Strozzi and other Florentine expatriates who had been there since the start of the siege. In Montalcino they proclaimed the republic of Siena in exile.

Around 6,000 inhabitants were left in Siena, the sorry remainder of a population of more than 40,000 at the beginning of the siege. The survivors now fully understood the sentiment behind the Roman proverb about France and Spain. After capitulating to the Spanish, Siena began life afresh, repopulating its city with new vigor. The siege army, for its part, set up camp outside the town walls of Montalcino. Catherine de' Medici again sent Blaise de Monluc to deal with the situation. Yet this siege was carried out without the venom of the previous one. The game was up, the last move made. With the exception of the town of Lucca, Cosimo I de' Medici was now lord and master of the whole of Tuscany.

## 1557: epilogue

With Philip II of Spain in financial difficulty, Cosimo I de' Medici decided to call in the two million ducats that Florentine bankers had lent to Spain some years previously. As Philip was unable to pay up, the following political solution was reached: the debt would be considered honored if Siena and all its lands were ceded to the duke of Florence. As resistance was relatively comfortable this time around, the exiled republic of Siena in Montalcino managed to hold out for a further two years before giving in.

Monluc's memoirs of this period are lacking in detail. Food found its way into the town, as did wine. Following the peace treaty of Château-Cambrésis, signed by the French and the Spanish in 1559, Montalcino finally capitulated to Florence and with it the Sienese republic in exile. Piero Strozzi moved to France where he entered the service of Catherine de' Medici. Blaise de Monluc, finding himself idle now that the sieges were over, turned his attention to the massacre of the Huguenots.

Anastasio Fontebuoni and Bartolomeo Fontebroni
*The Battle of Montalcino*
Palazzo Vecchio, Florence

Although Montalcino broke the peace treaty with Siena in the 13th century by offering refuge to Guelphs who had fled the city, it later became Siena's most loyal ally. Following the siege of Siena by Florence, which stretched out over four seasons and reduced the population of Siena to a fraction of what it once was, a few of the most powerful families of Siena set up a government in exile in Montalcino. Yet after a second brief siege even Montalcino capitulated, making Florence ruler of all Tuscany. The painting of the battle in the Palazzo Vecchio celebrates Florence's heroic victory.

# Lucca

## A wall against fear

Opposite page, top:
Paolo Sinibaldi
*Geometric Plan of the Town of Lucca*, 1845
Archivio di Stato, Lucca
Stampa n. 494

The map shows the town within its walls. At the top we can make out the course of the River Serchio.

### The town walls

The walls that encircle the town of Lucca like a giant bean are still in one piece. There are only a few towns left today, most of them small, compact villages, which can lay claim to a complete set of municipal defenses. The walls of Lucca have stood idle for over 300 years, never once challenged by marauding troops or siege armies. As they were never put to the test, we will never know whether they would have been up to the job they were designed for.

The destruction of city walls began in the mid-19th century, with the devastation gathering pace particularly after 1945 in the course of post-war "restoration"; the bits the bombers had missed were bulldozed by the building boom. The damage caused during

There are 11 bastions dotted along the wall at irregular intervals, each one built to an individual design. Their lack of uniformity stems from the fact that they were built in different periods: construction spanned 150 years. Their prime function was to protect a curtain wall or gate. They were equipped with loopholes from which the attacking army could be bombarded with crossfire. Along the wall and close to each bastion are *casermette* or barracks where the guards lived.

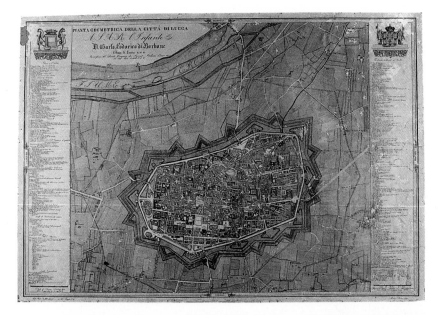

the Second World War to city fortifications in places such as Pisa, Florence, Bologna, Verona and Parma, to name but a few, provided developers with the perfect excuse to tear them down altogether; it was felt that they were of no historic value and only hindered city development. Lucca, a place of no strategic importance, was not bombed during the war. Its walls remained intact.

Post-war development and growth in Lucca thus took place outside its *enceinte*. Comparing an aerial photo of modern Lucca with an engraving from the 19th century, we can see that the town within the wall has remained unchanged, complete with its watchtowers and belfries. Yet along its exterior the wall is surrounded by entire armies of houses,

Right: *One of the Military Architects of Lucca's Town Walls*, from: Agostino Ramelli, *Le diverse artificiose macchine*, Paris 1592 Bayerische Staatsbibliothek, Munich

The architect is portrayed here in his military capacity.

Below: *The Military Architect Designing One of the Walls of Lucca*, from: Agostino Ramelli, *Le diverse artificiose macchine*, Paris 1592 Bayerische Staatsbibliothek, Munich

The architect is working with compasses and a set square while the builders of the wall state their requirements.

factories and wide roads, by the old stadium, the station and the cemetery. This is the first siege the walls of Lucca have had to withstand since they were built.

## New weapons, new defenses

The town walls of Lucca were built between 1550 and 1560, a product of the late Renaissance. At a time when firearms were in common use and close to being perfected, the old town walls from the 13th century soon proved totally ineffectual. The use of new and more fearsome weapons called for a complete overhaul of older fortifications. Towers and high, thin walls were not merely impractical; they were also a danger to the defending garrison. A well-placed barrage of cannon-balls was enough to bring the medieval masonry crashing down about their ears. What was needed were round, squat bastions and watchtowers. A phase of architectural development began which culminated in the bunkers of our modern defense systems.

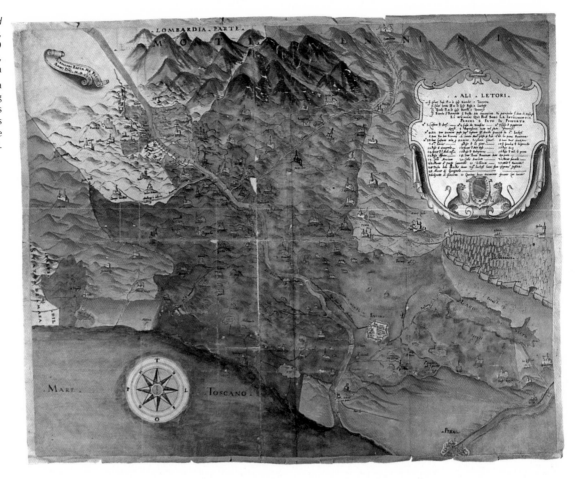

Alessandro Resta, *Lucca and Its Lands in the 16th Century*, 1569
Archivio di Stato, Fondo Stampe, Lucca

In the 16th century Lucca also had control over a long stretch of coast. Lucca was the only town to maintain its independence from Florence until the age of Napoleon.

Lucca implemented its new defense strategy with little regard for the cost of the operation. The best military architects of the day were commissioned and in 1513 building commenced. The first stage was to construct the Tagliata, a safe area running along the outside of the wall which was to be deforested and remain undeveloped. Plots of land were confiscated and villages that happened to be in the buffer zone demolished. Between 1515 and 1521 banks of earth were piled up in the Tagliata and a wide ditch formed. The imposing watchtowers were then erected and in 1544 the new wall itself began to rise, partly incorporating its medieval predecessor. The area of the town increased by 80 percent.

## An inland Amauroto

Sir Thomas More the English statesman and scholar, Lord Chancellor of King Henry VIII, describes the city of Amauroto, the capital of his island of Utopia, described in the book of the same name, as follows: "It is surrounded by tall, strong walls defended by a great number of towers and outworks. On three sides the walls are enclosed by a dry ditch which is wide and deep and protected by hedges of thorns. Along the fourth side the river forms a moat." This passage reads like a description of Lucca's town fortifications. Why Amauroto, the nucleus of a peaceful island where all live in perfect harmony, has a town wall when it is defended on all sides by sea, More does not say. Indeed, why were the walls of Lucca built? Why did its citizens put up with the destruction of entire villages? Why did they agree to finance the walls through taxes to the tune of an incredible 900,000 *scudi*, spread out over no fewer than four generations? The people of Lucca were obviously fairly prosperous and extremely concerned for their safety.

Two stone panthers perch on the south face of the Porta Santa Maria. As if keeping watch over Lucca and its inhabitants, their gaze seems to be directed towards its coat of arms, affixed to the wall above the higher central arch of the town gate.

## Mighty soldiers

There has been a walled town at Lucca since the Roman period. We have evidence that there was a square city boundary, parts of which still exist, dating back to 180 B.C. The Greek historian Strabo mentions Lucca in connection with its "mighty soldiers." Lucca acted as a military outpost to Rome, defending the region against the Ligurians. The Romans could have chosen Pisa as their northern ally but were unwilling to trust a rival with access to the sea (Pisa lies at the mouth of the Arno, the twin of the River Tiber). Lucca, however, fulfilled two important functions: it kept a watchful eye on neighboring Pisa and held the Ligurians in check.

## Old friend, new foe

Lucca, hinged between the Etruscans and the Ligurians, was an ancient center of trade. The only area of business the town had yet to breach was ocean trading. Its access to the sea was, however, blocked by Pisa. The two towns,

barely 12 miles (20 km) apart, thus became bitter rivals, their animosity outliving the fall of Rome and running on well into the Middle Ages. Lucca was constantly forming alliances with towns claiming to be Pisa's arch-enemy. At the beginning of the 13th century one of these was Florence. Following a long siege, Florence managed to take Pisa in 1407, ruling over its captive for almost a century. In 1494 Pisa scraped up the courage to revolt, and for a brief period won back its independence. Yet in 1509 it again fell to Florence, this time remaining firmly in the larger city's clutches.

It seems strange that Lucca only began planning its new wall after its ancient rival Pisa had been finally defeated by Florence. Who were the people of Lucca frightened of now? The fall of Pisa left just two independent republics in Tuscany that were not subject to Florentine rule: Siena and Lucca. Florence laid siege to Siena in the mid-16th century. Lucca now had a very good reason to fear Florence more than it had ever done before.

Right: Porta San Pietro is Lucca's oldest town gate, designed in 1563 by the military architect Alessandro Resta. It was built where the main entrance of the medieval church once stood; decorative elements from the portal have been integrated into the Renaissance arch.

The Lucca town wall originally had only three gates, as these formed the weakest link in the defensive chain. Three more openings were made in the fortifications between 1811 and 1931. Porta San Pietro was the only gate through which visitors could enter the town, provided they first handed their weapons over to the guards. At night all the gates were locked up until the next morning.

Below: Porta Santa Maria. The Madonna and Christchild between the two panthers, over the main doorway. The doorway is named after her.

## Good walls make good neighbors

There is not a single walled town in history that has been able to successfully ward off a stronger enemy. This does not mean that city fortifications are superfluous, however. If citizens are to be expected to defend their city, then some kind of enclosing wall must be erected. For the republic of Lucca the construction of the most modern town wall of its time had a function that was largely therapeutic. The edifice was designed to calm the anxieties of those within, who were terrified that now that Pisa had been captured the enemy would start to blockade Lucca. Allowing people to observe the construction

Left: The entire town wall is undermined by underground passageways. These long, straight tunnels lead to crypt-like rooms with vaulted ceilings.

Left: Lucca has an entire system of underground streets built to ensure that people, goods, food and munitions could be safely and continuously transported in the event of an attack. If defense was necessary, Lucca envisaged not just the military but the entire town taking part. As this was never the case, the mobilizing of troops and civilians was restricted to sporadic practice drills and maneuvers.

of the wall was sound psychology and helped stem their mounting fear.

The town also put out diplomatic feelers, thanks to which the republic was able to retain its independence. Putting itself under the protection of ever greater and more distant powers, Lucca held out until 1799. In its years of autonomy the town paid more in protection money than it had for the building of the wall. Then came the Napoleonic Wars.

## The café in the wall

The town fell to Napoleon, who, upon receipt of 87,803 Milanese *lire* from Lucca, told the town: "Create a small state. Live peacefully and have no concern other than for the good of your own people." Once again the town

walls had proved as surplus to requirements as those encircling More's Amauroto.

Following the Congress of Vienna, Mary-Louise of Bourbon, the duchess of Lucca, decreed that the walls be turned into a public walkway. A shady avenue of trees was planted along the entire circumference. The largest of the wall barracks above the Porta di San Pietro became a concert café – one of the more inspired ideas of the 19th century.

Strolling along the almost 3 miles (5 km) of wall today is like traveling through time. On one side lies a unique medieval city surrounded by an indomitable Renaissance wall, both completely intact; on the other, an entire garrison of 19th- and 20th-century buildings lays siege to the town that built a wall against fear.

An avenue of trees was planted along the entire stretch of Lucca's town wall in the 19th century. The wall itself has been perfectly preserved, as this aerial view demonstrates.

# Life in the 13th Century

Chiara Frugoni

## Darkness

In the typical medieval town of the 13th century people's daily rhythm was very similar to that of animals in the wild. As soon as the sun set, darkness flooded their houses. Very little could be done by the sparse light given off by tiny lamps and candles, so evenings were more or less devoid of activity. The streets outside were also plunged into paralyzing blackness. It is very hard for us to imagine just how gloomy it was, living in our neon-lit cities with electricity on tap.

The only light in the black of the medieval night, and the only guide for people stumbling along the rural roads, were the lamps that shone out from shrines scattered along the wayside. It was actually against the law to be out at night, because the impenetrable darkness provided bandits and brigands with perfect cover to ambush their victims. Town bylaws were passed in an attempt to prevent citizens from going out after dusk. People left their houses only in special circumstances, one being if a doctor was called to tend to the dying.

## The cold

The lack of glazed windows in the Middle Ages meant that in winter the biting cold found its way into all corners of the house. The wooden shutters fit badly and were little use against the cold and damp. During the day the shutters had to be left open to admit light; in the winter these also let in the cold, and in summer, the insects. The latter is an inconvenience we have almost forgotten, something we now associate mainly with summer days out in the country. In the Middle Ages the streets were like huge open sewers, swarming with insects. People tried to protect themselves and their houses from the vermin by hanging wax cloths in the windows. As these were not transparent, they blocked out much of the light, making the poky medieval home, reeking of all kinds of vile odors, even more inhospitable than it already was.

Most medieval towns and cities were surrounded by walls. Building fortifications was a costly and complicated business, so they were kept as limited in extent as possible. Living space in the town was extremely scarce and

Opposite page, top:
*Room in an Inn*, late 14th century
Miniature on parchment, Giovanni Boccaccio: *Decameron*, IX, 6, ms. 5070, fol. 337r
Bibliothèque de l'Arsenal, Paris

To curb the spread of fleas and lice at the inn strangers slept in the nude, with everyone sharing one large bed.

Below left:
Gentile da Fabriano
*Worshipping the Kings* (detail), Murder Scene, 1423
Tempera on wood,
303 × 282 cm
Galleria degli Uffizi, Florence

This poor soul trying to creep out of the city gates has fallen victim to two soldiers.

Below right:
Agnolo Gaddi
*Women on the Balcony* (detail), 15th century
Fresco
Cappella del Sacro Cingolo, Duomo Santo Stefano, Prato

expensive. Houses were small and cramped, so people tried to spend as little time as possible indoors. Community life was an interplay of relationships between all kinds of people, brought together by a common desire to leave their houses and take to the streets as early in the day as they could. Craftsmen went out to work, women to market, and children played out on the streets. Those left at home tried to spend as much of their time outside as possible, leaning out over their balconies and roofed loggias jutting out from the wall. Squashed up very close together, often almost touching, these verandas were one of the focal points of public street life.

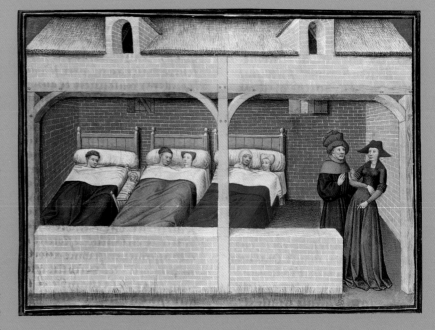

## Vermin

We are so accustomed to having our own private space that we can hardly imagine a life where you could never be on your own. Yet it was precisely this lack of privacy that forced people to take such an active part in the community life of the medieval town.

Even in bed, people were not alone. To make optimum use of the available space, beds were built big enough to accommodate seven or eight people. Almost everybody slept in the nude. During the day, people's bodies were crawling with vermin; fleas and lice made life particularly uncomfortable. At night most of the irritating pests were left in people's clothing. This was hung up in a neighboring room on tall poles to protect it from attacks by the ever-present rats. Few people wore nightclothes; this is why miniatures of people in hospital – even the dying – show them completely naked. This was also true of the inns and hostels. If the landlord was short of space, he would ask his guests to share a bed, even if they were complete strangers.

## The three public spaces of the town

In private houses no distinction was made between different living areas, and the limited space served a number of purposes. During the day the bedroom was turned into a sitting room, where people perched on trunks around the bed conversing. The women often sewed or embroidered as they did so. Public spaces, however, were allotted a specific function. There

were various centers: the *Piazza religiosa*, the *Piazza politica* and the *Piazza del mercato*. We may ask why there was need for a special "religious space," for example, with the enormous churches available in the towns. The success of the mendicant orders was so great that the new, spacious, unaisled churches soon proved unable

Below: *Agiluf in the Servants' Bedroom,* 1427
Pen and watercolor
Giovanni Boccaccio:
*Decameron,* III, 2, ms. It. 63, fol. 94v
Bibliothèque Nationale, Paris

People slept two or three to a bed.

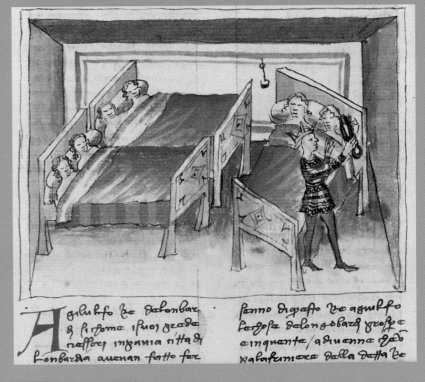

99

*Market at the Porta Ravegnano in Bologna*, beginning of the 15th century
Miniature on parchment
Matricolae Societatis Draperorum, ms. 93
Museo Civico Medievale, Bologna

Outside the limited privacy of the home three public spaces dominated medieval life: the *Piazza religiosa*, where priests, mostly from mendicant orders, preached to their congregation; the *Piazza politica*, where the latest news was discussed, newspapers still a thing of the future; and the *Piazza del mercato*, where people made their daily purchases and took part in community life.

to cope with the hordes of worshipers flooding to services. Priests thus preached on the squares outside the church, such as the Piazza Santa Croce in Florence. Preachers such as St. Bernard (1090–1153) showed extraordinary charisma and a great gift for speaking in public. Bernard's incredibly visual sermons were the work of a genius. He spoke of the damned in Hell, who were frazzled like fish coated in flour in an enormous pan. The new brotherhoods broached not only religious subjects but also topics from day-to-day life, ones close to people's hearts. St. Bernard, for example, criticized the various luxuries women indulged in. He disapproved of pearls and gold jewelry, urging his female followers to turn their thoughts from themselves to God. He also voiced his opinions on economic matters, claiming that jewels were "dead" money which failed to reap further financial reward. This possibly refers to the large sums of capital that were invested in pearls and gold at that time, leaving less "real" money to circulate in the urban economy as a result. The congregation, hearing their own problems mentioned and discussed, were totally captivated by the speakers. For the mendicant orders, this combination of religious, political and civil themes was the key to their success.

The political *piazza* was also heavily frequented. Here the community met up to discuss civic affairs. As there were no newspapers (and in any case most people were illiterate), the populace flocked to hear the town criers proclaim the latest decrees passed by the mayor and publicize all kinds of news by word of mouth. This was where the arrival of a new doctor in town was announced, where the skills of the horologist who had finally managed to repair the city clocks were praised. These clocks, bafflingly complicated in their workings, often ran too fast or too slow and were not taken too seriously by the townspeople. As a rule, people had only a rough idea of the time of day.

## The lives of women: fire and water

Women left the house to go about their day-to-day tasks as the domestic heads of household. What are now simple chores, such as lighting the fire or turning on a tap, were extremely laborious in the Middle Ages. Water, for example, had to be fetched from the well on the town square or at one of the town crossroads. Here women met up with other wives and mothers waiting to take their turn. Standing in line, they passed the time chatting and catching up on the latest news.

Another reason for leaving the house was to find fire. Kindling fire was an extremely strenuous business. The embers had to be kept

Giovanni di Corraduccio
*Martha in the Kitchen*,
beginning of the 15th century
Fresco
Convento di Sant'Anna, old refectory, Foligno

Many of the domestic chores that are now quickly and easily accomplished were extremely arduous in the Middle Ages.

Anonymous
*Knight and Lady Playing Chess*, second half of the 14th century
Fresco
Camera della Castellana di Vergi, Palazzo Davanzati, Florence
The wife of Prince Guernieri playing chess with the knight Sir Guglielmo, who is trying to seduce her. Detail from the cycle of frescoes which tell the French tale of the chatelaine of Vergi.

glowing under the ash at all times, so that the fire would never go out. If on rare occasions it did, the task of relighting it fell to the woman of the house. As this was such a complicated procedure, the woman usually took a poker or tongs round to her neighbor and either collected glowing embers from her fire or carried a burning rag back to her own fireplace a few yards away.

With no matches or cigarette lighters in the Middle Ages, starting a fire was no easy task. Flints were rubbed together to produce sparks which ignited tinder; this had to be bone dry and extremely fine. Some sources describe an incredibly elaborate method of preparing tinder which involved boiling and drying the bark of a walnut tree and then beating it until very dry, fine,

sponge-like fibers were formed. The person laying the fire hoped that the tinder would catch light as soon as the sparks hit it. In practice much skill and patience went into making a good, blazing fire. Thus great care was taken to make sure it did not go out; this was a procedure people did not want to have to repeat too often.

Obtaining food was another of the essential tasks carried out by women. As there was no means of keeping food cold, very little food could actually be kept in the house. Women thus had to go out for the day's supplies, buying bread, meat and vegetables. Yet even in the Middle Ages, life was not all work. Another important reason for leaving the house was for pleasure and entertainment.

## Entertainment

People rushed out to the *piazza* to listen to a storyteller or a traveling minstrel, maybe one with trained animals that performed tricks for the crowd. Even a sermon intended to educate the masses could prove entertaining and informative. To show how wise they were, preachers often included news of the latest discoveries in their lectures. The sermon given in Florence by the Dominican friar Giordano di Pisa in 1303 is one such example. His proclamation "The invention of the eyeglass is a good thing!" tells us that there were reading aids already in use at this time. The growing demand for books and other reading matter among the laity of the 14th century meant glasses became a coveted asset. Again, it was the mendicant orders, and the Dominicans in particular, who encouraged people to read religious texts.

## Hygiene

One of the issues which undoubtedly affected the quality of life of medieval citizens was that of hygiene. During the Middle Ages people actually washed more than in other centuries; in the 17th century, for example, ablutions were performed without water. Medieval burghers were quite keen on washing – provided it wasn't too much trouble to fetch water. Hands and faces were frequently cleaned but a full bath was rarely taken. There were public bathhouses where the water was heated for guests. As so much effort was required to fetch such vast amounts of water and warm it up, baths were often used more than once. The same applied to washing pots and cleaning vegetables; it was done, but economic use of water was always a top priority.

Another problem was drinking water. In the Middle Ages people knew that water from moldy cisterns was bad and made you ill. They had also come to realize that spring water was better than water from the river, although no serious conclusions were drawn from this information. Naturally people had no idea that there were such things as microbes and that the quality of water could be improved by boiling it. In China, people did boil their water to make tea, thus sparing the country the large-scale epidemics that decimated much of the population elsewhere in the world.

Yet general standards of hygiene remained extremely superficial. The streets were breeding grounds for disease. Municipal bylaws specified that no diseased animals should be sold for food, and that great care must be taken to keep meat and fish clean. The fact that these stipulations were so detailed and emphatic suggests that transgressions of the law were frequent. All kinds of human and animal waste were thrown into the street and covered with nothing more than a thin layer of ash. Food scraps were devoured by animals, doing away with the need for street sweepers (pigs, however, left behind as much mess as they removed). The only real relief was provided by rain, which washed away the waste and foul smells.

Keeping clean was not an easy undertaking. Clothes were changed less frequently than they are today. As sleeves were the parts of the garment which dirtied most quickly, these were habitually cut off and replaced. The Italian proverb "That's a different pair of sleeves" stems from this custom. Robes and shifts were treated

*Two Bath Maids Washing King Wenceslas's Head,* 1390–1400
Miniature on parchment
The Wenceslas Bible, ms. 2759, fol. 174v
Österreichische Nationalbibliothek, Vienna

The general standard of hygiene required that women washed their hair each Saturday. Otherwise people washed at least once a day.

with greater respect and not washed too often to preserve the cloth. As they were expensive, they were wrapped in sweet-smelling herbs and kept rolled up tight in wooden chests. They were passed down from generation to generation, meaning that fashions seldom changed. It is thus impossible to date pictures from this period with any accuracy. Clothes remained the same over many decades, making it difficult to use them to pinpoint a brief span in time. This has only become possible during more recent history, as fashions have changed with greater frequency.

## Medieval color

Medieval illustrations give us the impression that the Middle Ages was an era of glorious color. In reality only the rich could afford garments with lasting, expensive dyes. It is no coincidence that red cloth was worn only by doctors and judges; the manufacture of red pigment was extremely costly, as was the production of a vivid blue. People usually dyed their clothes with natural plant extracts that faded with washing. Places that brought a splash of color to life, such as churches, were thus a welcome diversion. The vibrant tones of the wall paintings and of the windows stained in red, blue and green and lit up by the rays of the sun were appreciated more than we can imagine. Paints, dyes and inks were thus highly valued; they made it possible to experience the bright, animated color so seldom seen in everyday life.

## Accidents

We can glean much of our information on everyday life in the Middle Ages from the many

*The Birth of Julius Caesar by Cesarean Section*, beginning of the 14th century Miniature on parchment *Les faits des Romains*, Nouvelle Acq. Fr., ms. 3576, fol. 197 Bibliothèque Nationale de France, Paris

According to Pliny (Hist. Nat. VII, 7), the name Julius Caesar comes from the Latin verb *caedere*, to cut. The emperor was brought into the world *a caesa matris utero*, by Cesarean section, a method of delivery named after him.

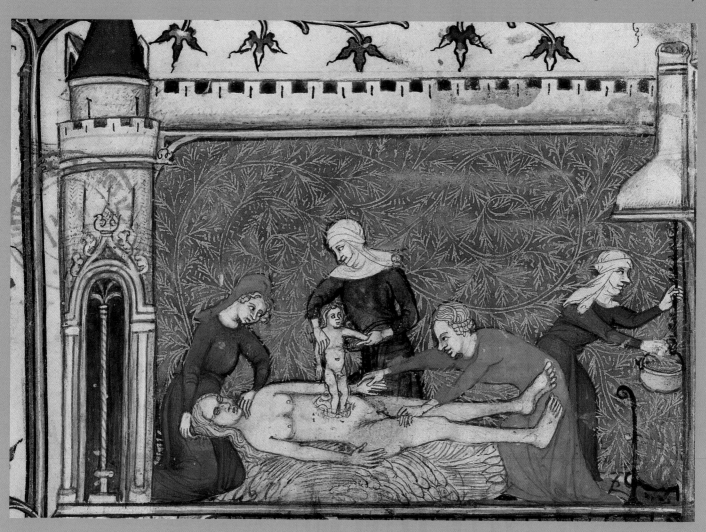

miniatures still in existence. Among the occurrences they depict are accidents at the workplace or a child falling from a balcony as the wooden railing breaks. Accidents at work were so common during this period that an entire host of saints was called upon to protect individuals going about their daily business. Building houses in the Middle Ages was a particularly dangerous occupation. Scaffolding, for example, was not erected as a frame, its base firmly affixed to the ground, as this was too costly. Instead, holes were left in the masonry exterior into which wooden beams were inserted. Planks of wood were laid across these for laborers to stand on. The entire structure was extremely unstable and simply hung in mid-air.

A plate in the museum in San Gimignano illustrates the procedures of the medieval building industry and the perils craftsmen had to face. The picture is dedicated to a miracle performed by St. Fina and shows how the saint swoops down to Earth to lend a poor carpenter a helping hand. She grasps his arm just as a plank snaps in two, saving him from certain death as he plunges to the ground.

Another story tells of a mason who falls from a wall but manages to grab hold of the stones in falling, then spending all day clinging to the construction for dear life. As his strength ebbs away, two angels miraculously fly to his assistance.

## Cesarean section and surgery

Another interesting illustration is of a Cesarean section, only practiced in the Middle Ages when a woman died during childbirth. The operation was not carried out to save a life but to allow the stillborn baby to be christened. Christening was extremely important; an unchristened baby was thought to be the bearer of cardinal sin and its mother delivered of a child of Satan. People believed neither would be admitted to Heaven. The tragedy of death was thus intensified by the sorrow that that the departed could not be buried in consecrated ground. In many miracle tales the dead child comes to life for a few moments during its christening and then finally dies. These stories were nothing more than

comforting anecdotes which endeavored to mask the pain of death, bearing promise of a better life both on Earth and in Heaven. They also enabled the man who had lost all that was dear to him, his wife and child, to go to the cemetery and pray at the grave, finding solace in the knowledge that both were in Paradise and had not been damned to an afterlife in Hell.

Another miniature shows women operating on a woman in labor and delivering her of her child. This demonstrates that female medical knowledge was not limited to the application of herbal potions but also encompassed surgery. Surgical skill was also required of nuns in convents when the deceased was thought to be a saint and thus had to be embalmed. The nuns Chiara of Montefeltro and Margherita from Città di Castello, who both won over their contemporaries with their great religious fervor, are a good example here. One of the two claimed to bear the stigma of the Passion in her heart, with the other convinced that in the same place she had a small crib harboring Mary, Joseph and the Christ Child. On the death of the holy sisters their bodies were closely examined. Corresponding marks were found and the two were embalmed as saints. As

Anonymous
*An Apothecary*, 1488–1495
Fresco
Issogne, Castello, Val d'Aosta

Women amassed great practical knowledge on how to care for and heal the sick through their daily chores, with physicians learning their trade from books. This picture illustrates how science was linked to religion. The medical ingredients are stocked on the shelves; behind them are the votive tablets.

Taddeo di Bartolo
*San Cristoforo*, c. 1414
Palazzo Pubblico,
Anticoncistoro, Siena

People believed that creating images of saints would encourage them to assist and intervene in everyday life. St. Christopher, who was usually depicted on the exterior of a building, was thought to be able to prevent sudden death. St. Christopher was also the patron saint of travelers who passed by the city building on their journey.

saintly relics were said never to decay, people went to great lengths to preserve the corpse as best they could.

## Medieval medicine

In the Middle Ages it was the women who had the most comprehensive medical knowledge. As caring for and healing the sick had "automatically" fallen to the females in the family for centuries, women had inherited a rich catalog of healing traditions and tried-and-tested herbal remedies passed down from generation to generation. The range of potions and methods went far beyond the proverbial chamomile tea; special herbs were used both to relieve and cure symptoms. In a different process of learning, the physicians of the day gleaned most of their knowledge from books; their practical medicine, however, was often restricted to merely holding urine up to the light and taking the patient's pulse.

Pictures are an important source of information on medieval medicine and should be carefully considered in any assessment of the topic. Close study of a picture of an apothecary in Piedmont, for example, reveals some interesting and unusual facts. We can see the beautiful vessels containing various medicines we would expect to find at a chemist's. But we can also see, hanging on the wall behind these, several wax votive tablets for sale. People went to the chemist to buy natural medicines. If these failed to achieve the desired effect, disappointed clients placed their faith in the supernatural. Religious belief was a driving force, often rendering the medical undertakings of mere mortals utterly superfluous. The following episode from the reign of Louis IX is a good example of this. Fighting for her life under water for several minutes, a young girl was saved from drowning by the speedy reaction of one woman. The woman took necessary steps to revive the girl although we are not told precisely what these were. The report plays down the lady's brave actions and turns its attentions instead to Louis IX. The reason for this is quite obvious. The document is intended to celebrate Louis IX and praise both his miraculous and saintly powers.

An attempt is made to detract from the role played by the woman and to vividly underline the king's supernatural abilities. This clearly illustrates how people's trust in the theory and practical experience of medicine was constantly undermined in the Middle Ages. The public were to be persuaded to continue to believe in the power of God, religion and saintly miracles. Modern insight has taught us, on the other hand, to read between the lines and to recognize the true capabilities of the woman in this story.

## The weight of religious belief

People were continually searching for ways and means of demonstrating and proving the intervention of the supernatural. One document records a procedure in which handkerchiefs were weighed before they were taken down into the crypt and dropped onto the floor close to the saint who lay buried there. After a certain period had elapsed the handkerchiefs were weighed a second time. These had naturally become damp during the night, an attribute people associated with the material coming into contact with the saint's body. Their increased weight was proof that the fabric had absorbed the magical powers of the resting saint. Contemporary spiritualists act along similar lines when they take a picture and claim to be able to charge it with positive energy by performing a special ritual. In the Middle Ages people wanted proof that an object could be given supernatural powers, in this case through the handkerchief becoming heavier with its new, saintly burden. In their eyes, this turned the supernatural into a measurable quantity.

## Medieval lack of faith

Of course not everybody believed in the powers of the paranormal. It is very difficult, however, to find out much about people who opposed the norm. Whereas today we are free to voice our own opinions, in the Middle Ages non-believers were ferreted out, arrested, interrogated and then punished. The trials for heresy and witchcraft only give us a vague idea about those who demonstrated a lack of faith in medieval religion. Only those with extremely strong moral convictions who were prepared to endure terrible sanctions aired their views in public. From this sketchy evidence it is not clear how widespread the phenomenon of unbelief actually was.

Religion played a major part in the day-to-day life of medieval people and dominated their imaginations. The church was omnipresent, infiltrating all classes and all phases of life. One of the reasons for this was the difficulty people had in finding explanations for certain geophysical and climatic phenomena. As nobody knew how freak weather and natural catastrophes came about, such phenomena were often interpreted in religious terms. Earthquakes, hailstorms and comets were signs from God. As people had little means of physically defending themselves against the force of the elements, it was necessary to construct sturdy psychological defenses in addition to those which could be erected by human hands.

Life in the Middle Ages indeed hung by a thread. Sudden death was never far away: at the hands of bandits along the highways, in the event of war or during periods of civil unrest. People could be struck down by a falling beam, break their neck in a fall or tumble to their death from their horse or a bridge. Sudden illness could prove fatal, appendicitis quickly developing into peritonitis. This permanent state of insecurity gave rise to one of the most persistent fears of the era: that of dying without receiving absolution. People were driven to find suitable antidotes for their predicament. They had visions, spent hours in worship, and said frequent prayers. They hoped that one of the saints would hear them and perform miracles in their favor.

This obsession with personal salvation is personified in the numerous larger-than-life images of St. Christopher projected onto the walls of churches, palaces and town fortifications. The general belief was that if you saw an image of the saint you would not die suddenly on that day. This custom indicates just how afraid people were of dying without having made a final confession, because a death without absolution was synonymous with damnation.

## Letters out of fruit

Another topic we can learn much about from medieval illustrations is how people in the past

*La virtù della grammatica,*
beginning of the 15th
century
Fresco
Sale delle Arti Liberali e di
Pianeti, Palazzo Trinci,
Foligno (Perugia)
Children were taught to read
with letters made of fruit.

In pictures of the Virgin Mary with her child we can see how children in the Middle Ages started to learn. They wrote on slates that resembled wooden boards coated in plaster. The child practiced reading sounds such as "ba," "be," "bi," "ca," "ce" and "ci," etc., as the first stage in the learning process. If the child was lucky enough to grow up in a family that considered reading important, he was later sent to school. There he studied from a primer or a manuscript containing the psalms. First children had to learn a number of psalms off by heart and then try and recognize them written down.

In many respects this method of teaching was an early form of integral learning. At the same time as learning to read, the child was also instructed in a "foreign" language, namely Latin. In the 14th century the population spoke *volgare*, a form of vulgar Latin diluted with loan words, which was to become the forerunner of modern Italian. Besides learning to read and speak Latin, the child also had lessons in religious education.

At that time, reading and writing, two skills we now automatically link with one another, were seen as two completely different entities. There were people who could read, but not write. This was partly due to the fact that there was not much paper to be had; what little was available was so expensive that it was considered too precious to waste on writing exercises. Writing was also not thought to be absolutely necessary. Merchants had to have enough writing knowledge to note down their accounts, but otherwise it was more important to be able to read a prayer-book or a novel. Women were the most avid readers. In the prologue to his *Decameron*, Boccaccio comments at length on whom his book is intended for. Women who only busy themselves with spinning and sewing are exempt from his list. He refers to them as souls who are subject to the whims of their fathers or brothers and have to stay at home with no distraction from, or recompense for, the pain and sorrow in their lives. The *Decameron* is thus dedicated to women who can read.

educated their children. One picture portrays a mother teaching her child to read. She has cut letters out of fruit which the child may eat if he recognizes the letter correctly. It is clear that fruit was very popular. If this method of teaching had persisted to the present day, many of our children might still be illiterate!

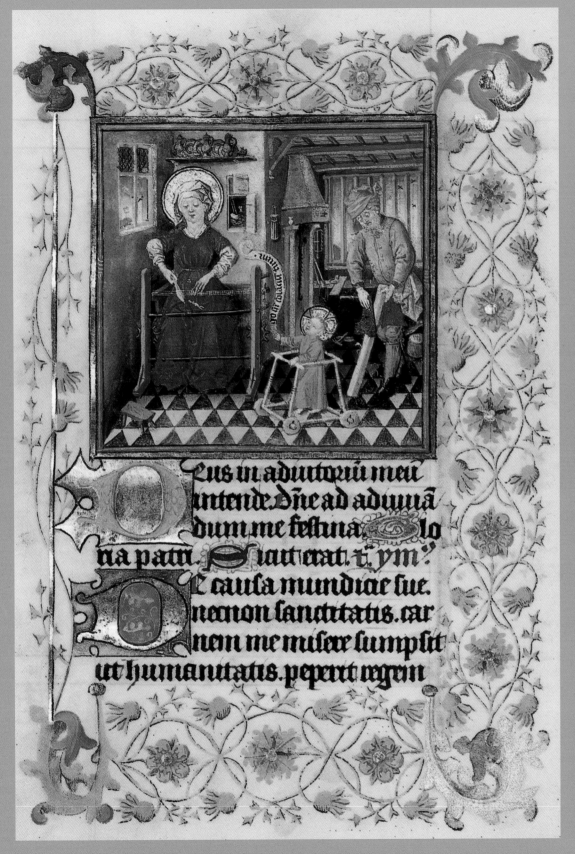

Master of Catherine of Cleves
*The Holy Family at Work*,
c. 1440
Miniature on parchment
Book of hours, ms. 917, fol. 149ʳ
The Pierpont Morgan Library, New York

The Holy Family was usually portrayed when an artist wished to illustrate the hierarchy of family life and particularly the role of the child. In this book of hours Baby Jesus toddles back and forth in his playpen from mother to father. He tells his mother: "Ego sum solacium tuum" (I am your consolation and your faith).

# Vicopisano

Pisa's lookout post

View of Vicopisano from the River Arno.

## Brunelleschi's castle

For many centuries Vicopisano was *la Sentinella di Pisa,* Pisa's lookout post. The hilltown clings to the easternmost ridge of Monte Pisano facing Florence. A long time ago the River Arno curled around the foot of the castle, enabling passing boats to be stopped and searched. Behind the castle the mountain formed a natural defensive shield. There was also a complex system of watchtowers from which quick and urgent messages could be sent to Pisa with the aid of fire, smoke and mirrors. To the north expanses of unnavigable swamp stretching as far as Lucca, an ally of Florence and thus an enemy of Pisa, provided further protection.

Until the beginning of the 15th century the free *comune* of Vicopisano acted as loyal sentinel and toll post to its mother town Pisa. By October 1406, however, the ancient maritime republic was on its knees, forced to allow the Florentines to capture the city in a moment of triumph. Prior to taking Pisa, Florence had had to crush Vicopisano. After a period of starvation that lasted nine long months, on July 16 the Florentine army took the town, "razing all the houses to the ground." The Florentines now set about turning Vicopisano into an allied outpost from which they could keep a beady eye on the defeated Pisa, sending a governor and an army of troops to the hill-fortress. In 1435 they commissioned Filippo Brunelleschi, who had made a name for himself both as a great architect of civilian and military buildings and as an expert on water installations, to build a new set of fortifications.

The complex of walls and towers we can see in Vicopisano today is the product of the integration of the town's ruined older fortifications into Brunelleschi's 15th-century system of defense. The result is a unique whole with

Opposite:
The keep of the fortification built by Florentine architect and sculptor Filippo Brunelleschi (1377–1446).

110

Above: The connecting wall between the keep and the river tower, built by Brunelleschi in 1435, is clearly visible here.

Right: Giorgio Vasari and workshop
*The Capture of Vicopisano*, 1565
Salone dei Cinquecento, Palazzo Vecchio, Florence

For Florence the capture of Vicopisano was an important step towards seizing control of Pisa. The painting depicts the Florentine siege of Pisa's sentinel in the war of 1494–1509.

Opposite: The outer wall is divided into sections linked with drawbridges. These enabled the defending garrison to block off parts of the system one after the other to deter their attackers.

Once in command of Vicopisano the Florentines planned to alter the course of the Arno, which now lay about 2 miles (3 km) from the town. They had a drainage canal dug around the edges of the Lucca swamp. The area was laid dry, providing Vicopisano with a vast plateau of fertile ground.

Without water surrounding it, Vicopisano was no longer viable as a defensive outpost. The inhabitants adapted and became farmers. Pisa, which had receded further and further back from the coast, its harbor silting up with mud and sand, turned its attentions to education, developing into one of the major university towns of the Italian peninsula.

a number of clever strategic advantages. A wall complete with wall-walk and machicolations links the fortress, situated at the highest point of the town, with one of the eight towers that punctuate the wall enclosing Vicopisano. As this connecting wall runs right up to the castle, in the event of an attack the defending garrison could position themselves at any point along the city defenses. Drawbridges placed at the intersections of towers and wall-walk allowed the various sections of the fortification to be blocked off one by one from its lower reaches to its center. The *alure* along the top of the massive connecting wall and the edge of the castle wall could thus be cut off from the keep. This enabled the town soldiers to resist attack for as long as was necessary. In the course of the second war between Florence and Pisa this system was tried and tested on several occasions. In 1494, when Charles VIII attacked Italy and Florence found itself in great difficulty, Pisa saw its chance and, mustering its last reserves, ran the occupying Florentine army out of town. The citizens of Vicopisano immediately seized control of their walls, towers and fortress.

The war between Florence and Pisa raged for 15 years, finally ending in June 1509 in Pisa's capitulation. Vicopisano, occupied by Florence in 1498 and won back by Pisa in 1502, again fell to Florence in 1503.

Above: Leonardo da Vinci
*Landscape near Pisa*,
c. 1502/03
Red ochre on paper,
21.1 × 15 cm
Codex 8936, fol. 7v
Biblioteca Nacional, Madrid

This precise topographic
sketch was made in
preparation for the extensive
canal project commissioned
by the Florentine republic.

Right: One of the eight
towers flanking Vicopisano's
fortifications.

Unlike the other seven, this
tower has archways on all
four sides.

## Rerouting the Arno

In 1503 Leonardo da Vinci worked for the republic of Florence on a project which envisaged altering the course of the River Arno. He was 51, and had spent the previous 20-odd years among crowds of admirers at the duke's palace in Milan, his every need catered for by his host's generous sponsorship. With the end of the Milan duchy and the demise of his mentor Lodovico *il Moro*, Leonardo suddenly found himself out of work and out on the streets. After brief sojourns in Mantua and Venice the artist went back to Florence and offered his services to the republic. A few years prior to his return the Medici had been driven out of Florence, young Piero in particular being held responsible for the city's fate following the death of Lorenzo II *il Magnifico* (the Magnificent) in 1492. The greatest blow to the Florentines was their loss of control over the ancient coastal republic of Pisa, seized at the beginning of the 15th century. After 90 years of Florentine rule, Pisa had rebelled and managed to win back its independence. For the new republic of Florence recapturing Pisa was a matter of life and death. Pisa was synonymous with access to the sea and control of the inland waterways; in other words, exactly what Florence needed

to become a powerful center of international trade. It was against this backdrop that Leonardo presented his plans to reroute the Arno. The river was to be dammed a few miles short of Pisa and redirected south towards Livorno. The project required an enormous dam to be built and around 6 miles (10 km) of canal to be dug out, stretching from Pisa to an area of swamp known as the Stagno, whose canals ran into the harbor at Livorno. Pisa would have been left gasping for water like a fish on dry land and nothing more would have stood in the way of Florence's rise to maritime riches and power.

The republic of Florence approved Leonardo's idea, financing his plans and providing vast amounts of timber and 2,000 laborers at ten *soldi* a day each to construct the dam and dig out the canal. According to the notes made by contemporary chronicler Jacopo Nardi not even half of the work had

Leonardo da Vinci
*The Pisa Plateau*, c. 1502
Black chalk, pen, ink and
paint on paper,
33.8 × 48.8 cm (facsimile)
Royal Collection Picture
Library, London

To provide Florence with
waterways and access to the
sea, in 1503 Leonardo
developed a project which
envisaged building an
enormous dam just short of
Pisa and rerouting the River
Arno along 6 miles (10 km)
of canal towards Livorno.
Pisa would have been left
completely dry if the project
had been implemented.

been completed in twice the number of days originally allotted for the project. The republic also had to pay the troops stationed around Pisa who were continuing to lay siege to Florence's defiant neighbor. Leonardo's undertaking was bleeding Florence dry. The problem was solved by a flash flood in 1503, when the Arno burst the banks of the dam, tearing the construction from its anchorage and filling the area between Pisa and Livorno with water. Once the floods had subsided, the River Arno continued to flow peacefully along its original course – through Pisa to the sea. It was at this point that the Florentine republic terminated its contract with Leonardo and all work on the project ceased.

In the more recent past Leonardo's plans have again been put into practice – this time with some modifications. In 1966 a great inundation swamped much of Florence and Pisa, destroying large sections of the cities and many of their priceless art treasures. Along the course of Leonardo's original canal a new one, the Arnaccio, has been dug in the direction of Livorno, this time not from military design but for the good of the civilian population. The rapids of the Arno now have an overflow outlet that should protect Pisa from further flooding. Ironically, the only place the Arno can now burst its banks is in the city that first tried to alter its natural course: Florence.

# Milan

## Castello Sforzesco

### The Visconti state

In the 14th century Milan vied with Naples for the position of biggest city in the Italian peninsula. Close behind these great medieval cities were Venice and Genoa, Florence and Rome. Although there are no exact figures, it is known that 14th-century Milan had over

Far right: Francesco Sforza had his ducal palace built on the foundations of the old Visconti fortress in 1450. The castle is an almost perfect square, its walls over 650 ft (200 m) long. Half of the bailey is taken up by the parade ground. The enormous round twin towers on the city side of the stronghold housed cisterns of drinking water. They are mirrored by two equally huge square towers on the other side of the fortification. In the 1480s and 1490s Lodovico *il Moro* commissioned a number of artists to work on the building, among them Bramante and Leonardo da Vinci.

Right: This strange creature, the *biscione*, once adorned the Visconti coat of arms. A young boy emerges from the mouth of the dragon serpent.

100,000 inhabitants. This growth was the result of economic and demographic expansion over a period of 100 years; expansion that was to continue for a further two centuries. The Milanese state flourished between 1280 and 1350 under the *signoria* (overlordship) of the Visconti family. Their territory included 30 towns and stretched down to the Florentine border in the south. The fate of

Right: Baldo Martoselli
*Grammar*
786 fol. 1, detached sheet
Biblioteca Trivulziana, Milan

The success of Francesco Sforza as a military commander depended largely on his tactical ability, which led him to avoid pitched battle and gamble on internal conflicts in the enemy camp. Having no male heirs, Filippo Maria Visconti put his faith in the famous captain in order to keep his state, and gave him the hand of his daughter Bianca Maria. The subsequent reign of Francesco Sforza in Milan (1450-1466) was a period of peace and prosperity.

Below: The castle, surrounded by a wide moat, is built on the foundations of its predecessor. The military area with the parade ground and barracks acted as a buffer between the city and the duke's private quarters. To the west of the residential apartments is the heavily fortified Rocchetta, which served as a final place of refuge.

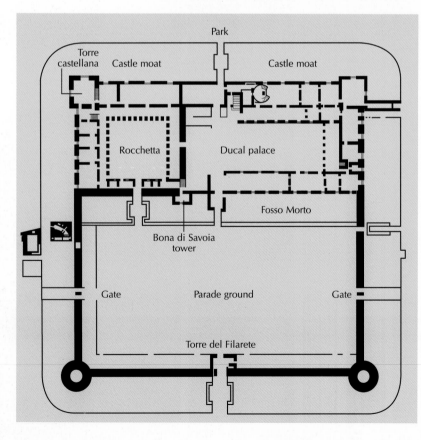

this new state remained uncertain for a long time, however; its boundaries foggy and fluid. As the Visconti were rich enough to employ mercenaries there was no need for a state army. At that time Milan itself had neither a castle nor a fortress.

## A diarchy of brothers

In 1355 the two sons of Matteo Visconti II, Bernabò and Galeazzo II, decided to rule their land and people as a diarchy, i.e. to share power. They split the city and state of Milan into two halves: an unusual undertaking, particularly for the 14th century. A few years later, Galeazzo, who owned the western half of the city, had a large square castle built along the north-west wall. It actually straddled the town wall, with half of the fortress in the city and half outside it. It had a dual function, being designed not only to defend the Visconti from the potential enemy without but also from the enemy within, a sensible measure given the long and proud tradition of the Free Commune of Milan (*comune*). When the Visconti dynasty died out 100 years later, the city did not hesitate to proclaim itself a republic. The first decree passed by the Repubblica Ambrosiana (1447–1450) targeted the Visconti stronghold; the "enemy within" was now free to demolish the castle at the Porta Giovia.

## Rebuilding the castle

The castle as it stands today was erected by Francesco Sforza in the 15th century on the foundations of the Visconti fortress. The ground plan of the present edifice, with walls over 650 ft (200 m) long and a surface area of just under 10 acres (4 hectares), thus corresponds exactly to that of its predecessor. On the city side of the castle are two enormous round towers in its corners which held two large cisterns of drinking water. Two massive square towers dominate the silhouette on the opposite side of the Castello. The entire complex is surrounded by a moat. A second moat, whose stagnant water earned it the name Fosso Morto or "dead ditch," cut the

The tower at the main entrance to the castle was designed by the Florentine sculptor Antonio Averulino, otherwise known as Filarete (*c.* 1400–*c.* 1469). The Torre del Filarete at the castle exit to the city, defended by a drawbridge, once contained the fortress's supply of gunpowder, which is why it was also called the magazine. It was destroyed by an explosion in 1521. The present tower is a copy erected at the beginning of the 20th century.

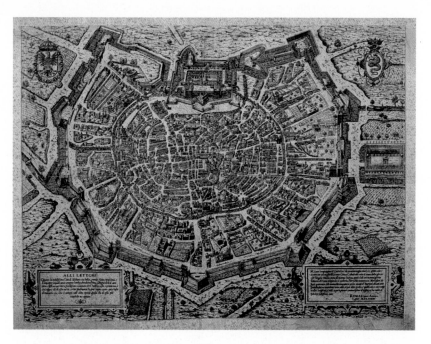

Above: Antonio Lafrery (ed.)
*Bird's-Eye View of Milan*,
Rome 1573
Copper engraving
Achille Bertarelli Collection,
Castello Sforzesco, Milan
This city map from the late
16th century shows the
Spanish fortifications around
the perimeter of the Castello
Sforzesco. Napoleon had the
defensive walls pulled down
in 1800.

Far right: Master of the Pala
Sforzesca
*Pala Sforzesca* (detail),
Lodovico *il Moro*, 1494
Tempera and oil on wood,
230 × 165 cm
Pinacoteca di Brera, Milan

Lodovico was one of
Francesco's sons; he was
called *il Moro* not because of
his dark skin but because of
his character. *Il moro* is the
mulberry tree, said to be
particularly pliable, flexible
and tough. Lodovico was
considered an educated and
eloquent man, but also vain,
disloyal and superior. During
his reign Leonardo da Vinci
was the dominant mind at
his court.

bailey into two halves. To the south was
the military parade ground, with barracks
lining the exterior walls. The north section of
the fortress, accessed by a drawbridge across
the inner moat, was reserved for the ducal
apartments.

The residential quarters consisted of the
duke's spacious palace and the impenetrable
Rocchetta. The latter was a fortification in its
own right within the castle walls. The square
tower or Torre Castellana in the west corner
of the structure housed the state jewels.
Today all the rooms of the fortress are open to
the public and are used as a museum,
archives, libraries and historic institutes.

## The gunpowder tower

Once work on the new fortification was well
under way, Florentine architect Antonio
Averulino, also known as Filarete, was
summoned to Milan. He was entrusted with
constructing the central tower, which opened
out onto the city gate. This formed the main
link between the castle and the city. As
dangerous ammunition was kept in the Torre
del Filarete, it was known as the gunpowder
tower or magazine. Its name proved apt in
more ways than one; in 1521 the explosive
contents accidentally caught fire, blowing the

tower to smithereens. The present Torre del
Filarete is a copy erected by the architect
Beltrami at the beginning of the 20th century.

Following the murder of Duke Galeazzo
Maria Sforza in front of the Santo Stefano
church, in 1477 his widow Bona di Savoia had
another tower built above the moat in the
castle bailey as a safe house for herself and her
children in times of danger. Between 1480 and
1490 Lodovico *il Moro* made a number of
further additions and improvements to the
fortress, inviting artists such as Bramante and
Leonardo da Vinci to contribute to the various
projects. The Ponticella di Lodovico, for
example, is attributed to Bramante. The beautiful loggia of the ducal palace is the work of
architect Benedetto Ferrini. Leonardo also
painted a ceiling of vines here, today sadly
barely visible.

## The Spanish walls

During the course of the 16th century the
duchy of Milan fell first to France and then to

Leonardo da Vinci
*Trees with Branches, Roots and Rocks*, 1497/98
Fresco
Pinacoteca del Castello Sforzesco, Milan

In 1482 Leonardo da Vinci (1452–1519) arrived at the court of Milan, remaining there until the end of the century. One of his tasks was to decorate the Sala delle Assi in the ducal chambers, sadly now in a poor state of repair.

Spain. Under the Spanish the exterior of the Castello Sforzesco was much altered. When Charles V had new town walls erected he also built an enclosing fortification around the castle. Six huge pointed ramparts and six ravelins joined to the *enceinte* made the fortress resemble a giant 12-point star. The two larger upper walls formed a forked ditch. From the air, the entire castle complex looks like a crab clinging to the city wall.

In the wake of Napoleon's Second Coalition War to gain supremacy of the Continent, the Italian republics collapsed. In 1802 the Sforza's castle came under Napoleonic control. So that the stronghold would not fall into enemy hands on his retreat he ordered it to be destroyed. The Spanish walls were demolished. Only the return of Austrian troops prevented the castle itself from being leveled. By 1814 the fortress was again a barracks. The Austrian General Radetzky was the first to use the castle as it was originally intended. During the March riots of 1848 he fired on the city from the fortress walls. The cannons boomed for five days. The troops stationed at the Castello then marched into town to amuse themselves.

By the end of the 19th century the castle was in such a state of disrepair that the authorities almost gave up on it and pulled it down. After much discussion, however, they decided to restore it. The result was controversial, to say the least. The people of Milan still go out of their way to avoid the absurd construction.

## The Sforza: grandfather, father and son

The Sforza *signoria* ruled Milan from 1450 to 1500. The empire that father Francesco Sforza had spent his life consolidating and

Opposite:
Anonymous
*Marriage of Bianca Maria
Visconti and Francesco
Sforza*, 1463
Illumination on parchment,
10 × 14 cm
San Sigismondo Codex
Archivio Parrocchiale di S.
Sigismondo, Cremona

The miniature depicts the
wedding of 40-year-old
Francesco Sforza to 16-year-
old Bianca Maria Visconti in
1441. Sforza had demanded
the girl's hand in marriage
from her father,
Filippo Maria Visconti,
in return for his military
services to the duke.

Below: Pisanello
*Filippo Maria Visconti*, 1440
Bronze medal, diam. 120 mm
Museo del Bargello,
Florence

Filippo Maria Visconti
(1412–1447), a soldier to the
core, was the most powerful
ruler of his age. The greatest
threat to his territory was the
maritime city-state of Venice.

expanding was squandered and destroyed by his son Lodovico *il Moro* within a very short space of time, yet during their reign the Sforza of Milan were the most influential rulers in Italy. Their rise to power began with Francesco's father, Muzio Attendolo.

The son of a well-to-do family of farmers from Cotignola near Ravenna, Muzio laid down his hoe at the age of 16 to join a volunteer corps passing through the village. The soldiers marched away from the farm with not only the farmer's son but a few pilfered geese and pigs as well. After he had served for several years, Muzio left the army to become one of the most famous and best-paid volunteer captains of his day. Under the name of Sforza, he won land and titles fighting both for and against Queen Joan II of Naples. He lost his life in the same way as Emperor Frederick Barbarossa; in his eagerness to save one of his soldiers from drowning, Muzio forgot to remove his armor before jumping to the rescue and himself perished in the rapids.

From the countless children he had by his three wives and numerous mistresses Muzio chose his favorite illegitimate son Lucia Trezarias Francesco as his heir. Francesco was raised at court in Ferrara from an early age and then sent to Naples as a royal page. Muzio

completed his son's education by taking him with him on his various campaigns and crusades. His method of upbringing would bear fruit later.

## Francesco (1401–1466)

As a leader of mercenary troops Francesco's main strategy was to avoid out-and-out conflict wherever possible. His tactics were to stall both his employer and his enemy. One of the ways he did this was to take control of strategic roads. He occasionally took on a battle to keep his soldiers on form, with victory usually assured.

Francesco also made sure that he chose the most powerful man of the age as his employer: Filippo Maria Visconti, lord and master of Milan. Visconti had no sons and therefore no direct heir to whom to bequeath his beloved duchy on his death. A series of crushing defeats at the hands of the Venetians convinced him that the only person who could save him was a military genius like Francesco Sforza. Sforza agreed to defend the duke after Visconti had promised him his only daughter Bianca Maria, then six years old. Filippo Maria later tried time and again to break his promise; time and again Sforza tore up the basic contract they had made and threatened to enter the services of the duke's rivals, the Venetians, Florentines and the pope. In 1441 Francesco finally managed to lead his bride, now 16, to the altar.

## The Milanese

When Filippo Maria Visconti died in 1447 Francesco Sforza was not in town. He was waiting for the moment when the Milanese would call on him for aid. Growing unrest in the city itself sparked off a full-scale republican revolution. The castle at the Porta Giovia, the seat of the tyrannical Visconti, was razed to the ground; it stood in the way of the reintroduction of the republican *comune* tradition. When Venice tried to profit from the political vacuum and extend its boundaries at the expense of Milan, the leaders of the Repubblica Ambrosiana were forced to turn

MARCHIO
CAROLVS FRANCISCVS
VICECOMES

Above: Leonardo da Vinci
*The Sforza Coat of Arms in the Sala delle Assi*, 1497/98
Fresco
Pinacoteca del Castello Sforzesco, Milan
Leonardo painted the coat of arms of the Sforza family as a boss covering the intersection of the ribs in the vault.

Top right:
*The Coat of Arms of the Visconti*
Biblioteca Trivulziana, Milan
Francesco Sforza adopted the title and heraldic symbol of his predecessor.

to Francesco Sforza for help. He came, conquered the Venetians and marched on Milan with his victorious army. He stopped short of the city gates and set up camp outside the town, however, respecting the Milanese ban on his entering the city. Even when new troubles broke out on the interior of the walls, Sforza refused to get involved. Despite his restraint, the presence of his troops just outside the town walls was seen as a threat and the inhabitants began to get nervous.

At the end of February 1450 the Milanese finally opened their gates to Francesco. Sforza entered and had his soldiers distribute fresh bread. One of the conditions of his entrance to the city was that he did not rebuild the demolished fortress. Sforza agreed. Just four months after signing the treaty he broke his word, however, and turned the place where the castle had stood into an enormous building site. The commander erected the Castello Sforzesco and henceforth proclaimed it the residence of the ducal family. He adopted all the trademarks and traditions of his predecessors the Visconti, from the title and coat of arms bearing the dragon serpent, the *biscione*, down to the names of his children.

As head of state Sforza avoided violence and bloodshed both in the city and in the surrounding countryside. His period of rule saw the longest period of military peace in Italy. His policies earned him loyal allies in Cosimo *il Vecchio* and Florence. The Treaty of Lodi (1454) had all the trimmings of a gentlemen's agreement, with the five most powerful states in Italy – Milan, Venice, Florence, Rome and Naples – pledging through their rulers to pursue a policy of compromise and compensation, if not actually of friendship. The administration and chancellery of the duchy of Milan was allotted to the Simonetta family. Francesco Sforza died in 1466. The eldest of his legitimate children, Galeazzo Maria, inherited the most flourishing state in Italy.

## Lodovico, the autocrat

Lodovico *il Moro* is "certainly an excellent prince through his eloquence, intelligence and the many facets of his soul and character, worthy of his gentle and mild epithet if he had not blackened this praise with disgrace over the death of his nephew (…)." This was according to a contemporary diplomat and historian, Francesco Guicciardini of Florence. He adds: "But on the other hand he is of a vain nature with restless and ambitious thoughts, full of scorn for his promises and loyalty; and so presumptuous in his self-esteem and superior manner (…) that he was convinced he could direct everyone's thoughts in a particular direction with his intrigue and charms and wiles."

Lodovico *il Moro* was one of over 30 sons sired by Francesco Sforza. A year after his father had conquered Milan, Lodovico was born at the castle while it was being rebuilt. As he was the first to enter the world in the fortress, he considered himself the firstborn of all his brothers, even though many of them were older than him, and thus had greater claims to be their father's heir. He was given his nickname *il Moro* by his father, not because of his dark skin but because of his character. *Il moro* is a mulberry tree, said to be particularly pliable, flexible, resilient and tough.

Egnazio Danti
*The Duchy of Milan,*
1580–1583
Galleria delle Carte
Geografiche, Vatican

The map shows details of four battles fought in Lombardy, with the history of the Milanese noted in the cartouche on the top right.

Above: Nicola Cianfanelli
*Leonardo Explaining His
Skill and Mechanical
Inventions to Ludovico
Sforza*, 19th century
Fresco
Tribuna di Galileo, Florence

In a letter from Florence
addressed to Lodovico,
Leonardo offers the duke of
Milan his services, stressing
his skills as a military
engineer and constructor of
war machines. He also states
that "in times of peace" he is
prepared to work as a
decorator and painter.

Opposite, top:
Leonardo da Vinci
*Crossbow, c.* 1485
Pen and ink on chalk on
paper, 20.5 × 27.5 cm
Codex Atlanticus,
fol. 149r-b (ex 53r-b)
Biblioteca Ambrosiana,
Milan

Opposite, bottom:
Leonardo da Vinci
*Letter to Ludovico Sforza,*
1481
Pen and ink on paper
Codex Atlanticus, fol. 391a
Biblioteca Ambrosiana,
Milan

## A dubious character

Lodovico was 15 when his father died. His oldest brother, Galeazzo Maria, heir to the duchy, promptly had him removed from Milan. Ten years later, however, the situation changed. On St. Stephen's Day three young men from Milan stabbed Galeazzo Maria Sforza to death outside the church of Santo Stefano. Galeazzo's demise represented a new kind of political assassination. The conspirators were not only driven by private motives but also by a humanistic and literary ideal: the Romano-republican murder of tyrants. Lodovico was now 25 years old. He was an educated man and a patron of the arts; he lived a life of luxury and was a friend of Leonardo da Vinci. Yet the legitimate heir to the duchy was now little Galeazzo, his seven-year-old nephew, whose legal guardian was his mother, Bona di Savoia. The man responsible for the protection of the boy and his rights was Chancellor Cicco Simonetta. On May 25, 1477, Lodovico and three of his brothers tried to seize the guardianship of Galeazzo from their sister-in-law, Bona di Savoia. Their attempt failed, thanks to Simonetta's quick reaction. The

rogues were exiled. Swimming through the river one of the brothers drowned, suffering the same fate as his grandfather. Lodovico was banished to far-away Bari, where he gave substance to his nickname. Bending in a new direction, as malleable as the mulberry, he changed tack completely. He began a long and very clever exchange of letters with his sister-in-law, finally persuading her to accept his presence in Milan as her adviser. As soon as he had re-entered the gates, however, he began to put his real plans into action. He first rid himself of Simonetta, whom he had tried and beheaded as a traitor. He then had himself named Galeazzo's guardian; the boy loved his uncle and desperately wanted to follow in Lodovico's footsteps.

## The fateful invitation

As ruler of the richest duchy in Italy, within the space of a few years Lodovico managed to completely destroy the tentative peace agreed in the Treaty of Lodi. The duke was not alone in disturbing the status quo; Italian politics at the end of the 15th century were unusually turbulent.

Lodovico's opponents very quickly realized that he was striving to become ruler over the whole of Italy. To this end he formed an alliance with the king of France, Charles VIII, assisting him financially in his campaign against the kingdom of Naples which the French monarch, as heir of Anjou, claimed as his by right.

The duchy of Milan occupied a key position for anyone wanting to march an army from the north to the south of the country. Hoping to weaken all his Italian rivals in one fell swoop, Lodovico flung open the gates to a French invasion, a move so perilous that Francesco Sforza had been violently opposed to it. On the evening before Charles VIII's campaign was due to start, Ferdinand of Aragon, the king of Naples, sent Lodovico some heartfelt advice in the following letter: "Deliberate on the past, and observe how often internal disputes between the Italian states have led to foreign powers being called in to traverse the mountains into Italy and oppress and tyrannize the country so terribly that the consequences can still be felt."

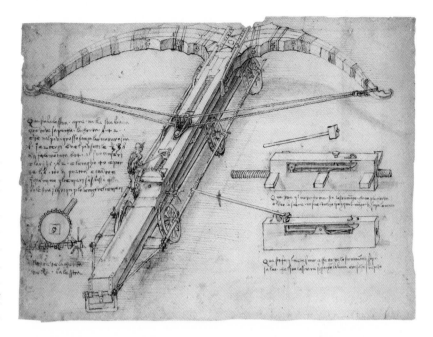

## An army of soldiers and whores

In the late summer of 1494 Charles VIII crossed the Alps at the head of an army of 40,000 soldiers and 800 prostitutes. A well-organized propaganda campaign highlighting the evils of the murderous French artillery had spread a wave of terror across the entire peninsula. Lodovico rode with his royal household to Asti to welcome the king. While Charles VIII was in Lombardy, the young Galeazzo Sforza, the rightful duke of Milan, died. The cause of death, according to contemporary sources, was a gradual overdose of poison.

## A bull in a china shop

Not in the least bothered by the turn of events, Charles VIII continued with his campaign, proceeding through Italy with all the grace of a bull in a china shop. The proclamations the French king had sent out to the rulers of Italy prior to his advance stated

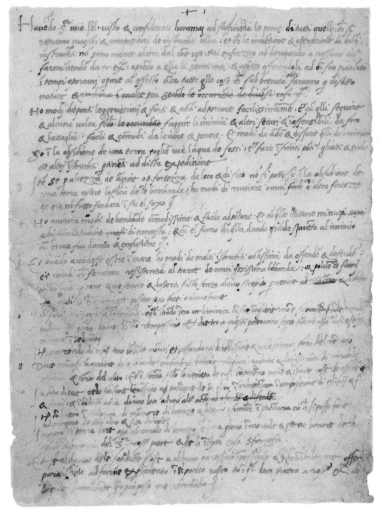

clearly that he was only interested in Naples and not in the states he had to pass through to get there. Those on the monarch's route still had to decide whether to grant the most modern army in the world permission to cross their territories or resist their unwelcome guests. The internal balance of the states the king had to march through along the route crumbled on this issue long before the French had even arrived. The news of the regent's long stay in Lombardy alone was enough to wreak havoc in Italy and shatter its fragile political mosaic.

The advancing French army left behind scenes of social catastrophe and military devastation. The population was struck down by a strange illness never previously heard of; the Italians dubbed it the "French disease" and the French, infected by soldiers returning from Italy, the "Neapolitan sickness." Its medical name is syphilis.

Even Naples did not offer any resistance to the French invasion. King Alfonso II, successor to Ferdinand, who had died in 1494 just before the French arrived, fled the capital. Charles VIII marched into Naples and found himself caught up in the political vacuum of southern Italy. He finally realized that he could not govern the country without a strong territorial state in the north under his control. The prime candidate was Milan – not as an allied power but as vassal to the king.

Egnazio Danti
*The Battle of Fornovo*
(detail), 1580–1583
Galleria delle Carte
Geografiche, Vatican

With great diplomatic skill Lodovico *il Moro* persuaded all of the powerful states of Italy to form an Italian League against Charles VIII. At Fornovo, seeing he was outnumbered by his adversaries, the French king abandoned hundreds of cartloads of booty to the League's mercenaries and was able to ride off unscathed.

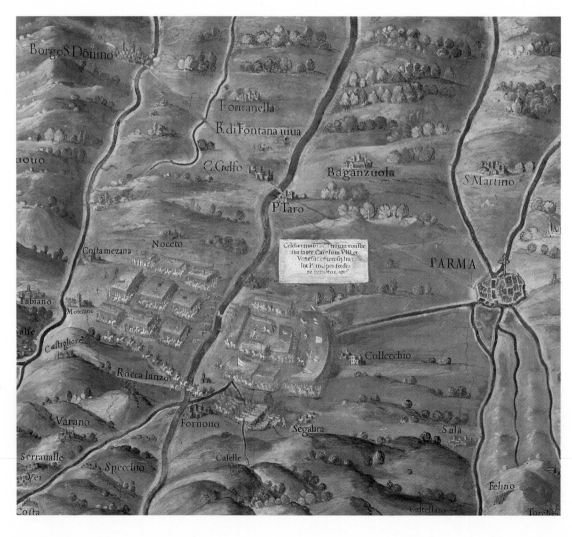

## Diplomatic contortions

While Charles VIII was still in the south Lodovico correctly predicted the king's next move and engaged in the sort of complex diplomatic negotiations that were later to become accepted practice in Italy. The duke's skill and sensitivity in negotiation helped him form an anti-French league (*Lega Italica*) comprising nearly all the states of Italy.

Charles VIII, suddenly betrayed by his "allies," hurried back north. In Fornovo in the Ligurian Apennines, he found himself in grave danger from the armies of the Italian League who were blocking his passage home. For the first time the French king had the chance to exercise his brilliance as a military commander. He ordered his troops to abandon the hundreds of cartloads of booty they had pillaged on their travels. As the king had anticipated, the men in the various mercenary companies of the *Lega Italica* greedily pounced on the loot, leaving the French army to steal away unobserved.

## Capitulation and refuge

Three years later, in 1499, Louis XII, successor to Charles VIII, also sent an army to Italy. This time the king did not advance to the south; this attack, arranged with Venice, was meant to punish Milan. The remaining Italian states watched the battle from a safe distance. As the French neared the city *il Moro* fled, taking the state treasure with him. He sought refuge with Emperor Maximilian in Tyrol. The emperor promised to come to his aid in exchange for a loan to help finance his war against the Swiss.

In the meantime, Milan had capitulated to the French. Louis XII seized control of the town and stationed one of his garrisons at the Sforza's castle.

## A sorry end

With the remains of his ducal gold and jewels Lodovico hired the services of 10,000 Swiss infantry and set off to win back Milan. He was greeted by crowds of jubilant subjects. He also managed to regain control of Novara, forcing the French to retreat to Asti.

What happened next is unique in European military history. The 10,000 French infantry men and Lodovico's 10,000 troops were all, in fact, Swiss. During the siege of Novara the two sides made contact and decided to leave their paying masters in the lurch. "They did not want to raise a hand against their relatives, against their brothers or any others of their nation," explained Guicciardini. The Swiss mingled "as if they were but one army who wanted to immediately leave for home. No amount of pleas, tears or countless promises from the duke could prevent them from carrying out this malicious deed. He finally begged them insistently to at least convey him to a safe place; yet as they had agreed with the commanders of the French army that they would disperse and not take him with them they refused his petition, decreeing that he should merge among them dressed in the uniform of one of their soldiers in order to save himself, if luck were to be on his side and he should not be recognized."

Far left: Antonio and Piero Pollaiuolo
*Galeazzo Maria Sforza,*
*c.* 1471
Tempera on wood,
65 × 42 cm
Galleria degli Uffizi,
Florence

When Francesco Sforza died in 1466 he bequeathed a thriving state to Galeazzo Maria, the eldest of his 30 children. Galeazzo Maria had his younger brother Lodovico *il Moro*, then 15, removed from Milan. Ten years later Galeazzo Maria was murdered by political assassins and Lodovico returned to his home town.

Lodovico was "identified as he ran off, clothed as a Swiss soldier and armed in amongst the throng. He was immediately captured, a sorry spectacle which even moved many of his enemies to tears."

He was taken to France, where he spent ten years rotting in the tower dungeon of Loches Castle as the king's "guest." Little is known about this period. It is assumed that *il Moro* was not incarcerated in a cage, as was customary with detainees at this particular establishment. He was allowed an hour's walk in the courtyard. He could write letters in which he suggested using the rest of his jewels to buy his freedom. The French king refused to even consider this, however.

The dungeon in the tower of Loches, where Lodovico *il Moro* spent his last ten years. The tower had been used as a top-security prison for very special "guests" of the French king since the 15th century. The standard procedure was to lock the prisoner up in an iron cage and throw food down to him from above. The captive usually died before he drowned in his own excrement. In 1489 nobleman Philippe de Commynes, advisor to the late Louis XI, was accused of being party to a conspiracy and spent six months in Loches. He described it as a "pitiless dungeon covered inside and out with iron brackets, with terrible fittings at head height and one foot above these." Lodovico *il Moro* was privileged enough to be incarcerated in a normal cell with permission to walk the courtyard. At the beginning of his sojourn he insisted on being able to talk to the king in order to clear up any misunderstandings but was refused an audience. No further details on Lodovico's final years at Loches have been recorded.

# CAROLVS VIII GAL:REX

## The Death of Charles VIII in Amboise

Philippe de Commynes (1447–1511)

Anonymous
*Portrait of Charles VIII,
King of France,* 16th century
Collezione Gioviana,
Galleria degli Uffizi,
Florence

In 1494 the king of France
marched on Naples with an
enormous army then
considered to be the most
modern in the world.
Although he was only
interested in the southern
state, he created anarchy
throughout the Italian
peninsula. His death was
sudden and unheroic.

The French diplomat Philippe de Commynes from Burgundy is one of the greatest writers of early modern history. He accompanied the Burgundian Charles the Bold (1467–1477) and from 1472 onwards the French kings Louis XI (1461–1483) and Charles VIII (1483–1498) on their travels as a royal reporter, witnessing both the private and military affairs of his masters. De Commynes began writing his chronicle *Mémoires* in 1489. This voluminous historical work was printed in 1542, and subsequently translated into a number of languages. It included a moving account of the death of Charles VIII:

"At a time when he enjoyed such great fame in the world and stood in such good grace with God, on 7 April of the year 1498, the day before Palm Sunday, he left the chambers of Queen Anne of Brittany, his wife, to watch a game of badminton with her in the baileys of the castle. It was the first time that he took her with him. Together they stepped onto the Haquelebas Gallery, which had suffered damage during construction work and was considered to be the most undignified area of the palace; it was situated directly at the entrance, the place where everyone answered the call of nature. Although the king was small, he hit his head on the lintel as he entered. Afterwards he watched the players for a long time and chatted with his royal household.

I was not there, but his father confessor, the bishop of Angers, and his closest chamberlains have told me what happened. I had left eight days previously and set off for home. His last words spoken in full consciousness were that he hoped that he would never commit a mortal or venial sin if he could. As he said this, he fell backwards and his voice faded. It must have been about two hours after midday. And he lay in this place until eleven at night. Three times he regained consciousness for a brief period, as his confessor told me, to whom he confessed twice in this week. Anybody who wished could come to the gallery and observe the king lying on a humble sack of straw from which he did not rise again until he breathed his last. This was at nine o'clock. The father confessor, who was with him all the while, told me that when he regained his powers of speech three times he said: 'My God and you, Holy Virgin Mary, and you, Saints Claudius and Blaise, stand by me!' In this way a king as powerful and strong as he departed this world in such a wretched place – he, who possessed so many beautiful castles and had one of such splendor built, did not deserve to end his life in such lowly surroundings.

How keenly we recognize that the power of God is great and our life very poor, that we can put such effort into the things of this world and that kings can last no longer than a simple peasant."

# Imola

## Caterina Sforza's dowry

Far right: The end wall of the castle seen from the east. According to historic documents the first fortification at Imola dates back to c.1000. The present fortress, constructed by engineer Danesio Maineri in the 15th century, quickly became something of a model for military architects. The Renaissance stronghold incorporates the ruins of an earlier 13th-century castle which was also equipped with large towers.

### Between us and them

The little town of Imola lies on the Via Emilia between Bologna and the Adriatic Sea. The Via Emilia runs along the northern edge of the Apennines. Built by the Romans, the perfectly straight road stakes out the boundary between "us and them."

As with nearly all of the other towns erected along the Via Emilia, the fall of the Roman Empire signaled the decline of Imola, then known as Forum Cornelii after Lucius Cornelius Sulla. At the end of the 4th century St. Ambrose counted Imola among his *cadaveri di città*, his "dead cities." The populace of

Above: View of the moat, now filled in.

Forum Cornelii dispersed in three or four different directions, as the Via Emilia had nothing left to offer them but danger. Some moved to the sea and others into the mountains, with the rest prepared to try and build a new life on the plains. Only a few remained to brave the barbarians, bandits and mosquitoes. The entire Romagna area, to which Imola

132

Above: The embrasures running along the entire circumference of the large circular room at the top of the tower enabled the surrounding area to be kept under all-round surveillance.

The 13th century saw the construction of a castle with towers – a project financed by loans from Bolognese bankers. Some remnants of this medieval castle can still be seen in the present Renaissance complex.

For a long time Imola was under the influence of Bologna. It was also in permanent dispute with its neighbors Faenza and Forlì. In the 15th century, like the rest of the Romagna, it found itself taking center stage in the battles waged between Milan, Venice, Florence and the pope.

## The Sforza

The Visconti of Milan stormed the town in 1424 and again in 1434. Their successors, the Sforza, gained legal possession of Imola through marriage in 1470. Under their rule an area on the edge of town was turned into a giant building site for a state-of-the-art fortress to replace the old medieval castle. Military engineer Danesio Maineri, the man responsible for the fortifications of the duchy of Milan, was commissioned to design and build the new castle. Danesio was from a family of architects but was himself an engineer whose forte was the technical study of weaponry. He had also spent a long period training with the duke's artillery. The new fortress was quite revolutionary compared with other fortresses of its day with regard to its facilities for firearms. Maineri also incorporated as much of the old castle as he could into his new edifice.

belongs, was criss-crossed by repeated migrations. Most of the new settlers came north from the Balkans and crossed the Po Delta to find themselves face to face with their first major geographic obstacle, the Apennines.

## The return

We know nothing about Imola during this insecure period in its history, because few documents dating from prior to 1000 make any mention of it. A fortified site is known to have existed from this point onwards. There are also comments marking the return of various communities who had moved away in previous centuries. It is assumed that the name of the town was derived from that of one of these communities.

Right: The round defensive towers were state of the art, designed for use with firearms.

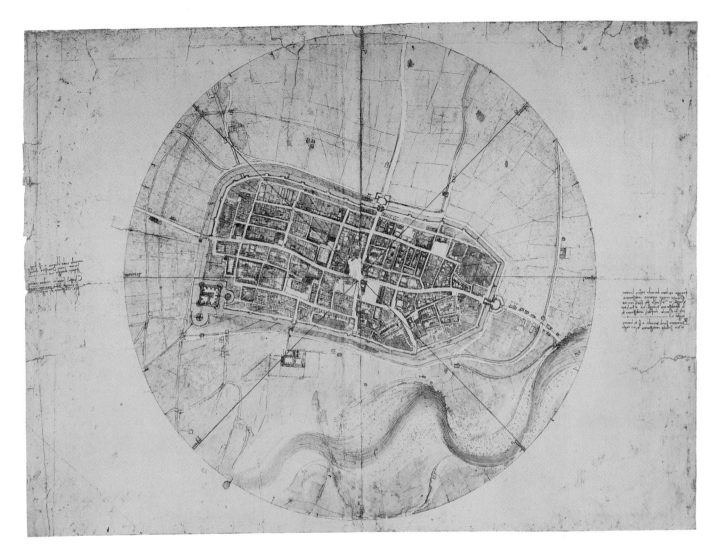

The sketches and reports he sent to the duke of Milan indicate that Maineri was particularly interested in the restoration of the older walls and defenses. Work went on for about a decade and the result must have been truly astounding. The castle became a model fortress that inspired many of Italy's military architects, especially those who lived in the regions controlled by the Papal States. Even Leonardo da Vinci drew a plan of the town and its fortifications during his few months in Imola in 1502.

## Leonardo's map

Leonardo da Vinci's map of Imola is heralded as a cartographic masterpiece. This was the first map whose individual proportions exactly matched those of the actual geography. Leonardo operated according to a strictly scientific method when collecting data for his town plan. He first surveyed every single street, every square and every palace with absolute precision. With the aid of a goniometer he had made himself he then measured the radial corners of the city's primary components from the highest points of the town. Finally he compared his two sets of measurements and used the data he had compiled and verified with this method to draw up his plan. Leonardo completed his map of Imola in the summer of 1502 while he was working as military architect to Cesare Borgia. The fortress, linked up to the town walls, is on the bottom left of the plan.

Leonardo da Vinci, *Map of Imola*, 1502 Codex Windsor, reproduction of a facsimile in the Museo Vinciano, Vinci

Leonardo da Vinci completed his map of Imola for the Borgia in 1502. It is heralded as a masterpiece of contemporary cartography. The plan was draw from precise scientific measurements and calculations made on site.

## Caterina Sforza, the golden contessa

On May 1, 1477, the town of Imola was in a state of nervous anticipation. Men and women, old and young, had dressed themselves in their Sunday best. The sun was shining, the streets decorated with flowers and children's choirs were practicing songs and sonnets. The entire community was eagerly awaiting the arrival from Milan of Caterina Sforza, the countess of Imola. She rode through the city gates at sunset.

Caterina had left Milan on April 24, "an hour before lunch," stopping off en route in Pavia, Reggio, Modena and Bologna. Just 14 years old, she showed no signs of exhaustion even after traveling for eight days. Every night she wrote a letter home full of news of her journey. From Imola she described how she dismounted outside the portal to the palace and was immediately surrounded by a crush of people, pushing her backwards and forwards in an attempt to embrace her, an experience she found "not unpleasant." She told of a banquet held in her honor and the dances the people of Imola performed for her. "In their dances they make many changes of step, curtseying and moving much. They stamp their feet and hop in the air." Caterina was a young woman of captivating beauty and charm. She wore a heavy chain around her neck and a wrap of gold brocade, a short cloak and sleeves of black velvet. Her skin was snow white, her eyes and hair jet black and her manner kind and relaxed. The day after her arrival the peasants on the market place humbly murmured "Contessa, contessa!" when she presented them with a pale hand to kiss. "They do not cease their celebrations until the stones themselves rejoice at my arrival," she wrote. Caterina was mature for her age, a child forced to grow up fast. On St. Stephen's Day about four months before she embarked on her tour her father, Count Galeazzo Maria Sforza of Milan, had been stabbed to death in front of the cathedral by three young men claiming to be acting in the name of the republican ideal. This form of political crime was new to Italy, but it was soon to become widespread.

## A little girl's secret

After spending a few days in Imola, Caterina rode on to Rome where she was to be married. She was in no great hurry, seemingly happier to be on the road than in the papal city. She had left Milan only once before in her life when she and her family had been invited to stay with Lorenzo *il Magnifico* in Florence. In Rome she would be greeted by the groom, Girolamo Riario, the man known as Pope Sixtus IV's "nephew." Riario was in fact the pope's son and Caterina's senior by a few decades. For three years Caterina and Riario had been joined in marriage, a state secret Caterina had kept closely guarded. The matrimonial union was perfectly legitimate, yet as Caterina had been under age at the time special dispensation had been required from the pope. Without this both the validity of the marriage and, most importantly, of Caterina's dowry, the town of Imola,

Melozzo da Forlì
*Sixtus IV Names Bartolomeo Platina Prefect of the Biblioteca Vaticana,* 1477
Fresco, 370 × 315 cm
Pinacoteca Vaticana, Vatican

Pope Sixtus IV (1414–1484) was the first of the "terrible popes" of the Renaissance. He was heavily influenced by the monastic order of the Franciscan Minorites. Elected pope in 1471, he concentrated his energies on strengthening and increasing the worldly power of the church, often to the benefit of members of his own family. He was also a patron of the arts; the Sistine Chapel in the Vatican (1473–1481) is attributed to him.

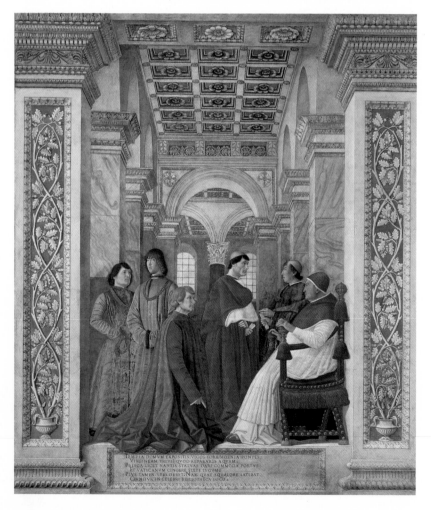

would have been contestable. After the ceremony had been performed with the utmost secrecy, and before several trustworthy witnesses at the insistence of the bridegroom (who wanted to secure his dowry), Riario returned home to Rome. Caterina remained at the castle in Milan to play with her horses.

Imola was in one of the areas the Church had claimed as its own. The ecclesiastical version of history records both Emperor Constantine and King Pippin giving the region known as the Pentapolis to the Church many centuries earlier. Since then Imola had been passed from one ruler to another, falling to the Sforza family in the 15th century. By marrying off his "nephew" to the daughter of Galeazzo Maria Sforza, the pope was only reclaiming what had been his in the first place. The Sforza acted as if they wished to give Imola to the pope as a present by way of Caterina's marriage. Their real objective, however, was quite different.

Up to now Caterina had been a mere pawn in the game of politics, carefully deployed by her father, Galeazzo Maria. Now that he was dead it was up to Caterina to make the next move.

## The murder plot

In August of 1484 the 22-year-old Caterina was in Rome, now the mother of three children and eight months pregnant with her fourth. Girolamo Riario, governor-general of the Church and to all intents and purposes lord of Rome, had in fact been the most powerful man in the city for three years. Having increased his hold on the Romagna through the acquisition of Forlì, he was now trying, with the support of the pope, to also gain possession of Faenza and Rimini with an eye to creating a territorial state. In league with the Orsini, Riario had initiated the persecution of the Colonna family in Rome. Fires, plundering and street battles had the city in utter turmoil. The pope's "nephew" was one of the most hated men in Italy. In 1482 he had the powerful Cardinal Lorenzo Colonna dragged off to the Castel Sant'Angelo and beheaded. This deed was so terrible that it incensed even the Orsini, who had been enemies of the Colonna for centuries.

Anonymous
*Caterina Sforza in the Final Years of Her Life* (detail),
16th century
Galleria degli Uffizi,
Florence

The daughter of Galeazzo, Maria Sforza, was married to Girolamo Riario at the tender age of 11, a political union that gave the Church possession of Imola. Throughout Italy Caterina was famous for her beauty and ivory skin and particularly for her legendary courage and ability to stand her ground.

Melozzo da Forlì
*Sixtus IV Names Bartolomeo Platina Prefect of the Biblioteca Vaticana* (detail), Girolamo Riario, 1477
Fresco
Pinacoteca Vaticana, Vatican

The man people called the "nephew" of Pope Sixtus IV was actually the pontiff's son. Together with his father, Riario planned the assassination of Giuliano and Lorenzo de' Medici in 1478 (the latter survived the vicious attack). Caterina's mean and violent husband was himself assassinated in Forlì in 1488.

Master Wenceslas
*September* (detail),
beginning of the
15th century
Fresco
Torre d'Aquila, Trent

Following the death of Pope Sixtus IV in 1484, Riario was threatened with execution. The college of cardinals ordered that he leave Rome. Caterina, heavily pregnant, promptly seized control of the Castel Sant'Angelo and had its cannons pointed in the direction of the Vatican palaces. She was granted possession of Forlì, Imola and various other estates on condition that her family moved to the Romagna.

This was not the first time that Girolamo Riario had struck terror into people's hearts. After carefully analyzing the murder plot which had resulted in the death of his father-in-law Galeazzo Sforza, in 1478 Riario made similar plans to eliminate Giuliano and Lorenzo de' Medici. The assassination took place in the cathedral in Florence on April 26. Giuliano died but Lorenzo managed to escape the knife of his executioner. *Il Magnifico* then waited for the moment when he could avenge the brutal butchering of his brother.

## Cannons threaten the conclave

Pope Sixtus IV died in 1484 during one of his frequent temper tantrums. On the very same day an angry crowd attacked and pillaged the Riario-Sforza palace on Via della Lungara and set it alight. Even the trees in the garden were felled and torched. The college of cardinals demanded that Girolamo Riario, absent from the city with his army, return immediately to Rome. His luck had obviously changed; he now faced deposition or even execution. Failing to heed Caterina's advice, Riario obeyed the cardinals' orders and hurried back to Rome in a state of sheer panic.

On the evening of August 14 a heavily pregnant woman rode up to the gates of the Castel Sant'Angelo and dismounted. The castle garrison, among them a dozen soldiers from Imola, allowed the lady to enter. In the name of her husband Caterina Sforza took command and immediately had the castle cannons positioned so that they could fire on the palaces of the Vatican, where the conclave was to meet to elect the new pope. Threatened by the cannons, the conclave was unable to convene. They decided to wait, hoping that Caterina would soon give up. Days went by without the situation changing. Riario's nerves snapped first. He distanced himself from his wife's plans and pledged to the cardinals that he would persuade Caterina to capitulate by August 24. During the night of August 24 the sound of joyous celebration, with music and singing, was heard coming from the Castel Sant'Angelo. The hours passed and still Caterina did not show. On the evening of August 25 a delegation of eight cardinals presented themselves at the castle gates and requested an audience. Caterina granted their request, thinking she could take the clerics hostage if the need arose. During the night a contract was drawn up and signed by Caterina and the cardinals. The document guaranteed the Riario family possession of Imola, Forlì and all their other estates outside Rome. On the condition that the family moved to the Romagna, well out of Rome's way, a considerable sum was to change hands. The money was to recompense Girolamo Riario for his services as governor of the church.

On the morning of August 26 the eight cardinals left the Castel Sant'Angelo. By sunset Caterina had also appeared. Two days later the Riario-Sforza entourage left for Forlì where they arrived on September 4. The countess had barely dismounted from her horse when she gave birth, prematurely, to a little girl.

### The situation worsens

Forlì, April 14, 1488. Caterina, now 25 years old, was as famous throughout Italy for her legendary courage as she was for her ivory skin. A year previously she had given birth to her sixth child, a boy she named Francesco after his grandfather, after riding 25 miles (40 km) across rocky mountain trails. She had now traveled to Forlì from Milan with her sister Stella and her mother Countess Lucrezia Marliani, once Galeazzo Maria Sforza's official mistress. Caterina was pregnant again.

Caterina may not have been quite as popular in Imola and Forlì as she had been in her youth, but she was still highly thought of – which was more than one could say of her moody, violent and vindictive husband. Over the years he had become extremely parsimonious, as well. In an attempt to gain favor with his subjects the pope's "nephew" had once abolished all forms of taxation for the towns of Imola and Forlì. He now reinstated the old tax laws and passed new ones on a daily basis. Content to manage the financial side of his estates, Riario left the actual administration to Caterina.

On the evening of April 14, 1488, after a meal with Caterina, her mother and her sister,

Girolamo Riario was in unusually high spirits. He walked over to the window to breathe in the spring air. Suddenly three of his friends were ushered in. The first to enter was Checco Orsi. He held a letter in his hand, beneath which was a dagger. Riario's last words were: "Checco, my friend, what good wind brings you here?"

### Milk for the countess's children

Caterina heard noises in her room. Before she had even seen any signs of intruders she assessed the seriousness of the situation and dispatched a servant to Milan to fetch help from her uncle, Lodovico Sforza. She then gathered her mother, sister and wet nurses together and locked herself and the other women in the nursery. The news spread through town like wildfire. From the palace the traitors proclaimed that the tyrant Riario was dead, hurling his body out of the window to spur on the crowd below. Armed troops

*Fortified City – Representing Rome – Prophecies of the Pope*
Harley 1340, fol. 12
The British Library, London

This miniature is an allegory of the ideal city of Rome. The Holy City showed itself vulnerable and conquerable, however, when it was forced to submit to Caterina Sforza.

working for the conspirators seized the palace. Caterina, the other women and the children were taken captive and brought to the leaders of the coup, who were now installed at the house of the Orsi family. En route to her prison Caterina shouted into the crowd that the duke of Milan knew what was happening and would destroy Forlì if anything happened to her children. Her threat had the desired effect. That same night the town councilors held an emergency meeting, agreeing that they would have to ask the pope for aid if they were to ward off a dreaded attack by the Milanese.

On the morning of April 15, the papal regent of neighboring Cesena, Monsignor Savelli, arrived at Forlì. He hurried straight to the countess and assured her that neither she nor her children would be harmed. Caterina was not in the mood for politics, however. She demanded that the monsignor first bring milk for her children, as the two wet nurses were so terrified that they were no longer able to feed. Only then would she be willing to participate in any talks.

## A turn in the course of events

The castles at Forlì and Imola were not party to the uprising against Riario, and the commanders remained loyal to Caterina. The countess declared she would only persuade the

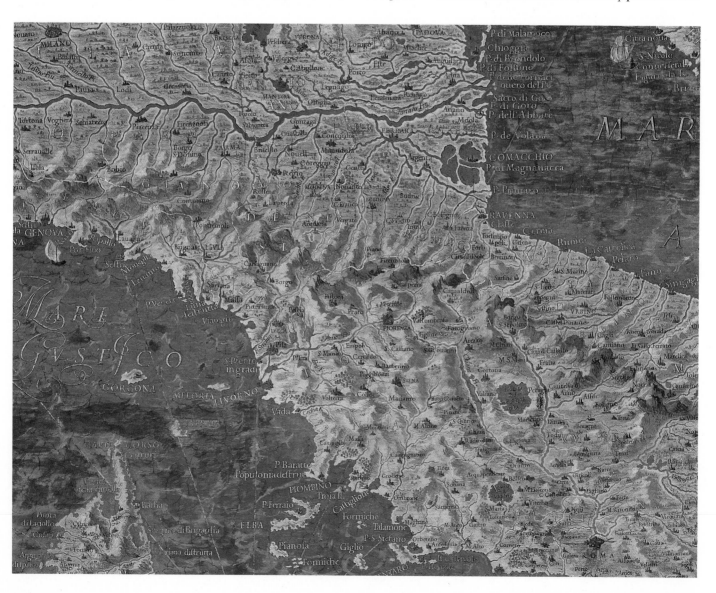

Egnazio Danti
*Italia moderna* (detail),
1580–1583
Fresco
Galleria delle Carte
Geografiche, Vatican

This fresco shows Italy during the last quarter of the 16th century.

Anonymous
*Allegory of Justice and Punishment*
Illumination
Biblioteca Nazionale, Turin

Caterina Sforza refused to relinquish Forlì, even when her enemies threatened to murder her children. In this allegory of justice and punishment, Justitia, shown here as a woman, also stands up to the forces of tyranny.

castle garrisons to capitulate if she could talk to them in person and if an absolute guarantee was given that no harm would come to her family while she was absent. After long hours of negotiation Monsignor Savelli decided, against the counsel of the Orsi, to allow Caterina to enter the heavily armed castle of Ravaldino. On April 16 the drawbridge was slowly lowered and Caterina was given three hours to talk the garrison into submission. She had barely disappeared behind the castle walls when the drawbridge was raised. Monsignor Savelli could only watch in horror as the cannons were turned round to face Forlì.

The castle was now under Caterina's command. Hours passed. The new rulers of the town were at a complete loss. After much deliberation the Orsi hit on a solution. They grabbed Caterina's children, dragged them up to the castle walls and held knives to each of their throats. A slim figure then emerged on the ramparts. Caterina raised her skirts,

exposing her genitals, and yelled at her black-mailers. "If you want to murder my children, then here's the wherewithal to make more!" She turned round and slipped back into the castle as suddenly as she had appeared.

Caterina held out for two weeks, occasionally firing a rebellious shot into the air to show she was still in a fighting mood. Her children did not have their throats cut but were regularly given their milk.

On the morning of April 29 an army 12,000 strong appeared on the horizon, halting five miles from the town walls. Troops from Milan had finally come to Caterina's aid. The pope's army failed to show, causing the Orsi brothers and other conspiracy leaders to flee Forlì that very same night. Shouting out the name of Caterina's firstborn, "Ottaviano! Ottaviano!", the people of Forlì spilled onto the streets. The drawbridge of Ravaldino Castle thundered open and out came the victorious countess, her head held high.

## Noble Knights, Rabble-rousers and Bankers: a Mixed Society

Katrin Boskamp-Priever

Andrea Mantegna
*The Gonzaga Family*, 1474
Fresco
Camera degli Sposi, Palazzo
Ducale, Mantua

Lodovico Gonzaga II
(1414–1478) had a portrait
painted of himself, his wife,
Barbara of Brandenburg
(1422–1481), his children
and his court by Andrea
Mantegna, royal artist to the
Gonzaga of Mantua.

Even as an old man Ser Mazzeo carried on going to the royal place in Palermo once a year during the lemon harvest to give King Frederick II of Sicily a present. The elderly spice merchant was pushed about by rude servants, and by the time he had been admitted to see the surprised monarch he looked rather disheveled. Offering his apologies for his appearance, in a clever speech embellished with a story from the Bible Mazzeo admonished the king about the disorderliness of his court. The king took the old man's words to heart. From that day onwards, as Florentine writer Franco Sacchetti (1335–1400) claims in one of his short narratives, King Frederick kept "his court in much better check."

As is often the case, in real life things were quite different. The merchant displayed great courage in the way he chastised the king. The story could have ended on a much less positive note, with Ser Mazzeo being arrested and thrown into prison. Medieval Italian society was based on the inequality of the various castes and of their legal rights. The feudal class system is best understood if we see it as a pyramid. At the tip is a handful of powerful rulers: the emperor or king, the church and the nobility. The level below them consists of knights, the lower nobility and civil servants. The people in the next stratum down had relatively few rights and represented a broad section of the population; these people could be townspeople, farmers or craftsmen, although who was actually counted in this class depended on the region and the period in which they were living. Those excluded from the hierarchical order, which the people of the Middle Ages believed was determined by God, were known as the marginalized: the poor, the sick, beggars, Jews, heathens, gypsies, minstrels, entertainers, travelers and slaves, and also those with disreputable occupations, such as slave drivers, knackers, executioners, tinkers, knife grinders and charcoal burners. There were strict rules governing contact between the different classes with regard to manners, clothing and modes of speech.

The advent of Norman rule in Sicily heralded the arrival of the feudal system in southern Italy, where it took on a singular form very different from that of its counterpart north of the Alps. In 1140 the Norman king of Sicily, Roger II, issued a statute book, the *Assizes of Ariano*, in an attempt to legitimize his claim as overlord and Christ's ruler on earth. King Roger's *Catalogus baronum*, in which he lists in detail the duties of his vassals, is also unique. This, together with the creation of a functioning civil service, was a large step towards the centralization and rationalization of the state. The Normans now had to take the "multicultural" population of their empire into account, translating documents into languages that Arabs, Byzantines, Berbers, Saracens, Jews, Greeks and Latin-speakers would understand. Roger II's grandson, the young Frederick Hohenstaufen II, who was crowned emperor in Rome in November 1220 and proclaimed ruler of Sicily in May 1221, tried to reorganize his kingdom into a strict system of feudalism and establish an efficient body of state administration. Among the emperor's many innovations were the reforms he made to criminal, civil, feudal and vassal law and to education (he founded the University of Naples in 1224). He also adopted a polished financial and economic policy. During this period the Caracciolo, Carafa and Pignatelli, three of the oldest noble families in Italy, assumed a leading role, their influence and importance growing in the south of the country, particularly Naples.

The alliance between the cities of Lombardy and Tuscany which Frederick II failed to crush at the end of his life gathered in strength during the interregnum (1254–1273), the period in which there was no Holy Roman Emperor on the throne. This had a considerable influence on the differentiation of the classes in Italy's towns and cities. The strata of the *comune* which set the tone consisted of members of the public (*popolo grasso*) and also of individuals from the ancient aristocratic families. Entire cities were thus effectively run by noble *signorie*, such as the Malatesta

Giovanni Stradano (Jan van der Straet)? *Tournament in Florence on the Square Outside Santa Croce,* 1561–1562 Fresco Quartiere di Eleonora da Toledo, Sala del Gualdrada, Palazzo Vecchio, Florence

The frescoes lining the private apartments of Eleonara da Toledo (1522–1562), Cosimo I's first wife, are of great historical interest as they illustrate scenes from life in 16th-century Florence. This *veduta* depicts a jousting tournament in front of Santa Croce. People crowd the wooden stands erected around the edge of the square and jostle for space at the windows and balconies of the surrounding houses to get a better view of the bloodthirsty spectacle.

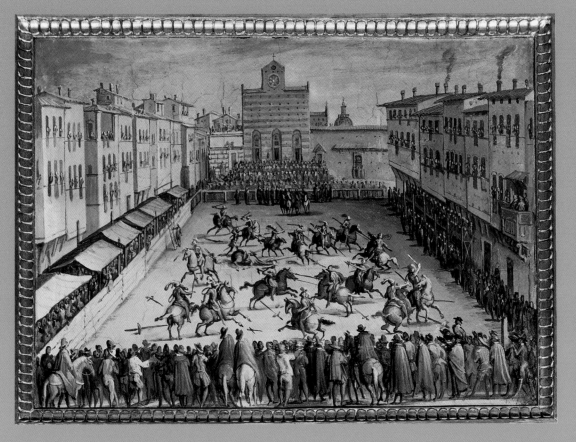

in Rimini, the d'Este in Ferrara, the Montefeltro in Urbino and the Gonzaga in Mantua.

Society was still dominated by a courtly code of chivalry that upheld the primacy of marriage, defendable by personal and bloody vendettas if necessary. Aristocratic men were drawn to tournaments, jousting, hunting, falconry and of course the glorious adventures the Italians could seek both on land and at sea. Young nobles were knighted according to a special ritual known as the *accolade*, in which a sword was ceremoniously belted around the waist. The tasks of a knight were honorable and considered a mark of distinction. Like many of the elements of life at court, medieval jousting tournaments were modeled on those of the French aristocracy. Knights from far and wide came to participate in these mass skirmishes, fighting to a specific set of rules for fame, honor, riches and the patronage of the ladies.

Yet during the 14th century the Age of Chivalry fell into decline – much to the chagrin of many contemporaries, among them Franco Sacchetti, who complained that entering the knighthood was no longer a question of "noble blood," as was the case in the kingdoms and principalities north of the Alps. "Oh you unhappy orders of knights, how have you deteriorated," wails Sacchetti. "Craftsmen and merchants down to bakers (...) wool-carders, profiteers and robber pawn merchants" had all been made knights and were simply not fit for the job. "What an ugly, what a stinking knighthood this is!" the poet laments. This merging of groups previously segregated by rigid rules and codes of conduct was a widespread phenomenon. During this period families rose from the lowly depths of the craftsmen's guilds to become members of the *nobili* or city elite. The Bentivogli of Bologna, for example, were once a hardworking family of butchers. The city's guild registers list no fewer than eight of them before 1400, with all of their businesses apparently flourishing. In the same era the Medici were ordinary moneychangers who earned their spurs in the minor offices of the *comune* of Florence.

As many of the established noble families (*case lunghe*) or those which had climbed the social

Antonio Pisano (known as Pisanello) and other artists *Playing Tarot Outside,* *c.* 1445 Fresco Stanza dei Giochi, Casa Borromeo, Milan

This painting, commissioned by Vitaliano Borromeo (1391–1447), may have been worked on by several artists. Three of the walls in the Hall of Games show ladies and their knights playing ball and card games.

ladder (*case curte*) were followers of either the Guelphs, the Ghibellines or some other splinter group and thus in a permanent state of conflict with each other, expending much of their energy in petty feuding, in many cases the *podestà* or top officials of a city had to be called in from outside to run the municipal administrative, judicial and defense systems. The *podestà* of Florence, for example, resided at the Bargello. Both the citizens and their governors were protected by a town garrison headed by the *gonfaloniere (della giustizia)*. He was employed to ward off attacks from external enemies and from the city magnates, the noble families excluded from holding community office because of their leanings towards violence and their overtly aristocratic way of life.

If a vassal – usually a knight – had sworn an oath of personal loyalty, service and obedience to his lord, either a prince, the king or the emperor, then this *condottiere* was a mercenary general bound by a contract to carry out a particular task in the name of a *comune* or local potentate. The *condottieri* were often well rewarded for their labors. In gratitude for two generations of loyalty

Above: Giovan Pietro Birago
*Condottiere Francesco Sforza Debating with Scipio, Pompey, Caesar and Hannibal*, end of the 15th century
Miniature (fragment)
Galleria degli Uffizi, Florence

Francesco Sforza I (1401–1466) entered the service of Filippo Maria Visconti, the duke of Milan, in 1425, becoming his successor in 1450. Seated here between Caesar and Hannibal, he is seen debating with other great army generals of the Roman period.

Right: Andrea del Castagno
*Condottiere Niccolò Marucci da Tolentino on Horseback*, 1456
Fresco (transferred),
833 × 512 cm
Duomo Santa Maria del Fiore, Florence

In recognition of the services of the *condottiere*, the city of Florence commissioned this portrait to be painted. This image of Marucci on horseback resembles a marble statue and was painted for the cathedral in Florence.

to the Hohenstaufen emperors, first in Henry VI's army fighting for the reconquest of southern Italy and then under Frederick II, in 1226 the Montefeltro were given the town of Urbino, which they subsequently ruled for several centuries. One family of *condottieri* to take to the political stage relatively late on, their origins going back only to the late 14th century, were the wild and unruly Sforza. Their military career commenced under Muzio Attendolo Sforza (1369–1424), and they gained possession of the territories of Milan from the defunct Visconti in 1450 thanks to the clever tactics and military strategy of Francesco Sforza (1401–1466). There were of course far less glorious and honorable ways of advancing one's social position and securing one's place in the centers of power. The Medici in Florence are one such example. The various members of this extremely complex dynasty had long been in disrepute as

notorious campaigners, rabble-rousers and conspirators. At the beginning of the Duecento they were one of the major non-aristocratic families of the *popolo grasso*, admitted to local government in Florence only because they were not knights, and neither did they have a title. It wasn't until later in their history that the Medici discovered their talent for business. Giovanni de Bicci (1368–1429) turned the assets bequeathed by Vieri de Cambio (1323–1395) into a powerful and influential Florentine bank, giving Giovanni's son, Cosimo il Vecchio (1389–1464), free rein to indulge in a series of prudent yet influential political dealings and patronage.

The contemporary writer Franco Sacchetti also seems to have considered it wiser to act with an eye to business rather than engage in open combat. In his narrative *German Knights*, a nobleman set off for Padua from the household of

Above: *Hartmann von Aue*, beginning of the 14th century Miniature on parchment Codex Manesse, Pal. Germ. 848, fol. 184v, Universitätsbibliothek, Heidelberg

The miniature depicts one of the most famous minnesingers and poets of the Middle Ages wearing an ornamental helmet.

the Bardi of Florence, the 14th-century proprietors of an enormous banking and finance company. In Padua he was elected *podestà*. As he was extremely short, his friends gave him a giant bear figure to put on the top of his helmet. Riding through Bologna one day he came across a group of soldiers. One of them, a big strong fellow called Scindigher, gazed on the splendid headpiece with envy. In bold tones he proclaimed that the helmet was really his and that Bardi was sporting a false trademark. When the German giant challenged the Italian to a fight the latter calmly refused, incensing his aggressor even more. Bardi decided to "(...) resolve the matter with money and leave honor out of it." He asked Scindigher if he would like to buy the helmet. The man agreed and paid Bardi five florins. Bardi bought himself another helmet for two florins, making three florins profit out of the whole affair. He rode off satisfied and "avoided the fight in which he was not particularly tempted to participate."

Yet even this tale, which so poignantly illustrates the difference in the way Italian and German knights saw themselves, does not appear to tally with many real-life situations. Unlike the Medici, the Bardi of Florence were magnates, one of the ancient noble families that had been banned from election to local government since the end of the 13th century. The usual reason given for the ban was that the magnates constantly violated the rules governing community life in the cities with their violent acts and militant behavior. In many respects these rules or statutes were the city's lifeline; official written records of citizens' rights, the comprehensive *diritti comuni* were introduced relatively early on and were fairly widespread, which is unique for Europe during this period. The statutes were a conglomerate of various laws that affected all sections of the population (the *popolo*), the guilds (*arti*) and the commercial enterprises (*mercanti*) and that could also hold sway over the *comune* controlled by the town, city or republic, over the rural settlements (*terre*) and the castles (*castri*) out in the *contrado*, the surrounding countryside. In Siena various generations of the Salimbeni dynasty, bankers since the 13th century, sent colorful figures into battle to fight for the domination of towns, villages and

Pedro Berruguete (also attributed to Justus van Gent)
*Double Portrait of Duke Federico da Montefeltro with His Son Guidobaldo, c.* 1476
Oil on wood,
134.4 × 75.6 cm
Galleria Nazionale delle Marche, Urbino

Federico da Montefeltro (1422–1482), the illegitimate son of Guidantonio da Montefeltro, was a well-paid *condottiere* who was much in demand. Guidobaldo, Federico's longed-for heir, was born in 1472 following five daughters. Federico is shown in full armor and decorated with ermine honors, with his helmet resting at his feet. Both an army general and a scholar, in the eyes of medieval society he was the ideal ruler.

castles. In appreciation of their loyalty as Guelphs supporting the curia and the French king, they were given the castles of Orgia and San Quirico in Sienese territory. First branded as magnates and exempt from office but later integrated into the city's system of local government, the Salimbeni were loyal to the new regime until 1355. As owners of the castles of Tintinnano, Castiglione Ghinibaldi outside Monteriggioni, Strozzavolpe near Poggibonsi, Montorsaio, Castiglioncello del Trinoro and Castel della Selva in Val d'Elsa the family had built up a dense network of fortresses on Sienese land which, coupled with a considerable income from their various fiefs, propelled them to a position of great power. The Salimbeni were financially so secure that they could afford to maintain their own army, competing with the militia of the *comune*. The Salimbeni are just one typical example of the coexistence of feudal and modern forms of rule in medieval Italy.

Opposite:
Perugino
*The Miracle of St. Bernard* (detail), An Ambush on the Street, 1473
Tempera on wood,
76 × 56.5 cm
Galleria Nazionale dell'Umbria, Perugia

Captain Giovanni Antonio Tornano is being murdered by hired assassins armed with daggers and swords. Like his horrified, wailing companion he is powerless to ward off the surprise attack. In the background St. Bernard heals his head wound.

# Ferrara

## The castle of the Casa d'Este

### A lonely outpost

In the days of ancient Rome Ferrara did not exist. At that time, northern Italy's ruling city was Ravenna, perched in a wide lagoon where the main branch of the River Po flowed into the sea. Rome had its eastern Mediterranean fleet stationed in Ravenna's

Right: The castle of the d'Este family has five entrances, all of which are defended by a ravelin and a drawbridge. At the end of the 14th century the castle moat was linked up to a canal which ran along the city walls.

Far right: The castle was built between 1385 and 1395 by architect Bartolino Ploti da Novara. Niccolò II d'Este, the duke of Ferrara, decided to erect a castle in the center of town after his family was threatened by an uprising staged by citizens angry at the levels of taxation.

large harbor. When the troubled Roman Empire began to crumble the city's significance actually increased. It became the gateway to the East, a place where information and goods were exchanged, where different languages, religions and art forms intermingled. During the Byzantine exarchate of the 6th century, Ravenna was a capital city. Its huge turnover of merchandise and great

Egnazio Danti
*The Duchy of Ferrara*,
1580–1583
Fresco
Galleria delle Carte
Geografiche, Vatican

Ferrara was founded by the
Byzantines on the left bank
of the Po during the 7th
century to defend the river
and the hinterland of
Ravenna, where the Eastern
Church had relocated its
headquarters. In 1152 the
river changed course after a
flood, shifting several miles
further north.

number of inhabitants even made it the most important city in Italy for a brief period.

During the 7th century a settlement named Ferrara gradually evolved along the left banks of the Po. Situated in the hinterland of Ravenna, it was treated as a military outpost guarding the sovereign territory of the Byzantines. Ferrara's main function was to defend the river and to protect Ravenna from the Lombard threat. When Byzantium finally relinquished its grip on Italy, Ravenna sank into a state of lethargy. Ferrara was now nothing more than a lonely outpost, a motley collection of thatched wooden huts

huddled around a tower and exposed to constant flooding.

## Betrayed by the river

In later years new tribes from the east settled in the area and a harbor was built at a bend in the river, acting as a pivot between the sea and the hinterland. The new facility proved safer and easier to defend than the port at Ravenna. Ferrara soon blossomed into a flourishing center of trade with its own town walls and a tower to the northeast. Its southern defenses ran along the banks and islands of the River Po.

After years of prosperity, in 1152 the city's history again took a turn for the worse. Following weeks of unusually heavy flooding the river changed course, leaving Ferrara high and dry. As a result of this hydrogeological phenomenon, which locals called the *Rotta di Ficarolo* (the breach in the Ficarolo dyke), the main branch of the river wandered several miles north. The inhabitants of Ferrara felt betrayed by both their river and by Fate.

## The fall of Ferrara

The *Rotta di Ficarolo* was, however, welcomed by the Venetians. For a number of years they had warily observed the rise of Ferrara and its port, increasingly aware that both posed a threat to Venetian trade in the Adriatic, particularly to their monopoly on salt. A war loomed on the horizon, the object being to destroy Ferrara's saltpans. The *Rotta di Ficarolo* brought the conflict to a peaceable end. Ferrara reverted once again to an insignificant provincial town, subject to the feudal rule of a handful of powerful Italian families.

## The d'Este family

One of these powerful dynasties was the d'Este family. Originally from Venice, where

The castle was built around the existing Torre dei Leoni or "lion tower," which was integrated into the brick complex.

they owned vast estates, they settled in Ferrara with the help of the Venetians. On February 17, 1264, Obizzo I d'Este was made head of the town for life. In 1287 the trade and crafts guilds were disbanded and the local constitution abolished. The margravate of Ferrara was founded; covering an area which stretched down to Modena and Reggio Emilia, the new state acted as a buffer zone between northern and central Italy.

The success of the d'Este *signoria* lay in the rigid system of taxes they compelled the urban and farming community to pay and in their right to control the passage between north and south. For pilgrims from the northeast traveling to and from Rome the city was an obligatory stop on their journey. As opposed to the neighboring states, Ferrara also operated a cautious policy of neutrality.

## An uprising with consequences

For a long time the margravate of Ferrara survived without the need for extensive fortifications. It was defended by the old Torre dei Leoni, to the northeast of the town walls; this had a sturdy *enceinte* built around it and could be stocked with heavy artillery in the event of war.

## Taxes and cannons

The decision to build a more robust stronghold was made by Niccolò II d'Este in 1385, following a rebellion in Ferrara against the extortionate levels of taxation. To save his own skin Niccolò had sent his chancellor Tommaso da Tortona out to placate the crowd, only to see him lynched by the seething mob. After the uprising had been bloodily suppressed, Niccolò II commissioned architect Bartolino da Novara to build a new fortress to provide the city's rulers with greater protection in the event of further trouble. The outer walls were incomplete, the foundations only just laid, when the town again rumbled to the sound of Niccolò's artillery. Weaponry also featured later on in Ferrara's history when the town was home to a thriving metal industry. The cannons made

at the d'Este foundries were famous throughout Europe. They were one of the duchy's main sources of income, together with the grain and taxes supplied by the local inhabitants.

The nucleus of the new castle built by Bartolino da Novara was the old Torre dei Leoni watchtower-cum-fortress on the northeast section of the town walls. Three additional towers the same height as the existing edifice were erected in a square. Low buildings joining the towers surrounded an inner bailey; these and the towers were topped with battlements resting on neat rows of corbels. All entrances were supplied with additional defenses to protect the vulnerable drawbridges. A wide moat was dug around the castle and connected to the canal flowing along the town walls. A walkway was built to link the fortress to the nearby Palazzo dei Signori, the d'Este's private residence. In later years a second floor and a roof were added to the walkway, guaranteeing quick and safe passage between the two buildings. During the reign of Duke Ercole I towards the end of the 15th century, the entire d'Este family moved into the castle.

## The extension of the town

Under the same Ercole I, and after 200 years of peaceful neutrality under the protection of the Venetian lion, in 1482 the Este were persuaded to enter into an alliance with Milan, Naples and Florence. Venice correctly interpreted the move as a threat to its own safety. Venetian troops promptly marched on Ferrara. Only by signing a particularly harsh

peace treaty was Duke Ercole I able to protect his town from a ghastly fate at the hands of his new adversaries. Once the danger had passed Ercole began hatching new plans which envisaged doubling the size of the town to the north. Under the expert guidance of the great architect Biagio Rossetti the duke had a second town wall erected as part of the *Addizione erculea* (the Herculean extension). The area the wall enclosed provided ample building space for the *metà mancante*, the missing half of the city. Once this extraordinary project had been completed, the Castello Estense no longer straddled the town wall but instead dominated the center of Ferrara. Unfortunately the costs incurred by the duke for his *Addizione* – not to mention those imposed by the conditions of the peace treaty – were so astronomical that the d'Este dynasty now faced financial and political ruin.

Erecting the new section of town wall and extending the town to the north robbed the castle of its military function. Following a devastating fire at the castle in 1554 the decision was made to turn the stronghold into a huge residential palace. Many years passed

Opposite: The castle moat ran into a canal which followed the line of the town wall, enabling the castle inhabitants to access the town canal directly from the moat by boat.

Left: The d'Este adopted a policy of neutrality befitting their status as *signorie* of a buffer state representing the interests of Venice. In the 15th century the d'Este foundry began making cannons, which were highly prized throughout Italy and Europe.

Below:
Egnazio Danti
*Ferrara after the Addizione Erculea*, 1580–1583
Fresco
Galleria delle Carte Geografiche, Vatican

Following his defeat by the Venetians, Duke Ercole I d'Este had the town doubled in size to the north. This extension of Ferrara was called the *Addizione erculea*.

*Heraldic Lions with Decorative Headpieces,*
14th century
Bas-relief
Torre dei Leoni, Castello Estense, Ferrara
The white stone bas-relief on the lion tower depicts two heraldic lions with decorative headpieces holding a coat of arms.

before the complex took on its current appearance. Court architect Girolamo da Carpi was authorized to design and build the new palace. He added an extra floor, dismantled the military wall-walks and battlements and replaced the latter with white stone balustrades mounted on the old consoles. The arrow loops and two-light windows also disappeared, with larger window openings emerging in their place. The upper stories were decked out with terraces, overhanging loggias and balconies. Two huge salons were created in the palace interior. The decorations on the facade were fashioned from white Veronese travertine, which boldly offset the red brick of the tall buildings. Several centuries later the watchtowers were extended, the new carillons banishing the lingering air of militarism from the castle for ever.

### Enter the popes

Renovation had only just finished when in 1595 the last duke of Ferrara, Alfonso II d'Este, died. As he left no male heirs the pope demanded that the duchy of Ferrara be returned to the Church. The papal claims were based on what is known as the Gift of Pippin from 754 which stated that the Carolingian king awarded the Church absolute supremacy over the former exarchate of Byzantium. Since then the Este had legally ruled the area as an investiture of the pope. With the legitimate line of the Este dynasty now extinguished, Pope Clement VIII wanted his town back – a coup long planned by papal diplomats.

The Este felt obliged to leave Ferrara and at the beginning of 1598 moved to Modena.

Opposite:
Dining room in the Prolegati wing.
The Prolegati wing was the raised passage connecting the castle and the old d'Este residence. In the 16th century, the passage was doubled in height and roofed over. The rooms thus created were richly decorated. The dining room now houses the office of the city prefect.

Over a period of 200 years these avid patrons of the arts had amassed an impressive collection of masterpieces which they tried to take with them. What they were forced to leave behind was plundered by the papal nuncios. Devoid of its riches, Ferrara reverted once more to a minor provincial town sustained by local agriculture.

The most significant architectural contribution by the Church to Ferrara was a star-shaped, state-of-the-art fortress constructed along the south-west wall. The old belvedere, one of the "greatest delights" of the d'Este, had to be torn down to make room for the new fortification. This is also no longer intact; in the throes of an armed uprising against the pope and the Austrian troops, on June 21, 1859, the people of Ferrara angrily demolished the hated symbol of pontifical domination.

### Giulio's eyes

Ercole I d'Este died in 1505, leaving four sons: the firstborn, Alfonso, who succeeded him to the ducal throne, Ippolito, later a cardinal, Ferrante, and Giulio, who was illegitimate. The latter two, feeling themselves unjustly barred from any claims to power, planned a conspiracy. They were found out, thrown into prison and sentenced to death. The punishment was later amended to life imprisonment in the castle dungeons of the old Torre dei Leoni. For many decades the two brothers slowly rotted away in their gruesome underground cell while life at court went on as usual above their heads. In 1540 Ferrante died of debilitation and deprivation. Giulio survived and in 1559 was finally pardoned by Alfonso II, his grandnephew. After spending 50 years of his life incarcerated in the tower, the 81-year-old had gone completely blind.

The initial cause of Giulio's blindness dates back to his youth when the young man was still fully able to indulge in the merriment and entertainment of the ducal court. Historian Francesco Guicciardini, one of Giulio's contemporaries, describes the episode as follows.

"At Ferrara however / where shortly before, Duke Hercules of Este had died / and his place

taken by his son Alfonsus / a sad incident occurred towards the end of the year 1505 / which is similar to that / seen prior to the days of Thebis in Greece / but with a much lesser cause / although the immeasurable desire of love is not much worse / than controlling fervent lust.

The cardinal of Este, one Ferrar Hippolytus / was so passionately and ardently in love / with a young woman / who was related to him by blood / and she was no less inflamed by Hippolytus's illegitimate brother Julius / and she confessed to the cardinal himself / that she was attracted to Julius / first and foremost by the beauty of his eyes. Upon this the cardinal went blind with rage / and waited for a convenient time / and when Julius was out hunting one day / he accosted him on the field / and had him dismount / whereupon his bodyguards were ordered to gorge out his eyes / and when they went close to him in this barbarity / he could bring himself / to watch this inhuman act of barbarism: upon which deep animosity arose between the brothers hereafter. So ends the one thousandth five hundredth and fifth year / after the birth of Jesus Christ."

In one of the ensuing chapters of his *History of Italy*, Guicciardini discloses that his first report was exaggerated. Giulio's beautiful eyes were not "taken out" but "merely" brutally beaten. His sojourn in the Torre dei Leoni did the rest.

## La Prima Donna del Mondo – Isabella d'Este
Katrin Boskamp-Priever

Isabella d'Este was born on March 17, 1474, in Ferrara, the oldest of seven children. Her parental home was a chivalrous center of the arts, a place where magnificent banquets and conquering heroes were celebrated. When she was still barely a toddler, Ercole I d'Este (1431–1505), Isabella's father, betrothed his daughter to Francesco Gonzaga (1466–1519), the margrave of Mantua. Following his disastrous campaign against Venice in 1482 Ercole devoted himself to more artistic pursuits, such as architecture, music and the theater. Isabella's creative environment was instrumental in the development of her own excellent cultural tastes and talents. She inherited her father's great love of music and was herself a musician; she went to see the plays he directed and wrote detailed accounts of them in her correspondence which has been preserved, unusually, in its entirety. She received an outstanding classical education and years of training in Latin from her tutor Battista Guarino, one of the major humanist figures of northern Italy. Isabella also profited from the presence of various literary courtiers at the d'Este palace, such as Boiardo, Ariosto, Tito Vespasiano Strozzi and Niccolò da Correggio, who extolled the extraordinary intelligence and charisma of the little girl in their hymns of praise. "A life of leisure without education (literature) is a living grave," her teacher told her, urging her to continue her studies once she was married. We do not know whether her later function as patron of the arts in Mantua permitted her to do so. Her library did, however, include the writings of the ancient poets, Savonarola's sermons and works by Italy's foremost contemporary authors.

Anonymous
*Ercole d'Este*
Galleria Estense, Modena

Ercole I d'Este was duke of Ferrara from 1471 to 1505. He promoted the arts and particularly favored architecture. Under his rule, Ferrara became the seat of one of the most brilliant courts in Europe. The doubling of the circuit walls (later called the *Addizione erculea*) is associated with his name.

Tiziano Vecellio
*Portrait of Isabella d'Este*,
1534–1536
Oil on canvas, 64 × 103 cm
Kunsthistorisches Museum,
Vienna

Isabella is shown here at the
age of 60; her features are
youthful but her posture
emanates all the grace and
dignity of a mature woman.
Ercole I's daughter was
engaged to Francesco
Gonzaga at the tender age of
six, moving to the court of
Mantua ten years later.
A modern and extremely
well-educated woman for
her day, Isabella was a great
patron of the arts for over
50 years. Her favorite room
was her study with its library
of works by Aristotle,
Plutarch, Dante, Petrarch,
Lorenzo de' Medici and
Baldassare Castiglione.

# Fontanellato

## The castle of the Sanvitale

Francesco Maria Mazzola, known as Parmigianino
*Diana and Actaeon* (detail), Two Resting Nymphs, 1522/23
Fresco
Saletta di Diana e Atteone, Rocca di Fontanellato, Parma

The two nymphs are a detail from a magnificent allegorical wall fresco which Parmigianino, one of the forerunners of mannerism, painted in the castle interior.

Far right: The castle has three round towers of varying heights and an old square watchtower at the heart of the fortification. The Sanvitale tended to fight their battles through diplomacy rather than with arms, so there is no evidence that the castle ever had to function in its full military capacity. The clear water in the castle moat was legendary and supplied the kitchens with an abundance of delicious freshwater crabs.

## On the Via Emilia

Fontanellato is near Parma on the old Roman Via Emilia. Nearly all the towns in the Emilia region were built along the straight road running from Piacenza to the Adriatic. The first written evidence of a small fief called Fontanellato dates back to the 13th century. Since the 14th century the little town has been inextricably linked to the name Sanvitale, the family who built the castle here and lived in it from 1386 until the last in the immediate line died in 1951. Over the course of these six centuries Fontanellato has constantly mirrored the historical fates and fortunes of its parent town, Parma. Best known today for its ham and its cheese, Parma was once a Roman city with baths, theaters and an amphitheater. It was later a Byzantine metropolis and the place where the imperial state treasure of the exarchate was hoarded, hence its label *chryso-polis* or "city of gold." During its period as a free *comune*, Parma battled successfully with Frederick II. The city later belonged to the

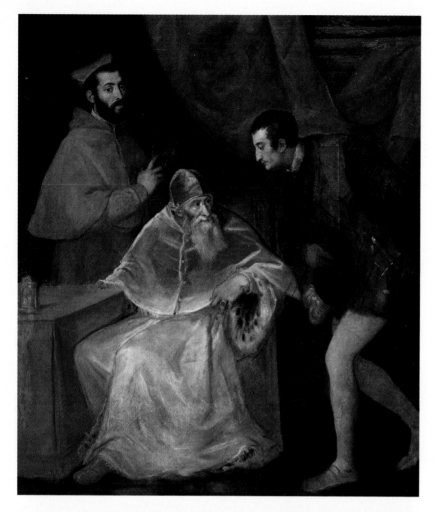

duchy of Milan, which was governed by the Visconti and the Sforza. Only when Milan had fallen were Parma and Piacenza able to form an independent duchy of their own, presided over by an entire dynasty of the sons, grandsons and great grandsons of Pope Paul III (Alessandro Farnese, 1468–1549). Embalmed as a neutral buffer state, Parma was later subject to first Spanish and then French rule. In 1815 the Treaty of Vienna awarded the modest duchy to Marie Louise, Napoleon's second wife and the daughter of the Habsburg emperor. It was to be her consolation prize for having to endure a torturous yet politically prudent marriage to a man like Napoleon.

## Water and time

On the north side of the Apennines, in an area rich in natural springs, the Romans built their Via Emilia cutting along the base of the mountains. At the foot of an ancient watchtower on the Roman road the town of Fontanellato gradually evolved. The tower had been built on the shores of a lake fed by a deep underwater spring. The water is crystal clear and has a constant temperature of 50–53°F (10–12°C). Until the beginning of the 20th century the town canal and castle moat were both supplied by the lake – not only with water but also with delicious freshwater crabs. Documents from the 16th and 17th centuries testify that people were forbidden to let their pigs bathe in the moat and canal "(...) because said pigs are a pest and eat the crabs, on penalty of one gold *scudo* for each pig." The town canal has now been filled in and the castle moat is no longer as clean and sparkling as it once was. The crabs have been usurped by dark shadows lurking in the depths – carp, perhaps.

The castle itself is square with three round towers of varying heights and a fourth square tower in the north-west corner. The latter is the old watchtower, *il Maschio*, the ancient nucleus of the first fortification on this site. On the south side of the complex stands a second quadratic tower from the 17th century, soaring up in front of the castle's only gate, whose original drawbridge was later

Left: *Map of the Town of Parma*, 1460
Archivio di Stato, Parma

The little town of Fontanellato was inextricably linked to the name Sanvitale for over 600 years. Its history closely mirrored that of its parent town Parma.

Bottom left: *Fontanellato Castle*, detail from a map from 1460

The map includes a remarkably accurate topographical illustration of the old castle complex. The fortress was surrounded by a ring of houses whose number barely exceeded 113 in the course of the years.

replaced by a stone arch. The gigantic clock tower has hands and a double quadrant so that the hours, half hours and quarter hours can be easily read. The Sanvitale who resided at the castle from the 15th century onwards loved timepieces above all else. So that the chimes of the three different bells could be correctly interpreted, Count Alessandro Sanvitale even wrote a special little handbook entitled *The Constant Passage of Time*.

The quadratic inner ward of the castle is paved with stone and skirted by a double colonnade on two sides. There has hardly been a time in the long history of the complex when it has not been under some form of renovation. As a fortress the castle was not particularly well suited to the needs of its inhabitants. We also do not know if the fortification was ever besieged, but it is unlikely.

## A church and a theater

A small cluster of houses slowly sprang up around the castle. In 1800 there were 113 of them; the number has hardly increased to this

day. The new settlement consists largely of small villas surrounded by square lawns and has gradually crept out onto the plateau as far as the *Autostrada del Sole*. The tourist brochure claims that "(…) the desire to build a church" – naturally one of great beauty with a sumptuous wooden sacristy from the 18th century – "was not apparent until *c.* 1437." In 1681 the town expressed the need for a theater. One was promptly designed by Count Alessandro Sanvitale, who had it erected behind the

Opposite, top:
Tiziano Vecellio
*Paul Farnese III with his Grandsons*, 1546
Oil on canvas, 200 × 173 cm
Museo di Capodimonte, Naples

This famous picture by Titian shows Paul III with two grandsons. Nepotism was one of the most conspicuous features of Alessandro Farnese's pontificate. The pope founded the duchy of Parma and Piacenza with the sole purpose of handing it to his grandson Pier Luigi. Paul III was also the pope of Counter-Reformation and the Council of Trent. Obsessed by the fear that Protestant ideas could spread in Italy, in 1540 he approved Loyola's Society of Jesus and centralized the power of the Inquisition in Rome.

Opposite, bottom:
The double colonnade or covered walk in the inner ward. The castle is devoid of both dungeons and barracks. The castle of the Sanvitale family was home to the freethinkers of society, particularly in the 16th century.

Reception room at
Fontanellato Castle.

The principal room of
Fontanellato Castle.
The interior of the castle,
which remained inhabited
until 1951, retains
a rather intimate,
everyday atmosphere.
One of its most remarkable
features is the long ancestral
gallery which dates as far
back as the Middle Ages.

stables. The building later caught fire and burned down. In the 19th century the theater was reconstructed from a model of the original.

## Fish and meat

The Sanvitale used their castle first and foremost as a place of residence. There was only ever a handful of soldiers in residence at any one time and the fortification had neither a dungeon nor a torture chamber. The furnishings that have accumulated over the centuries still adorn the interior today. Among them are many personal effects, most of which belonged to the women, dotted about the various chambers as if the lady of the house had just left the room. In the dining hall a spacious 16th-century fireplace and two unusually large paintings preside over the huge ceramic plates from Faenza, the priceless English soup bowls

and the Augsburg porcelain. The paintings, a *Still Life with Fish* and a *Still Life with Meat*, depict a frugal meal and a lavish banquet respectively.

After walking through the armory and the reception and billiard room you come to the *Galleria degli Antenati*, the ancestral gallery, where the portraits of around 50 members of the Sanvitale dynasty clutter the walls. The Sanvitale born from the 16th century onwards all have their own distinguishing features and mode of dress. The people in the earlier portraits look as if both their clothes and physiognomy have been borrowed from that of their successors lined up along the opposite wall. In a seemingly reversed order of chronology, here grandfathers seem to inherit their physical traits from their grandsons. The most accurate of the Sanvitale portraits, that of Galeazzo Sanvitale, was painted by Parmigianino and hangs not in Fontanellato but in the Museo di Capodimonte in Naples.

## The freethinkers

The Sanvitale were unusual in that they managed to remain in one place for so many centuries. They were not only persistent; they were also of a gentle and generous nature and extremely open-minded. Although many members of the ancient family were professional soldiers, they usually fought their battles far from home in France and Flanders. The Sanvitale annals hold no accounts of the family murders that were so common in this era, when husbands, wives, mothers, fathers, brothers and even children were victims of internecine strife. Instead, the Sanvitale family chronicle reminisces about keen enthusiasts of botany, philosophy and technology and even includes a poet or two.

During the 16th century the court at Fontanellato was a focus of cultural activity. The Sanvitale were interested in people who thought differently from the rest and offered sanctuary to those the Inquisition accused of heresy. They themselves were suspected of Nicodemism, of deliberately attempting to reconcile opposing philosophical and religious theories. In 1525, when Parma was under Church rule, in the letters they sent to Rome the locals complained about the exceptionally high number of Jews who "have been brought to this area by several feudal lords who are not bothered if they are in opposition to God." Their comments referred specifically to Fontanellato. The founding of the Farnese duchy saw the passing of laws prohibiting Jews in Parma and Piacenza from owning land or even staying in town for longer than three days. Following the Council of Trent the small state became a bastion of the Counter-Reformation. The number of Jesuits in both Parma and Piacenza steadily grew, causing speculation that the priests in these towns outnumbered the houses. Across the entire duchy male Jews were forced to wear yellow caps and women veils of the same color.

## Barbara Sanseverino Sanvitale

The name of the woman whose smile is no less charming than that of the Mona Lisa is Barbara Sanseverino Sanvitale, Countess of Colorno, portrayed by an unknown master during the 17th century. Barbara Sanvitale was considered to be one of the great female figures of the Italian Renaissance. Her contemporaries admired her for her intellect, knowledge, and rare beauty. The poet Torquato Tasso dedicated countless sonnets to her. She was the driving force behind the Accademia degli Amorevoli, attended by the keenest minds of the day. At the age of 15 Barbara Sanseverino married

Francesco Maria Mazzola, known as Parmigianino
*Portrait of Galeazzo Sanvitale,* 1524
Oil on canvas
Museo di Capodimonte, Naples

Under Galeazzo Sanvitale, Fontanellato became a cultural and intellectual center where freethinkers and "heretics" hounded by the Inquisition could take refuge. With his progressive and philosophical way of thinking, and his keen interest in Greek and Roman civilization, Galeazzo proved himself a match for Florence's grand patrons.

Right: Anonymous
*Barbara Sanseverino
Sanvitale, Countess of
Colorno,* early 17th century
Oil on canvas
Rocca di Fontanellato, Parma

Barbara Sanseverino was greatly admired for her intelligence and beauty. The keenest minds of her day attended her Accademia degli Amorevoli. Accused of conspiracy against Duke Ottario Farnese, she was beheaded with other nobles in 1611.

Right: Atop the coat of arms of the Sanvitale family, a red diagonal on a gold background, stand two griffins which in Greek mythology were often shown protecting Artemis, the goddess of the hunt. The figure in the center here appears to combine Athena, the goddess of peace and wisdom, with Nike, the goddess of victory.

Count Vincenzo Sanvitale, who left her a widow not long afterwards. As she loved freedom and travel, the countess spent much of her time in the major cities of Italy accumulating the pearls of wisdom she then passed on to her eager followers at her provincial courts in Colorno, Sala and Fontanellato.

For a time Barbara Sanseverino found herself under the protection of Ottavio Farnese, the duke of Parma, who greatly desired her. In 1611, however, Ottavio's son Ranuccio I, now himself duke, accused her of conspiring with fellow noblemen to murder him and his father, wanting to put an end to the Farnese dynasty. The key figures behind the alleged murder plot were arrested, tortured, sentenced to death and beheaded on a public market place on May 19, 1611. The entire population of Parma flocked to the scene to look on in horror. The countess's head was the first to roll. The executioner had to wield his axe twice to sever the head from the body. The heads of six of the county's noblemen followed that of the countess. The grisly spectacle took place, appropriately enough, on the square outside the Pia Unione di San Giovanni Decollato, the Holy Union of the Beheaded St. John, and lasted several hours. With the heads impaled on spikes, a Jesuit priest addressed the crowd, listing the many sound reasons that had prompted the young Duke Ranuccio to exercise supreme justice – against his will. The priest was followed by a Counter-Reforming Franciscan who had heard the countess's confession on her way to the scaffold. He revealed that at the last moment Barbara Sanseverino had confessed and expressed regret, authorizing the monk to publish her confession, through which she had received absolution. Executing the countess and her fellow conspirators enabled the Farnese to establish a firm hold over the duchy of Parma and Piacenza for several decades.

## The penitent hunter

Two of the creatures on the Sanvitale coat of arms are griffins, mythological creatures which are part lion and part eagle. One room in the Rocca di Fontanellato is also devoted to the

Francesco Maria Mazzola, known as Parmigianino
*Actaeon Catches Sight of Diana* (detail), 1522/23
Fresco
Saletta di Diana e Atteone, Rocca di Fontanellato, Parma

Actaeon unwittingly catches sight of Diana bathing. To punish him she turns him into a stag and leaves him to be torn apart by his own dogs.

notion of transfiguration, depicted in a fresco inspired by the third book of *Metamorphoses* by the Roman poet Ovid. Publius Ovidius Naso, to give him his full name, was born in Sulmona in 43 B.C. and died in exile in Tomi on the Black Sea in 17 or 18 A.D. Enthralled by the Greek idea of a fluid distinction between man and beast, Ovid was motivated to write down his version of the Greek and Roman myths, describing in hexameters the metamorphosis of members of the various species. He begins his work with the words: "I tell of the shapes of bodies which have taken on a new form (…)."

Fontanellato's very own metamorphosis takes place in the smallest room of the castle. The tiny chamber which originally had no windows was transformed by Francesco Maria Mazzola alias Parmigianino. Heralded one of the great masters of Italian mannerism, the artist smothered the bleak walls with exquisite frescoes. Commissioned by

Galeazzo Sanvitale and completed in 1523, the work portrays one of the stories from Ovid's *Metamorphoses* in a slightly varied form. After a day out hunting with fellow hunters and his dogs, Actaeon finds himself near a pool where Diana, the virginal goddess of the hunt, is bathing. To punish him for seeing her naked and to prevent him from telling his friends what he has seen, Diana sprinkles Actaeon with water from the spring. The unsuspecting hunter immediately begins to turn into a stag. He flees. The dogs he himself has raised and taught to hunt catch up with him. He tries to calm them down, calling out their names. Yet the only sound to come out of his mouth is a hoarse roar which excites his animals even more. They tear Actaeon to pieces. The hunter's final realization is that his fatal mutation must have been brought about by the water the naked goddess splashed him with.

Francesco Maria Mazzola, known as Parmigianino
*Diana Turns Actaeon into a Stag*, 1522/23
Fresco
Saletta di Diana e Atteone, Rocca di Fontanellato, Parma

The two key moments in the tale are shown here: Diana splashes Actaeon with the water that will transform him, and the hunter turns into a stag. In the next scene his dogs will rip him apart.

Opposite:
Francesco Maria Mazzola,
known as Parmigianino
*Paola Gonzaga* (detail),
1522/23
Fresco
Saletta di Diana e Atteone,
Rocca di Fontanellato, Parma

Tucked in between the
mythological figures is a
portrait of Paola Gonzaga.


Right and below:
Francesco Maria Mazzola,
known as Parmigianino
*The Transformed Actaeon*
and detail, 1522/23
Fresco
Saletta di Diana e Atteone,
Rocca di Fontanellato, Parma

The dogs have set upon
Actaeon who has been
changed into a stag. The
children shown in the detail
are often thought to
represent the early death of
Paola Gonzaga's second
child.

A Latin inscription running along the walls beneath the fresco accuses the virginal goddess of cruelty. Actaeon came across Diana purely by chance; he did not intend to watch her bathing. The inscription concludes: "Only if guilty should a man be punished, not for a coincidence. A deed such as this does not befit a goddess."

The fresco also contains a portrait of Paola Gonzaga, Galeazzo's wife. Among the cherubs decorating the vaulted ceiling are her two children. The baby boy stares into space and clutches a small twig of cherry, the symbol of the grave, in his hand. His little sister holds her brother in her arms and tries to pull him back towards her. It is known that Paola Gonzaga's second child died very young. The entire fresco has thus been interpreted as an allegory of maternal pain and the comfort that can be drawn from the incessant transformation and reincarnation of life.

Sandro Botticelli
*Inferno XVIII*, 1482–1490
Colored drawing on
parchment, 32 × 47 cm
Engravings gallery, Staatliche
Museen – Preussischer
Kulturbesitz, Berlin

In dank, stony ditches in Hell
Dante and Virgil watch
naked sinners – here the
matchmakers and seducers –
being mercilessly beaten and
whipped by horned devils.

Opposite:
Grosse Heidelberger
Liederhandschrift
*Henry VI as a Minnesinger*,
beginning of the 14th
century
Miniature on parchment
Codex Manesse, Pal. Germ.
848, fol. 6r
Universitätsbibliothek,
Heidelberg, Germany

The most significant
manuscript of texts and
music to come out of the
Middle Ages, the *Codex
Manesse*, was produced late
in the history of medieval
High German minnesong.
The poems are ordered
according to the social class
and standing of their authors;
the manuscript thus opens
with a miniature of Emperor
Henry VI (1190–1197) and
his songs.

## Minnesong and Troubadours –
## Italian Literature in the Middle Ages
Katrin Boskamp-Priever

*Book in Honor of Augustus* (*Liber ad honorem Augusti*) is the name of the chronicle Petrus de Ebolo (*c.* 1160–1219/20) wrote for Henry VI (1190–1197), in which he tells of the emperor's battle for his Sicilian inheritance in evocative text and vivid illustrations. The book's pictorial dedication shows the poet kneeling on the steps of the throne as he hands his work to the monarch, with the imperial chancellor to Henry VI and the man who commissioned the work, Konrad von Querfurt, recommending the poet's services to his lord. The court of Henry's father-in-law, King Roger II, had also had chronicles written in Latin, most of them specially commissioned works, by authors such as Alexander von Telese, Falco von Benevent and Romuald Guarna, who was made archbishop of Salerno in 1135. The poets documented the events of their age, each focusing on the personality and heroic deeds of his particular lord and master.

The majority of those who wielded the quill were clergy attached to the court or resident at the royal monastery, most of them educated, schooled in Latin and of noble blood. Producing books was a laborious undertaking in which texts were notated by hand in large, roman letters onto expensive parchment (paper did not come into use until the 14th century). This was then folded into sheets and elaborately bound in intricately worked wood, leather, ivory or precious metal. It could take years to manufacture a single volume. The medieval emperors, in deliberate imitation of their Roman forebears, were great patrons of the arts, generous in their sponsorship like Frederick II Hohenstaufen (1212–1250), the king of Sicily. His father, Henry VI, had gone down in the annals of history as a poet; the *Codex Manesse* (*c.* 1304/1330), the largest and most famous collection of medieval ballads, contains a miniature of the king on his throne and also several *Minnelieder* he is believed to have penned. In Sicily the *lyrica dei trovatori*, the lyric poetry of the troubadours, modeled itself on the courtly romance and epic song of northern France, Provence and Aquitaine. In northern Italy the courts of the princes with whom Henry VI was in

The illuminated manuscript page includes text in Old French.

Above: Giovanni Boccaccio *Decameron*, 1414
Miniature on parchment
Cod. Pal. lat. 1989, fol. 29v
Biblioteca Vaticana
Apostolica, Vatican

Embedded in text and elaborate ornamentation, this miniature tells the tale of a young woman from Gascony who is attacked in Cyprus. She manages to reach the royal court, and kneeling before the king on the right of the illustration, she tells him of her misfortune and demands an explanation for the bad treatment she has received.

artistic and literary activities at his palace in Palermo.

Other major figures to dominate the Sicilian school of medieval poetry were the first notary of the imperial chancellery, Pietro della Vigna (*c.* 1190–1249), Jacopo da Lentini and Rinaldo d'Aquino. Their songs were written in Sicilian dialect, *lingua volgare*, peppered with Provençal and Latin expressions. The result was poetry which, in partial imitation of French structures, keenly reflected the personal impressions and everyday experiences of its authors, set down in a language which was neither Latin nor Provencal but an early form of Italian. Like the French troubadours the Sicilians created *Minne*, works dedicated to courtly love or an ideal frequently extolled in the French epic, such as in the *Lancelot* of Chrétien de Troyes (*c.* 1135–pre-1190). Minnesingers and troubadours traveled from tournament to tournament, fervently composing songs in honor of their ladies in an effort to win their favor.

Two important works which greatly influenced subsequent generations were the *Cantico di frate sole* (*Canticle of the Sun*) by St. Francis of Assisi (1181/82–1226) and the *Laude* or passionate songs of Franciscan monk Jacopo da Todi (*c.* 1236–1306) written in a kind of rhythmic prose, both good examples of the religious poetry of the 13th century. During the same period Florence, Bologna and other northern Italian cities saw the evolution of the *dolce stil novo*, an idealist form of lyric poetry influenced by the Sicilian school which

regular contact were also entertained with minne-song and epic poetry. It is possible that Henry commissioned the first German Lancelot epic by Ulrich von Zatzikhoven, the story of the legendary King Arthur, the knights of the Round Table and the Holy Grail. The Hohenstaufen dynasty itself was also the subject of narrative poetry; Emperor Frederick II, for example, was celebrated by minnesinger Reinmar von Zweter. He was as well versed in the arts as his father, writing a famous book on falconry entitled *De arte venandi cum avibus* (*The Art of Hunting with Birds*), composing songs in vernacular Italian and exerting a considerable influence on the

is dedicated to the topics of love and women yet is slightly more refined in its linguistic medium and richer in the use of motif. The poems of Ghibelline judge Guido Guinizelli (1240?–1276), of Guido Cavalcanti, a nobleman of Florence (c. 1259–1300), of lawyer, judge and envoy Cino da Pistoia (c. 1270–1336/37) and other friends of Dante Alighieri (c. 1265–1321) were advocates of the new style. Dante even developed a new language for it, the *volgare illustre*, a form of Italian vernacular which was perfectly suited to tackle the sophisticated themes of the genre. With his *Divine Comedy*, a fictitious journey through the Inferno, Purgatory and Paradise, an opus was created which is still counted as one of the most significant works of world literature. Another great epic to come out of Tuscany is the *Novellino* by a Ghibelline from Florence, a series of 100 stories which cover a range of subjects from antiquity and the Bible to medieval epic poetry and life in the 13th century.

The popularity of Provençal lyric poetry also spread to the court of King Robert of Anjou (1309–1343) in Naples, drawing Giovanni Boccaccio (1313–1375), the son of a court official, in its wake. Boccaccio first encountered the courtly romance at the palace, a genre which was to be echoed throughout his early works. His epic poem *Filostrato* borrows its main theme from the Old French *Roman de Troie* (*Trojan Novel*) by Benoît de Sainte-Maure. Back in a Florence ravaged by the plague, Boccaccio completed his *Decameron*, a collection of short stories linked by a common theme, probably in 1351. Ten people running from the plague spend ten days on a farm not far from Florence and pass the time telling stories – a literary formula emulated by the likes of Geoffrey Chaucer in his *Canterbury Tales*, Goethe in his *Unterhaltungen deutscher Ausgewanderter,* and Gottfried Keller in his *Sinngedicht*, to name but a few. A strong, moral, realistic compendium packed with the pain and promise of love, full of tales of honor and dastardliness, the *Decameron* is an amalgamation of diverse themes and motifs. The *Minne* ideal still holds a certain significance in the book, yet its driving force is undoubtedly Boccaccio's description of love in its fully physical capacity. A friend and contemporary of Boccaccio was Francesco Petrarca, or Petrarch (1304–1374), a

tireless traveler and frequent guest at many of the courts across Europe. In his books he takes the theme of love several steps further. His subjectivity, his emphasis on the secret life within and his perception and understanding of man's most personal emotional responses in the *Canzoniere* and the *Trionfi*, the poems of love dedicated to his ideal and idealized Laura, make Petrarch the first modern lyric poet. In his Latin poems, however, the forms and ideas of ancient Greece and Rome and the sphere of the spiritual carry considerable weight. In the works influenced by the teachings of Virgil, Horace and Plato, Petrarch paves the way for humanism in Europe.

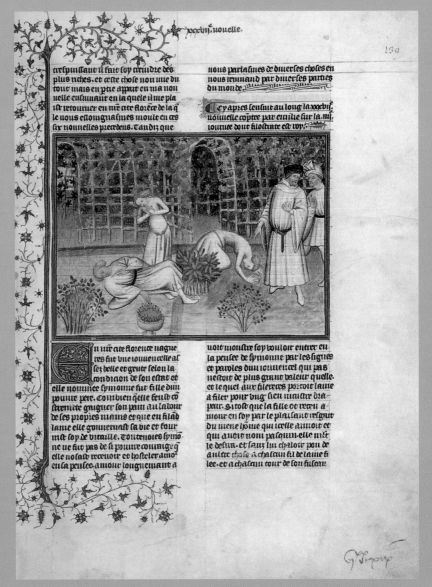

Above: Giovanni Boccaccio *Decameron*, 1414 Miniature on parchment Cod. Pal. lat. 1989, fol. 29v Biblioteca Vaticana Apostolica, Vatican

In a garden with a trellis running across the background, Simona weeps for Pasquino, who has been poisoned by sage. Simona dies of heartbreak while telling the story.

Opposite: Cimabue *St. Francis* (detail), c. 1280 Wood Museo di Santa Maria degli Angeli, Assisi

# Gavi

## The fortified vineyard

Above: An additional turret on the watchtower provided a clear view of the surrounding area.

### Protection from the north

Seen from above, the castle in Gavi Ligure looks like a tortoise. Yet as the perspective changes, it turns into a giant rhinoceros or a gigantic crab clinging to the side of the hill. Gavi is in the Ligurian Apennines on the Po Delta side of the mountains, now in the Piedmont region and part of the province of Alessandria. Historically, Gavi had links to Genoa on the other side of the mountains to the south, not actually all that far away as the crow flies. The castle front thus faces south – towards Genoa – when in fact it should have faced northwards. In the Middle Ages the primary task of the fortress in Gavi Ligure was to keep the old maritime republic's passage to the northern Continent open. The edifice was then only a fraction of its present size.

The nucleus of the castle occupies the highest point on the rock. The later fortifications straddle several levels of defensive terraces and long stone ramparts, with numerous dwellings propped up against them. The entire complex resembles a fortified monastery. The garrison was equipped to accommodate and feed up to 900 soldiers for several years without any assistance from the outside world if necessary. Before the castle was extended there was room for just 60 men.

Proof that numerous garrisons could be housed in the castle in Gavi Ligure at any one time is provided by the five cisterns in the cellars, some of them enormous, and a complex hydraulic system for collecting and purifying water. Extension of the medieval castle began in 1625 and took several decades to complete. The republic of Genoa hired the famous military architect Gaspare Maculano, known as *il Fiorenzuolo*, to implement its plan.

Far right: The castle ramparts during the grape harvest. The vineyards climbing the terraces of the castle in Gavi Ligure are its most distinctive feature. Grapes were first planted at Gavi Castle as part of an experiment to combat the vine pest. The vineyards now produce an excellent white wine.

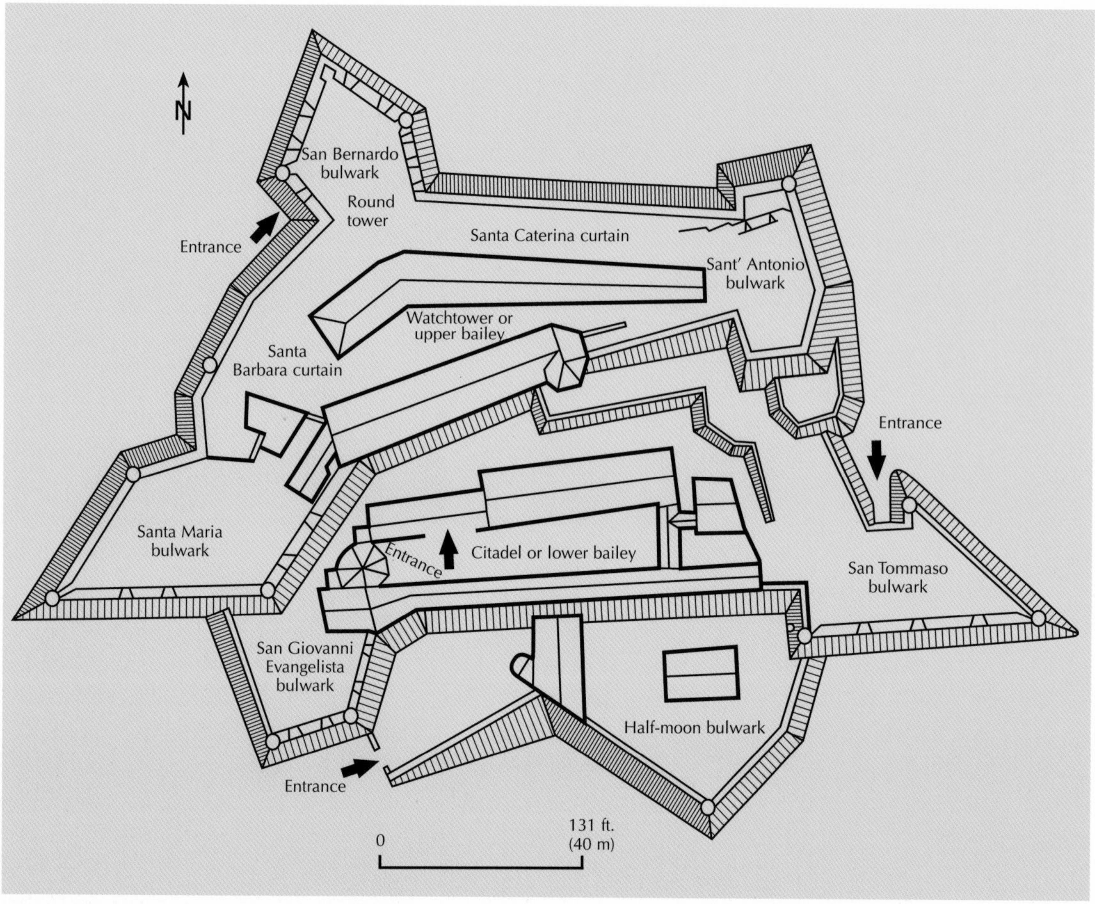

N

San Bernardo bulwark
Round tower
Entrance
Santa Caterina curtain
Sant' Antonio bulwark
Watchtower or upper bailey
Santa Barbara curtain
Entrance
Santa Maria bulwark
Entrance
Citadel or lower bailey
San Tommaso bulwark
San Giovanni Evangelista bulwark
Half-moon bulwark
Entrance

0    131 ft. (40 m)

Gavi Castle is split into three levels. The oldest section is at the top of the hill and serves as a watchtower for the entire complex.

From a military point of view the project was superfluous, as Genoa's conflicts at that time with the powers of the hinterland, Milan and Savoy, were more often fought by diplomats than soldiers. Nevertheless the old, tired republic obviously still felt it necessary to flex its muscles one last time.

The next garrison of soldiers to take up residence in Gavi was stationed there by none other than Napoleon during his campaign in Italy. A few years later, in 1815, the Treaty of Vienna decreed that the republic of Genoa be disbanded. Genoa had to relinquish its territories to the future ruler of Italy – Savoy. The House of Savoy turned castles that had lost their military value into prisons, a practice that quickly spread across the whole of Italy including Gavi. The recently unified nation of Italy did not find it hard to fill its many castles and fortresses, many of which looked back on a glorious past, with unwilling detainees.

In 1923, by pure coincidence, Gavi's sorry fate took a turn for the better. The vineyards of Europe were infested with the vine pest *Phylloxera*, which decimated the grapes in a cancerous wave of destruction. An institute dedicated to finding an antidote to the problem was set up at the castle. On the grand terraces of the mighty ramparts vines were planted and grafted. These were Gavi's best years. The vine pest was eliminated and the vineyards remained. Visitors to Gavi in October can now watch grape pickers harvesting the year's vintages beneath the bulwarks and gun loops.

## Two recent escapes

During the Second World War (1939–1945) Gavi was a military prison. Two notable episodes from this period bring a sparkle to the otherwise dull and pedestrian history of this lonely fortified outpost. Both tell of great escapes.

176

## Major Jack Pringle

Major Jack Pringle, an American from the 8th Army, was captured in Libya at the end of 1941. After spending several months imprisoned in the desert he was taken to the castle of Gavi in Italy. On his arrival at the station, where he was placed in the custody of four *carabinieri* and an officer, he was informed that in the last 600 years nobody had managed to escape from the fortress. He was also told that there were 20 officers and 300 guards responsible for the 180 prisoners at the castle. He reported his future place of detention as "a truly impressive and imposing place, very difficult to describe … Walls, ramparts and towers on three levels made it look like a giant wedding cake." During his admission to jail he was subjected to the "only real search during my years in prison. The seams of my clothes were undone, the heels of my boots removed and my toothpaste squeezed out of the tube." He was allotted a clean, dry cell which looked south. The food was good. The same went for the wine, a Bianco di Gavi, of which the prison authorities allowed their charges a single bottle daily, with extra rations available for those willing to pay for them. The prison also had the best chocolate in Italy, manufactured in Novi Ligure a few miles north of Gavi. Again, internees could buy as much of it as they wanted – provided they had the money.

It was not difficult for Major Pringle to find new friends among the English and American prisoners of war held at Gavi. The Italian guards and officers, too, soon became more than mere acquaintances. Pringle amassed a mine of information and quickly realized that there really was "absolutely no way to escape; we were sitting in a box of stone."

One day a fellow American prisoner confided in him. "He was a soldier from my regiment. His name was Hadley, he was a chef and lived in a cell which bordered on a lower courtyard. Hadley's room was directly under mine and was in the building facing the village. He lay on a top bunk in his cell, which had two bunks on each side and could thus sleep four. One night when he turned over in bed he banged his head

From the castle ramparts there are grand views of the wide valley and town of Gavi Ligure, now in the province of Alessandria.

The castle in Gavi Ligure, seen from the south.

The castle was erected on the ruins of an old fortification dating back to the ancient Roman period. In 1202 it fell to the republic of Genoa, its new function being to guard the port against attacks from the Po Delta. During the course of the 17th century the stronghold was completely rebuilt and extended.

on the wall. He heard a hollow noise unusual for the thick stone walls. He spoke to the leading seaman on the bunk below him about it who answered that it was perhaps his head which sounded so hollow. Eventually they both tried to make a hole in the wall at that point. They found a secret passageway several feet wide leading down into the depths."

Hadley then went to talk to Major Pringle. A commando of a dozen of the most reliable of the prisoners was formed. The first to explore the passageway was Major Pringle, clutching a torch made of "flannel pajamas soaked in olive oil." He was lowered down to the bottom of the hole where he discovered a huge cistern full of water. He swam back and forth across the pool, examining the walls more closely. The prisoners then busied themselves for weeks studying the external topography of the castle, measuring it and

collecting snippets of information. Once they had all they needed they began working on their escape route. The wall they had selected for partial demolition was opposite the end of the passageway, a huge partition made of enormous blocks of granite and about ten feet (3 m) thick. The men had to swim over 30 feet (10 m) to get to it. Work was done in shifts; a small raft was made for transporting materials. Supporting themselves on a bit of protruding masonry, the soldiers began to chisel away at the stone with an iron leg from Hadley's bed. They later applied the principle of temperature fluctuation so that the granite was easier to work. They lit a fire on the stone outcrop using material they had collected outside. They then cooled the stone down with water and began scraping with Hadley's bedpost. The project went on all winter through to the beginning of spring, with the men working three shifts day and night. During these months the chocolate consumption at Gavi prison reached a record level. As planned, the prisoners crept to freedom across the roof of the room where the guards slept. They waited for a wet, foggy night in April to make their escape.

Eleven of the 12 who had made the breakout were rounded up in the fields surrounding the castle the next morning. Pringle, the only one to reach Genoa, was obviously a pro. From there the major worked his way down to southern Italy where he met up with his wartime comrades, had a brief holiday back home in the United States, and then returned to Europe to continue fighting. In Austria Pringle was recaptured and imprisoned. Again he was able to escape. His enemies caught up with him in Germany and threw him into prison, where he escaped twice. He made his last dash for freedom from his final place of detention in Czechoslovakia, just before the end of the war.

## General Efisio Marras

In March of 1944 the gates of the castle in Gavi opened to admit three new prisoners, all of them Italian soldiers guarded by an Italian SS unit. They had come a long way to get there. Although barely a year had passed since Major Pringle's escape, the situation in Italy had changed completely. The state of Italy no longer existed. The south of the

The huge underground cisterns held an inexhaustible supply of water for the castle garrison.

179

country was ruled by a provisional monarchist government in league with the Allies, who occupied the lower half of the peninsula; a parliament fronted by Mussolini and dependent on the Third Reich held sway over the north. The German army effectively controlled central and northern Italy.

Even the castle in Gavi no longer functioned quite as it did. It was still a prison, yet both internees and personnel were now all Italian. Only the castellan, Signor Rabbia from Gavi Ligure, had remained, still fighting his own personal battle against the vine pest as he had done for the last 20 years. Italy was in the throes of a world war and a civil war. A battalion of the Fascist republic of Salò guarded the castle, imprisoning soldiers who had refused to be a party to Mussolini's state in northern Italy.

The entrance to the castle with its round watchtower.

The new arrivals were General Efisio Marras, head of the Italian military mission in Berlin since the end of the 1930s, Rear Admiral Carlo de Angelis Chalet de la Frémoire and Air Force colonel Giuseppe Teucci. The latter two men were military attachés to the navy and the aviation corps respectively at the Italian embassy in Berlin. All three were experts on the military situation in Germany. They were the men responsible for maintaining the close links forged between the general staff of Italy and Germany during the first four years of the war. They knew all the secrets of the "brutal friendship" between the two regimes. The bluntest and shrewdest reports on the structure of the German military and on the procedures of the state and army hierarchy of decision-makers and command-issuers were written by General Marras. His communiqués predicted the failure of the invasion of Great Britain and of the campaign in Russia, the opening up of the Eastern Front, and the final defeat of the Nazi regime months before these events occurred. Although it was common knowledge that General Marras had little time for the two regimes and their leaders, Mussolini had shown some favor towards Marras; the general was the only person who could provide il Duce with watertight information on Italy's German allies. The fact that Mussolini always did exactly the opposite of what Marras urged in his dispatches is another matter entirely.

## From Oranienburg to Gavi

On September 8, 1943, the monarchist government of Italy and the Allies signed an armistice. Marras, de Angelis, Teucci and almost the entire civilian staff at the Italian embassy in Berlin promptly professed their

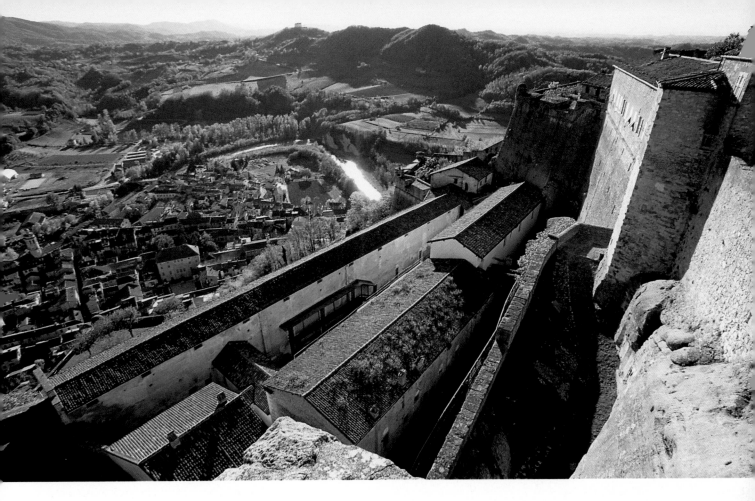

View of the barracks set into the castle walls from the upper bailey.

loyalty to the monarchy. On September 10 the diplomatic corps and the members of the Italian military mission were packed off to Italy with their families on a special train. At a station in Bavaria the three officers were politely requested to leave the train and taken to a camp at Garmisch-Partenkirchen. They were then sent back to Berlin and interned in a camp in Oranienburg, where they spent six long months. As soon as the German authorities considered the Fascist government in Salò to be stable enough, Efisio Marras and his two officers were transported to Italy and handed over to the battalion at the castle in Gavi Ligure, where they were to be tried for high treason.

On October 12, 1944, General Efisio Marras, Rear Admiral Carlo de Angelis Chalet de la Frémoire, and Colonel Giuseppe Teucci escaped from the castle in Gavi, along with a second general, two NCOs and 12 soldiers held captive in the fortress. Two Breda 37 machine guns, two sub-machine guns, numerous rifles, five crates of grenades and the safe containing all the documents on the castle's resident battalion disappeared with them. The amount of contraband they took suggests that they could not have used the same escape route as Major Pringle.

With the war at an end, in December of 1945, various details were given from a statement made by Signor Giovan Battista Rabbia, the castellan stationed at Gavi. He stated that the prisoners had left the castle through the main gate; he had accompanied them personally and helped them to load their "luggage" onto waiting vehicles provided by the partisans. It was a wet, misty night. Rabbia claimed that the battalion guards had not noticed a thing.

Rabbia's daughter, Signora Graziella Rabbia, is now castellan of the castle in Gavi Ligure.

# Bracciano

Castello Orsini-Odescalchi

## A possible approach

Leaving the center of Rome and driving north along the Tiber and around Monte Mario, you come to the Via Cassia. The next 11 miles (18 km) take you over and under highway feeders, bridges and beltways, past refuse dumps and fortified residential areas armed with video cameras and guard dogs. Eventually you come to the little town of La Storta, which evokes sad memories of the Second World War. Here the road forks. The surroundings become less depressing after a further 11 miles (18 km), where you find yourself on a road described by many travelers of the 19th century with passionate enthusiasm. With a little imagination, it is just about possible to appreciate their sentiments.

Bracciano is actually a lake that, like many of those in Lazio, fills a volcanic crater. Its surface area is the same as that of Old Rome, the area of the metropolis within the ancient city walls. The water in the middle of the crater is very deep. Looking north you notice that the lake is skirted by a ridge of low, black, jagged mountains: the old edge of the crater. The lake takes its name from one of the three medieval towns that overlook it. They form a regular triangle along its shores, with Bracciano in the western corner and Anguillara and Trevignano in the other two.

Above: View of the castle and the town of Bracciano.

In the 18th century the castle and much of the Roman property belonging to the Orsini family was acquired by Prince Odescalchi, hence the fortress's double-barreled name.

Opposite: Orsini-Odescalchi Castle towers above the Lago di Bracciano, one of the crater lakes common to Lazio.

View of the curtain walls and solid towers on the east side of the castle.

After the castle came into the possession of the Orsini in 1419, Napoleone Orsini began rebuilding. His son, Gentil Virginio Orsini, continued the renovation, introducing a number of modern features which transformed the 12th-century fortress into a comfortable and secure stately residence.

The enormous castle of the Orsini, which now also bears the name of Odescalchi, the prince who acquired it in the 18th century, dominates the lakeside. The main building and the walls and five towers enclosing it are made of huge square blocks of lava basalt whose gray-black is echoed by the surrounding rocks. Even the surface of the water is a metallic dark gray. The castle is irregular in plan and consists of two very different rectangular complexes linked by courtyards and a central building. The older east wing closest to the town and the lake dates back to the 12th century.

Through the offices of Pope Martin V, for which he levied the symbolic tithe of one vulture per year, the old fortress came into the possession of the Orsini family in 1419. The Orsini were one of the two great feudal families of Rome whose lands stretched from Apulia to Abruzzi and from Lazio to Campania. The family was naturally in permanent conflict with the second ancient dynasty of Rome, the Colonna. Both parties

governed a large section of the city, and the feud plunged the inhabitants into a state of civil war. The Orsini were at constant pains to form an alliance with the Church. The pope, for his part, could not have survived in Rome without their support. Each was dependent on the other; with their castles and estates the various branches of the Orsini family oversaw the main routes leading into the city. With the fief of Bracciano they also gained control over the Via Cassia, the main road linking Rome to Umbria and Tuscany.

After Napoleone Orsini had been made lord of Bracciano, he began rebuilding the castle. His aim was to turn it into a modern fortress and comfortable residence worthy of his great name. To the existing structure a second was added which fulfilled all the military requirements of the second half of the 15th century, an age where weapons and defense systems were undergoing rapid development. The resulting combination was successful. The project was completed by Napoleone's son,

Gentil Virginio Orsini, who had been brought up at the court in Naples and was brother-in-law to Lorenzo *il Magnifico*. He busied himself with the decoration of the stark edifice. He commissioned top artists and architects, among them Francesco di Giorgio Martini from Siena. Thanks to the new master's attention to detail and eye for design, during the second phase of its restoration the severe, menacing character of the castle was greatly softened and given an unexpected elegance. Under Gentil Virginio the fortress at Bracciano became the favored residence of the Orsini and one of the great Renaissance courts of central Italy.

## The death of Gentil Virginio

Like all the other regions that the Neapolitan expedition under King Charles VIII (1494–1496) passed through, the Papal States and the city of Rome were devastated by the French army. Pope Alexander VI was in

Left: F. Sansovino *Portrait of Gentil Virginio Orsini*, from: *L'Historia di casa Orsini*, Venice, 1565.

Gentil Virginio Orsini was brought up at court in Naples. The humanist Giovanni Pontano, who was one of his teachers, later uttered harsh criticism of his former pupil. In a letter dated July 24, 1487, from Pontano to Giovanni Albino he writes: "But I have a bad opinion of all fat people, especially if they are Guelphs. Guelphs and fat people are generally patter merchants whose actions go up in smoke (...) their blood is only good as fat." Gentil Virginio was also said to be extremely mean.

Left: In the room of hunting trophies there is also a fresco which has been removed from the wall and placed on canvas. It shows scenes from the life of Gentil Virginio Orsini. The fresco is attributed to Antoniazzo Romano and his 15th-century school of painters and was originally in the entrance vestibule from the inner ward.

Antoniazzo Romano
(1452–1508)
*Meeting between Gentil
Virginio and Pietro de'
Medici*
Fresco
Castello Orsini-Odescalchi,
Bracciano

This picture was painted in
honor of Gentil Virginio's
appointment as captain
general to the Aragonese
troops of the kingdom of
Naples (1489).

league with the Aragonese royal family, then the rulers of Naples. The French king Charles VIII claimed, however, that Naples was ancient French territory which rightly belonged to the French crown. In 1494 Gentil Virginio Orsini bore the standard of the Church and was captain general of the Neapolitan army. His task should have been to halt the advance of the French and defend both Naples and the Eternal City. Yet as the French neared Rome, Gentil Virginio sent his sons to meet Charles VIII and invite the king to the Orsini castle. Charles agreed and on December 19, 1494, moved into the fortress in Bracciano. Orsini's sudden change of heart caused Naples' position to rapidly worsen, forcing King Alfonso to flee the city.

About two years later, in February 1497, when the political French whirlwind had subsided, Gentil Virginio Orsini and his son Gian Giordano lay rotting in a cell in the Castel dell'Ovo in Naples. Having broken their alliance with the pope and the king of Naples and defected to the camp of Charles VIII, they were both accused of deceit and treason – not once but twice, for Gentil Virginio had also sheltered the French king on his return. His crime cost him his rights and all of his estates, confiscated in a bull issued by the pope on June 2, 1496, "because he dared to contest the rights of the Church." He was also excommunicated and thus damned for eternity. One morning Gentil Virginio was found dead in his cell. According to Alexander VI he had died "of catarrh." The general consensus is that the cause of death was poison supplied by the pope's infamous cellars. Gentil Virginio's son Gian Giordano promptly went on a hunger strike. His refusal to eat or drink lasted just one day, for the next morning a declaration arrived from the pope pardoning the accused. Gian Giordano was

set free and the rights and lands of his father were restored to him. The pope had acted generously for a number of different reasons; his troops had suffered a military defeat at the hands of Orsini soldiers, the Orsini faction had threatened Rome with an armed uprising and the Venetians had paid 50,000 gold *scudi* into the papal coffers to have the two prisoners released. For Gentil Virginio, who had emptied the bottle of wine the prison authorities had given him on the spot, the pope's pardon came too late. His son, however, was a moderate drinker and thus survived.

## Gian Giordano's wedding

Presumably scarred by the terrible experiences he had suffered in the Neapolitan dungeons, Gian Giordano pursued a more prudent line of politics than those which had cost his father his head. The younger Orsini sought to solve disputes with his enemies

through compromise, doing all in his power to avoid armed combat. Despite being overtly extravagant, a trait that earned him the nickname of "public fool," he proved that he could plan with an eye to the future. His policies began to bear fruit following the death of Pope Alexander VI – who made the mistake of drinking his own wine. After a brief reign by Pope Pius III, which lasted a mere 26 days, Giuliano della Rovere, Pope Julius II, ascended the pontifical throne. In an attempt to restore law and order to Rome and the Papal States the new pontiff hit upon the idea of reconciling the Orsini and the Colonna. In doing so he would make himself father-in-law to the heads of both families. He married off his "niece," Lucrezia Gaia della Rovere, to the young Marcantonio Colonna. The wedding was celebrated with great pageantry in the church of the Santi Apostoli in Rome on January 2, 1506. A long letter from

Cardinal Dovizi to the duke of Ferrara has been preserved in which the prelate describes the bride's velvet and brocade clothing, her necklace, bracelets and diadem in great detail. The ceremony, writes the cardinal, with its "two banquets and two comedies which were held in the presence of a great number of cardinals," lasted no less than 48 hours.

By pure coincidence, it was around this time that Gian Giordano Orsini was widowed. He was now fairly elderly and the father of four girls and one boy. Pope Julius immediately offered the bereaved husband his daughter's hand in marriage. Felice della Rovere was little more than a child and deemed "a flower of rare beauty." The pope suggested that the ceremony be kept modest and simple to dampen the criticism of jealous rivals. The pope's wish was that there be no pomp, no banquet and no elaborate gowns. In view of the bridegroom's age and the recent death of his wife, there were also to be no presents, plays, concerts or festivities. Although Gian Giordano felt that Julius II was being a little mean with his daughter's dowry, he agreed to the union. The marriage was held at the beginning of June 1506 and proved a truly memorable occasion. On the day of his wedding the head of the Orsini household rose at the crack of dawn and went hunting. At the appointed time he turned up at the Palazzo della Cancelleria in his hunting clothes, dirty, sweaty and unshaven. The nuptial rites had barely ended when Gian

Above: Frieze with cherubs and the Orsini coat of arms. In the center, surrounded by leaves of acanthus, is the family emblem on its red and blue background. A cherub holds it on either side, with a two-headed satyr at the top.

Opposite top:
Zuccari
*View of Bracciano*
Fresco
Castello Orsini-Odescalchi, Bracciano
This view adorns one of the walls in the castle interior.

Opposite bottom:
A covered veranda in the residential quarters.

Giordano ordered those present to leave the room and wait outside until the marriage had been consummated where it had taken place. There was no time to ask the Holy Father what he thought of the whole affair.

The newlyweds finally emerged from the palace. They made their way to the Palazzo Orsini on Monte Giordano on foot, their guests trailing behind them. The bride, holding onto her husband's arm, did not look the slightest bit ruffled, but appeared content. In keeping with the pope's wishes, no banquet had been laid on in the palace. As there was also no cutlery and the wedding party had to eat with their fingers, simple kebabs were served. Gian Giordano ate in earnest silence, concentrating fully on his repast and leaving his visitors to talk amongst themselves. During the course of the meal a servant stood holding a hat above Gian Giordano's head. As soon as the bridegroom had finished eating, he grabbed his hat, kissed it and put it on. He then dismissed his guests.

Concert on the Piazza San Giovanni (detail), c. 1450
Painted front of a chest of the Cassone Adimari
Inv. no. 147
Galleria d'Arte Antica e Moderna, Florence

With the banner of their employer hanging from their trumpets, as many heralds as possible were used to demonstrate the social standing of their lord and master.

## Music and Dance in the Lives of the Italian Nobility

Margit Bachfischer

"Above all take great care that neither his highness the king nor anyone else could suspect that we are behind the disappearance of these singers." With these words Galeazzo Maria Sforza ordered his ambassadors in Naples to poach some of the local singers for his Milan court band in 1472, luring their services with the promise of "a good stipend and a good reward." Until the death of the duke in 1476, the Sforza orchestra employed over 40 musicians.

As the Middle Ages progressed, the manner in which a nobleman kept court became increasingly synonymous with his standing and prestige as a ruler. The more pomp and ceremony he could provide, the more powerful and affluent he appeared to his subjects. It is thus no surprise that when flicking through the account books of the great Italian courts we regularly find singers for the royal choir, court trumpeters and heralds, minstrels, fools and dwarves on the temporary or long-term payroll. The immense power wielded by a potentate was to be proclaimed as loudly and as impressively as possible, with the intention of making him seem even greater than in reality. The trumpet, with its sharp and penetrating tone, was particularly well suited for such a task, but not everyone was permitted to use it; the instrument was the prerogative of the patriciate and a select handful of influential citizens. No self-respecting nobleman traveled or even appeared in public without making a great show of it, frequently engaging minstrels to broadcast his pending arrival. Bands of heralds – the bigger the better – with the banner of their lord dangling from their trumpets were another popular status symbol. King Alfonso II of Naples even took his singers hunting with him. One undertaking by Galeazzo Maria Sforza vividly underlines just how much importance was attached to having a band of musicians accompany a man of substance on his travels. In 1471 Sforza planned to ride from Milan to Florence. Unfortunately, his own trombone, shawm and fife players were in prison sitting out a sentence. Finding himself lacking an entourage befitting his station, he postponed his journey until the marquis of Mantua could at least lend him his 40 lute players as an emergency replacement.

Nothing was too much trouble for the families of the Italian nobility when it came to seeing who could put on the biggest display of pageantry and earn the most recognition from their peers and underlings. When Ercole I d'Este began building up his court orchestra, one of his concerns was that it should provide Galeazzo Maria Sforza with some healthy competition. The latter, however, outdid his rival, in 1473 investing four times as much in his musicians as the duke of Ferrara. Musical revenge came after Sforza's death; Ercole

Far right: *Instruments of the Trecento*, 14th century Illumination "V.E.III", Napoli, Ms. VA 14, fol. 17 Biblioteca Nazionale, Naples

This illustration shows the instruments typically used in the 14th century: fiddle, psaltery and lute (top), tambour, portative organ and clapper (middle) and bagpipes and shawm, kettledrums and trumpets (bottom).

took on several of the singers and minstrels formerly employed in Milan and became proud owner of the largest court orchestra in Italy. He continued to build up his number of string, wind, and brass players; in 1484 11 trumpeters were in his service alone at the palace in Ferrara. The importance of the brass was mirrored by their salary. In Ferrara they were paid considerably more than the singers and the other instrumentalists, flautists, harpists, and lutenists among them.

In the 14th century one of the most popular ensembles was a group of high or alto instruments, which during the course of the 15th century became one of the standard features of courtly musical entertainment. The group usually consisted of three winds, a combination of shawm, bass shawm, cornett or trombone. The *alti* played at competitions, tournaments and to herald the arrival of important people; they accompanied ceremonious banquets and courtly dances out in the open or in the great halls of castles and palaces. Alto ensembles (often known as *pifferi*) usually improvised, with one of the group playing the melody and the other two weaving countermelodies around it. The occasional score of some of these three-part instrumental pieces has, however, been preserved, such as those performed in 1480 during the engagement celebrations for Isabella d'Este and Francesco Gonzaga and in 1490,

Below: *Dancing a Roundelay in Noble Company*, c. 1460 Illumination in the 13th-century *Roman de la Rose* Ms. Fr. 16153, fol. 7 Bibliothèque Nationale, Paris

Three minstrels play the shawm for four noble couples dancing a roundelay in a garden.

interspersed between classical comedies staged at their wedding.

In 1465 Borso d'Este was asked if he would lend his court *pifferi* to the aforementioned Galeazzo Maria Sforza. Borso was sadly unable to oblige, because he needed them himself for the feast of St. George; although d'Este conceded that musicians were "not absolutely vital," he nevertheless felt they were of significance "for our honor and that of our country."

Occasions demanding such elaborate celebration were usually major Church festivals, important political occurrences or exceptional personal events. Christenings, weddings, funerals, regional and imperial diets, the successful return from a crusade or long journey and important visitors were all good reasons for holding a usually fairly flamboyant feast. These affairs were merry orgies of food, drink, dance, song, games, theater performances and various other forms of entertainment. The party often went on for several days and banquets lasting several hours were the norm. The festivities were often held in the great hall; depending on the scale of the jamboree, however,

the dances, musical and theatrical performances and the banquet often had to be moved outside. The guests were then accommodated in tents and huts erected in front of the castle or palace especially for the occasion. Although most courts had instrumentalists in their employ, wandering minstrels often found lodgings and paid work for the duration of the festival. In 1376 a street singer named Francesco da Vannozza and in 1377 and 1394 an *Enzellino piffaro* are recorded as having stayed at the d'Este palace. Traveling musicians such as Lodovico da Padova and Prando da Verona spent some time entertaining the duke's guests in Ferrara in 1445 and 1450. The gentlemen of the nobility occasionally helped each other out when it came to providing musicians. The minstrels were usually packed off with a letter of recommendation to their new employer, where they received a friendly welcome and a generous pay packet.

The focal point of most medieval festivities was the feast itself: the banquet and all the ceremony which went with it. The acoustic backdrop was provided by dancers, musicians, jesters and actors. An alto ensemble normally accompanied servants bringing in the countless platters of food for a meal in which each course vied with the next to tempt the guests' palate. It was considered essential that music be played during the courses, both as a magnificent embellishment to the sumptuous cuisine and to enhance the general sense of enjoyment. The performers often positioned themselves close to the guests at the table. Documents frequently tell of singers and instrumentalists wandering back and forth across the room during a banquet. Musicians were most commonly placed on a wooden stage or balcony. If the alto ensemble became too loud, the musicians swapped their shawms and cornets for bass instruments or quieter fiddles, harps, lutes, flutes and small drums. The practice of alternating between alto and bass ensembles, usually seated in separate alcoves and galleries, is known to have persisted until about 1600. The great value attached to the interplay of different sounds is illustrated by the wedding banquet held in honor of Ercole d'Este and his bride, Renata of France. The 17 courses were accompanied by a number of ensembles playing various permutations of instruments. One

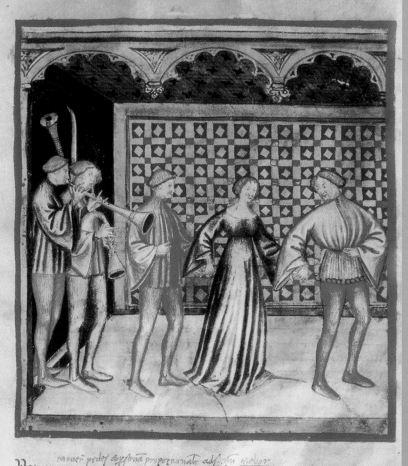

Sonare et balare

course was consumed to the dulcet tones of the court choir, for example, another fiddled into the room by a virtuoso string player; they were followed by a singer with a lute, dancers weaving around the tables, a musical dwarf and the performance of a madrigal, to name but a few.

The banquet was invariably interspersed with interludes of music, dance, theater and storytelling, even between courses. These *entr'actes* usually included heroic songs and street ballads or stories told to a musical accompaniment. Local traveling singers such as Ferrarino da Ferrara and Matulino da Ferrara appeared at the palaces of the Este family between 1208 and 1264. At the most important festivals men in positions of power were

Above: *Sonare et balare*, end of the 14th century
Miniature from the *Tacuinum sanitatis in medicina* (the Cerruti family book of remedies)
Cod. ser. nov. 2644
Österreichische Nationalbibliothek, Vienna
Dancing is described as being particularly beneficial to one's health.

Opposite: Simone Martini, *St Martin is Made a Knight* (detail), c.1320/25
Fresco, 265 × 200 cm
Lower church at the basilica of San Francesco, Assisi
Group of singers and instrumentalists.

particularly keen to have their virtues extolled in front of their guests. Complaints were sometimes made about performers who were not long-winded enough in their hymns of praise. As opposed to the wandering minstrels, musicians in the court's permanent employ had to keep their criticism to themselves. They were required to laud their employer at all times and scorn anyone who dared condemn him. At a feast in Ferrara in 1468 street singers such as Francesco Cieco and Giovanni Orbo applauded the merits of Borso d'Este. Feuds between the various Italian courts and cities were also recorded in music. Bartolino da Padova, for example, who had followed the Carrara of Venice into exile in Florence, repeatedly mentions the Visconti of Milan in his madrigal texts. Both troubadours and court musicians were frequently richly rewarded after performing at royal banquets. In 1300 Galeazzo Visconti celebrated his marriage to Beatrice d'Este in Milan. The Chronicle of Asti notes that at least 7,000 expensive items of clothing were distributed among the performers contributing to the lavish ceremony. A few centuries later the 500 musicians and minstrels engaged for another princely wedding in Milan were allegedly given magnificent robes in appreciation of their services.

Although the banquet was the main attraction of any medieval feast, the dancing was almost as important. Dances acted as a form both of representation and of entertainment. In the *Tacuinum sanitatis* of the 14th–century Italian Cerruti family, dancing is even alleged to have healing properties. Dances were performed in groups, with people dancing more in pairs from the 14th century onwards. In courtly circles the rank and standing of the dancers determined who went first. The slow, ceremonious step of the *bassa danza* was generally distinguished from the sprightly caper which followed. One of the most popular dances of this period we know of is the saltarello, a quick, lively after-dance usually in simple triple or compound duple time. The steps and figures of the courtly dance were mostly learned from a dance master and were subject to regional variation and the fads of fashion. Any festive occasion at court, whether it be in Burgundy, Milan or England, was not complete without the guests being able to stride or hop along to the fashionable dances of the moment. Sadly, the only characteristic of these dances to have survived into later centuries is the steady alternation of slow and fast. Alto ensembles provided the music both outside and inside. Accompaniment was also frequently supplied by the pipe

Below left: Andrea Bonaiuti (Andrea da Firenze) *The Way to Spiritual Salvation* (detail), c.1365–1367 Fresco Santa Maria Novella, Cappella degli Spagnuoli, Florence

This fresco scene from life at court in the Trecento shows musicians with bagpipes and a fiddle and a group of young girls obviously dancing to the rhythm of the tambour.

Far right: Francesco del Cossa *Triumph of Venus* (detail), 1469/70 Fresco Palazzo Schifanoia, Salone dei Mesi, Ferrara

The fresco depicts a spring festival for the month of April, at the center of which are Nature and Love and, in close conjunction with them, Music. The couple kneeling down are surrounded by girls and boys with lutes and flutes or "quiet instruments" whose soft, gentle tones were particularly appreciated in small, private circles.

and drum, which could be played simultaneously by a single minstrel. Like the leader of the dance, the minstrel set the rhythm, the direction of movement and sometimes also the steps for the dance.

The roundelay or round dance, which dancers and onlookers alike frequently sang to, was also extremely popular in the Middle Ages. The roundelay – or *ballata* in Italy – was either a stepping or a hopping dance. A lead dancer often executed the steps, directions and rhythms for others to copy. In the early 14th century Giovanni del Virgilio told of how in an Italian *ballata* a solo singer would sing the verses of the dance song and have everyone join him in the refrain. The dancers often performed steps standing on the spot while they listened to the soloist, stepping sideways in a circle during the chorus.

Another source chronicles how guests at a banquet organized by Francesco Sforza at the court of Milan in 1459 in honor of a visit by the legate to Philip the Good of Burgundy retired after the feast while people sang to the strains of "quiet instruments." Festivities at court thus resounded to both the loud, representative anthems of shawms, trumpets, pipes and drums and to the calming, gentle music of strings and flutes. In his *Decameron* Giovanni Boccaccio aptly describes a palace garden full of flowers, orange and lemon trees, rose bushes and a fountain near which people sang and made music. During a royal jamboree people could thus take a walk through the palace gardens, join in a round dance, listen to the soft strumming of a lute player, perhaps skip along to a few more dances in the great hall or be lulled off to bed by the "sweet art" of quiet melodies.

One musician who became unusually famous was Pietro Bono. A virtuoso on the lute and the lyre, Bono was in service to the d'Este family at the court of Ferrara and an asset the d'Este were undoubtedly extremely proud of. He often performed at court festivals together with the tenor singer Malcise. Bono was occasionally granted permission to play at rival Italian courts. In 1456 he was allowed to join the entourage of Francesco Sforza in Milan for a brief period. As one contemporary poet writes, Pietro Bono not only enchanted his audience with his heavenly singing and playing; his repertoire also included a number of love stories

which he told to music. His talents were probably not only in demand for special events but also for the more mundane occasions in the life of the nobility. Minstrels were also contracted to fulfil a private function at the palaces and castles, performing chamber music, singing and playing their employers to sleep, entertaining them and driving away boredom. One chronicler relates the everyday habits of Beatrice d'Este, who arrived at Lodovico Sforza's court at the tender age of 14: "She spends day and night engaged in song and dance and all kinds of pleasures." Masked balls with hundreds of colorful costumes came into vogue at the court of Milan where "singing and sweet music of all kinds and of such melodious delight [were] heard that they seemed to have come to this eminent court from Heaven itself."

Johannes de Sacrobosco
*The Italian Bath, c.* 1470
Miniature
Ms. lat. 209, fol. 10
Biblioteca Estense, Modena

The families of the patriciate and the nobility naturally kept to themselves when they took their summer baths, leaving their underlings to use the town bathhouses. The garden at the back of the city palace with its decorative fountain provides privacy for the pleasures of the bath – which included music, as the singers and band of minstrels with their many instruments illustrate.

# Trento (Trent)

## Castello del Buonconsiglio

The Lion Courtyard in the Magno Palazzo, seat of the prince-bishops in Trento, with the arcade designed by Alessio Longhi.

Opposite: Buonconsiglio seen from the north-west, with the cylindrical tower dominating the Castelvecchio and the Magno Palazzo in the background. The castle's original name of Malconsiglio, "ill counsel," was changed to Buonconsiglio, "good advice," long before the Council of Trent convened here in the 16th century.

### A castle is renamed

The original name of Buonconsiglio, the castle in Trento, was "Malconsiglio." The word may have come from Malconsey, a rocky elevation surmounted by a large round tower, the Torre d'Augusto, which once guarded the town below it. The River Adige flowing south forms a 45-degree bend around the foot of the hill.

Another explanation for the name Malconsiglio is that it was derived from the word *Mahl*, an ancient Germanic court trial. Merged with the Latin "consilium," this became the vernacular Italian *malconsiglio*, which translates literally as "ill counsel" or a rash, badly considered verdict. This seems a rather inappropriate name for a small theocratic state ruled by a prince-bishop for eight centuries! Some sort of ill omen was obviously attached to it, for one of the ecclesiastic sovereigns ordered his subjects to rename Malconsiglio "Buonconsiglio," meaning "judicious, fortuitous, welcome advice," long

before December 13, 1545, when the fateful Council of Trent was convened in the town.

The fief of Trento was given to the local Church in 1004 by the Saxon ruler Henry II. It remained a prince-bishopric until 1803, making it the longest-lasting political territory of the second millennium in western Europe. Napoleonic cannons finally put an end to the ancient domain.

Perched in a key position between central Europe and Italy, the little state of Trento provided access to and from the peninsula, acting as a permanent filter, pivot and bridge between Germany and Italy. The historical head of this extremely durable territorial arrangement was the prince-bishop who, as half-emperor and half-pope, was two tyrants rolled into one, both protected and contained by the sturdy defenses of his state boundaries. For 800 years the principality was ruled with a rod of iron by generation after generation of prince-bishops. A temporary break in the domination of the religious rulers occurred during the second quarter of the 13th century, when Frederick II was wrestling with Rome for absolute supremacy. During this period construction began on a castle along a bend in the city wall beneath the old Torre d'Augusto. In later years a second tower, the square eagle tower or Torre dell'Aquila, was erected further south, linked to the castle by the wall. This, the oldest section of the fortress, is known as the Castelvecchio, or old castle. When the fief of Trento again fell to the Church in 1255 after the death of Frederick II, Bishop Egnone chose Castelvecchio as his place of residence. All of his successors followed suit, spending their lives in a fortified palace watched over by two massive towers.

### The dreamer

A member of a very old noble family that also owned large swathes of land in what is now Switzerland, and in Slovakia, Prince-Bishop George of Liechtenstein (1390–1419) made a number of major changes to the Castelvecchio in about 1400. Suffocated by the old fortress, he had a strong wall built along the south face which looked out over the town

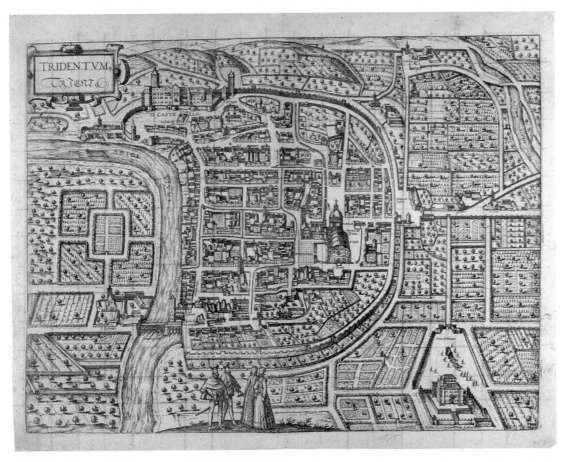

Hans Hogenberg
*Perspective Views of Trento*,
1588

The castle hill in the top left
corner towers above a sharp
bend in the River Adige.

and a garden laid out in the space created between this wall and the castle front. He then delegated the interior decoration of the Torre dell'Aquila to an artist known as Master Wenceslas, thought to be from Bohemia and thus from the fief's eastern estates. Traces of his fresco work still exist in other cities near Trento. The master also designed a garden along the walls of the Torre dell'Aquila. In a room on the second floor of the tower he created the wonderful *Ciclo dei Mesi* (Cycle of the Months). This extremely vivid work of art depicts the life of the nobility alongside that of the peasants over the course of one year. The two groups are only shown together once, during the month of the harvest, when they join forces to press the grapes.

## The agitator

Rebuilding work on Castelvecchio plodded on through the 15th century. During the reign of Johann Hinderbach (1465–1486) the inner ward was embellished with a colonnade in the Venetian Gothic style. Four loggias were added, one above the other, their walls and ceilings completely covered in frescoes by Bartolomeo Sacchetto. A doorway was knocked through the wall bordering on the town in the same period. The opening was called the Porta di San Vigilio after the first bishop sent by Rome to Trento to spread the Word of God.

Johann Hinderbach is remembered not only for the architectural amendments he made to the castle. He also altered the makeup of the community, organizing a meticulous pogrom that resulted in the banishment of Trento's entire Jewish population. The Jews had been accused of kidnapping and killing a Christian child for one of their rituals. Their terrible punishment was exacted even though there was not a single shred of evidence against them. The unfortunate boy was later made a saint, St. Simonino, and is now pictured as a cherub in

Opposite bottom:
A further building, the
Magno Palazzo, was added
to the castle under Cardinal
Bernardo Clesio
(1485–1539). This splendid
palatial residence was
erected in a very short time,
between 1528 and 1536.

Above: Heinrich Schickhardt
*Buonconsiglio Palace in 1598*
Cod. hist. 40148a,
fol. 9v/10r
Württembergische
Landesbibliothek, Stuttgart

the Catholic rendering of Heaven. Although for Pope Sixtus IV conspiracies and assassinations, such as the murder of Lorenzo de' Medici in Florence, for example, were standard procedure, he did not support this particular pogrom and sent a team of investigators to Trento to see what was going on. The lord and master of Trento was not that easily perturbed; even while the commission was making inquiries he continued to run the Jews out of town.

### The realist

When in 1514 Bernardo Clesio, a man of boundless energy and infinite ambition, was elected prince-bishop, there was not much left to renovate in the old castle. Along the city walls between the castle and the Torre dell'Aquila, however, there was a large gap. Clesio was a man who loved filling in empty spaces. With the bishop checking every architectural decision and every penny spent by his team of builders, a brand-new edifice was erected next to and separate from the Castelvecchio. Building was begun in 1528, with the main construction work finished a mere four years later and the interior fully decorated and furnished by 1536. The result was a magnificent princely palace worthy to receive Ferdinand of Habsburg and his bride Anna of Hungary on an official visit to the capital of their former fief.

Architects and artists from Italy and Germany contributed to the grand project. The decor was entrusted to the capable hands of Bartolomäus Till Riemenschneider, Girolamo Romanino from Brescia, the brothers Dosso and Battista Dossi, painters at the court of Ferrara, and the Venetian Marcello Fogolino, among others. The most famous names in art worked alongside dozens of craftsmen and hundreds of laborers and German engravers at work on the coffered ceiling. They were joined by sculptors and stonemasons, ornamental plasterers, bronze smiths, ceramics experts and an entire army of the best Italian and German masters of the day. In 1539 court poet Andrea Mattioli wrote a detailed description in verse of Bernardo Clesio's Magno Palazzo, as it was now called. All that joined the Magno Palazzo to the Castelvecchio was a covered walkway between the top two floors of the respective buildings.

Under Prince-Bishop Johann Hinderbach the inner ward of the Castelvecchio was also redesigned to include decorative colonnades in the Venetian Gothic style.

The plaques above the arches in Alessio Longhi's Lion Courtyard depict various rulers.

## The successors

At the end of the 17th century the last undeveloped section of the castle plot was filled with the Congiunzione Albertiana, erected in the name of Prince-Bishop Francesco Alberti Poja. Like his predecessors, Poja also wanted to leave his mark on the structure. A new building subsequently went up on the last empty piece of land between the Castelvecchio and the Magno Palazzo. The result attempts the impossible – to forge a union between two very different styles of architecture – and is not terribly successful.

In the following years the principality of Trento and with it the prince-bishop gradually paled into insignificance. The ever greater and ever more immediate influence exerted by the House of Habsburg on northern Italy slowly robbed Trento of its position of power. During the Napoleonic Wars Buonconsiglio became a place of refuge for French troops and their horses. The bishops of Trento, hounded from their home and stripped of their title, made a permanent move. When the French left the castle they took everything that wasn't nailed down, firing a few heavy volleys at what was left for good measure. In the 19th century Buonconsiglio was an Austrian prison for Italian political prisoners. In 1848, 21 patriots were executed in the castle ditch during Italy's campaign for independence. The area around Trento remained Austrian until the First World War. In the 1920s the castle was heavily restored. A second phase of restoration concentrating primarily on the decor and ornamentation is still under way.

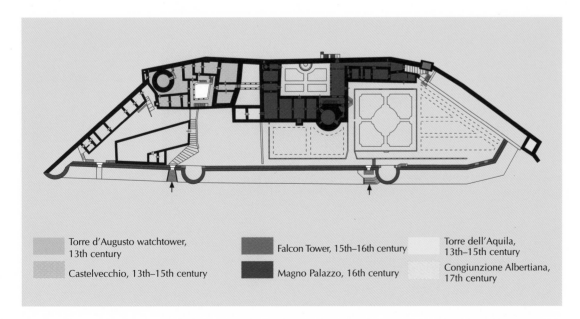

Plan of the irregular complex.

The Magno Palazzo takes up the center of the plan, with the Castelvecchio, the oldest part of the building, on its left. Gardens were laid out along the town side of the site relatively early on in its history.

Torre d'Augusto watchtower, 13th century

Castelvecchio, 13th–15th century

Falcon Tower, 15th–16th century

Magno Palazzo, 16th century

Torre dell'Aquila, 13th–15th century

Congiunzione Albertiana, 17th century

Left: The great semicircular tower built into the Magno Palazzo.

Opposite top:
The small Gothic loggia with its trefoils looking out onto the town was knocked into the wall at the instigation of Prince-Bishop Johann Hinderbach in the 1470s. Never besieged during its history, Castelvecchio was no longer required to function in its defensive capacity; all the architectural work done on it during the 15th century was purely for the purpose of turning the fortress into a palatial residence.

Opposite bottom:
View of the facade of the Castelvecchio showing the position of Hinderbach's Venetian Gothic loggia.

Following pages:
Dosso Dossi
Fresco, 1536
Magno Palazzo
Castel del Buonconsiglio, Trento

Chapel vestibule painted by Dosso Dossi, who had formerly worked at the court of Ferrara and was strongly influenced by Giorgione and Raphael.

## Dosso Dossi

Katrin Boskamp-Prievier

Sons of a native of Trento, the real names of Dosso Dossi (*c.* 1489–1542) and his younger brother Battista (1490/95–1548) were Giovanni and Battista di Niccolò de Lutero. They took their alias from the domicile of their father, the Villa Dossi near Mantua. Dosso Dossi was heavily influenced by Giorgione and Raphael and worked for a long period at the court of the Este family in Ferrara, which had a glittering cultural life very similar to that of the

Dosso Dossi
Fresco, 1536
Magno Palazzo, Castel del Buonconsiglio, Trento

A figure in a spandrel from the frescoes painted by Dosso Dossi in the chapel vestibule of the Magno Palazzo, the decoration of which was completed in 1536. The tiny cherub spreads out his arms in a gesture of goodwill.

French courts of Provence. Dosso Dossi is recorded as having been in Ferrara as early as 1514, having possibly been referred to the Este court by the Gonzaga family in Mantua, where Dosso is known to have been in 1512. By 1531, when Dosso and Battista Dossi were commissioned to work on the Magno Palazzo or Palazzo Clesiano by Cardinal Bernardo Clesio, they were counted among the top

masters of the Ferrara school of the 16th century and had a long career as fresco painters and interior decorators behind them. Their artwork adorned the villas and palaces of the Renaissance rulers of northern Italy, among them the ducal palaces in Ferrara and Modena. Under contract to Francesco Maria I della Rovere, the duke of Urbino, the brothers designed the interior of the Villa Imperiale

near Pesaro, where Agnolo Bronzino and Raffaele dal Colle also worked. In Trento, too, a number of major artists were busy with the embellishment of the palace interior. The frescoes on the vaults in the atrium and loggia and the artwork on the marble staircase were done by Girolamo Romanino. The tower room was festooned with frescoes by Marcello Fogolino. In the linking passageway Battista Dossi covered the ceilings with paintings of the Olympic gods. The heavy coffered ceiling in the Sala Grande is the work of Dosso Dossi; between a painted plinth and ledge Dosso has created illusionist architecture with plump cherubs and clouds dancing across a blue sky. He filled the Camera degli Scarlatti with painted busts of Roman emperors and the library with ancient philosophers and scholars.

Dosso Dossi
Fresco, 1536
Magno Palazzo, Castel del Buonconsiglio, Trento

The frescoes on the coffered ceiling of the library in the Magno Palazzo are also by Dosso Dossi. The great scholars of the ancient world are interspersed between the cherubs.

## Bernardo Clesio

Bernardo Clesio, who was elected bishop of Trento at the age of 29, was a major player in the Europe of the first half of the 16th century. He came from an ancient family of government officials. His father Hildebrand had been a councilor in Vienna; his mother, Dorothea Fuchs of Fuchsberg, gave birth to 13 children: nine boys and four girls. Bernardo first studied rhetoric as a lay bishop in Verona, then jurisprudence in Bologna. He was unanimously voted bishop by the cathedral chapter in Trento in 1514. This marked the beginning of a brilliant political career.

After the death of Maximilian of Habsburg in 1519, Clesio was one of the party of scholars that wanted to see Charles V crowned emperor. Working on the legal issue of how the royal inheritance should be divided, Clesio was one of the most entrusted advisers to Charles and his brother Ferdinand, and thus played a decisive role in establishing the Austrian line of the

Habsburg dynasty. Clesio became Ferdinand's consultant in diplomatic and financial matters. He upheld relations between the House of Habsburg and its main financial backers, the Fugger family of bankers. He held the top posts in Vienna: councilor to the court, chairman of the court council and privy councilor. In addition to his senior secular posts, he was promoted to cardinal in 1530 at the instigation of Charles V.

When Pope Clement VII died in 1534, the emperor and his brother, the archduke of Austria, tried to bring Clesio into play in the election of the next pontiff. The Fuggers provided the royals with 100,000 ducats to help influence the decision of the conclave. Their attempts were unsuccessful, however; with France behind him, Alessandro Farnese (Paul III) was proclaimed the new Holy Father. Later, Clesio was to prove an indispensable adviser to the pope, particularly during the Wars of Religion. The prince-bishop

Girolamo Romanino
*Portrait of Cardinal Bernardo Clesio, c.* 1532
Fresco
Sala delle Udienze, Magno Palazzo, Castel del Buonconsiglio, Trento

The fresco by Girolamo Romanino (*c.* 1484–*c.* 1559) from Brescia, who was greatly influenced by Giorgione and Titian, is in the entrance to the audience chamber. It shows Cardinal Bernardo Clesio writing one of his dreaded letters.

had very strong views on the Protestant Reformation. He believed that it was necessary to counter the reform movement with a crusade, in which he believed all the great powers of Europe should participate. Clesio was also one of the very first advocates of an anti-Protestant council. The new pope made him a member of a commission that would prepare a bull convening such a council. When the bull was issued in 1536 Clesio said the grand opening prayer. However, it took much longer to set up the council than was originally thought and Clesio was unable to witness its completion. He died on July 30, 1539.

Clesio's diverse political, religious and financial activities kept him away from his episcopal palace and diocese. Yet he imposed a stern rule from afar, managing his affairs through his dreaded letters. In May 1525, when the Peasants' War began spreading to Tyrol and the area around Trento, Clesio returned home to make a stand against the farmers. He showed no mercy in his dealing with the insurgents, executing them by the dozen months after the rebellion had been ruthlessly crushed. Clesio kept a constant eye on the construction of the Magno Palazzo at Trento, which was to be on a par with the greatest courts in Europe, following the project in the tiniest detail from his distant abodes. He chose the artists who worked on the palace personally. The costs, estimated to have reached 10,000 Rhenish guilders in 1527, were six times this amount by 1533. In 1531 Clesio wrote a letter to his master builder, claiming that with the money which had already been consumed a high building could have been erected in Vienna "similar to those with many bulwarks, towers, ditches and other almost unbelievable fixtures currently in fashion, and not as much is spent on these as will be spent on our damnable building." In the end it wasn't the money but the time his new palace was taking to be built that finally made Clesio lose patience. It looked as if the Magno Palazzo might not be finished in time for the visit of Archduke Ferdinand and his new wife, scheduled for September 1536. On July 12 Clesio wrote to his chief architects: "as you show yourselves to be so slipshod in carrying out our contract, we will speak with each of you personally as to this additional negligence and to your past carelessness, and it would surely have been better if you had never received this commission." By the end of August everything was completely finished.

Bernardo Clesio' s coat of arms in the ceiling outside the chapel.

Girolamo Romanino
Fresco (detail)
Castel del Buonconsiglio, Trento

This fresco, which was also painted by Girolamo Romanino in 1532, depicts one of the daily occurrences on the building site of the Magno Palazzo. A higher official is paying two laborers their wages. The paymaster in his elegant robes and large feather hat, a bored and rather absent expression on his face, listens as the two laborers, obviously dissatisfied with their pay, plead their case.

Master Wenceslas
*Cycle of the Months*, April to
June, *c.* 1400–1407
Fresco
Torre dell'Aquila,
Castelvecchio, Castel del
Buonconsiglio, Trento

On the second floor of the
tower, in the private
chambers of Prince-Bishop
George of Liechtenstein, is
the *Cycle of the Months*
fresco painted by Master
Wenceslas in the first decade
of the 15th century. Country
folk and the nobility are
shown engaging in typical
activities for each month of
the year. A banner gives the
signs of the zodiac in their
positions relative to the sun.

## The World in a Single Room

Clemente Manenti and Katrin Boskamp-Priever

Along the top of the town wall which adjoins all the various buildings of the Castello del Buonconsiglio is an old wall-walk leading to the Torre dell'Aquila. The walk, accessible from what used to be Bernardo Clesio's private apartments, has been roofed over and turned into a long, narrow corridor. It takes you straight to the room on the second floor of the tower that houses the *Cycle of the Months* fresco by Bohemian artist Master Wenceslas. This cycle is the sole remnant of the sumptuously decorated private chambers that George I of Liechtenstein, the bishop of Trento, had installed in the eagle tower. George came from the Austrian-Moravian noble family of

Liechtenstein-Nikolsburg and was born at Neuspaur Castle in south Tyrol in 1360. In 1377 he enrolled at the University of Vienna and in 1381 was made dean of the Cathedral of St. Stephen in the same city. In 1390 he went to Rome as an envoy. His election as bishop of Trento by the cathedral chapter in 1390, probably heavily supported by Duke Albrecht III, was followed by a period of office marred by tension between the bishop, his diocese and his vassals. His reign was terminated when George was sent back to Vienna in 1407. The *Cycle of the Months* must thus have been painted during this period.

The passageway leading to the tower seems to have been erected with the purpose of preparing visitors for the surprise which awaits them there. Those who enter feel as if

Master Wenceslas
*Cycle of the Months* (detail),
April, *c.* 1400–1407
Fresco
Torre dell'Aquila,
Castelvecchio, Castel del
Buonconsiglio, Trento

The months April and May
heralded the start of work out
in the fields for the farming
community.

Master Wenceslas
*Cycle of the Months* (detail),
May, *c.* 1400–1407
Fresco
Torre dell'Aquila,
Castelvecchio, Castel del
Buonconsiglio, Trento

The spring month of May
was enjoyed by the nobility,
who sang and played games
in the fresh air.

they have reached the very top of the building, and not just the second floor, standing under an open sky with a fictitious landscape stretching out before them. Pictures cover all four walls. Thin, spiraling pillars divide the frescoes into sections illustrating scenes from life at court and the various chores of the peasant community for each month of the year. Allegorical depictions in cyclic form such as these were common in the Middle Ages. Although the content of these frescoes was usually more or less identical, interesting discrepancies between them are noticeable, possibly due to differing climates, indicating that the artists attempted to create a realistic reproduction of their environment.

In Buonconsiglio the paint on the third month of March has peeled away where the spiral staircase enters the room; the fresco was probably destroyed when the stairs were rebuilt. The cyclic panorama is thus incomplete. The blue sky in all of the pictures, reminiscent of the sheet-like sky backgrounds of Bohemian art, has a blazing sun for all of the seasons. A banner inscribed with golden Gothic lettering gives the astronomical positions and signs of the zodiac that the sun passes through. Against a scenic backdrop true to the principles of medieval representation, where proportions are not realistic but joined in narrative unity, are the main figures which bring the picture to life.

211

Master Wenceslas
*Cycle of the Months* (detail),
July, *c.* 1400–1407
Fresco
Torre dell'Aquila,
Castelvecchio, Castel del
Buonconsiglio, Trento

July was the month in
which the farmers had
to cut the hay.

Master Wenceslas
*Cycle of the Months* (detail),
July, *c.* 1400–1407
Fresco
Torre dell'Aquila,
Castelvecchio, Castel del
Buonconsiglio, Trento

The nobleman spent his July
trying to win the favors of his
sweetheart.

The cycle begins to the left of the entrance and follows the pattern of the months of the year. January is a time of winter fun, with a snowball fight taking place between people who are evidently aristocratic ladies and gentlemen. The peasants' hunt is a more serious affair. The February scene is painted around a window and shows a tournament.

Underneath, pigs are being slaughtered, a typical winter motif that features in many medieval depictions of the months and cycles of the year. Opposite the entrance, April and May herald the arrival of spring. This signals the start of the toil in the fields for the farmers; in the extremely varied, serene landscape we see peasants sowing the land, plowing the fields and breaking up the soil. Oxen or horses tug the plows through the ground. We can also observe the gallant merrymaking of courtly nobles in their lush floral paradise. Against a colorful backdrop of flowers and blossom, knights and their ladies take a leisurely stroll, profess their love, admiration and affection for one another and engage in scholarly debate. In June the farmers are extremely busy tending their livestock and mowing their meadows. The aristocracy, brightly dressed in the latest elegant fashions with long drop sleeves, have time to amuse themselves and promenade through the grounds. For the hardworking peasants life is very different; July sees them making hay, hunting and fishing. In August and

September the nobility pursue the sport of falconry and October is spent harvesting and pressing the grapes. November is the month of the dangerous bear hunt and in inhospitable December the farmers cart off the wood they have cut or collected to sell it in town.

With great attention to detail the artist has placed his figures in a colorful, fairytale world of forests, craggy hills, castles, cities and a multitude of animals and plants. A fundamental strain of inequality runs through these pictures. The peasants are portrayed stooped low over the soil: digging, hoeing, sowing, gathering and harvesting. They are probably serfs, people destined to spend their lives engaged in hard physical labor. Even in the months where work in the fields was scarce there was wood to chop or collect and tie into bundles for transportation. Whatever chores these people are engaged in, they are always shown in pairs and bent double, their heads covered to protect them from the burning sun; their simple clothes, squat figures, sturdy limbs and rough faces characterize them as members of the lower classes. The lords and ladies of noble blood show no

sign whatsoever that they are aware of the frenetic activity going on around them. Whether on foot or on horseback, they are tall and slim and shrouded in soft, vibrant robes, engrossed in games, hunting or amorous dalliances or busy raising their successors. Here we see two completely

Above: The lives of the two classes are kept strictly separate in the various scenes.

Below: While the farmers were hard at work in the summer months, the nobility had time for leisurely strolls.

Master Wenceslas
*Cycle of the Months* (detail),
September, *c.* 1400–1407
Fresco
Torre dell'Aquila,
Castelvecchio, Castel del
Buonconsiglio, Trento

In September the aristocracy
devoted much of their time
to falconry.

different groups of people existing side by side, with no contact and apparently no conflict between them. Each person is in his or her right place and they all seem satisfied with their lot in life. This seemingly static world underlines the cosmic and divine order determined by a higher authority. Only once, during the celebration of the new wine, which here is also to be interpreted as a Christian symbol uniting all spheres of society, do the rich and poor, the upper and the lower classes, come together and intermix.

Although the fresco was completed in the early years of the 15th century, the theme and form of expression belong to the Middle Ages. It depicts an unchallenged world ordered by God, so to speak, where everyone accepts the place allotted to him and goes about his daily business – or pleasure – without question or complaint. This idyllic depiction of an almost autumnal, gentle, dreamy Middle Ages probably tarried well with George I's vision of the world, although it is puzzling when seen in the historical context of the ill-fated, not exactly joyful reign of the prince-bishop, now buried in the

cathedral in Trento. Without doubt, George I of Liechtenstein had found in Wenceslas an outstanding master of his trade to paint the frescoes. The cycle is a prime example of what has become known as the "soft" style or International Gothic of *c.* 1400. With brilliant skill and endearing naivety the artist portrays charming scenes of nature and of humans engaged in their daily chores with fresh, spring-like colors. In his seasonal depictions of work he demonstrates an astounding sense of realism. As in other works of this kind from the 15th century, here, too, the months of the Middle Ages are scenes full of figures which make up a generic landscape. Details such as the depiction of horses instead of cattle plowing the fields, the plants illustrated or the Gothic nature of the architecture, point to a northern Alpine origin and training. The master stuck to common models in his allocation of tasks to months, only deviating in his original scene of the bear hunt. Here, Wenceslas may have succumbed to the influence of Italian art during his time in Trento or before. The choice of topic, attention to detail and additive juxtaposition are sure

Master Wenceslas
*Cycle of the Months* (detail),
October, *c.* 1400–1407
Fresco
Torre dell'Aquila,
Castelvecchio, Castel del
Buonconsiglio, Trento

For the farmers, the autumn
months were devoted to
fishing, hunting and
harvesting and pressing the
grapes.

Master Wenceslas
*Cycle of the Months* (detail),
September to December,
*c.* 1400–1407
Fresco
Torre dell'Aquila,
Castelvecchio, Castel del
Buonconsiglio, Trento

Almost naive in its joy of
narration, the fresco
juxtaposes the bustling
activity of the peasants with
the leisurely pastimes of the
nobility. The world depicted
here, ordered by God and
the cosmic powers, is
unusual for the beginning of
the 15th century.

indications of the method of narration
favored by the Middle Ages; the fine brush-
work suggests an experienced illuminator and
miniaturist.

# Baron Cristoforo Madruzzo, Prince-Bishop of Trento and Lord of Castel del Buonconsiglio

Hartmut Diekmann

The stone mouth forms the entrance to the gardens of Bomarzo. The inscription "Every thought shall fly" entices the curious to step inside a wild botanical landscape and let the imagination run riot.

The Parco dei Mostri at Bomarzo on the border of Lazio and Umbria huddles beneath the imposing villa of the Orsini. After the death of his wife in 1557, Vicino Orsini sank into a deep depression and had his elegant gardens turned into a monstrous park haunted by bizarre figures and dark thoughts. The work was carried out by simple craftsmen from the surrounding countryside, once part of Etruria. Names of artists who contributed to the crazy project include the architect Vignola, the landscape gardener Michelangelo Jacobo del Duca, and the painter Taddeo Zuccari.

## The gardens of the underworld

In the gardens of Bomarzo, the Parco dei Mostri or "monster park" near Viterbo dating from the second half of the 16th century, wild spirits haunt the forests and follies. Bomarzo is a place of pilgrimage for artists past and present and was the creative paradise of the Surrealists of the 20th century. Visitors who dare to stay in the crooked house for more than a minute or two start to feel the world spin. Nothing is square; dizziness takes hold. If the more intrepid manage to stay long enough to decipher the inscription, they will read: "Calm will make my spirit wiser, thus (this house) is dedicated to Cristoforo Madruzzo, the prince of Trento." Above the crooked house an enormous stone mouth symbolizing the entrance to the kingdom of the dead yawns open. Above it is another saying in red: "Ogni pensiero vola," "every thought shall fly." Inside the cave is a table left by the stone-mason when he was hewing the monster's throat out of the rock. It is said that this table is where the aforementioned Cristoforo Madruzzo often sat with his host, Vicino Orsini, to talk about death and unhappiness. The year was 1566.

Vicino Orsini was married to Giulia Farnese, a member of a dynasty to which Pope Paul III belonged. Vicino was also very close to his cousin, Orazio Farnese. Not wanting to leave his friend to fight alone when conflict erupted between the French king and Emperor Charles V, Vicino accompanied his beloved cousin into battle and was forced to watch him die at his side. Vicino was taken prisoner, maltreated and tortured. As his good connections to the Holy See were worthless after the death of Pope Paul III in 1549, he was not released until 1557. When he returned home to Bomarzo, he found his wife, whom he loved

dearly, on her deathbed. He was overcome by melancholy and depression, shrouding everything about him in darkness. He turned his elegant gardens into a realm of morbid fascination. He chose the turtle as his spiritual companion on the journey to the kingdom of the dead. Weighed down to the ground by its heavy shell burden, the turtle seems to bear the seal of death in its Italian name, *tartaruga*, reminiscent of "Tartarus," the Greek underworld. His partner in darkness was his friend Cristoforo Madruzzo, whom he had met in 1546 on his way to meet Emperor Charles V as envoy of the pope. Vicino stayed in Trento *en route* and was the guest of the young baron. The meeting was not without its consequences for Madruzzo; in his years of mourning Orsini remembered his host in Trento and visited him again in 1557, later writing to him to ask him to come to Bomarzo.

This was a request that went beyond the bounds of friendship. It seems as if the disturbed Orsini was not quite clear as to the implications of his appeal. Cristoforo Madruzzo was much more than a kind neighbor. He had a brilliant career behind him and was at the pinnacle of his powers. Simply listing his various posts and qualifications sheds light on just how outrageous Orsini's plea was.

## The friend

Cristoforo Madruzzo was born on July 5, 1512, in Calavino, Trentino province. At the age of 17 he was parish priest of Tyrol, in 1534 canon of Augsburg, in 1535 canon of Trento, in 1536 canon of Salzburg and in 1537 canon of Bressanone. And this was just the beginning. In 1539 he was made bishop of Trento, in 1540 imperial prince and in 1542 cardinal and administrator of Bressanone. He had his portrait painted by Titian during this period. In 1545 he was host to the opening of the Council of Trent. In 1550 he was coadjutant to the archbishop of Salzburg and in 1551 again host to the Council. In 1556 Emperor Charles V made him governor of Milan. In 1560 he became a cardinal of the Curia, in 1561 bishop of Alba and in 1562 bishop of Sabina. In 1564 he received the title of bishop of Preneste and in 1570 that of cardinal-bishop of Porto. People said he collected bishoprics as others collected coins.

Tiziano Vecellio
*Cristoforo Madruzzo*, 1552
Oil on canvas,
210 × 109 cm
Museu de Arte São Paulo –
Assis Chateaubriand,
São Paulo

Baron Cristoforo Madruzzo, born of a German mother and Italian father and thus raised in two languages and cultures, made an astonishing career for himself after studying in Bologna. When in 1566, at the age of 54, he received a letter from his old friend Vicino Orsini calling him to Bomarzo, he had earned a reputation for collecting bishoprics like coins. He relinquished his ecclesiastical and political offices and moved to be near Orsini's villa.

His mother was German, Euphemia von Sporenberg. She taught her son her native language, and Madruzzo's Italian father instructed him in his. He built up a first-hand knowledge of Italian culture through his studies at the University of Bologna. He was very good at making friends with whom he stayed in close contact throughout his life. He himself felt he was something of a go-between, caught between the Germans and the Italians. An expert on the mentality and traditions of both nations, at the Council of Trent he was able to eloquently describe the quirks of the Italian character to the Germans and, especially, to explain the nature of the Germans to the Italians.

At the pinnacle of his career at the age of 54, this incredibly successful man received the letter from the lonely, disturbed Vicino Orsini. Madruzzo

Albrecht Dürer
*Castel del Buonconsiglio,*
*c.* 1494
Watercolor
The British Museum, London

Dürer painted his watercolor around 50 years before the first Council was held. The castle, here seen from the south, has lost much of its sinister character.

Sebastiano del Piombo
*Clement VII, c.* 1526
Oil on canvas, 145 × 100 cm
Museo Nazionale di
Capodimonte, Naples

Pope Clement VII was one of the people who feared the Reformers less than a pending Council and the political and internal ecclesiastical unrest that would undoubtedly follow in its wake. He thus did nothing to promote the convening of the assembly.

made an astounding decision; he gave up his ecclesiastical offices and titles, even his position as imperial prince, and handed them over to his nephew Lodovico Madruzzo. He was made a cardinal of the Curia in Rome and, retaining most of his Church posts in Italy, he moved to Soriano a few miles from Bomarzo. Various hypotheses were put forward to explain why he gave up his international offices; one was that they were no longer able to satisfy him as he had failed to attain the highest position in the Church: that of pope. Another was that he had not been particularly successful as administrator of Milan. And finally, despite great effort on his part, he had not been successful in being nominated legate by the pope.

Cristoforo met with unanimous admiration, however, in his role as host of the Council of Trent. He ran up frighteningly high debts in order to give his guests a special welcome and ensure that they wanted for nothing. Educated, eloquent, a man of luxury, great compassion and yet of driving ambition, Bishop Madruzzo was the best possible "front man" for the Council. He was the perfect embodiment of German excess and Italian finesse and courteousness. The papal legates were overwhelmed when at Easter in 1545 he threw an inaugural banquet in their honor. According to one contemporary estimate it consisted of 74 courses,

a feat which earned him the nickname "Grand Gourmet." He liked to present himself dressed as the prince he was, his red bishop's miter the sole indication of his religious office. His seat of residence, Castello del Buonconsiglio, was also a place of regal opulence – although some Council delegates would have preferred to be received with slightly less elaborate episcopal honors.

On one occasion the papal legate himself felt it necessary to curb the prince-bishop's worldly overabundance. Madruzzo had invited the bishops present at the Council to a wedding celebration for one of the local nobles. When the time came for the bridal dance, he asked the bishops if they would like to open the round together with the newlyweds. At the last minute the papal legate was compelled to intervene.

## The Council of Trent: struggling to be born

The Council took its time in coming together. Since the start of the Reformation 28 precious years had passed during which it might have been possible to unite the divided Church. For several years it had even been believed that the Reformation, which had started in 1517 in Germany, was a reform

Claudy
*The Council of Trent,* 1565
Copper engraving

28 years passed before the pope finally called the Council of Trent in 1545 after securing the agreement of Emperor Charles V. At the outset the number of participants was so small that the inauguration should have been postponed. Yet those present were all well aware of the fact that the voices calling for reform within the Church had become almost deafening.

movement within the Roman Catholic Church and would not lead to a permanent split in the Church. When it became obvious that this was not so, the need for reform from within became more and more pressing, to strengthen the Catholic Church to the point where it could fight back against the gains of Protestantism. However, for a number of reasons, most of them political and/or national, many of those involved were reluctant to get the Council off the ground. Even Pope Clement VII (1523–1534) was one of the many who feared a council more than he feared the Lutherans themselves. He is quoted as saying: "A few drunken Germans will throw the Council and the entire world into confusion. But let them! I shall flee to the mountains and then the Council can elect a new pope, no, a dozen, for each nation will want its own." He undoubtedly also feared that the political quarrel between France and the House of Habsburg would dominate Council proceedings and lead to a split within Europe and the Christian world. Hemmed in by the empire of Charles V, with the kingdom of Naples to the south and Milan to the north, he saw himself as France's political ally, France looking for a way to liberate itself from the restrictive presence of Charles's neighboring estates in Spain and Germany. The Lutherans were just what Francis I needed to keep Emperor Charles occupied in Germany. Neither of these monarchs was interested in seeing the Council take place, and especially not on German soil as the German princes had demanded. Both would have been at the mercy of Charles V and would have run the danger of having to face the Lutherans who had reconciled themselves with the emperor. This would have signified an enormous triumph for the emperor. As if this wasn't enough, these potential problems were augmented by almost deafening calls for drastic reform of the Church, a topic which for over 100 years had been a major bone of contention. Clement VII, an illegitimate child who had become pope under dubious circumstances, did not want to come under the scrutiny of a stricter moral code imposed during a council. All this was reason enough for him to take no action whatsoever in the Council's favor. The Council and the preparations for it were to be constantly fueled by political calculation. Fear of reform led to greater and greater divisions within the Church.

Coat of arms of Pope Clement VII
Castel del Buonconsiglio, Trento

The pontificate of Pope Paul III (1534–1549) saw a change of heart towards the Council. He elected pro-reform cardinals onto the committee whose demands considerably exceeded what Rome considered acceptable. In a document entitled "Consilium de emendanda ecclesia" ("Suggestions for Improvements to the Church"), their spokesman, Cardinal Contarini, compiled 13 pages of reforms: from abuse of the papal office – the careless ordination of unsuitable bishops who accumulated numerous titles and offices and resided in Paris, Rome and Venice, leaving their flocks without a shepherd – to the spiritual neglect and waywardness of the clergy and their failure to honor the vow of celibacy. Not surprisingly, the Curia in Rome was not keen to heed his suggestions. Pope Paul IV even placed Contarini's draft reforms for the Church on his "Index of Prohibited Books."

## The rocky road to Trento

Many hoped that with the coming Council tensions would be resolved, Christendom reunited and the Church rigorously reformed from top to bottom. Charles V was determined that the Council should take place. He had gone to Rome in 1524 to raise the issue, only to be told it would be better if he did not actually mention the word "council." When the desire for reform was also clearly expressed by Cardinal Contarini in Rome, Charles tried to bring about a theological reunification of the Lutheran and Roman Catholic factions. He invited the parties to take part in a discussion in Regensburg in 1541. Here, the two groups managed to agree on the question of justification. They agreed that justification was "living faith, a faith exercised through charity." Opinions regarding the essence and significance of the Church and thus of the Communion, however, remained irreconcilable.

From then on Charles V pursued a clear, simple policy. He sought military victory over the Lutheran leaders so that he could force them to meet around the Council table on their defeat. There he wanted to make concessions to them regarding the administration of the chalice to the laity and the marriage of priests and hoped that in doing so he would be able to reunite the two sides. The Lutheran bishops, for their part, had told him in no uncertain terms that they would only join a council when the pope agreed to accept the authority of that council and reach decisions on the basis of the Holy Scriptures alone without deferring to any other authority. It was only when the Protestant princes actually walked out of the Council in 1552 voicing these arguments that Charles fully realized the political weight they carried.

In the meantime Protestantism had spread to Italy. Fears arose that a deep cleft would be driven through society. The Roman Curia believed that Germany should be left to the Protestants and that the Church should concentrate its efforts on saving the Latin countries of Italy and France from the onslaught of Lutheranism. If a council were to be held, then its main task should be to defend the Catholic Church. Reform would be a secondary concern.

Anonymous Swiss artist
*The Council of Trent – Meeting of the Church Assembly in Trento Cathedral*, 1769
Painted from a contemporary original

In later years the meetings of the Council included 100 delegates who were eligible to vote, 90% of whom were cardinals and bishops. The Roman Curia saw not reform but the defense of the Catholic Church as the main objective of the Council. Three papal legates decided which texts should be put up for discussion; the entire operation was thus controlled by the pope.

220

With the emperor's agreement a convention of the Council was scheduled for the year 1542, but it was evident that it would not be possible for it to go ahead until Charles V and Francis I signed their peace treaty, in 1544. Trento seemed a suitable site; it was not in Germany, where the French would have refused to go, but it was also not one of the Papal States, where the emperor would have refused to go. It lay within the Empire yet was an independent principality, ruled by the aforementioned Cristoforo Madruzzo. In the first half of the 16th century Trento had about 6,000 inhabitants and ample space to accommodate the 100 Council delegates and their entourages. The population was bilingual. The pope invited his guests to convene at the Council on March 15, 1545, but hardly anybody came. The opening was repeatedly postponed, because nobody could believe that the Council was actually going to take place. People were not prepared to risk undertaking the long journey to Trento from France or Spain only to find that the invitation had been a

bluff – and the German bishops did not dare leave their dioceses for fear of their falling into the hands of marauding Protestants.

## The opening

The number of participants present on December 13, 1545, was so small that the inauguration should have been postponed once again. Yet those responsible were well aware that if they didn't start now, the Council would never take off. A mere 25 archbishops and bishops paraded into Trento Cathedral with six heads of monastic orders. Those present were nearly all Italian or Spanish. The Spaniards were imperialists, full of confidence and extremely mistrustful of Rome. They expected the Council to make clear decisions pertaining to the reform of the Church. The Council log records frequent arguments, some of them violent, between the Spanish and the Italians. France had not sent any delegates because it believed the Council was pro-imperialist. The German princes had not come for the reasons given above.

Left: *Paul IV*
Contemporary copper engraving
Archiv für Kunst und Geschichte, Berlin

Pope Paul IV (1555–1559) placed the drafts of reforms for the Catholic Church on his "Index of Prohibited Books." He could only countenance reform if it came from above.

Right: Tobias Stimmer
*Gaspare Contarini*, 1575, from: P. Giovio, *Elogia virorum bellica virtute illustrium*, 1596
Woodcut
Archiv für Kunst und Geschichte, Berlin

Cardinal Contarini compiled his 13 pages of suggestions for the improvement of the Church entitled "Consilium de emendanda ecclesia" in 1537. Among the faults he found were abuse of the papal office, accumulation of titles and offices, spiritual neglect and waywardness and failure to honor the vow of celibacy.

221

Whereas earlier councils had been extremely well organized, in Trento no hard and fast points of procedure had been decided on in advance. The points of order, whether votes should be taken according to nation or private individual, whether the Council should concern itself with reform or instruction: all this had yet to be ascertained. What was clear was that the right to vote was granted only to the bishops, the heads of the monastic orders and the abbots. Parallel to the Council were meetings of what became known as the Theological Councils, where 50 to 100 theologians discussed the topics dealt with at the Council proper. Many of the ideas the theologians came up with filtered through to the consultations of the main Council delegates.

## Council delegates at work (session 1)

During its main meetings the Council eventually consisted of up to 100 delegates who were eligible to vote. Cardinals and bishops constituted the largest group at 90%. Six heads of the monastic orders and a few abbots completed the Council plenum. The theologians acted as consultants. The Council met as a plenary session or Congregation under the chairmanship of one of the three papal legates. They could exercise the authority of the pope, yet often had to seek his approval on certain matters, sending messengers hurrying off to Rome on time-consuming journeys.

Three sub-Congregations were formed. These prepared the most important points for discussion and decision and were chaired by one of the papal legates. They were advised by the theological Congregations of the various universities.

Finally, there were the deputations: delegations of Council members whose job it was to formulate the Council's decisions. These sub-Congregations and deputations failed to achieve the desired results, however, and in 1546 they were replaced by conferences of prelates and theologians.

As the Italians were in a clear majority, for a while the Council considered voting by nationality, as had been the practice at earlier councils.

Egnazio Danti
*Venetian Estates*
Fresco
Galleria delle Carte
Geografiche, Vatican

The map shows the hinterlands of Venice. The cities of Padua, Verona, Brescia, Cremona, Mantua and Trento are particularly well-pronounced.

ROLVS · MAGNVS · IMPERATOR · AVGVS

The Council was chaired by the three papal legates. They alone had the right to make suggestions. The pope thus determined which texts were presented to the assembly, vetoing those that were not to his liking. He could even decide when and where the Council convened. Discussions no longer took place in corridors or in the aisles of churches but in the meetings of the Congregation. The Council met at either San Vigilio Cathedral or the church of Santa Maria Maggiore. The raised choir was segregated from the nave, providing the Council with a secluded place to work. On hot

The fresco in Castel del Buonconsiglio makes references to Charlemagne. Under the battle scene the cardinals of the Council are presented in an even row.

223

Tiziano Vecellio,
*Charles V at Mühlberg*, 1548
Oil on canvas, 332 × 279 cm
Museo del Prado, Madrid

After a decisive defeat of the
Protestants at the Battle of
Mühlberg Emperor Charles V
wanted to force the
Lutherans to attend the
Council. His plans were
foiled when Pope Paul III
decided to move the Council
to papal territory in Bologna.

summer days delegates convened to the crypt. Council documents also show that meetings were held at the castle of Prince-Bishop Madruzzo.

Many attempts were made to hinder the Council in its work or influence its proceedings. The fact that they were chaired by a total of four different popes did not ease the difficulty of the delegates' task. Pope Paul IV, for example, could only envisage a reform of the Church if it came from the top, which is why the Council did not convene under his pontificate.

In its first session from 1545 to 1547 the Council managed to reach decisions on the subjects of justification, original sin and the Eucharist. It thus succeeded in its capacity as an instructive body; as a vehicle of reform, however, it failed on several counts. It was not able, for example, to reach an agreement on whether a bishop should be obliged

to reside in his diocese or not. The problem was formulated in such a way that the Council had to decide whether the bishops were appointed by the pope or were granted their episcopal powers directly by God. In the first instance the bishop was a higher Church functionary and member of a mobile class. In the second, the bishops were seen as shepherds tending their flocks, a vocation in which even the pope himself could not intervene. Here, the Council elegantly sidestepped the central issue – bringing about a reduction in apostolic power.

The reform bishops tried time and again to put an end to the popes' arbitrary appointment of men of the Church. The Holy Fathers, in their persistent and outrageous nominations of totally unsuitable candidates, provided their critics with plenty of ammunition. As soon as Pius IV ascended to the Holy See, for example, he named his 22-year-old nephew Charles Borromeo archbishop of Milan, although the young man wasn't ordained a priest until three years later. This appointment nevertheless proved to be a prudent choice for the Church in the long run; Julius III's appointment of his monkey trainer as cardinal in later years, however, once again underlined the ailing state of the Renaissance papacy.

In 1547 the first session of the Council ended with Paul III's authoritarian decision to move the assembly to Bologna and thus to papal territory. Isolated cases of typhoid fever provided him with a convenient excuse for his actions. In Germany the emperor had just secured a military victory over the Protestants at the Battle of Mühlberg. The chances were good that the Lutherans could be forced to attend the Council in Trento; getting them to papal Bologna would, however, prove impossible. Emperor Charles V was livid, and forbade his delegates to travel to Bologna. In Trento, Cristoforo Madruzzo was also beside himself with rage. Other participants also found their stay in Bologna less than pleasant, the city being nowhere near as hospitable as Trento under its magnanimous prince-bishop. Many longed for the Council to revert to its original venue

### A hiccup in the proceedings (session 2)

During the pontificate of Julius III (1550–1555) the second session of the Council took place under the papal legate of the first, Cardinal del Monte. The second session was also attended by the German electors of Brandenburg and Saxony, the dukes of Württemberg and the free imperial city of Salzburg. Yet they announced that they were to participate only if discussions rested on the basis of the Holy Scriptures. Charles V's interest in the continuation of the Council had waned noticeably when in 1552 Duke Maurice of Saxony joined forces with the king of France and attacked the emperor in Innsbruck. The Council gladly interpreted this as a sign that it should disband, and did so of its own accord.

After the death of Julius III and the brief 21-day pontificate of Marcellus II, in 1555 Giovanni Piero Carafa was elected Pope Paul IV. He believed that reform was possible without a council. His reforms came from above – from the Vatican itself – and included intensifying the activity of the Inquisition, to whom the former papal legate of the first Council session, Cardinal Pole, and later the savior of the Council, Cardinal Morone, fell victim, prisoners for many years in the Castel Sant' Angelo in Rome.

In his fight to counter the Reformation Paul IV constantly undertook new measures against the Jews. On his orders Cardinal Contarini's

"Consilium de emendanda ecclesia" was placed on the "Index of Prohibited Books." In 1559 the duke of Alba marched into the Vatican City and brought the pontificate of Paul IV to a quiet end.

## Conclusion (session 3)

The final session of the Council took place under very different conditions. Pope Pius IV (1559–1565) was determined that the Council

Above:
Lucas Cranach the Younger
*Elector Maurice of Saxony and His Wife Agnes*, 1559
Oil on wood, 44 × 69 cm
Gemäldegalerie Alte Meister, Dresden

The electors of Brandenburg and Saxony also took part in the second session of the Council of Trent chaired by Julius III.

Left: Venetian artist
*Illustration of the 23rd Meeting of the Council of Trent in S. Virspilio Cathedral on 15 July 1563*, second half of the 16th century
Oil on canvas, 117 × 176 cm
Musée du Louvre, Paris

In 1563 the Council assembled prematurely for its final meetings. Pressured by the forthcoming papal elections, topics such as indulgence and purgatory were treated superficially. The Council closed at the end of 1563.

Opposite:
André Pieyre de Mandiargues writes that there are people who would have liked to shroud the cruel and potentially erotic monsters of Bomarzo in darkness. He also says that in chaos – and with the aid of nature – there have been places of truly strange beauty created at the hands of man and that the valley of Bomarzo is one of these. Scholars have often puzzled as to the purpose of Bomarzo; perhaps it was designed as a backdrop for the balls or mysteries of the Renaissance. Maybe, however, it was merely a reflection of the dark thoughts harbored by the extremely sensitive and melancholy Vicino Orsini.

should continue to meet. Charles V had abdicated (1556), the Empire and Spain were no longer an item, Ferdinand I reigned in Austria and Philip II in Spain. In France the Calvinists were gaining ground; the government was threatening to hold a national council at which they wanted to come to an understanding with the Calvinists. England was lost to the heathens as far as the Catholic Church was concerned. In Germany Protestantism had been legally recognized at the Peace of Augsburg (1555); German Catholicism had been completely subdued. Contemporary Italian reports make the following observation: "The Protestants are wide awake, the Catholics asleep; one has the impression that they – and not the Protestants – think belief will prevail without action, so little do they do to prevent the collapse of the Catholic religion in Germany."

On January 18, 1562, the Council convened once again. On November 19, 1560, the pope had pronounced 1562 a holy year in Rome in order to get the proceedings off to a good start. He proclaimed the following Wednesday, Friday and Saturday fast days, ending in Communion on the Saturday. The faithful were asked to pray that divine grace may sink into the hearts of the Lutherans that they might recognize their erroneous ways. When the cardinals and bishops paraded ceremoniously into Trento two inscriptions hung above the triumphal arch: "Blessed is he who comes in the name of the Lord" and "To the restorers of Christian unity." Prince-Bishop Cristoforo Madruzzo had had the banners installed in the hope that he could point the clerics towards religious unification. Yet it was far too late for that. Issues of Church reform were the focal point of the arguments in this session of the Council. Events had proved that to date absolutely nothing had been achieved with regard to the question of residency. The French, who had sent a large delegation to the Council, had insisted that the bishops should only be appointed by the grace of God. Their opponents, particularly the Italians and the Curia, wanted this to remain the prerogative of the pope.

In a preliminary vote those in favor of ordination by the right of God doubled those backing the pope. Counting the vast number of abstainers, however, the latter outnumbered the former. The decision rested with the pope, who, as if to make matters worse, forbade any further discussion on the subject. Unfortunately that was not all he did. True to form the pontiff made cardinals of a

14-year-old and a 16-year-old from the Medici and Gonzaga families. He also bestowed the office of bishop on two cardinals he knew would never actually reside in their own dioceses. Motivation among the pro-reformers reached an all-time low. The French demanded that bishops be elected by the clerics and the people, as was the procedure in the early Church. The sides were only appeased and the necessary majority ensured thanks to the outstanding diplomatic skill of the new legate of the Council, Cardinal Giovanni Morone. The cathedral chapter, the king and the pope were now obliged to confer on the candidates proposed for a prospective career in religious office.

When in December 1563 the Council assembled prematurely for what was to be its last meeting, delegates numbered 206, two-fifths of the possible maximum. Speed was of the essence, as Rome feared that the pope would soon die and wanted to avoid a situation where the Council might elect a new pope while in session. Topics such as indulgence and purgatory, both of which held particular significance for popular religious belief, were thus treated superficially. At the end of 1563, the Council of Trent closed shop for the last time.

## Remembering an old friend

With the delegates gone, one man was left behind: the duke of Trento, who had sacrificed much of his wealth in his role as host. On several occasions he had been forced to turn to the Curia, his funds exhausted by his generous hospitality. Once the ecclesiastical world had moved on, Trento reverted to what it had been before the religious jamboree: a small town and stop-off point on routes north and south. Madruzzo now had time to ponder one of the many positive aspects of his character which had stood him in good stead all his life. For 20 years his role as host of the Council had required that he neglect his ability to be a good friend. The letter from the devastated Vicino Orsini reminded him of his greatest passion. He gave up all the offices and titles he held outside Italy and moved to be near Bomarzo. He dedicated himself to new thoughts and ideas: the dark visions of his friend and his own visions of a giddy past, full of images of sumptuous living and painful defeat.

# The Coastal Region and the Islands

# Genoa

## The fortress in the hills

Previous page: Genoa is surrounded by 19 castles and many small fortresses. Sperone Castle is situated at the most strategically important point above the city, in the Apennine foothills which surround the harbor basin.

### The longest walls in Italy

Genoa's walls do not surround the city, but have been constructed on the mountain ridge behind it. They form two sides of an enormous triangle, the third side being formed by the Gulf of Genoa and the coastline. The walls are a total of eight miles (13 km) in

Above: Sperone Castle. At 1,650 feet (502 m) above sea level, the castle looms over the city and harbor. It is an imposing complex of buildings on three levels, enclosed in a ring of walls. The enclosed fortified area is over 2.5 acres (10,000 m²), of which about a third is built on.

Right: Diamante Castle

length, with a number of strongholds at the most important points. The whole construction is a comprehensive defense system comprising 19 main castles and numerous small fortresses, which protect the city and its extensive hinterland. This walled boundary joins a line of much older watchtowers, some of which still stand. These watchtowers were placed along the coast of two Rivieras: the Riviera di Ponente, which ends in Ventimiglia, and the Riviera de Levante, which extends as far as La Spezia and Sarzana. Genoa's walls are thus a late work,

GENVA
MARITIMAE·LIGVRIAE·CAPVT
NAVALIS·MILITIAE·STVDIO
ET·CIVIVM·VIRTVTE
ATQVE·OPVLENTIA
IN·CLYTA
MVNITISSIMIS·NVPER
EXAEDIFICATIS·MOENIBVS
TVTAM
CLARISSIMAE·REIPVBLICAE
SEDE·PRAEBET

having been started in 1629 and finished 20 years later. The castles that already existed were altered radically to fit into the new defensive system, and during the 18th century new ones were built.

## At the edge of the world

Genoa is a very old city, having flourished even in pre-Roman times. At that time the city traded intensively with the Etruscans and the Greeks. In the 8th century B.C. the Greek poet Hesiod described Genoa as the "last city at the edge of the world." At the time of the Punic Wars Genoa was conquered and ruled by Rome, and its destruction by Hannibal and the Carthaginians in 205 B.C. was an act of reprisal directed against Rome.

For the Romans, the conquest of the Ligurian hinterland proved more problematic. From their strategically placed villages and towns, the inhabitants waged a terrible guerilla war on the Roman legions that had to pass through Liguria on their way to Gaul. In an attempt to pacify the region, the Romans carried out mass deportations of the Ligurian people near Benevento in 180 B.C., sending them to Campagna. They also built two large new roads in Liguria: the Postumia, which ran from Genoa down to the plain of the River Po across the Apennines, and the Aemilia Scauri, a continuation of the Via Aurelia on the Tyrrhenian coast.

## The seaside republic

In 641, during the Gothic Wars, the ancient Roman walls of Genoa were destroyed. The walls from the late Middle Ages later fell victim to the Saracens, who seized possession of the city in 925. In 1155 the inhabitants of the city erected a new wall to protect it from the depredations of Frederick Barbarossa, who was waging war against the Lombard cities. Genoa's first chronicler, Caffaro, described the haste with which the people tackled this work: "Men and women, who worked unceasingly day and night, dragged stones and sand so that in only eight days these walls were seen to shoot upwards. No other city would have achieved this." These walls were later improved and strengthened in order to keep up with the rapid development of the city.

## The last leap

At the beginning of the 16th century new walls were built around the city in the shape of a horseshoe. After several decades they turned out to be useless; not because Genoa suddenly found it had no enemies, but because the walls were obsolete from the beginning.

The development of firearms forced the city of Genoa, situated between sea and mountains, to completely revolutionize its defense technology. This was because an attacker only had to occupy a few of the surrounding hills to be able to launch an attack on the city. If the walls were to offer protection, they had to be moved to the mountain ridge. This was duly done in 1629.

Opposite:
Egnazio Dante
*General View of Genoa*
(detail)
Fresco
Galleria delle Carte Geografiche, Musei Vaticani, Rome

A bird's-eye view of Genoa clearly shows its unique location: like an elongated triangle, the mountain foothills encompass the seaport. In the foreground two warships, equipped with cannons and a full crew, draw attention to Genoa's military strength.

Left: Diamante Castle.

This is the northernmost, highest castle, 2197 feet (670 m) above sea-level, and it lies the farthest away from Genoa, deep in the mountains behind the city. It is situated in a strategically important position, from which access to the city could be controlled. Diamante was built in the middle of the 18th century, in an historical context that was completely different to the one that led to the construction of the walls. In 1800 the castle was besieged by Austrian troops fighting the Napoleonic Wars, and was successfully defended by the French.

Bottom: Cristoforo Grassi
*View of Genoa*, 1481
Oil on canvas
Museo Civico Navale Genoa

Located between the two Rivieras on the gulf, Genoa was, along with Venice, a major maritime power during the 15th and 16th centuries in particular. This gave rise to continuous hostility between the two rivals.

## The Women's Crusade

Above:
Gratian
*Decretum Gratiani*:
Miniature of the chapter on marriage, around 1530
Illumination on parchment, 485 × 295 mm
British Library, London

In the year 1300 the women of Genoa announced their intention to go on a crusade, not only for religious reasons, but also to safeguard the wealth of the city. As a maritime power, Genoa lived on wars. Thousands of children from Germany, Switzerland and France had gone ahead of the women on their own crusade. They had stopped off in Genoa on their way to the Holy Land, in the hope that the sea would part in front of them. The Children's Crusade was handed down the generations in the form of the legend of the Pied Piper of Hamelin.

Towards the end of 1300 something very unusual happened in Genoa. A group of the city's noblewomen, some of whom belonged to the Guelphic faction and some to the rival Ghibellines, buried their differences and joined forces to collect money to finance a crusade to the Holy Land. This was at a time when the crusading movement was at its lowest ebb.

For more than a century, Jerusalem's Holy Sepulcher had been in Muslim hands. The most important territorial defensive posts in the Middle East had been lost. Not only six large crusades, but also a myriad smaller crusades, had failed miserably. The orders of knights that had taken part in the Crusades turned to frenzied profiteering, openly competing with each other. The crusading movement fell into a state of economic and military anarchy, which led eventually to the bloody annihilation of the Templars. Christendom was reduced to the state where it had to pin its hopes for retaking the Holy Land on the barbarous Mongols. This was the sorry situation during the papacy of Pope Boniface VIII.

The pope, for his part, had found a new way to assert the Church's temporal dominance and fill the Vatican coffers at the same time: the jubilee. It was easier and more lucrative to bargain with the souls of living and dead Christians, than it was to hold on to the dream of an armed reconquest of Jerusalem.

But the Genoese women's crusade would not be satisfied with merely whipping up enthusiasm and collecting money. The women were determined to undertake the journey to the Middle East themselves. Some had even had suits of armor made for themselves, several of which are now exhibited in the Royal Armory of Turin. It is evident that the suits have never been worn, however.

### The courageous women of Genoa

Even in antiquity the women of Genoa had been regarded as exceptional. Hesiod, Herodotus and Pausanias described the Ligurians as skillful and quick, as bold seafarers and strong warriors. Diodorus Sikulus described them in some detail: "they live modestly, are accustomed to trials and tribulations, and work. They cross the Sardinian and African seas and, in doing so, brave every danger. Their women are like them, strong, agile and as brave as wild animals." Many centuries later, in the 1430s and 1440s, the Catalan traveler Pero Tafur described the Ligurian women as large, nimble and dark-skinned. According to Tafur, the larger a Genoese woman was, the smaller her dowry. Although their husbands were frequently away for long periods of time, these women remained faithful, Tafur said. As they had to cope with living on their own at times, they were capable of anything, even a crusade.

### The children from Germany

In the year 1212 Genoa was one of the great intermediate stops of the Children's Crusade. Having set off from Cologne along the course of the Rhine, thousands of children between the ages of ten and 17 crossed Switzerland and at long last arrived in Genoa. They firmly believed that the sea would part as they marched through the city. In the same year another horde of children set off from Vendôme in France with the same goal. They followed the Rhine and reached Marseilles. The sea did not part in either Marseilles or Genoa, however. In Marseilles, some of the children boarded the ships of merchants who promised they would take them to the Holy Land. Two of these ships sank near the island of San Pietro, not far from the south coast of Sardinia, and all aboard were drowned. The people of Pisa later built a small church on the island, which they named Novelli Innocenti (Young Innocents).

The other ships sailed to Algeria, where the children were forced into slavery. The best-looking ones were sold to the court of the Egyptian sultan, who treated them well. They became interpreters and advisers for his diplomatic relations with the Christian world. One of them eventually returned to France, and told the story of the fate of the children.

Initially, the children who had traveled from the Rhine valley to Genoa were received with a certain amount of suspicion. After the children had waited in vain for many days for the sea to part, they were given the choice of either settling permanently in Genoa or returning to their homeland. Many remained in the city, while some began their journey home. A third group traveled down the coast to Rome, where they were granted an audience with Pope Innocent III. The pope greeted the delegation warmly, but advised the children to return home. They did not heed his advice, and the *sciame angelico* (host of angels) continued their journey over the Apennine mountains. In Ancona the children boarded a ship for the Balkans. They were never heard of again.

## Work of the Devil

What force had driven thousands upon thousands of boys and girls to this hopeless, foolish adventure? In the 13th century the whole of Europe endeavored to find an answer to this question. The answer was extremely unconvincing. The English theologian Roger Bacon finally declared that the children had been driven to this escapade by a *homo malignus* (envoy of the Devil). In Germany, this interpretation led to the origin of the legend of the pied piper, the flute player with magical powers.

The women of Genoa used the myth of the *novelli innocenti* for spiritual inspiration. They did not believe in miracles, though, knowing full well that the sea did not part. Perhaps they knew some of the German children who had settled in Genoa. Whether or not they did, the women certainly knew that Genoa had no future without crusades as the city's prosperity was intimately tied up with the crusading movement. For Genoa, there was truth in the saying "C'est la guerre qui fait l'argent" (it is war which makes the money). The women confided their plan to the merchant Benedetto Zaccaria, the foremost seaman at the time and an expert on the seas and countries of the Middle East. When the plan had progressed enough, it was made known to the pope. He was enthusiastic. "Oh what a miracle!" Boniface VIII shouted, "the women are going ahead of the men to rescue the Holy Land! The king and the princes are retreating, although they have been summoned. The women, however, although not called, are volunteering their delicate bodies!" The Women's Crusade never made it beyond the port, however. After initial enthusiasm, the pope began to impose specific conditions. He forbade the founding of new outposts in Palestine, in case they benefited certain merchants or communities. Benedetto Zaccaria, who had precisely this in mind, withdrew his support. Thus the magnanimous intentions of the women of Genoa soon came to nothing.

# Gradara
## The castle of the Malatesta

Gradara castle with its circuit walls, constructed by Sigismondo Pandolfo Malatesta in the 15th century. The oldest part, documented in 1182, is incorporated in the brick Renaissance shell. Sigismondo Pandolfo was the last of the Malatestas to exercise control over Gradara and Rimini. At the end of the 13th century, the ancient castle was the scene of the tragedy of Paolo and Francesca featured in Dante's *Inferno*. This story was familiar to everyone in Italy, even those who were illiterate.

### More towers than houses

Gradara lies on a small hill between Rimini and Pesaro, not far from the Adriatic Riviera. It is a small town, surrounded by walls, situated near the Via Flaminia, the Roman road that leads to Ravenna. Gradara has two town walls that are crowned with battlements. The outer wall surrounds the entire town, is around 2300 feet (700 m) long, and runs an irregular course as it follows the shape of the hill. Sixteen towers, also with battlements and no more than 40 paces apart, dominate this encirclement. The inner wall, known as the Girone, is only half as long as the first wall and encircles the castle and the old tower.

One enters Gradara through the central gateway in the clock tower known as the Torre dell'Orologio. One then follows a straight and gently rising street, which divides the town exactly into two, and leads to the Girone near the Torre San Giovanni. A drawbridge used to go over the ditch here, but now the ditch has been filled in. Through the inner gateway one climbs up to the grassy area in front of the castle. The fortress can be entered over another drawbridge that is still in operation.

### The rulers of a small town

Gradara owes its uniform appearance to its shape, the arrangement of houses and streets, the building materials used, and the color of the walls, towers, roofs and bastions of its castle. The town itself was built in the space of a few decades during the 15th century. The center of the entire fortification, the main tower within the castle and the east wing of the residence are, however, very much older. A document from the year 1182 verifies the existence of the tower. The base of the 125-foot (38 m) tower is built from large, rectangular cut blocks, some of

Above: View of the castle showing the two walls.

Opposite: View from the castle over the wider landscape.

Below: View between the two town walls: the first separates the city from the castle; the second outer wall surrounds the entire town.

Lord of Rimini and Gradara, who was the driving force behind the modernization of all the defenses, bringing them into line with developments in weapons technology. He erected the fortifications, the sturdy watchtowers around the main tower and the residence, as well as a solid octagonal rampart in the north-west corner of the town wall, which was known as the Rocchetta.

Gradara was given its present appearance at this time and the residence was transformed into a small palace. At the same time there was also work going on in Rimini. Sigismondo Pandolfo commissioned great artists and architects for the improvements needed there, notably Leon Battista Alberti, who was responsible for the Tempio Malatestiano, regarded as the model 15th-century building. Other great architects such as Filippo Brunelleschi and Matteo Nuti also stayed in Rimini at the end of the 1430s. Although it has not been proven, it is likely that some of them also collaborated on the construction in Gradara.

After the overlordship of the Malatesta, Gradara fell for a short time to a branch of the Sforza family. In 1493 Giovanni Sforza, lord

which bear Latin inscriptions. These are ashlars from Roman ditches that were laid along the Via Flaminia.

In the last decades of the 13th century the powerful Malatesta family, which also ruled over Rimini, settled in Gradara. The Malatesta were able to hold on to their property until the middle of the 15th century. It was Sigismondo Pandolfo, the last Malatesta and

of Pesaro and Gradara, married the young daughter of Pope Alexander VI, Lucrezia Borgia. This marriage guaranteed him the papal fief from his father-in-law. The bride and groom chose to live in the castle residence in Gradara.

As the marriage produced no children, however, Pope Alexander annulled it on the grounds of the husband's impotence. Furthermore, two years later the pope issued a bull in which he declared the Sforza's rule over Pesaro invalid. He then appointed his son Cesare, who was known as *il Valentino*, as Pesaro's new ruler. The former commander of a papal army, *il Valentino* invaded the dukedom of Urbino and the earldom of Montefeltro and tried to found his own state there. This escapade ended in 1504 with the death of Alexander VI.

## Paolo and Francesca

In the 13th century the Malatesta family from Verrucchio and the Polenta dynasty from Ravenna were amongst the most powerful houses in the Romagna. For generations there had been bitter rivalry between the two families. Around 1270 Guido Minore da Polenta was to become lord of Ravenna and Cervia, and the Malatesta became rulers of Gradara and the adjacent Rimini area. In 1275 the families finally came to an agreement. In order to seal the new pact of friendship, the heads of the families arranged a marriage: Guido's beautiful daughter, Francesca da Polenta, was to marry Giovanni, Malatesta's son – who was ugly, no longer so young, and lame in the hip, hence his nickname "Gianciotto" (the limping man). The future spouses had never set eyes on each other. As it was feared Francesca would refuse to go ahead with the marriage if she saw her spouse beforehand, it was agreed that the bride and groom should not meet until after the wedding. Consequently, a proxy marriage ceremony was arranged with Giovanni granting another person the power to act on his behalf. (This arrangement was customary among the feudal nobility at the time.) On the

appointed day Gianciotto's brother appeared in his place. Paolo was handsome, young and pleasant. Francesca happily went through the proxy ceremony then they all set out for Rimini, which was an hour from Ravenna on horseback. Not until she arrived in Ravenna was she introduced to her real husband.

The newlyweds moved to Gradara, into the castle of the old Guido Malatesta, vilified by Dante as "the old tyrant." (People later called him "the 100-year-old" as he lived for exactly 100 years, from 1212 to 1312.) Francesca looked after both her husband and her father-in-law. From time to time her brother-in-law turned up and stayed for a few days. Francesca had a baby girl, who joined the two sons from her husband's previous marriage.

In 1287 Gianciotto became the *podestà* or civilian commander of Pesaro, which was half an hour from Gradara on horseback. At that time Italian towns appointed their *podestà* for either six months or a year. Gianciotto was elected from a group of men, all of whom

Jean-Auguste-Dominique Ingres (1780–1867)
*Paolo and Francesca*

To seal a pact of friendship between the Polenta family, rulers of Ravenna, and the Malatesta, Francesca was married to Gianciotto, Paolo Malatesta's lame brother. The passionate relationship that developed instead between her and Paolo resulted in inevitable tragedy. In the 19th century Ingres presented the two lovers in this dramatic setting. He emphasizes the romantic moment shared by the lovers as their killer, Gianciotto, enters the room. He is already carrying a weapon as a sign of the impending murder.

were of noble lineage and lived outside the town. It was thought that only a stranger would be able to deal impartially with all sides in the event of disputes. To maintain his impartiality, the *podestà* was subject to numerous bans. He was, for example, barred from entering any public houses or from leaving his home in the evening without an official reason. He was also forbidden to bring his wife into the town over which he presided. At the beginning Gianciotto commuted between Gradara and Pesaro,

The so-called "Paolo and Francesca Room" in Gradara Castle.

As Gianciotto was increasingly absent, his brother, Paolo, would visit his wife. The story tells how the husband, catching them making love, ran through both of them with a single sword thrust. In Dante's portrayal the lovers are passionately joined together after death.

riding to work and back each day. Eventually he began to spend more and more time in Pesaro, staying the night there. At the same time his brother Paolo visited Gradara increasingly often. The two brothers exchanged roles, so to speak. One morning, after spending the previous evening with his children, his wife, his father and his brother, Gianciotto rose as usual at the first light of dawn and set off for Pesaro. After a while, however, he turned back. He caught Paolo and Francesca in bed together. Gianciotto drew his sword and with a single thrust he ran it through both of them.

### Dante the chronicler

This is the naked and cruel truth of what was then an everyday occurrence. It would not have been considered particularly remarkable if Dante Alighieri had not told the tale in the *Inferno*, in his *Divine Comedy*. From March 1282 to March 1283 Paolo Malatesta had been Florence's *capitano del popolo*, or military commander. Dante was then a 17-year-old resident of Florence, who admired the hand-some *capitano* when he was seen riding through the town. The news of the stabbing in Gradara caused a big stir in Florence at the time, spreading rapidly by word of mouth. As everyone was free to embellish the tale with new details, it remained the favorite topic of conversation for a long time.

Dante was later expelled from Florence. After 1316 he was often the guest of the Polenta family in Ravenna, and when he died in 1321 his remains were laid to rest there. Dante's account of Paolo and Francesca remained in the minds of many generations in Italy as a common occurrence of the past. It was even familiar to those who could not read or write. In his poetry Dante meets both lovers on his journey through the Inferno. They are passionately devoted to each other in the afterlife. He asks them how it all began. Francesca cries and tells the story. Paolo also cries, but he says nothing.

" 'Of what it pleases thee to hear and speak,
That will we hear, and we will speak to you,
While silent is the wind, as it is now.
Sitteth the city, wherein I was born,
Upon the sea-shore where the Po descends
To rest in peace with all his retinue.
Love, that on gentle heart doth swiftly seize,
Seized this man for the person beautiful
That was ta'en from me, and still the mode
    offends me.
Love, that exempts no one beloved from loving,
Seized me with pleasure of this man so strongly,
That, as thou seest, it doth not yet desert me;
Love has conducted us unto one death;
Caina waiteth him who quenched our life!,
Then unto them I turned me, and I spake,
And I began: 'Thine agonies, Francesca,
Sad and compassionate to weeping make me.
But tell me, at the time of those sweet sighs,
By what and in what manner Love conceded,
That you should know your dubious desires?'
And she to me: 'There is no greater sorrow
Than to be mindful of the happy time

In misery, and that thy Teacher knows.
But, if to recognise the earliest root
Of love in us thou hast so great desire,
I will do even as he who weeps and speaks.
One day we reading were for our delight
Of Launcelot, how Love did him enthral.
Alone we were and without any fear.
Full many a time our eyes together drew
That reading, and drove the colour from our faces;
But one point only was it that o'ercame us.
When as we read of the much-longed-for smile
Being by such a noble lover kissed,
This one, who ne'er from me shall be divided,
Kissed me upon the mouth all palpitating.
Galeotto was the book and he who wrote it.
That day no farther did we read therein.'
And all the while one spirit uttered this,
The other one did weep so, that, for pity,
I swooned away as if I had been dying,
And fell, even as a dead body falls."

Ary Scheffer
*Paolo and Francesca*
Oil on canvas
Musée du Louvre, Paris

In the 19th century, this
French artist took his
religious and romantically
conceived themes from the
works of Dante, among
others. For many centuries
the tragic love story of
Francesca and Paolo was
picked out as a central theme
in literature and art. Here the
couple blend together, as it
were, to become one single
figure. In the background
Dante and Virgil are
watching the tragedy. The
theme has become a symbol
of undying love.

## Piety in the Middle Ages

Hartmut Diekmann

Stefan Lochner
*The Last Judgment* (detail),
*c.* 1435
Oil on wood, 122 × 171 cm
Wallraf-Richartz-Museum,
Cologne
This detail shows the
entrance to hell, with a
usurer in the foreground.

Although the Reformation took place early in the 16th century, as early as the Middle Ages many diverse signs of the approaching religious changes were apparent. Forces within the Roman Catholic Church pressed for changes in matters of faith, just as external social developments likewise demanded changes from the Church. The Church responded to these challenges in surprising ways; it seemed almost to overreact to some, in an effort to purge itself and bring about a renewal and a return to the principles of the early Christian Church. Yet in other areas it adopted a pragmatic, ambivalent attitude that sowed the seeds for the rapid secularization of European society that was to take place in later centuries.

### Peter's Church and Paul's Church

The Roman Catholic Church was founded on the symbolic rock of St. Peter, and Peter's Church grew rapidly from humble beginnings to gain adherents in town after town and country after country. The Church acted in a positive way, trying to win new members by reaching out in a loving manner to "heathens." It obeyed the instruction "go out into the entire world and make disciples of all peoples; baptize them in the name of the Father, the Son and the Holy Ghost." Once the heathens had been overcome, however, they were no longer considered a threat, and no longer occupied the Church's thoughts. The gentle, caring Church of Peter slowly transformed into the mercenary, worldly Church of Paul. The Church became powerful and proud, but while gaining in worldly status it lost its soul.

"Paul's Church" came into being because of rank corruption among the clergy, reaching from the bottom to the very top. Ecclesiastical offices could be bought, from that of a parish priest to that of a cardinal. Popes granted high office to their "monkey keepers" or their infant nephews, and even salvation became a commodity, as expressed in the following lament: "What does it profit the Church if it gains the whole world and brings disgrace on its own soul?" The Protestant Reformation made the Church realize that it was no use pursuing "heretics" to the ends of the earth, if the most senior Church officials acted worse than any heathen or heretic. Heathenism was apparent in the thoughts and actions of the very popes, who by encouraging the practice of indulgences sold the faithful a clear conscience while deceiving them about the salvation of their souls.

"Paul's Church" looked to itself, converted its own soul, turned inwards and at the same time turned against the "heathens" identified within its Christian exterior. This process was not reached easily or in a straightforward way, however, and many contradictions and compromises appeared *en route* to the purification of the corrupt Church.

## Money or life, or money and life?

In the 13th century the Christian Church was at the peak of its power and area of influence. Within society, however, radical changes were occurring that would have far-reaching consequences all over Christendom. In the Western world at least, commerce and the cash economy became increasingly important. Trade flourished, merchants traveled from town to town just as missionaries had earlier to spread the faith, and markets overflowed with goods of every kind and from every land. The demands of the marketplace and of trade rendered the familiar techniques of barter inadequate. Money, as a means of payment, came increasingly to the fore.

Traditionally the Church had condemned money lending on the basis of Old Testament teachings on the immorality of earning interest, and had forced the trade on the Jews, deeming such an undignified occupation unfit for Christians. Originally, those who indulged in this practice had been condemned to go to hell when they died. The Church's uncompromising stance on this matter can be summed up by the following verse from the gospel: "No man can serve two masters. For either he will hate the one and love the other; or he will sustain the one and despise the other. You cannot serve God and Mammon" (Matthew 6:24). And the futility of trying to serve both God and Mammon was expressed in these verses: "This therefore I say, brethren: The time is short. It remaineth, that they also who have wives be as if they had none: And they that weep, as though they wept not: and they that rejoice, as if they rejoiced not: and they that buy, as though they possessed not: And they that use this world, as if they used it not. For the fashion of this world passeth away" (1 Corinthians 7:29–31).

Things could not have been spelled out much more clearly than that. The problem was that an increasingly mercantile world needed credit and creditors in order to survive. A slightly more equivocal approach to the problem of money lending therefore seemed necessary.

And so the 13th century began with a momentous decision: one that was to affect the Roman Catholic Church radically and permanently. In the year 1215 the fourth Lateran Council, convened by the pope to make decisions on doctrinal matters, resolved to make the oral confession obligatory for all believers. Thus the public confession became private. The punishment decided by the priest hearing confession was now based on whether the intention of the person making a confession was good or bad. A priest's main aim in hearing confession and setting a penance was to cleanse a person, rather than to atone for their sin. In the case of money lending activities circumscribed by the Church, confession was no longer all about usury, but about the usurer; it was no longer all

Pierre Eskrich
*The Papal Court,*
detail of the *Mappe-monde nouvelle papistique*
Wood carving, 170 × 135 cm
British Museum, London

Here the traditional Roman Church is portrayed as a "monarchy of good works" governed by the pope. Easily identifiable are St. Peter and the Vatican, where the pope sucks on the breast of "Lady Money," surrounded by his royal household.

Above: *The Devil and the Usurer*, c. 1210
Chartres Cathedral, south portal

The usurer in the Devil's clutches

Left: Two scenes from a money changer's room, late 14th century
Illumination on parchment
The British Museum, London

Due to the Old Testament ban on earning interest, money lending was seen as sinful.

Below: Luca Signorelli
*The Damned*, 1499–1504
Fresco
Cappella Nuova, Duomo, Orvieto

A scene from Dante's *Inferno* is depicted here.

for interest was still immeasurable, as this exemplary sermon verified:

"My brothers, my brothers, do you know of a sin that never rests, that is committed all the time? No? But there is such a one, a single one, and I shall name it for you. It is usury. Money lent at usury rates of interest does not stop working, it produces money without respite; it may be wrong, harmful, contemptible money, but it is nevertheless money. Usury is an untiring worker. Do you know, my brothers, any worker who leaves his work neither on Sundays, nor on holidays and not even while asleep? No? Usury works incessantly, continually – by night as well as by day, on Sundays and holidays, while asleep as while awake! Working while asleep? Usury performs this fiendish miracle, which is driven by Satan (...). This constant and endless sin will, however, be granted punishment with no peace and no end. As Satan's accomplice, never losing heart, usury can only lead to eternal servitude, to everlasting punishment in hell."

"Money or life" was the choice that the Church placed before all those who felt drawn towards usury. This condemnation grew ever feebler, however, even if it was repeated at council after council (in 1139, 1179, 1215, 1274 and 1311). Its ambivalence towards usury can be seen as the thin end of the wedge that created an everwidening gap between the stated principles of

about the punishment of the deed, but about the salvation of the wrongdoer.

Faith also became more individualistic. The Church saw itself confronted with a number of dissenting pious movements: the Cathars and the Waldensians were leaving the confines of their churches and were preaching throughout the land. Such groups wanted to establish a Church without churches, a "Church on the road." Their success was so marked that even bishops felt compelled to put sandals on, leave their palaces and go preaching throughout their dioceses to retain the loyalty of their flock.

At the same time money also changed its character. In the eyes of the great scholastic philosophers, money was unproductive. Unlike the fields, which were "naturally" productive, money brought forth nothing "naturally." It represented something else, and had no intrinsic value in itself. In usury, however, money demonstrated a wondrous fruitfulness. But the sin of lending it

Church and its pragmatic approach to the real world – a world that seemed to be growing ever more secular and commercial. It seemed that the Church would find it necessary to change the "or" in "money or life" into an "and," acknowledging the *de facto* function and importance of money in society.

But not all branches of the Church displayed this ambivalent – some would say hypocritical – attitude towards things material. This was a time when the mendicant orders opposed and resisted the burgeoning wealth and secular power of the Church. They also raised doubts about the traditional stark and uncompromising dichotomies between good and evil, God and the Devil, heaven and hell. Again, the example of usury provides a good example of how these doubts began to arise. Usurers were condemned to hell, but they were necessary for the smooth running of society. If usury was an essential service, how could those who practiced it be condemned? The Church needed a "get out" clause for this and other theological dilemmas, and the institution of purgatory provided this clause.

Purgatory was a distinctive spiritual innovation of the 13th century – a place where people who had sinned, but were repentant, could assemble and serve out time while awaiting redemption. Intercession from relatives on behalf of the dead person could shorten this period of time. The decisive factor as to whether someone went to purgatory as opposed to hell was, therefore, the degree of remorse they showed in their last hour of life. Thus even someone who had committed a sin such as usury could technically be saved, and ultimately enter paradise, if he displayed repentance before his death.

A story from the period tells of the marvelous salvation of a usurer. The story contains a mixture of strong feelings and strong theology, which together make a work of redemption:

Fragment of wing of the Palant Altar
*A Patrician Family Prays for Its Redemption from Purgatory,*
*c.* 1425
Tempera on oak, 82 × 45.5 cm
Suermondt-Ludwig-Museum, Aachen

This portrayal is the oldest known panel depicting purgatory. The donors are kneeling in the corners of the lower edge of the painting; they were hoping that through their donation they could "buy" their way out of purgatory.

Herr ihesu xpe das blut võ deiner buttern krönug vergoffen laß kome uber ons vnd uber vonßre kinder zu abwoeßchung sundtlicher mackeltt das wir also gerainiger dich müge anschawe in ewiger clarhait mit dē himlischen bürgern amen.

A usurer from Lüttich died. Under ecclesiastical laws he could not be buried in consecrated ground, but his wife pleaded for him as follows: "Is it not written, Reverend Father, that man and woman are of one flesh, and that, as the apostle said, the unbelieving man can be saved by his believing wife? What my husband failed to do, I shall do – as I am of his flesh – instead of him."

Thereupon she was permitted to bury her husband in the cemetery. She took up residence near his grave and prayed twice seven years for him, until her husband said to her: "Thanks be to God and thanks be to you, for today I have been redeemed."

Thus the Church and the institution of marriage saved a soul, and conveniently for the economy the usurer had been able to carry out his trade for many profitable years before his death.

Above: Bernhard Strigel
*The Funk Family's Epitaph*
Oil on wood, 58 × 99 cm
Museum Allerheiligen,
Schaffhausen

This is a portrayal of the family of the mayor of Memmingen, Johann Fund the Younger. The father with his sons is on the left, depicted on the side of the Blessed at the Last Judgment. The mother is with the daughters, on the side of the damned.

Opposite: *Paradise and Hell Landscape*, fol. 153 r.
Book of Hours for use in Rome, *c.* 1480
Victoria and Albert Museum, London

The idea that souls must make their way over long and narrow footbridges to get to heaven is common in early literature. Here they are inching their way across the unstable bridge to get to the shores of paradise.

# Massa

## Malaspina Castle

### Between the sea and the marble cliffs

Massa is situated on the high mountain slopes of the Apuan Alps. Even in summer these mountains are white: not because of snow, but because of the marble that is cut there. The sea is very close, and on clear mornings one can make out the pink outline of the island of Corsica.

Today the towns of Massa and Carrara form a single urban conglomeration. If one looks only at the built environment, then this part of upper Versilia can certainly be considered one of Italy's most scarred coastal sections. Nevertheless, it is also one of the most beautiful. For in this landscape it is not so much the

Right: Malaspina Castle rises on the slopes of the Apuan Alps above the town of Massa, which is famous for its marble deposits.

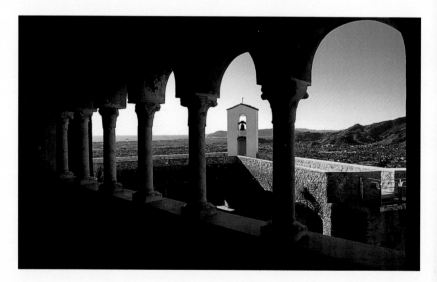

Above: The small arcade on the south side of the castle.

flat strips of coastline that count: it is the mountains, the sky and the sea. The fortification lies halfway up the hill above the town, and from it there is a wide view over the sea. Within the castle itself are the main tower and the remains of an older tower. Both of these towers are enclosed within a wall crowned with battlements. This wall also surrounds a Renaissance palace, situated at a slightly lower level, which

was rebuilt time and time again from the 15th century onwards. A bulwark from earlier times surrounds the entire complex. A marble plaque informs us that the castle complex was completed in the year 1570, "in order to resist the satanic invention of firearms." Although the Renaissance palace is not very big and is irregular in form, it does have some remarkable features: an inner courtyard, a roofed, colonnaded veranda, and rooms on the first floor that are also irregular in form but have beautifully arched ceilings.

## The margravate of Massa

In the Middle Ages the region of Genoa and Pisa, later also of Lucca and Florence, was disputed. The margraves of Massa, who had been appointed to office by the Ottone as early as the end of the 9th century, came from a Genoese family, the Obertenghi. Although their estates extended from the plain of the River Po, on the other side of the Apennines,

The rooms of the Renaissance palace, constructed by the Malaspinas inside the 15th-century castle, are small in size and irregular in shape, with delightful 'umbrella' vaults.

Above: the ceiling of the *Camera Picta*, entirely decorated with frescoes and ornamentation.

Below: among the motifs in the frescoes that decorate the walls are those of the dry thorn and the flowering thorn, representing the two branches of the family.

almost as far as Milan, and included Piacenza, the margraves of Massa-Obertenghi always remained seafarers. The Massa-Corsica family is descended from them, as are the Massa-Cagliari. The continental, more modest branch of the family produced the Massa-Parodi and the Massa-Gavi. At the end of the 11th century all the branches of the Obertenghi family experienced a real problem, however – while they continued to bring forth children, almost all were girls. This nightmare lasted for four or five generations. In order to retain their property, the last margraves did their best to arrange prudent marriages for their daughters.

The last male of the family line, Guglielmo di Massa-Cagliari, died in 1215 and all his titles and territories went to his eldest daughter Benedetta, the ruler of Cagliari. The second eldest daughter, Adelasia, had been married to Enzo, the illegitimate son of Emperor Frederick II. This meant that she

was allied to the Hohenstaufen king. Benedetta, on the other hand, was an ally of the pope. As these two powers were quite irreconcilable at the time, the Obertenghi could not stay in either Sardinia or Massa.

After the defeat and death of the last Hohenstaufen king, Conrad IV, the townspeople of Lucca had the castle of Massa demolished in the year 1269. Massa was later occupied by Castruccio Castracani, ruler of Lucca, who had the castle rebuilt. After Castruccio's death the land of the former margravate was divided up and auctioned off. Massa became a plaything in the hands of superior powers. It remained disputed and found itself under the "protection" of Genoa, Lucca, Pisa, Florence and Milan by turns. In 1359 the margravate rose up again, as there was general interest in establishing a buffer state in this region. Emperor Charles IV decreed the new margravate, which was now under the protection of Florence. Florence later

The elegant Renaissance courtyard, which was built at the foot of the castle of the margraves of Malaspina in the 15th century.

253

Opposite: The whole complex is surrounded by great ramparts with embrasures, which were erected in the 16th century. An inscription engraved in marble refers to the year 1570, when Antonio Alberico Cybo-Malaspina completed the castle complex.

Renaissance courtyard, detail
The Renaissance palace, situated at a slightly lower level, was rebuilt repeatedly from the 15th century, with some fine architectural additions, such as this beautiful window frame.

made sure that the new dynasty of the Malaspina family gained a foothold in Massa. The castle owes its present name to them.

## The Malaspina family

The rule of the Malaspina over the town of Massa was established on December 8, 1442. On that day the inhabitants of Massa, through their representatives, voluntarily submitted themselves to the ruler, Alberto Alberico Malaspina. The Malaspina was an old family that had owned various properties thoughout Lunigiana since the year 1000. Their first domicile was in the upper Taro valley at a place called Oramala, which means "disfavor" or "ruin."

According to legend, the name Malaspina stems from a certain Ancino, the progenitor of the family. Ancino killed his enemy, Theobert, king of the Franks, in close combat by allegedly thrusting a thorn into his heart. "Ah, 'mala spina,' what an evil thorn!" the dying Theobert is said to have cried out. The label stuck to the killer, and eventually became his family name.

Later, after the Malaspina had extended their estates to the coast, the family divided. The branch to whom the land to the right of the River Magra belonged called itself Malaspina "dello spino secco," or the Malaspina "from the withered thorn." The branch to the left of the river had the name Malaspina "dello spino fiorito," or the Malaspina "from the blossoming thorn." The new margrave of Massa, Antonio Alberico Malaspina, was a scion of the branch from the blossoming thorn.

## The third daughter

At first the town flourished under its new rulers. In the fourth generation, however, the Malaspina encountered the same curse that had befallen the rulers of Massa. Antonio Alberico II Malaspina, the third margrave of the branch of the blossoming thorn, managed to produce only daughters: Taddea 1, Taddea 2, Ricciarda, Leonora and Lucrezia. The first Taddea died in infancy. The second was an illegitimate child and as such was excluded from the line of succession. When Alberico died in 1519, the entire inheritance went to Ricciarda, the third daughter.

Alberico's will decreed that Ricciarda should govern the margravate until her firstborn son attained his majority. Ricciarda, a beautiful and strong-willed woman, was already married to a Fieschi, a descendant of the powerful Genoese family. She had a little girl by him. When Fieschi died in 1520, Ricciarda married another powerful Genoese, Lorenzo Cybo. He was the grandson of two popes (one on his mother's side, and one on his father's). The brother of a cardinal and cousin of Catherine de' Medici, the future queen of France, Lorenzo brought Ricciarda to Rome to live with Catherine, where he surrounded her with luxury. His greatest

wish was to acquire a share in his wife's fief and in the title of the margravate of Massa. To this end he plotted conspiracies with Pope Clement VII, without Ricciarda's knowledge. When she heard of this, she felt unable to forgive him. Not even the birth of an eagerly awaited son, baptized Giulio, could extinguish the hatred that had broken out between them.

## A loving maternal heart

As she drifted away from her husband, Ricciarda spent more and more time with his brother, the inappropriately named Cardinal Innocenzo Cybo. They embarked on an affair and she eventually bore him a son. As if to provoke her husband, she named her second son after his grandfather, Antonio Alberico. Ricciarda then began scheming to cut her husband and his issue out of her dynastic calculations. She wanted to disinherit her firstborn son Giulio in favor of her second son,

the child of the cardinal. Ricciarda, who apparently became more attractive with age, became acquainted with Emperor Charles V, who stayed in the castle at Massa during his frequent trips to Italy. She not only managed to induce the emperor to revoke the fief previously awarded to her husband Lorenzo, but she also obtained the privilege of deciding which of her two sons should be the legal successor. In doing so, however, she contravened the will of Alberico Malaspina. At this point Lorenzo Cybo gave up the fight and retreated to one of his country seats near Pisa, though he continued to goad his son into taking revenge on his mother.

## The poor child

Even before he had reached his majority Giulio Cybo, who had been well trained in the use of arms, attacked the castle of Massa, together with 50 men, and tried to take his mother prisoner and enforce the wishes of his grandfather,

The coat of arms of the Malaspina "dello spino fiorito," the branch of the family "of the blossoming thorn" that settled on the left bank of the River Po.

View of the castle from the south, with the walled-in courtyard.

Alberico, as expressed in the latter's will. Ricciarda locked herself in the main tower of the castle, however, and held out until her supporters came from Massa to free her.

Giulio did not give up, but allowed himself to be used by ruthless intriguers in the hope of exacting revenge on his mother. He joined pro-French emigrants from Florence, Genoa and other towns in a conspiracy to murder Prince Andrea Doria, lord of Genoa, whose daughter he had recently married. In January 1548, on the emperor's orders, he was arrested and brought to Milan, where he was tried on charges of conspiracy and leading a rebellion against the emperor. He was condemned to death and beheaded on the morning of May 18, 1548. On the evening before his execution the 23-year-old composed a sonnet in which he confessed all his mistakes, asked for forgiveness and submitted himself to God's mercy.

## The younger brother

After her death five years later, Ricciarda left the margravate of Massa to the son of the cardinal, now her only heir. Antonio Alberico Cybo-Malaspina ruled for 69 years and died in 1623 at the age of 91. As successors, his sons were of no use in that they all died before he did. One of his greatest concerns was to bring home the mortal remains of his unfortunate half-brother Giulio and inter them in the family vault in Massa.

During his rule the margravate was elevated to a dukedom. He founded a company to quarry the marble, promoted the arts and trade, improved the appearance of Massa, surrounded the town with walls, extended the castle's living quarters and had modern embrasures built into the fortifications. He put a marble plaque on the castle with the inscription: "In order to resist the satanic invention of firearms, Alberico Cybo Malaspina had this enormous bulwark erected in the year 1570."

The main tower of the castle, seen from the Renaissance courtyard.

The medieval castle was demolished in 1269 by the citizens of Lucca, and rebuilt half a century later.

# Cagliari

## A town within a town

View of the citadel and the Cagliari district

On the left one can see part of the Pisan walls and a Pisan tower from the 13th century, in the middle of a Spanish protective wall from the 16th century.

### A Phoenician town

What is known as *il castello* in Cagliari is not one single construction, but a *città murata*, a fortified town, which lies above another unfortified town and guards it.

Cagliari was originally founded by the Phoenicians as a trading center by the sea, and the city later came under the sphere of influence of the great Phoenician city of Carthage. Here, an enormous limestone spur rises above the lagoon, and together with extensive salt-works it forms a natural protective shield for the port and the commercial enterprises. The limestone spur was fortified as early as the time of Carthage. The only traces of these old constructions that remain, however, are now underground. Unlike Sicily, which was disputed by the Greeks and the Carthaginians for a long time and eventually divided up between them, Sardinia was never colonized by the ancient Greeks. This is why no acropolis ever rose on the white spur of Cagliari. The Greeks were content with giving the island a Greek name, *Ichnussa*, which is derived from *ichnos* (foot), and means "print of a human foot." The name was derived from the foot-like shape of the coastline.

### Rome and Barbária

After the Punic Wars in the 2nd century B.C., the Romans occupied the entire island. In doing so they met fierce resistance from the warlike tribes in the interior. The rebellion was put down through the construction of a road system, which dealt the death blow to the prehistoric culture that had survived hidden in the Nuragic ruins. The Romans named this interior Barbária. Some of the areas in the interior are very high in altitude and their inhabitants show marked differences from the rest of the population in the way they cultivate

the land and construct their houses, among other things. Even today these areas are known as Barbária. For centuries the interior remained "an island on an island." After the destruction of Carthage the Romans no longer had any rivals in the Mediterranean region. The sea became Mare Nostrum, or "our sea," and Rome never felt the need to fortify the hill looming above the port of Cagliari. Of the numerous Roman remains in the town there are thermal baths, villas and an amphitheater. There is, however, no trace of a fort.

## Byzantium

With the fall of the Roman Empire, Sardinia fell into the hands of the Vandals. There remains no trace of their presence, which lasted approximately 80 years, apart from remnants of their language.

In the 6th century, at the time of Justinian I, Byzantine Greeks came to Sardinia as part of a reconquest of the Mediterranean region, from the Eastern Roman Empire as far as Spain. The Byzantines subdivided the island into four areas of approximately the same size. They placed at the head of each unit a *logothet*, which in Latin is *judex* (judge). The *logothet* ruled over a finely organized and complex political and administrative system, the ultimate purpose of which was to levy taxes on the farmers in the interior – taxes that were channeled to Constantinople. But even the Byzantines did not worry about constructing fortifications to defend Cagliari. When Byzantium lost control of the western Mediterranean as the Islamic territories expanded, the four administrative units, the *giudicati*, were left to their own resources. These small, efficiently run states continued much as they had done, only without an overlord. The Arabs themselves were satisfied with repeated raids and plundering in order to take slaves, without ever undertaking a campaign to conquer. The *giudicati* paid their tribute to the Arabs, and remained intact.

In the 13th century, when the *città murata* was being planned, there were few citadels situated in the middle of "open" towns in western Europe, although the concept was well known in the Middle and Far East.

*De sphaera* (detail)
Illumination
Lat. 209 (= α.×.2.14),
fols. 10ᵛ–ll, 6ᵛ
Biblioteca Estense, Modena

The *città murata* united all aspects of civilian life: the piazza, the church, the government buildings and so on. During the day the inhabitants of the citadel mixed with those of the surrounding town. In the evening everyone returned to his or her own place. The miniature shows everyday life in a small town.

## The maritime republics

Later, the maritime towns of Marseilles, Pisa, and Genoa came to dispute the Arabs' right to the western Mediterranean. The people of Pisa managed to retake the Balearic Islands temporarily (1114), and they invaded Sardinia in the first two centuries of the new millennium. In Sardinia the *giudicati*, and the dynasties that had settled there during the Byzantine period, still existed. The Pisans advanced into the eastern part, the Genoese took the northern part and the Catalans the north-western part of the island. These three powers were desperately jealous of one another, however.

## The *città murata* of the Pisans

The *città murata* above Cagliari is the work of the Pisans. In many respects it is a prototype. This is because at the time when it was being planned there were few examples of walled towns situated within another open town in western Europe. This citadel brought together the functions and symbols of civilian, economic, religious, and military power: piazza, cathedral, market places, government buildings, as well as residential areas. The Pisans had extensive knowledge of the world. In Cagliari they had found a model of the ideal Mediterranean town, which was fortified but at the same time cosmopolitan. During the

day the inhabitants of the citadel mingled with the people from Santa Igía and other residential quarters in the lower part of the town, near the harbor. But when the sun went down, and a trumpet sounded, they returned to the castle. The townspeople, for their part, left the castle and the gates shut tightly behind them.

The ground plan of the citadel is in the shape of a spindle, and it is aligned north-south. It looks as though it has grown into the limestone cliffs on which it is built. Together with the vertical rock faces, the high walls and ramparts form an impregnable defense. High towers rise above the three town gates: the Porta di San Pancrazio in the north, the Porta dell'Aquila with the Controporta del Leone in the south and the Porta dell'Elefante in the west. Opposite this, the entire eastern part is built on the vertical cliffs. Six further towers, some of which have now collapsed, accentuate the walls. Three main streets, which were linked by a network of alleyways, used to go through the town lengthways and in the town center there used to be the piazza.

## The end of Santa Igía

The *città murata* was never conquered militarily. It was captured for the first time in the year 1256 by Genoa, as the result of a putsch-like political and military maneuver. After a

View of the *città murata* fortification crowned with battlements.

The tower, the *Porta dell'Elefante* gateway and the small stone elephant from which it derives its name.

long siege, two battles on land and one at sea, Pisa regained the fortified town. Torchitorio V, who was known as Chiano and was the commanding *judex* of Cagliari, had opened the gates to the Genoese. On Pisa's instructions he was murdered. Chiano was a young man of 19, who had wanted to avenge his grandmother Benedetta (see below). Santa Igía, the lower part of town, where Chiano's seat of government was located, was razed to the ground and covered with salt from the nearby salt-works. The *giudicato* of Cagliari, which included the southern quarter of Sardinia, was divided between the four most powerful families of Pisa.

## The Catalans are coming

A second conquest occurred with the citizens of Pisa capitulating without a fight. This was in 1326, two years after an Aragonese lord had landed on the island. In order to be able to compete with Venice for trade in the Orient, the Catalans needed all the islands in the central Mediterranean, from the Balearic Islands to the Peloponnese. They built, so to speak, pillars of a vast bridge on which their maritime Orient Express was to run. Pope Boniface VIII, who believed he was the "feudal lord" of the whole hemisphere, had created the "Kingdom of Sardinia and Corsica" in 1297 on his own initiative. By order of the *licentia invadendi*, he commissioned Giacomo of Aragon to take possession of the realm.

## The Pisans take their leave

Pisa was going through difficult times. It was preoccupied with a last attempt, together with the Ghibelline forces of Tuscany, to destroy the power of its old enemy, Florence. Thus Pisa could not fight an overseas war with the Aragonese as well. For two years the citizens of Pisa, in their *città murata*, resisted a half-hearted siege from their Aragonese enemies, who had set up a military base on the opposite hill, in Bonaria. Eventually the Pisans consented to an agreement requiring them to cede a large part of their Sardinian estates without a fight. This was on condition that the administration of the citadel, employing several 1000 people, could be retained. At the beginning their wish was granted. Later, however, most of the Pisans were forced to return to their hometown.

After the expulsion of the Jews from Spain, the synagogues in Cagliari were destroyed in 1492. The Jesuits later settled the same spot, in Santa Croce. By 1492 the last citizens of Pisa were already long gone. Responsibility for the events to come now rested with the new rulers.

# Benedetta

At the beginning of the 12th century, the western Mediterranean became a much traveled sea as a result of the Crusades and the vertiginous rise of the seaside towns of Pisa, Amalfi, Genoa, Marseilles, and Barcelona. In the middle of this stretch of water lay the half-forgotten island of Sardinia with its anachronistic *giudicati* of Byzantine character. Sardinia soon became the object of desire for the new maritime powers, for which the control of the Sardinian coast was of the utmost importance. The dynasties that ruled over the key towns on the western Mediterranean coast set about vigorously dividing the islands up amongst themselves. They became commercially active first, before developing politically advantageous marriage strategies with regard to the ruling dynasties of each island. Before long they had swallowed up the *giudicati*. Pisa emerged as the victor in the whole south-western region. But by what means had this maritime republic achieved its goal?

In 1214 Guglielmo II de Lacon-Massa, the *giudice* of Cagliari, who was called Salusio VI, died without any male descendants. Salusio, a Tuscan feudal lord, had ventured to sea in the pursuit of further territorial gains. He found them

Egnazio Danti
*Sardinia*
Fresco
Galleria delle Carte Geografiche, Musei Vaticani, Rome

The island is seen here from north to south, which makes it appear the wrong way around, with Cagliari in the wrong place.

Opposite: *The Porta dell'Elefante* in the west was one of three town gateways surmounted by massive towers.

The terrace of Umberto I was built on top of the Spanish protective walls. In the 16th century, when a Spanish viceroy ruled over Sardinia, the *città murata* was included in the new rulers' system of defense.

in Sardinia. After his death, Benedetta, the elder of his two daughters, married her cousin Barisone at the request of Pope Innocent III. The bridegroom became *giudice* and as such Torchitorio V. This was in accordance with the Byzantine tradition of calling the *giudice* Salusio or Torchitorio alternately. It was this Torchitorio who in 1216 allowed a group of traders from Pisa to build fortifications on a hill that already housed the remains of a Carthaginian fort. As he died soon afterwards, he did not find the time to regret this. Instead it was the young Benedetta, widowed with an infant, who regretted the decision. Pope Honorius III had just succeeded the pope who had brought about Benedetta's ill-fated marriage. She wrote a dramatic letter to Honorius, beseeching him for papal protection.

Furthermore, she revoked the authorization that her spouse had granted to Pisa to build the fortress on the hill. Consent had reportedly been wrung from him by a delegation consisting of a *console del mare* and a "retinue of many representatives of Pisa's aristocracy" using "threats, terror and flattery." No sooner had consent been given, wrote Benedetta to the pope, when the mayor of Pisa, *Podestà* Ubaldo Visconti, arrived on the island "at the head of an army" and occupied the *giudice*'s seat of power, had the ministers arrested and took over the functions of the *giudice*. The pope took Benedetta's appeal to heart. First of all he asked Pisa to withdraw all the armed men and demolish the new fortress, or at least hand it over to the locals. The only answer from the Pisans was to send hundreds of

families to Cagliari to begin building a great cathedral, which they dedicated to Mary. The consequence of this was that the pope imposed an interdict on all the people who had moved from Pisa to Cagliari. Pisa petitioned the pope to get the interdict lifted, and while negotiations were under way the pope suspended the interdict. This gained the wily Pisans some time.

## Lamberto Visconti

Lamberto Visconti was the brother of Ubaldo, whom Benedetta mentioned as the mayor of Pisa in her letter to the pope. Lamberto himself had set sail across the sea years before to make his fortune. The foundation of the new town Olbia was attributed to Lamberto. He had married the young Elena, heiress to the *giudicato* of Gallura, which was in the eastern quarter of Sardinia.

The marriage to the underage Elena had been performed secretly with her mother's consent but without the pope's permission. As a result Pope Innocent III excommunicated Lamberto, together with his mother-in-law and his spouse. This severe punishment was based on the fact that the pope had intended a different bridegroom for the girl. Lamberto's excommunication was later lifted, whereas those of his mother-in-law and wife were reaffirmed. As chance would have it, however, Elena died at the beginning of the year 1220.

After the funeral Lamberto made his way to Cagliari, where he persuaded Benedetta to marry him. In this way Lamberto Visconti became lord over half of Sardinia by uniting the eastern and the southern quarters. This position of power enabled him to legalize the Pisans' presence in the fort, or *castrum Kalari*, which within only a few years had grown into a town of 10,000 inhabitants. After Lamberto's death in 1226 the hapless Benedetta married once more, but herself died a few years later 1232. Her son Guglielmo, whose father was Lamberto Visconti, was barely 15 years old at the time. The Pisans were to enjoy a firm foothold in Sardinia for the next 100 years.

# Barumini

## A prehistoric fortress

Right: General view of the Nuraghe Su Nuraxi at Barumini with its village of huts. In the foreground the consoles of former parapets can be clearly seen.

Above: Limestone model of a Nuragic tower.

The 14-inch (36 cm) artefact, which today is in the National Archeological Museum of Cagliari, came from the assembly room of the Nuraghe Su Nuraxi. In excavations between 1949 and 1955, extensive fortified defense and dwelling towers, mainly from the Bronze Age, were unearthed.

### Sardinia's Nuraghi

The structures known as the Nuraghi in Sardinia are the product of an indigenous and long-established civilization that reached the peak of its development between 1600 and 800 B.C. For a long time it was believed that the Nuraghi – like the pyramids – were tombs. With the excavation of Barumini (1949–1955), however, this theory was proved wrong. Today it seems certain that they were fortified dwellings or castles. The ruins are large, stone towers of a conical shape, rather like squat tree stumps They are made up of big boulders arranged in rings that are layered on top of each other without mortar. Each ring is a few centimeters smaller in diameter than the one beneath it. The size of the stones also becomes smaller the higher the construction grows. Some of the towers are thought to have been over 66 feet (20 m) high. The Barumini tower once measured over 62 feet (19 m) and had a base 33 feet (10 m) in diameter. Stones forming the base ring were placed directly on the ground without foundations.

The inside of the tower can be reached through a rather long passageway, on the right-hand side of which there was a niche for a guard to stand in. A Nuraghe could hold up to three conically shaped rooms, one above the other, each of which had a high dome-shaped ceiling. Barumini's tower originally contained three rooms. The room on the ground floor, which has remained intact, has a height of just over 25 feet (7.7 m) and a diameter of 14 feet 9 inches (4.5 m). The thick walls take up so much space that the outer diameter is nearly twice the inner diameter. Access from one room to another is via a spiral staircase within the wall. The first step is positioned high up and a moveable wooden ladder was needed to reach it.

Above: On the aerial photograph of the Nuraghe Su Nuraxi at Barumini one can clearly see the central tower and its rhomboid bastion with four prominent corner towers. There is a another protective circular wall with seven towers surrounding the site. This site is in turn framed by the Nuragic village with its oddly shaped huts.

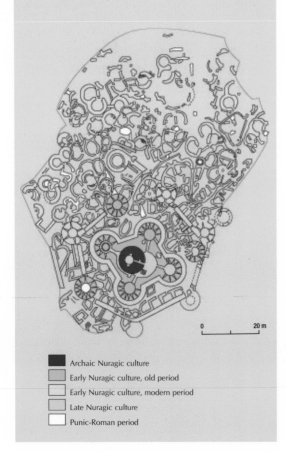

Right: The ground plan of the excavation site makes it possible to recognize structural details such as the embrasures, the inner courtyard and the fountains. The various construction phases of the Nuragic fortress are also illustrated.

0    20 m

■ Archaic Nuragic culture
▨ Early Nuragic culture, old period
□ Early Nuragic culture, modern period
▨ Late Nuragic culture
□ Punic-Roman period

The Nuraghi were immensely efficient when it came to their insulation properties. On a hot summer afternoon when the temperature is 104 °F (40 °C) the inside temperature of Su Nuraxi near Barumini will be between 53.6 and 59 °F (12 and 15 °C). In January the temperature is only a few degrees lower.

Nothing is known about the religious beliefs of the people who lived in the Nuraghi. We do know, however, that they took great care of the springs and sources of drinking water.

Of the 8,000 or more prehistoric monuments in Sardinia, a large number are Nuraghi with circular bases. Not a single one has remained intact, however. In all of the examples that have been discovered so far, the top has been found to have caved in. Small models made of stone, bronze and terracotta found in archeological excavations indicate that there were in fact coping stones on the top of the tower. Some of the stones found in excavations are in the shape of large consoles, which could have supported a type of ledge. A Nuraghe, with consoles and embrasures, basically resembles a medieval tower. The Nuraghi are spread all over Sardinia. They can also be found along the coastline, where they were obviously used as lookouts for enemies approaching by sea. The majority of them, however, are in the interior where they were distributed throughout the island in a checkered pattern. This arrangement or systematic order fulfilled strategic and military criteria. The Nuraghi often stand on the edge or in the center of plateaus, the boundaries of which are marked by basalt crests. These plateaus are known as *giare* and are common in central Sardinia. They are old volcanic craters that have been leveled with the passage of time. The Nuraghi were apparently spread out in a checkered pattern so that the entire territory could be surveyed from them, and optical signals sent from one to the other rapidly so that messages could be sent round the island as quickly as possible. Around many of the Nuragic towers the remains of other circular, but less thick, exterior walls have been found. These indicate that settlements grew up around them. This was true in the case of Barumini.

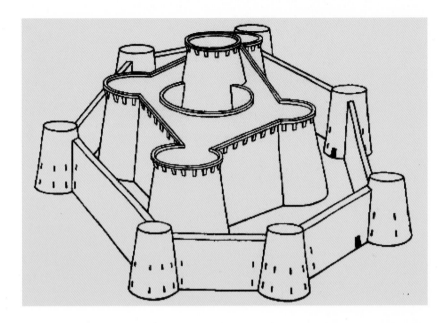

Above: An idealized reconstruction of the Nuraghe Su Nuraxi at Barumini shows how imposing and impregnable it must have looked.

This much is evident from many archeological finds, including oil lamps in the shape of small ships. For these Bronze Age people trade relations with other peoples must have been essential, because tin was required to produce bronze, and no deposits were found on the island itself.

## The Discovery of the Nuraghe Su Nuraxi at Barumini

Astrid B. Koberstein-Pes

As is so often the case in archeology, a chance event led to the discovery of the Nuraghi complex at Barumini. It was known that there were stone walls and rubble in the grass-covered mounds of earth. A trial excavation had taken place in 1946, but no one really knew what lay down there. In 1949 an unusually strong rainstorm washed away the top layer of earth, however, exposing parts of a colossal monument. The local historian, Giovanni Lilliu, recognized the significance of

The Nuraghe at Barumini was discovered relatively recently. The Nuraghe itself was completely covered by earth and formed a small hill on the southern edge of the *giara* of Gesturi. The children of Barumini were prohibited from playing on this hill. They were told that a giant fly slept in the belly of the hill and that it did not want to be woken up. This made the children want to go there even more. Among them was the child who would later become the archeologist Lilliu, who would wake the fly from its slumber. The excavation work, which began in 1949 and ended in 1955, unearthed a complex site. Around the tower there was an imposing rampart with many smaller towers on it. The fortification was surrounded by massive walls, on which other towers rose up.

We do not know what sort of enemy the builders of Barumini might have had in mind when they constructed such a formidable defensive site. One theory is that the island was organized into cantons, which frequently went to war with one another. Towards the end of the Bronze Age, around the 9th century B.C., Nuragic culture was already in decline. Many old fortresses had fallen into disuse and were being used as stone quarries to provide raw materials for the construction of nearby villages.

The inhabitants of the Nuraghi knew how to work metal and were masters of navigation.

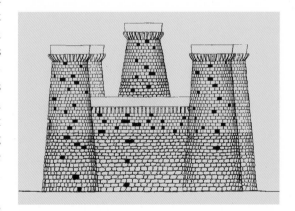

Right, top: An elevation of the Nuraghe Su Nuraxi at Barumini clearly shows its multiple stories.

Right, bottom: Idealized reconstruction of the front elevation of the fortress of Su Nuraxi at Barumini.

Opposite: The cross-section of the staircases and the corridors reveals pointed arches. Over the entrance areas there is a most carefully worked architrave (door beam) and an opening that lets both air and light in.

Right, top: View from the inner courtyard towards the sky. Spiral staircases were used to reach the upper floors. These staircases sometimes started so high up that they could only be reached using a ladder.

Right, bottom: The corbel dome, also known as a false vault, or a *tholos*, is the epitome of Nuragic construction. From the illustration it can clearly be seen how a cloister vault gradually emerges from the projecting stone layers and is ultimately covered over with a keystone.

Above: South view of the hill under which the Nuraghe of Barumini was hidden. The photograph shows the earthen bank a few years before it was excavated.

Far right: Bronze statuette from the shrine of Santa Vittoria di Serri, 8th century B.C. National Archeological Museum of Cagliari

The slender yet sturdily built Sardinian bronze statuette is impressive because of its detail. The "Nuragic prince" with his large cloak and mace lifts his hand in greeting.

Opposite, top: The excavation of Barumini: helpers used simple aids to move heavy stones.

Opposite, center: During the excavations oxen were also used to transport stone.

Opposite, bottom: View of the excavation site showing parts of the outer wall work as well as hut sites.

the discovery and obtained the first excavation permit.

During the stages of the excavation that took place between 1951 and 1956 the Nuragic fortress and adjacent settlements were completely uncovered. A five-stage chronological model was developed on the basis of stratigraphy and the types of finds made there. The excavations at Barumini became an archeological sensation, attracting attention far beyond Sardinia itself. International experts became involved and more and more excavations were undertaken all over the island.

## Nuragic society

Unfortunately, the master builders of the Nuraghi did not leave behind any heroic epics or written evidence that would help us gain an insight into their everyday life or draw our own conclusions as to how their society was structured. All that remains are the silent stone witnesses and the artefacts discovered in settlements, fortresses, tombs and shrines. It is important to realize that, although Nuragic culture appears uniform, from its very beginnings in around 1800 B.C. to its end it lasted almost 1,500 years. Within this period there must have been many a social change.

In the Nuragic fortresses and settlements are found large round huts with circular benches, which may have been assembly rooms or shrines. The gatherings that took place in these structures appear to have been accompanied by rituals in which Nuragic models made of stone, bronze or clay played a central role, as numerous finds uncovered nearby testify. The excavations did not reveal any marked differences in the social order. This could prove a hypothesis that tribal chiefs used to live in the Nuraghi. This appears to have been a community in which it was not the individual but the family as a whole that formed the most important element and the fundamental structure of the tribe. Presumably there were hierarchies according to age and sex. Village property such as land was used by the whole community. A social distinction could have existed as a result of owning more cattle, or having a higher position due to age or having achieved something special for the clan. It has not been possible, however, to perceive any differences in lifestyle

between individual tribe members. Cohesion was consolidated by common customs and traditions, and legal norms that were handed down; the community would have checked that these were adhered to. From the family community an extended family gradually evolved. This meant there was a tribal community, related by blood, which had the same origins, lived in the same area and used the same shrines and burial sites. The communal graves, or "giant graves" as they are called, also point to a collective consciousness. Even the cult of the dead was not merely a family concern, but affected everybody, and looking after every single member created a deep community spirit. The burial sites became a collective charnel house whose *exedra* served as a public area where ancestors were worshipped in front of the whole community gathered together. Over time there emerged simple forms of rule to control political and social life, and a federalist system of alliances developed. This system took the shape of autonomous communities with their own administration where the use of water, arable land and mineral resources was more or less regulated. It was not possible in the long term to keep the various extensive communities together. Territorial disputes and fragmentation, as well as the theft of women, cattle, or provisions gave rise to disunity and tribal feuds. However, just as monuments and commodities were developed further, so too did the social structure evolve. It did not become ossified, but instead adapted to changes over the course of the centuries and incorporated new influences, becoming more "modern." But in a closed society, social integrity can only be preserved if the economic basis meets the needs of every member of that society, and the society succeeds in either repelling outside influences or integrating them into the community in such a way that its basic nature is not changed.

In the 8th and 9th centuries B.C., during the transition from the Bronze Age to the Iron Age, there seem to have been changes in the social structure. The number of individual burials increased and fragments from 30

Right: Bronze statuette of an archer from the Abini shrine at Tehi, 8th century B.C. Height: 17 cm National Archeological Museum of Cagliari.

Of almost 500 well-known Sardinian bronze figures, it is the warriors that are the most famous. In this category archers are represented particularly often. What stands out is the cylindrical shape of the arms, legs and bodies, and the unconventional faces with their eyebrows and noses forming a T-shape. The warriors' weapons and protective clothing are always depicted naturally. This Oriental-style archer is wearing an ankle-length, armor-plated uniform, held in position by a belt.

Far right: Bronze statuette of an armed warrior from the Abini shrine at Tehi National Archeological Museum of Cagliari.

This type of armed warrior, with a round shield and sword or lance, is clothed in a double tunic made from cloth, and is wearing greaves or gaiters. He is fitted out with a breastplate, a leather glove, cuff-like neck rings and the characteristic horned helmet.

stone warrior statues found in Monti Prama could suggest the appearance of a new, powerful warrior caste. The increased use of metal will also have created social differences. During this time of radical social change, when there was a threat from Phoenician colonists, the many shrines sited near springs became more important and played a vital role in a unification attempt. Some of these shrines were enlarged over the course of time, and appear to have developed into major shrines. Examples are the distant sites of Santa Vittoria di Serri or of Santa Cristina di Paulilatino. The relics found here indicate that they were shrines, places of pilgrimage and sites of execution, treasure chambers and centers of commerce all in one. Here people could meet and participate in joint religious festivals and competitions, maybe even conclude agreements and settle disputes. It is certainly no coincidence that the spring shrines have turned out to be treasure troves for generations archeologists, full of bronze figures, weapons and tools, jewelry and fine ceramics.

## The bronze art of the Nuragic people

The votive gifts cast in bronze include figurines of all types of people: priests in long robes, armed warriors with leg armor and horned helmets, elegant archers, spear throwers and wrestlers, dignified male figures with large cloaks and (shepherds') crooks. There are simple folk such as musicians with reed pipes, sick people with walking sticks, men and women proffering round flat breads or jugs for sacrificial offerings, farmers driving oxen before them or shepherds with lambs on their shoulders. There are even mythical creatures and demons. But one thing is certain: the craftsmen who created these amazingly intricate bronze figures possessed enormous skill and artistic talent. The bronze statuettes were created by the "lost wax" method of casting. A wax model is made, then coated in finely ground clay and fired so that the wax melts, leaving a cavity that serves as a mold in which the figurine can be cast.

Since Sardinia was rich in lead, silver, iron and copper, and as these deposits came to the

Far left: Bronze statuette from the Abini shrine at Tehi, 8th century B.C.
Height: 19 cm
National Archeological Museum of Cagliari.

The production of the Sardinian bronzes, made using the "lost wax" method of casting, requires a high level of skill because of the complicated construction and the delicate patterning or piercing. The comical, demonic warrior figures with their four eyes, four arms, four round shields and two swords are not easy to interpret.

Left: Sardus statuette, second half of 3rd century B.C. National Archeological Museum of Cagliari.

A compact bronze figure of the deity Sardus Pater with a feathered crown and a tunic from the 4th/3rd century B.C. In Roman times Sardus was seen as a national hero as well as a god of the Sardinians.

surface in many areas, it comes as no surprise to learn that from early on there was a great deal of mining activity. Obsidian and hematite had been mined since the Stone Age. But the mineral riches of the island, as well as its key position between the eastern and western Mediterranean, also drew many foreigners to Sardinia. Mining during the Nuragic period was thus the cause, and not the effect, of intensifying Mediterranean connections. Copper bars and ceramic finds from the 13th and 12th centuries B.C. prove that Sardinia had trading relations with regions as far away as Cyprus. The Phoenicians probably took over the leading role in Sardinia's "eastern trade," formerly occupied by the Mycenaeans, towards the end of the 12th century B.C. The Nuragic people for their part seem to have been quick to learn, looking closely at what foreigners were doing or imitating their exported goods. And the Nuragic people's artefacts also found their way onto the export market: from the 9th century B.C. technically superior and artistically excellent Nuragic bronzes were being used as grave goods by the early Etruscans.

But what became of the people of the Nuraghi? From the 6th and 5th centuries B.C. they increasingly lost their cultural identity. In the long term the Nuragic people could not withstand colonization by Greeks, the Carthaginians, and the Romans. Parts of the population blended with former immigrants or lived in more or less peaceful coexistence with them. The indigenous culture was preserved far from the coast, where the native people retreated to the inner Sardinian mountainous region. The annexation of Sardinia by the Romans in 238 B.C. represents the end of the once-brilliant Nuragic period.

Right: Limbourg Brothers
*Plague Procession*, pre-1416
Illumination on parchment,
29 × 21 cm
*Les très riches heures du Duc
de Berry*, Ms.65, fol.71v/72r
Musée Condé, Chantilly

Painted from top to bottom,
this work was never
completed as the three
Limbourg brothers died from
the plague. The figures on the
left, the fallen one on the
right and the priests at the
head of the procession were
only added later.

Opposite: Jean Coene IV
*Triumph of Death, c.* 1500
Illumination on parchment,
30.8 × 22.2 cm
*Trionfi* of Anne de Polignac,
fol.33v
Heribert Tenschert,
Bibermühle

Perhaps the earliest
Petrarchan illustration in
France, this illumination
shows Laura, the poet's tragic
lover, laid out in white robes
symbolizing chastity
following her death from
the plague.

## The Castle as a Place of Refuge from the Plague

Eberhard König

Below: *The Plague of 1348:
The Black Death,
Death-Bed, c.* 1370
Illumination on parchment,
35 × 24 cm
Egerton 1070, fol.53 (WF)
The British Library, London

This unique picture shows
how courageously some
faced death. René d'Anjou,
the King of Naples and
Jerusalem, is laid out with all
his emblems.

The horror of the first plague epidemic, which started in 1347, was unparalleled. Like a gigantic wave, the pestilence devastated the whole of Europe, striking rich and poor alike. Thirty percent of the entire population is thought to have fallen victim to the disease; among them no less a personage than the French queen Jeanne, who died in 1349. While the upper classes were certainly vulnerable, the lower classes were sitting ducks for the spread of the malady. Weakened by hunger on account of the frequent crop failures of preceding years, they proved especially fertile ground for the depredations of the disease.

People living in close proximity and in un-hygienic conditions also reduced their chances of survival. This is why large towns and cities suffered unusually high casualty rates. The plague may well have depopulated entire villages or castles, too, but in the towns the virulence of

the pestilence was helped along by the frequent mass processions that were held from time to time in an attempt to invoke divine intercession against the plague. The concentration of so many penitents in one place provided an ideal breeding ground for the contagion. At least in the country there was a greater chance of isolating oneself.

Around 1370 two authors wrote about the plague experience in quite different ways. The vision of the "Triumph of Death" outlined by Petrarch (1304–1374) dwelt on the inescapable nature of death. The *Decameron*, by Giovanni Boccaccio (1313–1375) told the story of ten noble young people who met in the Florentine Dominican church of Santa Maria just after the epidemic had broken out. They then fled together to the countryside where they found themselves in an area free from horror and disease. To while away the time until the plague had finished its ravages elsewhere, they told each other stories that, being true-to-life, give us a full and in many respects critical view of life in 14th-century Italy: how folk lived, loved and cheated their neighbors, and how the clergy exploited the stupidity of ordinary people.

# Naples

## Castel Nuovo

General view of the castle complex from the northwest.

The Castel Nuovo has a trapeziform ground plan with three towers on the northwest side and two outer towers on the southeast side. Between the Torre della Guardia and the Torre di Mezzo is the resplendent marble triumphal arch of Alfonso V of Aragon, the ruler of the kingdom of the Two Sicilies, built in two stages between 1455 and 1471, separated by a break of five years between 1458 and 1463.

### Two uninhabited castles

Thirteenth-century Naples was a thriving town of 30,000 inhabitants, surrounded by a town wall and with two imposing castles. The Castel dell'Ovo was built on the island of Megaris on the site of a famous villa that had belonged to the Roman general Lucius Licinius Lucullus (*c.* 114–57 B.C.). This castle protected the town from any threats coming from the sea. The other castle, Castel Capuano, was further away, near the Porta Capuana and in the direction of Vesuvius. Frederick II enlarged and fortified both castles in the first half of the century. Castel Capuano became a residence for diplomatic and social occasions. The emperor never lived here, however, as he preferred his Norman royal palace in Palermo or his palaces in Apulia.

### Charles of Anjou

The third Neapolitan castle was given the name Castel Nuovo. It was built for Charles of Anjou, the brother of the French king, Louis IX (also known as St. Louis). After the death of Frederick II in 1250, Charles's compatriot Pope Urban VI gave him the task of subduing the kingdom of Sicily. Charles accepted this task with relish, tackling Frederick's heirs Manfred and Conradin one by one. The first heir fell on the battlefield in 1266, while the 16-year-old Conradin was lured into a trap, seized and then beheaded on the Piazza del Mercato in Naples. Manfred's four children were arrested and incarcerated in various castles of the kingdom. His daughter, Beatrice, languished in Castel dell'Ovo. Frederick's youngest son, Enzo, had already been in captivity in Bologna for 20 years. He remained there until his death in 1274.

## The third castle

Charles of Anjou settled down in Naples, which he made the capital of the kingdom of Sicily. In 1279 he ordered a third castle to be built in the town. The castle was erected between the first two fortresses, close to both the sea and the harbor, or the Porto Pisano as it was then called. A church and an old palace already stood on the chosen spot; both of these were confiscated and demolished. The Franciscan friars who had formerly celebrated mass in the church were recompensed with a church in another part of the town. The Castel Nuovo turned out to be quite different from the other two castles. It had six or seven slender, round towers, built in the French style, as well as moats and drawbridges. Moreover, from the very beginning it was designed as both a fortress and a residence. A French architect, Pierre de Caulis, was entrusted with its construction. De Caulis, who was also a priest, completed the project in a relatively short space of time. As early as 1282 the Angevin family was living in the castle. By 1284 construction work was complete, and the court was officially opened.

Of the Angevin castle only the chapel known as the Cappella Palatina and the foundations remain. The frescoes by Giotto, which adorned the chapel and other rooms, are gone. What we can see today is not the Angevin castle, but a fortress built on top of it by the Aragonese in the middle of the 15th century. The trapeziform foundations show, however, that the ground plan did not change. The area behind the castle used to be a garden with palm trees, and a large roof terrace full of exotic birds and plants looked out towards the Porto Pisano, which was situated beneath the Beverello, the main tower.

## Fiammetta

Information on the architecture of the castle has come down to us from literary sources. At the beginning of the 14th century a salon of great Tuscan writers gathered at the court of the "Wise King" Robert of Anjou, grandson of Charles I. Among them was Giovanni

Simone Martini
*St. Louis of Toulouse Crowns His Brother, Robert of Anjou,* 1317
Wood, 200 × 138 cm
Museo di Capodimonte, Naples

Robert of Anjou commissioned this panel in 1317 from the painter Simone Martini of Siena. The panel's purpose was to show the legitimacy of his succession to the throne of Anjou. Of the 14 sons of Charles II of Anjou Robert was the third, but his elder brother Louis became a priest and so ruled himself out of the succession. Louis later became bishop of Toulouse.

Boccaccio, then a banking apprentice, who lived in Naples and visited the court regularly. On the castle terrace he fell in love with King Robert's illegitimate daughter. He called her Fiammetta, and she became his muse and the inspiration for his stories. The memory of Fiammetta inspired Boccaccio's entire mature oeuvre.

Francesco Petrarca, or Petrarch, another member of the literary salon, wrote an interesting a description of the frescoes created by the great painter Giotto for the Angevin court in the 1320s and 1330s. Giotto spent five years painting this cycle on religious themes, including scenes from the New and Old Testament, as well as a series of famous figures from antiquity. All of these works of art, together with King Robert's legendary library, have been lost.

## Constance times three

At this time, the island of Sicily had broken away from the greater kingdom of Sicily. This

Opposite: *Robert of Anjou, King of Naples*
Illumination
Royal Ms. 6 E IX. 10r, WF
The British Library, London

Robert of Anjou (1275–1343), grandson of Charles I of Anjou, was crowned king of Naples by Pope Clement V on August 3, 1310. As leader of the Guelphs, he soon rose to become one of the most powerful princes of Italy. During his reign his court became an important cultural center, frequented by the poets Petrarch and Boccaccio as well the painters Giotto and Simone Martini.

Opposite: Prayerbook of
Alfonso V of Aragon, c. 1442
Add. Ms. 28962, fol. 78
The British Library, London
This miniature from the
prayerbook of Alfonso V of
Aragon tells of his battle with
the Moors in Spain. He
gained a definitive victory in
Granada in 1492. Alfonso
founded one of the greatest
libraries of his time at
this court.

happened at Easter in 1282, at the instigation
of King Pedro III of Aragon, and after a bloody
revolt known as the Sicilian Vespers. Pedro III
made a claim on the dynastic inheritance of
Frederick II, on fairly convincing grounds. His
father's aunt, Constance of Aragon, had been
the first wife of the Hohenstaufen emperor,
who in turn was the son of the Norman
Constance d'Hauteville. Pedro III had married
a third Constance, the daughter of Manfred,
Frederick's son. Pedro III not only snatched
Sicily away from the Angevins; within a short
space of time he had also acquired extensive
areas in Calabria and Apulia. The war that
broke out as a result lasted 160 years and
ended with a decisive defeat for the Angevins
(1442). During the last decades of the war the
Castel Nuovo changed hands many times and
by the end of the war it had been reduced to a
heap of rubble. Only the chapel with Giotto's
frescoes remained intact – for the time being,
at least.

### Vittoria

On February 26, 1443, Alfonso V of Aragon
(Alfonso I of Sicily) marched triumphally into
the town of Naples. He had ordered a section
of the southern wall to be removed especially
for this occasion. Although the town had been
in his possession for many months, he needed
symbolic recognition. Many chroniclers have
described his official entry into the town,
listing the names and ranks of the 70 most
important dignitaries, ambassadors and prelates who headed the triumphal procession.

The only aspect they did not agree on was the
number of horses used to pull the carriages.
What is certain is that theses horses were
white and that their reins were held by a half-
naked girl, who walked in front, wearing a
small crown in her flowing hair. She was the
famous Vittoria. Also, a painted wooden triumphal arch had been raised in the Piazza del
Mercato especially for the occasion. This arch
was supposed to resemble the marble arches
of the ancient Roman emperors. The
Neapolitans sniggered contemptuously at the
wooden construction, however. The triumphal procession ended at the cathedral square,
where the foundations for a permanent triumphal arch had been laid. While the reconstruction
of the Castel Nuovo progressed rapidly, the erection of the triumphal arch was repeatedly
postponed. Even when the castle was finished,
work on the arch had not even started.

### The unshakable castle

Alfonso summoned a host of Catalan and
Italian artists and architects to Naples.
Guillermo Sagrera from Majorca was
entrusted with managing the construction
work. After his death in 1454 the project,
which was now near completion, was handed
over to Guillermo's son and brother-in-law.
With the help of the great military architects
of the time the exterior wall of the castle and
its fortifications were continuously updated in
subsequent decades. Among these great military architects were Giuliano da Sangallo
from Florence and Francesco di Giorgio

In memory of his glorious
entry into Naples in 1443,
Alfonso V of Aragon had a
marble triumphal arch built
between two of the massive
towers on the castle's west
side. The frieze decorated the
architrave between the first
and the second arch.

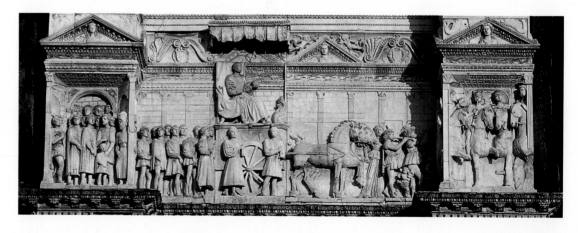

Preces pro intrantibus bellum contra paganos. a. Efftundc. ps damd
Deus venerint gentes in hereditatem tuam Gloria patri. a. Effunde iram tuam in gentes que te non nouerunt et in regna que nomen tuum non inuocauerunt.

The foundations, the facade and the Cappella Palatina are covered in peperite, a very hard volcanic rock which gives the castle its somber appearance. On top of the foundations there runs an overhang crowned with battlements, where the "field snakes," the notorious Aragonese guns, were positioned.

Martini from Siena. In his spare time Martini devised a hydraulic pump that was capable of supplying water to every floor of the castle.

The enormous strength of the Castel Nuovo was illustrated in 1456, when the castle withstood an earthquake, sustaining only minimal damage while the rest of the town was completely destroyed. Unfortunately, Giotto's chapel frescoes were irretrievably damaged. The last fragments of the frescoes fell victim to subsequent restoration work carried out by the Catalan Juan de Guares (1465). The *Tavola Strozzi*, which is kept in the San Martino Museum, gives an excellent impression of the port and the recently completed castle as they looked at the time.

## An unconventional king

Alfonso V died in 1458. He was a melancholic and stern ruler, who was unpopular with the Neapolitans as he spoke their language poorly and allocated all the top government positions to Catalans, Florentines, Genoese and Vene-

tians. Alfonso did not feel safe in the shadow of the volcanic Mount Vesuvius and in his will he specified that he was to be buried in Aragon and not in Naples. Despite his unpopularity, Alfonso was tolerant by the standards of contemporary rulers. He surrounded himself with the best minds of the time: men such as Enea Silvio Piccolomini, Lorenzo Valla and Antonio Beccadelli, to name but three. These men had such unconventional views that they would probably have been burned at the stake had they lived 100 years later. In 1458, one of them – Piccolomini – even became pope, however.

Alfonso's court offered refuge to learned Greeks, who had fled from Constantinople following the Turkish conquest of 1453, and to Jews who had been forced to leave Spain during the *Reconquista*. The king spent vast sums of money on ancient manuscripts. He financed Greek and Hebrew scholars and opened a language school. He would not go to sleep at night until a humanist scholar had read to him from an ancient text.

## The black castle

The Aragonese castle was built on top of the trapeziform ground plan of the old Angevin castle. Towers were built in the same places as in the old castle, and they retained the same names. Torre di San Giorgio, Torre di Mezzo and Torre della Guardia are the three large, round towers situated close together on the west facade. The towers on the north-east and south-east corners respectively also retain their original names: the Torre del Beverello, the largest and the highest tower, and the Torre dell'Oro, where the state treasure was kept. The towers and the walls connecting them lie on massive foundations, which are in the shape of a pedestal and rise out of a deep, wide ditch. A wide overhang, which protects a wall crowned with battlements, runs around the upper edge of these foundations. This is where people used to set up the castle's falconets, or "field snakes" as they were called. These Aragonese guns were on a par with the weapons of Ferrara – the most modern firearms of the age.

The foundations, the wide overhang, the long connecting wall on the north flank, the towers on the front, the Torre del Beverello, and the facade of the Cappella Palatina are covered with peperite, a very hard, blackish volcanic rock, which lends the castle its somber appearance. At the end of the 15th century an outer ring of protective walls was built around the castle. This outer ring was designed by Antonio da Settignano, who had taken over the castle extension and fortification work from his master, Francesco di Giorgio Martini. The first rampart complex was demolished after a few years, to be replaced by the so-called "Spanish ramparts," which had a star-shaped outline.

In the second half of the 19th century, when the castle had long since ceased to have any military purpose, these bastions were demolished, too. The grounds were converted into a public park, which in later years was tarred or concreted over to build new roads. Like so many old monuments in Naples, the castle today functions as a traffic island.

## The bones of the barons

The castle's inner courtyard is reached via a drawbridge. The most important building is located opposite the entrance. This is the Sala dei Baroni, the room of the barons near the Beverello. Next are the Cappella Palatina and the loggia from the 15th century, which lead to the royal residence. The Sala dei Baroni, the work of Guillermo Sagrera, is a large square room, 85 feet (26 m) long and 91.5 feet (28 m) high. The ceiling is made up of an octopartite stellar vault. In the middle of this stellar vault, instead of the customary keystone, there is a round eye that is open and lets light in. The room can be entered from the inner courtyard via a magnificent stone staircase. This room was

Above: The triumphal arch of Alfonso V of Aragon (detail).

The triumphal arch should in fact have been erected in the cathedral square, in front of the basilica of San Gennaro. The difficulties encountered by the Aragonese sovereign in completing the monument in the town center caused him to have the arch built as an entrance to his royal castle.

Below: The trapeziform ground plan of the Castel Nuovo. Between the watchtower on the right and the middle tower lies the entrance portal, in which the triumphal arch of Alfonso V of Aragon was built.

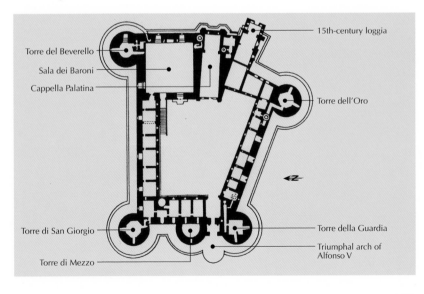

Torre del Beverello
Sala dei Baroni
Cappella Palatina
15th-century loggia
Torre dell'Oro
Torre di San Giorgio
Torre di Mezzo
Torre della Guardia
Triumphal arch of Alfonso V

Sala dei Baroni, vault.

The room of the barons, where the leaders of a rebellion were arrested, is the work of Guillermo Sagrera, the Catalan architect who oversaw the interior construction of the castle in the 15th century.

officially opened with a large reception on April 15, 1457, and in 1486 it was the beautiful setting for an ugly ploy. Alfonso's son Ferdinand I of Aragon, who was generally known as Ferrante, had invited some barons in the kingdom to a banquet to celebrate his reconciliation with them after they had earlier led a rebellion against him. Instead of sitting down for a feast, however, they were arrested and handed over to the executioner. From then on the room formerly known as the Sala Maggiore, the great hall, was called the Sala dei Baroni. The bones of the barons still lie in a chapel beneath the crypt.

Next to the facade of the Sala dei Baroni is the facade of the Cappella Palatina, which, unlike the former, is covered in black peperite with slender columns up its entire height. The Renaissance portal is the work of Andrea dell' Aquila, a student of Donatello. In a niche above the portal stands a tender Madonna figure by Francesco Laurana. Further up is a large rosette, the work of the Catalan Matteo Forcimanya from Majorca. This extremely fine web of stone replaced the original rosette that was destroyed by the earthquake of 1456.

## The time machine

The reason why it was decided to erect the triumphal arch of Alfonso V in the entrance of the castle rather than in the town remains a mystery. It is said that the location originally chosen, in front of the cathedral, displeased a local baron, Nicola Maria Bozzuto, as his nearby palace would be in the shadow of the

Cappella Palatina, rosette.

In 1470 the beautiful work of the Catalan artist Matteo Forcimanya from Majorca replaced the chapel from the Angevin period, which was destroyed by an earthquake, together with the Giotto's frescoes.

monument at certain times of the day. Furthermore the baron would be forced to drive around or through the triumphal arch in his carriage every evening upon returning to his palace. This explanation, while colorful, does not seem to be the true one.

Presumably what carried more weight was the opposition of the Church, which spoke out against a triumphal arch, especially one situated in the religious center of the town, opposite the cathedral. For many years, while construction work on the castle progressed apace, the townspeople gossiped about where, when and how the triumphal arch of King Alfonso, whom they had maliciously begun to call "the Magnanimous," was actually going to be erected.

It is not known who had the ambitious idea of erecting the marble triumphal arch between the two towers at the entrance of the castle. Normally such an arch would require a large empty space around it, but there was no such area in the castle. It may even have been the king himself; he would certainly have had to approve the plans for the structure. Thus there appeared a narrow, white and finely chiseled arch that made the best use of the little space between the two enormous, brown and somber towers, which seemed to be holding it prisoner. No one had tried such a thing before, but it worked. The result was extremely beautiful and highly symbolic: a jewel of the Renaissance, delicate and slender, wedged in between massive military constructions from the darker, and more dangerous, past.

In the decade between 1448 and 1458 dozens of Italian artists, architects, sculptors and engravers lived and worked in Naples. Among them was a certain Pisanello, the most eminent medallion engraver of his time. A drawing that has been ascribed to him gave

The archangel Michael keeps watch on top of the Aragonese triumphal arch. Within the arch there are bacchants with overflowing cornucopia and portrait-like features. The scene on the frieze and in the niches of the triumphal arch, situated above the lower arch, depicted Alfonso's triumphant entry into Naples. In the upper arch there is first a frieze with griffins, then niches with allegories of human virtues.

rise to the theory that he might have designed the triumphal arch. It would seem appropriate for an engraver, accustomed to portraying a whole world in the small space of a medallion, to come up with the idea of sandwiching the delicate arch between the squat towers.

The construction of the arch began in 1453, once the large round entrance towers had been completed at the end of 1452. Enormous blocks of marble, snow-white and free of veins, arrived from Carrara. An architect called Pietro Martino from Milan was called to manage the construction work. He brought with him the sculptor and engraver Francesco Laurana from Dalmatia, then an unknown artist. They were joined by Domenico Gaggini from Milan, Paolo Romano from Rome, Isaia da Pisa and Mino da Fiesole, as well as Andrea dell'Aquila from Florence and Antonio da Chellino from Pisa, both of whom were students of Donatello. In 1458 Alfonso V died. The work was stopped and the artists left. At that time the lower arch was finished, and the large bas-relief may also have been put up. This bas-relief was the work of many artists and it depicted a scene from the Aragonese sovereign's triumphant entry into Naples. It is assumed that many other elements had already been completed, and were only waiting to be put into place. For many years military operations and internal politics prevented the work from being completed, however. In fact, it was not until 1465 that work was resumed under Pietro Martino, who returned from Milan with a much smaller team of artists. Luciano Laurana, who had just completed work on the ducal palace in Urbino, also worked on the project. (He is not to be confused with Francesco Laurana, mentioned above). Because the project took so much time and employed such a large number of artists, the question of exactly who did what remains unanswered.

## The journey of the bronze doors

The Aragonese kingdom of Two Sicilies lasted just over 50 years. It was smashed by the French king Charles VIII, who claimed the Aragonese inheritance as his. King Ferrante, who had succeeded his father Alfonso V to the throne in 1458, could not withstand the strain of having a possible invasion looming over his head and died before the French ruler had even crossed the Alps to wage war on his kingdom. On his deathbed Ferrante composed a prophetic letter to Lodovico Sforza, the lord of Milan, who had thrown in his lot on the side of Charles VIII in his Italian campaign. When the French ruler arrived in Rome, Ferrante's successor, Alfonso II, abdicated in favor of his son and fled to Sicily. He died there a few months later. Ferrante II, known as Ferrandino, the small Ferrante, had come into a difficult inheritance in a desperate situation. He, too, left the town and

Opposite: The triumphal arch at the entrance to the Castel Nuovo was begun by Alfonso V of Aragon.

Below: There is s striking similarity between the base of the triumphal arch of the Castel Nuovo and the arch of Sergius (29–27 B.C.) at Pula in Sardinia. Pietro da Milano and Francesco Laurana may have brought precise drawings of the arch with them when they came to Naples.

289

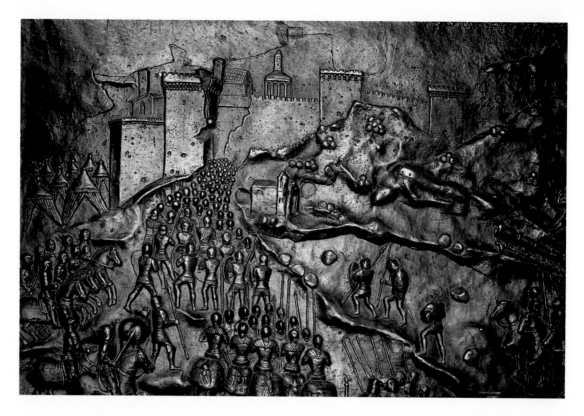

fled, first to Ischia, then to Messina. Meanwhile, Charles VIII marched into Naples without encountering any resistance. The humanist Giovanni Pontano, a former protégé of the old Ferrante, handed over the keys to the town. Charles VIII only stayed a few weeks in Naples. He had won it without a fight and spent his time there plundering its treasures before turning north again. In addition to the furnishings and the precious objects housed in the Castel Nuovo, Charles VIII also had the ancient scripts from the library of Alfonso the Magnanimous packed up. He then removed the bronze doors from castle entrance and had them loaded onto a ship, which was seized by the Genoese on its way to Marseilles. The doors later were later sent back to Naples.

No sooner had the Frenchman gone when Ferrandino returned to the humiliated and devastated town. He did not survive the catastrophe that had befallen his family, wiping out two generations within three years. Ferrandino died in 1496. His wife was the sister of Ferdinand (the Catholic) of Spain,

and on the strength of this connection Spain came to rule over the kingdom of the Two Sicilies. From now on the kingdom was ruled by two Spanish viceroys, one with a seat in Palermo, and the other in Naples.

## Bread and justice

The end of Aragonese rule heralded the inexorable decline of the Castel Nuovo and the whole of Naples. Charles VIII stole the decorations from the living rooms of the Aragonese residence, which were situated above the loggia and looked out to sea. For a while the living rooms housed the Spanish viceroys. Then they were abandoned in favor of the new royal palace that had just been built near the castle. Continuous earthquakes, pestilence and public revolt characterized the two centuries of Spanish rule. The earthquake was followed by the plague, and the plague by rebellion. The unpopularity of the rulers was due in no small part to the tradition that whenever an heir to the Spanish throne was born, or a Spanish king visited Naples, was crowned, married or died, the Neapolitans had to pay a "voluntary" contribution of 30,000 ducats to the Spanish crown.

Despite the many tribulations faced by Naples, the number of inhabitants rose steadily. Naples became the most densely populated city in Italy, and the second-largest metropolis of Europe, after Paris. In the middle of the 16th century Naples had a population of 210,000; its 20,000 priests, monks and nuns were not included in this figure. One century later there were already 360,000 inhabitants in the town. The dreadful plague of 1656 reduced the population by more than half.

In some of the popular uprisings that occurred in Naples the insurgents managed to gain control of the Castel Nuovo and other castles in the city. This happened during the two most important uprisings of the 16th century, in 1510 and 1547 respectively. The first uprising was about the price, the quality and the size of loaves of bread, and the second was directed against the introduction of the Spanish Inquisition. The Inquisition represented a decisive change compared with the traditional administration of justice, making use as it did of secret witnesses for the prosecution. Only the Inquisitors knew the real identity of these witnesses. On the basis of secret testimony people could be subjected to torture for as long as it took them to confess to their crimes. Moreover, the property of the accused was confiscated as soon as legal proceedings started. Because of this, members of the nobility also joined in the people's protest – after all, they had much more to lose than the poor. The philosopher Benedetto Croce put forward a novel reason why the Spanish-style Inquisition was unsuitable for Naples. He suggested that the method may work in a country such as Spain, where people spoke the truth, but in Naples, where giving false evidence was the norm, it just would not work.

In any case, these two revolts were successful. Later the Spanish-style Inquisition gained acceptance not only in Naples, but throughout Italy.

Opposite and left:
The bronze doors adorned the entrance portal to the castle. They depict scenes from the battle of Accadia at Foggia. When Charles VIII marched into Naples in 1485 he occupied and plundered the castle. In addition to other valuable objects, the bronze doors were taken. They did, however, find their way back to Naples eventually.

# The Conclave

### Charles, Celestine and Boniface

Three events that were unique in the history of the papacy took place between July and December of 1294 in the Castel Nuovo. A pope established his seat in the residence of a secular sovereign for the first time; a pope declared his abdication for the first time; and a conclave to elect a new pope sat in the castle of a secular sovereign for the first time. How did these extraordinary events come about?

### Past history

With the death of its founder, Charles of Anjou, in January of 1285 the kingdom of Sicily found itself in a desperate situation. Following the Sicilian Vespers the island of Sicily, which gave the kingdom its name, had broken away. Together with parts of Calabria and Apulia, Sicily went to the Aragonese. Charles II, the son and heir of the founder of the kingdom, was taken prisoner by the Aragonese during a sea battle in the Gulf of Naples, and was held hostage. In Naples itself, the capital city of the kingdom, a revolt against the Angevins had just been bloodily suppressed. In his will, Charles I of Anjou chose his 12-year-old grandson Charles Martel to be the provisional heir in place of his father, who was still the prisoner of the Aragonese. No one would have given much for the chances of the Angevin kingdom surviving, had the pope not been behind the boy.

Pope Martin IV, the Frenchman Simon de Brion, understood that he had to act as a clever mediator between the Angevins and the Aragonese. He filled the power vacuum in the kingdom by assuming *de facto* control. After the death of Martin IV the Franciscan pope Nicholas IV continued with the same policy. Exploiting the differences between the heirs of Pedro III of Aragon, he managed to obtain the release of Charles II in 1288. To secure his release, though, Charles did have to produce three of his sons and 60 French noblemen from his court as hostages. In addition, he had to pay a high ransom. With this exchange, the Aragonese were aiming to be recognized as

Henri Decaisne (1799–1852)
*Charles of Anjou*
(1226–1285), 1844
Oil on canvas
Musée Nationale du
Château de Versailles et de
Trianon, Versailles

The pope granted King
Charles I of Anjou the
kingdom of Naples, formerly
under the Hohenstaufen
family. Charles I had the last
Hohenstaufen prince,
Conradin, executed.

Right: Arnolfo di Cambio
(1245–1302)
*The Blessed Boniface VIII*
Marble
Museo dell'Opera del
Duomo, Florence

Cardinal Benedict Caetano
(1230–1303) owed his
election as Pope Boniface
VIII to his hostility towards
the Roman Colonna family,
and to the French. He had
studied law and was a very
worldly pope. In 1294 he
advised Pope Celestine V to
resign – the first time a pope
had ever done so. As soon as
he was elected pope, he
commissioned Arnolfo di
Cambio to build him a
mausoleum in St. Peter's
basilica. The structure was
completed while Boniface
was still alive.

the real rulers of Sicily and wanted nothing more than to humiliate their enemy. The Angevins, on the other hand, wanted to retain at least part of their kingdom. At the age of 41 Charles of Anjou was set free. On May 29, 1289, he was crowned King of Naples in Rieti by Pope Nicholas. It was clear that the realm of this king, who was known as *lo Zoppo*, "the cripple," could not have survived without the active support of the pope. When Nicholas died in 1292 the Angevin king did all he could to ensure that the new pope would be favorably disposed towards him.

## Cardinals at a dead end

The conclave that was to elect a successor to Nicholas IV was one of the longest and most arduous in history. The pro-French cardinals opposed the anti-French cardinals. Both parties were dependent on the two most powerful families in Rome, the Orsini and the Colonna. The conclave, in session in Rome, was moved no fewer than three times for fear that the cardinals would be kidnapped. The city was on the verge of civil war. After one year of fruitless meetings, the conclave resolved to move to Perugia. It was thought that here they would be free from the pressures exerted by the Roman parties. But even in Perugia it was impossible to resolve the impasse.

## A shrewd king

This situation prompted Charles of Anjou, accompanied by his young son, to go to Perugia and ask the cardinals whether he would be permitted to make a speech to the conclave. This constituted a serious impropriety, but they agreed to give the king of Naples a hearing. He declared that he approved the choice of Cardinal Benedict Caetano for pope. His appearance, which was unheard of, filled Caetano with indignation, as he did not belong to any party. He explained to the ruler that the Holy Spirit was the only permitted guest at a conclave. He then asked Charles II to leave and not disrupt proceedings any longer.

## A naive monk

Charles returned to Naples via a different route from his usual one, stopping at Monte Morrone

Reclining figure of the monument of Charles II of Anjou, end of the 14th century
Abbey of St. Denis, France

Like his Angevin predecessors, Charles II needed the active support of the pope to prop up his regime. To ensure adequate control of papal elections, in 1309 the French monarchy succeeded in getting the papacy moved from Rome to Avignon.

in the Abruzzi region on the way. An old monk called Pietro lived there in a community of hermits, and he was revered by the local people as though he were a saint. The king asked the monk if he would pray for a good outcome for the conclave. In addition, he was to write to the members of the conclave so the Holy Spirit might enlighten them. The old hermit prayed and wrote his letter. This had an outcome that no one could have predicted: Pietro da Morrone was elected pope! Upon hearing news of his appointment Christendom was filled with a feeling of jubilation. At last, a saint as pope! Even Charles, *lo Zoppo*, was happy.

The only person who was upset to hear the news was the man who was directly affected. Not only did Pietro da Morrone not really feel up to the task; more importantly, he was horrified at the thought of having to go to Rome for a ceremony with all those cardinals. He asked if the papal tiara could be placed on his head in the beautiful basilica of Santa Maria di Collemaggio in L'Aquila. His wish was granted and the ceremony took place on July 5, 1294. Pietro, who was now called Celestine V, gladly accepted Charles of Anjou's invitation to stay in Naples for a time, while preparing for the journey to Rome. Celestine V made his entry into the Castel Nuovo on a mule that was as white as the donkey on which the Messiah had ridden into Jerusalem. He declined the rooms that had been prepared for him and preferred to stay the night in a bare chamber above the Cappella Palatina.

## A crafty cardinal

The poor Celestine realized all too soon that he had wandered into a devilish trap. The wily cardinals tried to use him as a puppet, and exerted enormous pressures on him. On one occasion he was induced to appoint 12 new cardinals in one single day. There were seven Frenchmen and two Neapolitans among them, but not a single Roman. As a result of persistent pressure from Charles, the new pope also handed over the archbishopric of Lyon to Charles' 20-year-old son, Ludovico. Luckily for Celestine, Cardinal Benedict Caetano arrived in Naples at around the same time. This man, who was experienced

in worldly matters and who had approved the choice of Celestine, advised Celestine to do something that no pope had ever dared to do: to announce his abdication. On December 13, 1294, Celestine convened the consistory in the Angevin castle and declared his abdication. As canon law did not provide for such a deed, the law was changed there and then. Afterwards the conclave was convened again. On Christmas Eve a new pope was elected: he was none other than Benedict Caetano, who called himself Boniface VIII.

Cornelius Galle (1576–1650)
*Portrait of Celestine V*
Copperplate
Archiv für Kunst und Geschichte, Berlin

The former hermit was elected pope in 1294 against his will. After his resignation and his subsequent murder, he was elevated to the status of a martyr.

Opposite: The three towers on the west facade of the Castel Nuovo in Naples.

# Palermo

## The palace of the Normans

The Norman palace

First the Phoenicians, and then the Romans and the Byzantines settled on the hill upon which the Norman palace (Palazzo dei Normanni) stands today. The ancient conquerors of Sicily were followed by the Arabs, then the Normans and finally Frederick II. As soon as Roger II had been crowned in 1130 he set about renovating his royal seat. Arabic and Byzantine craftsmen were commissioned to do the work. At the heart of the complex is the Cappella Palatina, a colonnaded basilica with three naves. The mosaics within this church, along with Cefalù and Monreale, are unique. Much of the present complex was built in the 16th century. It was in a dilapidated state for many years, until preservation work commenced in the 1920s. Since 1947 Sicily's parliament has been located here.

### Ancient Ziz, the flower of Sicily

The origins of the Norman palace in Palermo go back to the tme when three different cultures met: the Islamic, the Greek-Byzantine, and the Norman. Very few architectural witnesses to such a unique combination have survived the ravages of time. Apart from the Norman palace there is the cathedral in Cefalù, several Palermitan churches and the *palazzetti delle delizie*, as the small pleasure palaces scattered around the old part of town are called. Changes made to the Palazzo dei Normanni during the middle of the 16th century are what give it such a distinctive appearance today. At that time the middle section of the royal seat was pulled down in order to build a new residence for the Spanish viceroys who ruled over Sicily. Other Norman constructions, on the other hand, remained intact and were incorporated into the new building.

The palace is in the heart of the oldest part of Palermo and rises on a hill situated between the old harbor and the mountain known as Monreale. Two rivers, now filled with debris, form the boundary of this district, which was built at the highest point of the city and fortified by the Phoenicians in the 4th century B.C. Traces still remain of these walls. The fortified upper town had the Greek name Paleàpolis, while the lower part of town that overlooked the harbor was called Neàpolis. Although Palermo was founded by the Phoenicians and not the Greeks, Greek cultural and commercial influence predominated. Even the name "Palermo" is derived from the Greek *panormos*, meaning "whole harbor." The Phoenician town was called Ziz, a word that means "flower:" Palermo was a Sicilian Florence that blossomed many centuries before the Tuscan town did.

Egnazio Danti
*Map of Sicily*
Fresco
Galleria delle Carte
Geografiche, Musei Vaticani,
Rome

The map shows the island
pictured from north to south.
Within the map can be seen
the detailed enlargements of
the seaports of Messina,
Syracuse and Palermo.

The upper town was fortified further by the Romans when they took over the town from the Phoenicians in the year 254 B.C., following the Punic Wars. The Roman masonry outlived even the Byzantine period, when Sicily was under the sphere of influence of Constantinople (535–831 A.D.). Sicily's key position can be recognized immediately by looking at a map of the Mediterranean. The island is situated between the western and the eastern sea basins, and is almost equidistant between the continents of Europe and Africa. Every Mediterranean culture from antiquity to the Middle Ages left its mark on this strategic island. As Goethe wrote: "Italy without Sicily makes no impression what-soever on the soul: the key to everything is here."

## The Muslim town

The Islamic invasion of the island began in 827 A.D., and it was to last 70 years. Palermo was the first important town to come under Arab rule, in 831. It became the capital of the Muslim emirate of Sicily. At first neither the emir nor the Islamic administration settled in the ancient fortified town. They did, however, tear down the old walls and build a new fortified town in the lower part, the Neàpolis. Near the harbor lies the district known as Kalsa, which has retained its Arabic character to the present day. Only later, once the Arabs

298

had gained control over the whole island, was the ancient Paleàpolis once again surrounded by a wall. Here the emirs built a residence set amid lakes and gardens. A covered road linked this residence to a mosque that had been converted from a cathedral. In the Islamic period the upper part of town was called Halqa.

During the two centuries of Islamic rule Palermo grew into a thriving and densely populated town. Its splendor was comparable with that of Córdoba and Cairo. The population of Palermo, which numbered about 30,000 at the time of the Romans, grew considerably. Medieval sources claim the town had 300,000 inhabitants, but this figure is undoubtedly exaggerated. More conservative estimates suggest that about 100,000 people lived in Palermo. The Arabs introduced the cultivation of sugar cane, date palms, cotton, hemp, and bananas into Sicily.

## The Norman town

Between 1061 and 1091 the Normans conquered the whole of Sicily and founded a kingdom there. These descendants of the Vikings had been called in by Italian potentates from their home in northern France to serve as mercenaries. Within a few years the warlike "Norsemen" had brought Apulia, Calabria and areas of Campania under their control. Next they prepared to cross the Strait of Messina in order to conquer the Arab emirate of Sicily. Within ten years they controlled the northern part of the island, and in 1072 they took Palermo.

Despite their track record as ruthless warriors the Normans succeeded in establishing a lasting state in Sicily, much as the Arabs had before them. This was due to their extraordinary skill in understanding the administrative, political and cultural heritage of the Arab emirs and of previous cultures, and building on this heritage. Under Norman rule, Sicily remained essentially what it had always been: a very mixed society in religious, cultural, ethnic, social and linguistic terms. Palermo was home to Greeks, Arabs,

an ancient Jewish community, Genoese and Pisans – all living together rather contentedly, as they had for some time. After the Normans had conquered the whole island, many new arrivals settled in various parts of the island. They were indiscriminately classified as "Lombards," although not all of them came from Lombardy.

## King Roger

As soon as they had conquered Palermo the Normans fortified the walls of the upper town and the castle by the sea. Later, after Roger II had obtained the crown of Sicily in 1130, he began constructing his own royal seat in Halqa. He retained the previous ground plan and took Arabic and Byzantine craftsmen and artists into his service. The Palazzo dei Normanni also retained its dual function of residence and castle, with its structured complex of buildings, towers, courtyards, large gardens and artificial lakes. The Cappella Palatina chapel rose up in the middle of the complex. Although the church was officially opened in 1132, it, or at least its extensive ornamentation, was not completed until 1443. This is attested by a Greek inscription, which can be seen on the base of the hemispherical cupola. The architecture of the

Marius Cartanus
*Topographical Map of Palermo* 1581
Copperplate
Società Siciliana per la Storia della Patria, Palermo

The ancient town was bounded by the Norman palace and the harbor, which cut into the settlement.

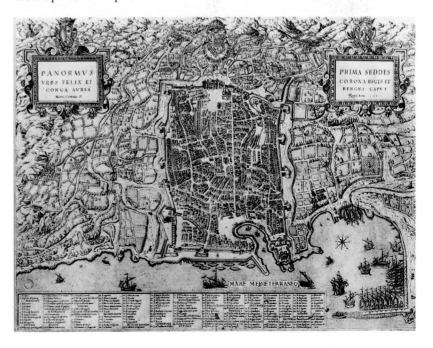

*Left: Christ crowns Roger II,*
first half of the 12th century
Mosaic
Martorana Church, Palermo

Roger d'Hauteville was
crowned King of Sicily in
1130 by Pope Anacletus II,
who belonged to the
powerful Roman-Jewish
Pierleoni family. Anacletus
was the only Jewish pope in
the history of the Church.
Although he was elected by
a majority of the cardinals,
another candidate called
Innocent II was nominated to
stand against him. Anacletus
was supported by only
Scotland and Sicily, and the
conflict between the two
popes ended in Anacletus's
isolation. In the end his
election was annulled. After
this, Innocent II
excommunicated Roger
d'Hauteville and armed an
expedition against him. The
pope was, however, defeated
and taken prisoner by the
Norman ruler. In order to
secure his release in 1139 he
had to recognize the
legitimacy of Roger's
coronation by Anacletus II.
The beautiful mosaic in the
Martorana Church is the only
extant picture of Roger
d'Hauteville. To destroy any
doubts as to his legitimacy as
a ruler, the mosaic shows
Roger receiving royal dignity
directly from Christ.

chapel and the ceiling in the nave is Arabic. The mosaics, which cover the floors, walls and the cupola, are the work of Byzantine craftsmen. At the entrance to the nave there is a large stone royal throne, which is also covered in mosaics.

Of the other Norman buildings, two square towers still stand. These are the Torre Gioaria and the Torre Pisana, which flank the chapel to the north-west. What has disappeared, however, are the two towers from the opposite south side, the Torre Kirimbi and the Torre Greca. All that is left of the Greek tower, which predated the Norman palace, are the foundations. The Torre Pisana is a strong and compact structure. Double walls surround the lower part on all four sides; between these walls there is a passageway. This protected space served as a strongroom, in which state treasure was once kept. Four enormous vessels that were built into the floor still stand here, and they can hold millions of coins.

On the upper floor is the Sala Nobile, a room 49 feet (15 m) high with a beautiful groin vault. The Sala Nobile was used for official and social functions. Regrettably, faint traces are all that remain of the mosaics originally adorning this room. The Torre Gioaria,

Opposite, top: The Cappella Palatina, Palermo

The cloister vault with the figure of *Christus Pantocrator*. The two fingers of the right hand are bent in a very unusual way.

Opposite, bottom: The Cappella Palatina, nave

Opposite the altar, in accordance with Norman royal practice, is a raised area for the throne; behind it is a mosaic showing the Pantocrator between Peter and Paul.

columns. This room takes one to the lovely Sala di Ruggiero (Roger's Hall), which became the belvedere of the Norman palace as it commands a fine view over the town and the harbor. Together with the Cappella Palatina, this space is the gem of the whole palace. The walls are lined with a high marble pedestal upon which an arch and a vaulted ceiling rest. The arch and the vaulted ceiling are completely covered with mosaics, showing animals such as leopards, peacocks and deer, and also palms and banana plants arranged symmetrically opposite each other.

## The gardens of Paradise

The wealth and variety of plants and animals depicted in the beautiful mosaics of Roger's Hall reflect in geometric and stylistic form what could be enjoyed from the windows and terraces of the Norman palace. The buildings lay in the green surroundings of an enormous "garden of Paradise," which was full of flowers and fruits, animals and birds, brooks, lakes and fountains. This reflects a strain of culture that the Arabs brought to Sicily; one that has its origins in faraway Persia, Mesopotamia and Egypt. With the spread of Islam along the Mediterranean coast, "gardens of Paradise" were created wherever the Arabs landed.

In Palermo the Normans not only surrounded their residential palaces with green spaces and water features, but Roger II also had the Arab gardens of Paradise that encircled the town restored and replenished. This is how La Favara, La Cuba, La Zisa and the great Altofonto park came into being. These walled-in gardens still have ruins dating from the Norman period. The gardens themselves have disappeared, along with the water that gave life to these idyllic microcosms. It is difficult to give credence today to numerous descriptions of the town written by writers back then. This applies, for instance, to Ibn Giubar, a Muslim from Valencia. He likened the gardens around Palermo to "necklaces of young women with swollen breasts." The Sicilian Abd Ar-Rahmàn also described the

Above: A front view of the Norman palace

The Torre Pisana dates from the Norman construction phase. On the ground floor is the treasure chamber.

Opposite: The Sala dei Venti and the Torre Gioaria

Below: The Sala di Ruggero

This animal mosaic clearly reflects the Arabic influence on Palermo.

whose name has Arabic roots, is the lowest and most solid tower. The Sicilian regional assembly currently has its conference room in this tower. Between the Gioaria and Pisana towers there used to be a narrow stone staircase, which was recently demolished to make room for an elevator. In the lower part of the tower there is a room, which was originally intended for a guard. This is the Sala degli Armigeri. On the upper floor is a courtyard known as Sala dei Venti. This courtyard is lined by large stone arcades supported by four

delights of La Favara, a place where "the branches of the garden bow over the clear waves to marvel at the fishes' game, and the birds fill the trees with their twittering. On the small island in the middle of the lake oranges hanging on emerald-green boughs put one in mind of glowing fire. The lemons are pale like a lover who has spent the night waiting. The two palms are lovers that have climbed the castle tower to escape jealousy. O palms that stand around the double lake of Palermo, quench your thirst with lavish water! Enjoy your fortunate lot; quench the thirst of our desire! That hostile incidents may stay away and lovers may find protection in our safe shadow and love may live unscathed!" Even the Tuscan writer Boccaccio described the Sicilian gardens in the preface of the third day of the *Decameron*. One of his most sensitive novellas (fifth day, sixth novella) is set at La Cuba. From Sicily the "gardens of Paradise" culture reached Naples, and from there it spread throughout the peninsula during the Renaissance.

Outside view of the *palazzetto delle delizie* La Zisa.

The Arabs left behind "gardens of Paradise" all around the town: parks that overflowed with all types of trees and plants, birds and water features. Roger II had the gardens, including the one at La Zisa, restored. Unfortunately the luxuriant splendor that has been described in many written sources no longer exists.

## Frederick II

When Constance d'Hauteville married Frederick Barbarossa's son, the Hohenstaufen King Henry VI, the Norman ruling dynasty of the kingdom of Sicily came to an end. At the end of 1194 Constance gave birth to a son, Frederick, who was to become the Hohenstaufen King Frederick II. Frederick was crowned king after losing his father at the age of three; his mother also died not long afterwards. The young king was brought up at the Norman court in Palermo, growing up at the palace his grandfather, Roger II, had built. He learned all the languages that were spoken in the town, as well as German as a foreign language. Even later when he became the Holy Roman Emperor, with unlimited power and boundless territories, Frederick thought of Palermo as his true home.

# Al-Idrisi's silver disc

The greatest geographer of the Middle Ages, Abu 'Abd Allah Muhammad ibn Idris al-Hammudi al-Hasani (known in the West as Dreses), lived in the Arabic-Norman royal palace in Palermo for 20 years between 1138 and 1161. In Sicily he was simply called Al-Idrisi. Al-Idrisi was a guest in Palermo at the court of the Norman King Roger II, who in 1130 finally attained the goal his father had desperately aspired to: he was crowned king of Sicily by the pope. Roger proved that he was worthy of the title. His court welcomed European, Egyptian, Greek and Arabic scientists and artists, and it very quickly became the most brilliant court in Italy. It was comparable to those of Cairo, Constantinople and Córdoba, the most magnificent of the age.

Al-Idrisi was a descendant of a great Arab ruling dynasty that had founded the town of Fez in Morocco but became impoverished and was reduced to an insignificant provincial court. Before he set off to travel the world, Al-Idrisi studied botany in Córdoba. On his arrival in Sicily many years later, he described Palermo in somewhat exaggerated terms as the greatest and most splendid in the world. For 40 years Palermo had been the capital city of the kingdom of the Hautville family. Before the Norman conquest, however, it had been built by Arabs over the course of two and a half centuries. In Palermo Roger II entrusted Al-Idrisi with the remarkable task of drawing the shape of the seas and the continents. This was to be done not on paper, but on a large silver disc, with the help of the best engraver of the time. The disc had a diameter of 6.5 feet (2 m) and weighed 330 pounds (150 kg). The outcome of his work resembled a flat globe. Al-Idrisi drew on his travel experience and scholarly knowledge to create this representation. He also made use of the wealth of information that was available in Palermo from traders, travelers, and sailors. He described Palermo as the only town where goods from all over the world poured in. Al-Idrisi also organized expeditions to the most remote places. He himself traveled all over

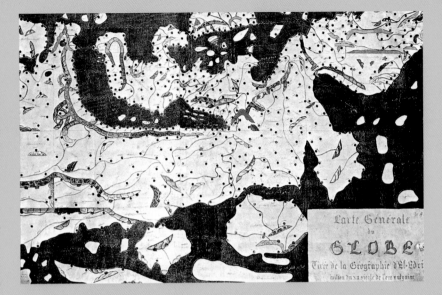

Sicily, making precise measurements of his new homeland. While the engraver transferred his drawings onto the silver disc, Al-Idrisi gathered together all the notes he had compiled during his lifetime into a book he illustrated with large maps. The title of the book was *Nuzhat al-musthaq fi ikhtiraq al-afaq* (*The Delight of Him Who Desires to Journey through the Climates*).

In 1154, after 15 years of work, the disc and the book were finished. Roger II, who died in the same year, just managed to see the work before his death. In addition to maps, the book contained numerous observations on towns and monuments, as well as on foreign people's customs and traditions. It also contained valuable information on areas that had not been fully explored then, such as the land we know today as Finland. How Al-Idrisi came into the possession of such knowledge is not known. After the death of Roger II he stayed on at the court for a while and wrote a second version of his work. He left Palermo as an old man and returned to Morocco.

A while later, during a rebellion against Roger's successor, William I, who was also called *il Malo* (the Bad), the Norman palace was plundered. Al-Idrisi's silver disc disappeared forever, but both editions of his book and the maps were rescued. A third, shorter, edition was later discovered in Constantinople. Thus the world's first travel guide was preserved for posterity.

The Mediterranean region and Europe, map by the Arab geographer Al-Idrisi (1100–1165/66) Archiv für Kunst und Geschichte, Berlin

The Moroccan Al-Idrisi (Dreses) had studied for a long time in Córdoba. He was able to draw on his great experience and his many journeys when compiling his map of the Mediterranean region and Europe. Commissioned by Roger II, the map was made on a large domed silver disc with the help of the finest engraver available. The silver disc was over six feet in diameter and was completed in the year 1154. Al-Idrisi worked for 15 years on the disc and on a book containing maps and accounts of his journeys.

# Sperlinga

The castle under a castle

## A mammoth made of stone

Sperlinga is situated in the middle of Sicily at a height of 2460 feet (750 m). The town is surrounded by high mountains such as the Madonie range to the west, the Nebrodi mountains to the north and the Etna massif to the east. A seemingly endless valley opens up to the south. In the middle of a region abounding in water and woodland, Sperlinga today has a population of barely 1,000. During the course of the 20th century successive waves of emigration swept most of the *Sperlinghesi* away. Now great numbers of the earlier inhabitants' descendants live in the United States, Canada, South America, Australia, Belgium, France, Germany or Switzerland. Sperlinga's houses, nearly all

Above: The approach to the fortress follows the cliff ridge.

built with local stone, appear to be a higgledy-piggledy muddle at the foot of a huge cliff of gray tuff that towers above the town like a mammoth, almost overwhelming it. The gigantic block of stone consists of two parts:

the first part is lower down and rounded off, the second part is higher and has a steep face. Sperlinga's entire history centers upon this geological giant.

In the Middle Ages the ideal place to build a fortress or a castle was on the highest and sheerest cliff face possible. This was the case in Sperlinga. At that time, Sperlinga was situated in the middle of 11 large fiefs, and in a strategically favorable position between west and east Sicily. When the medieval master builders got down to work, however, they found that much of their job had already been done. They could be content, therefore, with altering an existing construction to suit their needs. For this enormous cliff, consisting of soft tuff and therefore easy to excavate, had been hollowed out in all directions. It was a warren of man-made caves constructed in prehistoric times, presumably by the indigenous people of Sicily known as the Sicani. These first inhabitants of Sperlinga lived in the body of this stone mammoth. This is where they made their dry and sun-warmed dwellings, complete with pipes and wells to collect water, and well-ventilated workshops for working metal and wood.

## Seeds of the siege

During the 1140s an Arabic geographer called Al-Idrisi lived at the court of the Norman King Roger II and worked on his book of maps. He traveled around Sicily's coastlines and described the area down to the last detail. Al-Idrisi spoke of Sperlinga as if he were talking about a rich farmstead. He praised the quality of its water and its location. There was, however, no mention of a castle. Presumably, construction on the castle did not begin until the second half of the 12th century. Whatever buildings were constructed on the back of this mountain ridge over the course of time, it is mainly ruins that are left behind today. The underground constructions, however, are well preserved.

The castle can be reached by climbing a long series of steps cut in the stone. After the steps one walks through three gateways protected

by a drawbridge. In the arch of the second gateway is a Latin inscription chiseled into the rock. This inscription refers to events in the year 1282 and reads: "Quod siculis placuit sola Sperlinga negavit" (What the Sicilians liked, Sperlinga alone refused).

The fortified site is split into two levels as it follows the shape of the cliff. At the lower, long and rounded-off part of the cliff there is a guardhouse, a church with a single nave, and the remains of a feudal palace, which stand on the highest point of the cliff running west to east. A wall once encircled all of these buildings; only parts of it are still recognizable. The only building remnant is a single arch of the church which has remained intact over the centuries.

The ruins are spread out over a large area. There are inner courtyards and small squares; a network of rooms and passages lie below and their round openings lead into these squares. It is down here that the workrooms and workshops are to be found, and they all have their own ventilation systems. One of these passages cut into the cliff surfaces at a small terrace planted with trees on the north side outside the circular wall. This terrace is called the Giardino del Duca. This "garden of

Above: The rooms cut out of the rough stone in the belly of the enormous cliff were used as workshops or for food storage. The system of caves can be likened to an underground urban community.

Opposite: The openings to the caves, situated below the actual castle, lead to the outer wall of the cliff face. These "portholes" enabled the storerooms to be well ventilated and temperature-controlled. The entire castle complex was thus able to withstand long sieges.

Top: There was once a church at the castle's lower level, but all that remains of it is a single arch.

the duke" is the only place on the large cliff that holds any soil.

The other part of the fortress has a purely military function. The castle, which is as long and narrow as a sword, rises up with smooth and vertical walls on the ridge of the stone mass. Steps cut deep into the stone that have become worn away with time take one upwards. At the top an arch provides access to a passageway that runs a few hundred yards along the ridge and is flanked on both sides by walls crowned with battlements. From this passageway, one's gaze can roam freely over the landscape, as if looking out from a bridge. Almost 328 feet (100 m) lower down, at the level of the ruins lying below, large caves have been made in the cliff along its entire length. The openings to the caves are in a row and resemble a ship's portholes staring into space. In these spacious and well-ventilated store-rooms tons of provisions could be amassed, enabling hundreds of people to survive for a long time even if they were cut off completely from the outside world. In 1282 this did actually happen, after the revolt known as the Sicilian Vespers.

Right: The caves and buildings of Sperlinga closely follow the contours of the cliff.

Opposite: Both levels of the castle can be reached via two sets of steps cut into the stone. The massive vertical cliff faces make the castle impregnable, and the only links between one plateau and another are extremely narrow steps.

# "Sola Sperlinga" Negavit: the Sicilian Vespers

Arnolfo di Cambio
(1245–1302)
*Statue of Charles I of Anjou,*
1281–1284
Marble
Capitoline Museums, Rome

As king of Sicily, Charles of Anjou moved the capital from Palermo to Naples.

ILLE EGO PRECLARI TVLERAM QVI SCEPTRA SENATVS
REX SICVLIS CAROLVS IVRA DEDI POPVLIS

In the year 1282 a bloody uprising occurred in Sicily that would later be given the curious name of the Sicilian Vespers. Every year the population of Palermo gathered at church for Vespers, or evening prayers, on Easter Monday. It was as much a secular as a religious gathering. This year, Palermitans of all ages and races, languages and religions gathered on the square in front of the church of Santo Spirito outside the town walls. No one was absent.

## Sicily under the Angevins

In addition to the island of Sicily, in 1282 the kingdom of Sicily included roughly the southern half of the Italian mainland. The reason the entire region was called Sicily has as much to do with the skill of the Norman Hautville dynasty that founded the kingdom, as it does with the Swabian ruling house of Hohenstaufen, which inherited it from the Normans. Under the rule of both of these families people on the island of Sicily had always considered Palermo to be the capital and the center of the realm.

Charles I of Anjou, the brother of St. Louis, the King of France, had been crowned the new king of Sicily by the pope after the death of Frederick II of Hohenstaufen. Furthermore, he had defeated the heirs of the Hohenstaufen family in two successive battles (1266–1268). He then moved the capital from Palermo to Naples. It never occurred to the French sovereign to justify his reasons for this decision to the Sicilians, the actual inhabitants of the island. Neither did he feel the need to visit the island that had given his kingdom its name. Sicily was a "melting pot" of Greeks, Romans, Jews, Arabs and Lombards, and the Sicilians were deeply offended by their monarch's inexcusable behavior.

This island of Sicily, which had once been the heart of the kingdom and the "marketplace" of the entire Mediterranean, degenerated into an occupied province under Charles I of Anjou. The king forbade Sicilian noblewomen to marry without his "preventive permission." His aim was to force Sicilian women to marry French men, so that he could take possession of their fiefs. He barred the men from carrying weapons, which for a Sicilian was like going about one's business with no clothes on. What is more, the king monopolized trade in Sicily. He imposed taxes and export duties, holding the island in a stranglehold and bleeding it dry.

This situation grew worse when Charles took it into his head to conquer Constantinople, and started building a fleet that would enable him to do so by sea. In order to build Charles's fleet, the greatest ever assembled, the shipyards of Sicily, Naples, Pisa, Genoa, and Provence worked around the clock. The king treated the Sicilians like slaves and failed to pay them for their work. At Easter in 1282 the armed fleet lay off the port of Messina, ready for the great voyage to the East.

## Sicilianità

On Easter Monday there was a rumor going around outside the church of Santo Spirito that the king had had a seal made to brand on the forehead of any Sicilian who did not pay his taxes. But even tax evaders had made sure they turned up at the gathering on that day. When a unit of 200 French gendarmes arrived, a shiver ran through the crowd. The trouble started when a French gendarme began searching for weapons under the blouse of a young Palermitan woman. This caused a man standing next to the woman to draw a knife and thrust it into the heart of the thug. The cry of *Moranu li francisi!* (death to the French!) rang out over the square. Within a few minutes the 200 French policemen were massacred on the spot, and during the night the 2000 inhabitants of the French garrison were butchered. Neither women nor children were spared. After the barracks had been attacked, private houses were searched for French officers who had married Palermitan women. In cases where there was some doubt as to whether the men were, in fact, French, the poor wretches were forced to say "ciciri," a word that had no meaning but which would instantly mark someone who could not pronounce it properly as a non-Sicilian. *Moranu li tartagliuna* (death to the stutterers!) was the sentence. Only a few were able to save themselves. One who did was Giovanni di Saint Rémy, commander of the Angevin garrison of Palermo. He escaped through a window of the royal palace with his two servants, jumped on a horse and galloped away to the castle of Vicari outside of town.

## The twin towns of Palermo and Messina

The town assembly met that same night and five captains of the people were elected. A militia was formed, divided into three groups and sent out to the south, the east and the west in order to spread news of the armed rebellion. Palermo declared itself a free community and subordinated itself to the protection of the Church. In addition, ambassadors were sent to Rome to give a report to the pope. When the pope was

Francesco Hayes
*The Sicilian Vespers*, 1846
Oil on canvas
National Gallery of Modern Art, Rome

The Sicilian Vespers marked the beginning of a revolt by the Sicilian people to gain their independence. Four weeks after the Vespers, they had succeeded. Only Sperlinga allied itself with the French, who withdrew into the castle.

Matthäus Merian
Copperplate from Johann
Ludwig Gottfried,
*Historische Chronica*, p. 596
Frankfurt am Main, 1630
Archiv für Kunst und
Geschichte, Berlin

There was a rumor that the
king wanted to brand all
tax evaders. One horrific
night, hundreds of French
soldiers, their wives and
children were massacred by
the Sicilians.

told that they had arrived, he refused to receive them and threatened them instead with excommunication. The spark from Palermo, however, set the entire island on fire. Inhabitants of a nearby town called Caccamo stormed the castle at Vicari, where the French commander had fled. Giovanni di Saint Rémy was killed in the attack.

By April 3, Palermo and Corleone had joined together to form a league. On April 13, two weeks after the Vespers, the whole of west and central Sicily was in the hands of the rebels. Everywhere the French were massacred. The only exception was Calatafimi on the west coast. Here, the man in command of the French garrison, a deputy judge named Guillaume Porcelet, enjoyed the respect of the Sicilians because of his benign and compassionate rule. As a result, after their surrender the French were spared and escorted to Palermo, where they were permitted to board a ship heading for Provence.

After the first anti-French revolt had flared up it soon spread throughout the island and Messina

became the scene of a momentous decision. This is where a large unit under the command of the Angevin governor, Herbert d'Orléans, was guarding Charles's great fleet. Messina was the only town in Sicily where the people supported the king. At first the town merely waited to see how things would turn out. The people of Messina even sent out their own troops to occupy nearby towns such as Taormina. They did not respond to the passionate letter from the free community of Palermo, which suggested a league between the two twin towns. But soon after this the French themselves brought about a crisis among the pro-French clans of Messina. Herbert d'Orléans wanted to replace the soldiers from Messina, who had occupied Taormina, with French troops. In order to achieve this he engineered an armed clash between the two contingents. This ended ignominiously for the French, however, and they were captured. Messina had also sent out galleys to block the port of Palermo. The Palermitans then placed large standards on the walls in Kalsa, so that the emblems of both towns – the eagle of Palermo and the cross of Messina – could be seen flapping alongside each other. On seeing this, the sailors from Messina started a mutiny.

These events triggered an insidious civil war in Messina. The pro-French families, who ruled the town, were deprived of their power. On April 28 the revolt finally broke out there, too. The French occupying forces barricaded themselves in the fortress of Matagrifone and gave up control over the French fleet anchored in the harbor. On the same night, the beautiful ships, the pride of King Charles, were completely destroyed by fire. The following day Messina declared itself a free community and subordinated itself to the protection of the Church. The only response from the French Pope Martin IV was to impose an interdict on the whole of Sicily on May 7.

## Sicilia Felix

With the victory in Messina all of Sicily had become free and independent just four weeks after the Vespers. The town of Messina joined the so-called Federal Republic of Sicily, Sicilia Felix or "lucky Sicily." Over the course of time, however, the republic was beset by greater and greater difficulties. After a long period of paralysis that had been intensified by his disappointment over the failure of his military plans in the East, Charles I proceeded to reconquer the island, and he started by besieging Messina. He knew he had the backing of the pope and of France. In addition, he mobilized the Guelphs in Italy. In the long term he would have gained the upper hand over the motley crowd of Sicilian militia. But in the end Pedro III of Aragon intervened. Since he had married Constance of Hohenstaufen he could claim rights of inheritance to the kingdom. Under the pretext of preventing a maneuver in Tunisia, the Aragonese fleet had been hovering for some time off the North African coast. One day Pedro's entire army crossed the short stretch of sea to Sicily and dropped anchor in Trápani. Given the choice between two evils, the Sicilians chose the lesser evil. August 30, 1282, thus became the day when Catalan joined the many languages already spoken on the island.

## Sperlinga holds out

During the entire Vespers war, Sperlinga remained in the hands of the French. At the very beginning of the revolt, the Angevin garrisons scattered over the whole of Sicily gathered in the only fortress that could be defended for a long time. The inhabitants of Sperlinga also moved into the belly of the mountain, where their ancestors had lived. Sperlinga's population was made up of a mixture of the descendants of native inhabitants and the so-called "Lombards," people who had immigrated from Monferrato in the Piedmont region and intermarried with the local people at the end of the 11th century, at the time of the Norman conquest. The spacious storerooms of the castle were filled with wheat, oil and wine, oats for the horses, and whole flocks of sheep. Even when the French had been driven out of Messina, Sperlinga's resistance endured. Their hope that the Angevin ruler would once again cross the Strait of Messina and march across the island proved futile, however.

The siege gave rise to legends, which are still related today to those who visit Sperlinga. It is said that when, after many long months of siege the prospect of hunger started to arise, cheese was made from the women's milk and rolled down the hill. This was done to deceive the enemy about how much food was actually left. When the surrender was finally negotiated and the French soldiers were allowed to move off to the coast to embark, the community of Sperlinga, now larger than it had been at the beginning of the siege, also ventured out.

# Castel del Monte

## A clock and a calendar

Right: The facade of the Castel del Monte

From a military and strategic viewpoint the building, erected by Frederick II between 1240 and 1250, could never have been used as a fort. It appears to have been constructed according to specific geometric formulae, which have puzzled many people.

### Anything but a castle

Castel del Monte is one of the most famous castles in the world, which gives especial irony to the fact that it is not actually a castle. The name Castel del Monte was not in fact used until the end of the 15th century. It is not known what the building's original name was. From a military perspective, the castle lacks elementary features that would enable it to withstand an attack or a siege. Considered as such it makes no sense, in terms of either its location or its form. If anything, it resembles a

Above: Egnazio Danti
*The Salentine Peninsula*
Fresco
Galleria delle Carte Geografiche, Musei Vaticani, Rome

buoy, floating in the middle of the sea. It would never have occurred to an enemy army that had marched over the kingdom's borders from the north, covering 186 miles (300 km) through Abruzzi, to stop at the Castel del Monte and besiege it. The castle is situated on the edge of a wide plateau. It lacks moats, draw-bridges and external fortifications; instead it

has a church-like entrance, high windows and refined decor. There are no ledges, trap-doors, or battlements. Neither are there stables, kitchens, food stores, or dormitories to accommodate soldiers. It is therefore easy to say what Castel del Monte is not: namely, a castle. It is more difficult, however, to define what it actually is.

## An enigma

For more than a century people have been wondering why this proud octagon was built. All hypotheses are plausible, but none is convincing. This may be the very reason why this castle is so famous. It is an enigma made of stone, visible and tangible, that does not give any answers but merely throws up questions. Is it a sundial? Is it a temple to the favorite animal of Frederick II, the gyrfalcon, whose flight path many people have tried to emulate? Is it mathematical evidence for

something? The Castel del Monte was built between 1240 and 1250; this is known because a document dating from the year 1240 details the excavation carried out on the emperor's orders to obtain materials for the castle's construction. It is not known whether Frederick II ever actually used the castle, however. He was constantly on the move during the last ten years of his life. Maybe he did manage to see the building when he returned to Apulia towards the end of 1250, terminally ill. In December of that year he died.

## The exterior of the castle

The castle is on an isolated hill 1771 feet (540 m) high, which offers a pleasant panoramic view of the surrounding country. The building itself is a perfect octagon, with sides measuring 54 feet (16.5 m) each in length. At the top of each corner there are other octagonal

The double-arched windows on the upper floor are arranged so that the sun comes into each room twice a day. Here in the throne room the front of the window shown is aligned to the east. This basic layout gives rise to the theory that the Castel del Monte was a sundial built of stone, with a calendar thrown in for good measure.

towers set on massive foundations of the same shape. Halfway up and all around the exterior wall there runs a ledge separating the two stories into which the castle is divided. A second ledge somewhat further down marks the line where the towers sit on foundations at a height approximately six feet six inches (2 m) above the ground. The main entrance is also at this level, and two converging staircases lead up to it.

The front of the castle, where the main entrance is situated, faces east. On the opposite side in the west there is a side door. The whole building is made of smooth, perfectly cut ashlars of sand-colored limestone which, depending on the light and the degree of humidity, has a pink shimmer. The only other materials used were for decorating the windows, the portals and the interior; these were white marble and coral breccias in various shades.

Each outer wall of the octagon has two windows: a single-arched window on the lower floor and a double-arched window with trefoil tracery on the floor above. Only in the dividing wall on the north side is there a resplendent triple-arched window. A rosette was set in the tympanum above the windows. Coral-colored breccias were used to decorate the outside of the windows; these decorations consisted of small columns on either side of the window, capitals and arch trims. All of the original white marble columns in the middle of the double- and triple-arched windows are missing. They were removed in the middle of the 19th century and taken to Caserta to brighten up the park of the royal palace there. Even the marble paneling of the interior was taken out during the centuries when the Castel del Monte fell into disrepair. The same happened with the lavish floor inlays made from marble and slate.

## The interior

An eight-sided courtyard can be found inside the castle. Measured from inside, the walls have a height of 67 feet (20.5 m). The towers, therefore, barely rise above the flat roof of the

octagon. There are 16 rooms in the castle: eight below and eight above. They are all the same and all in the shape of a regular trapezoid, whose long side is formed by the outer wall and short side by the courtyard wall. Between pairs of columns in these rooms lie the tower rooms, where the changing rooms, toilets and spiral staircases are located. The spiral staircases lead to the upper floor and

Only on the north side was there a triple-arched window with a small double arch above it. All of the other windows incorporated a quatrefoil rosette.

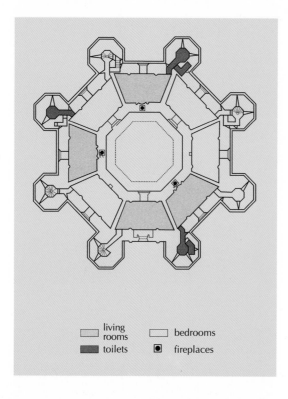

Right: The first floor is divided up in the same way as the ground floor, but the rooms are interconnected in different ways.

living rooms

toilets

bedrooms

fireplaces

Below: It is likely that a wooden balcony ran all the way around the first floor, under the French doors.

sometimes even up to the terrace on the flat roof. The spiral staircases turn to the left, thus echoing natural spiral forms such as that of the snail's shell. In medieval castles spiral staircases turning to the right were the norm, however, because the defender, coming from above, had the advantage when striking with

his saber in his right hand. Conversely, the attacker storming up the staircases was at a disadvantage, as he had to wield his sword with his left hand. Left-handed attackers did not come into the equation as far as medieval military architects were concerned. Besides, left-handedness was considered the work of the devil.

Three portals lead out from the inner courtyard. In addition, three high glass French doors on the upper story open out into the courtyard. Presumably there was once a round wooden balcony linking these openings. Other windows of various shapes have been built into the walls of the courtyard so that each room receives light from both the outside wall and the inner courtyard.

## Connecting passages

Although all eight rooms on the ground floor and eight on the first floor are the same size and shape, they do differ from one other in the way they are connected to the towers, the inner courtyard or the outer room. Two of the eight rooms on the ground floor open to the outside world through the main entrance or the side entrance. These rooms may not have direct access to the inner courtyard, but they are linked to the other rooms. There are, therefore, "through rooms," which have two or even three doors, and so-called "end rooms," which have only one door. The end rooms are superior as they are the only ones that contain a fireplace and provide access to a tower room, which is well ventilated by narrow openings and has a toilet that is flushed by the water that runs off the roof terrace.

## Light

There are two end rooms on the ground floor and two on the first floor. Altogether, then, four of the 16 rooms have been given this function. One of these rooms lies on the first floor and is described as the "throne room." Its double-arched window above the entrance looks out to the east, while a French door opens out to the west onto the inner courtyard. The rays of the morning sun, beautifully

framed by the double arch, filter through the window and the rosette on the east side. This window in the east is flanked on the outside by two large alcoves, which served as runners for the grill that used to be let down in front of the entrance.

The evening sun, however, comes through the French door on the opposite side, the one that opens into the courtyard. It is obvious that the throne room was used for official functions, as, unlike other end rooms, there is no fireplace or toilet here.

In all eight rooms of the first floor, just as in the throne room, the sun comes through twice a day. Sunlight thus fills one of the eight rooms each hour of the day. It is only the rooms on the first floor that have the privilege of receiving sunlight more than twice a day throughout the year. For the rooms on the ground floor, this is only the case in summer. The shadow that is cast by the side of the octagonal castle climbs too high on the opposite wall in winter. While on the first floor the sun's rays divide the day up into hours, the shadow that moves above the courtyard indicates the changing seasons. If the upper part of the castle was in fact planned as a sundial, the lower part is surely a calendar. Altogether there are two days in which the light distribution, both spatially and temporally, is in perfect alignment. These days are June 21, the summer solstice, and December 21, the winter solstice. As it is more likely that clouds will obscure the sun on December 21, a visit to Castel del Monte is advisable on June 21.

The sun's rays on the first floor indicate the time of day, while the shadow cast in the octagonal inner courtyard indicates the season. Sunshine penetrates the closed octagonal form of the castle to reach the ground floor twice a day in summer only, while on the first floor this is the case the whole year through.

On the ground floor and on the first floor there are two end rooms that do not lead through to any other rooms. In these special rooms there is both a fireplace and an adjacent toilet.

### Shelter for sheep, shepherds and bandits

In 1552 the Castel del Monte became the property of a noble Apulian family headed by the Count of Carafa. By 1656, just over a century later, dozens of noble families from Apulia inhabited the 16 rooms of the castle. Men, women, elderly people, children and servants all put themselves into quarantine here, seeking refuge from the plague epidemic that was devastating their town. Unfortunately, no Boccaccio has handed down to us the stories

of how their long evenings were spent here. After the plague had been endured, peace and quiet returned to the Castel del Monte. This was to change in 1799 when, after the collapse of the Parthenopian Republic, a group of Neapolitan Jacobins fleeing from Bourbon persecutors sought safety in Frederick's octagon. They no doubt did this believing the castle was a fortress. As this was not the case, their flight soon met with a bad end.

In the 19th century the castle fell into ruin, and sheep, shepherds, and bandits began using it as a refuge. The floor inlays and marble wall paneling were systematically ripped out. Only one tiny green stone was left of the mosaics that decorated the entire frame of the double-arched windows. Even the small window columns were taken away to Caserta.

The Italian state had scarcely been founded when in 1876 it bought the Castel del Monte from the Count of Carafa for the modest sum of 25,000 lire. The title deed states that the building turned out to be "completely unsuitable for any purpose owing to its present composition, its structural characteristics and the isolated and uninhabited place where it was built." The 25,000 lire were paid to the count not as a purchase price, for the castle was worth nothing, but rather as "simple evidence of recognition."

Several attempts have been made during the past century to renovate the structure and restore it to its former glory.

### The prisoners of the clock

As it turned out, the Castel del Monte was inhabited only sporadically and by chance over the years. Only three people lived in this building for a long period of time: 12,000 days in all. They arrived together in 1266 and left together in 1299. They were Frederick, Henry and Enzo of Hohenstaufen, and, as the sons of Manfred of Hohenstaufen and the grandsons of Emperor Frederick II, they were the legitimate owners of the castle. We do not know the age of Manfred's sons when they arrived at the castle, but their mother was 23.

After the battle of Benevento on February 26, 1266 had ended with the defeat and death of Manfred, Charles of Anjou's French soldiers seized Frederick's grandsons, their sister, mother and aunt in Trani in Apulia. The children and women were first taken to the nearby fortress of Lagopesole, and after that to the castle at Nocera, where Elena Comnena, the mother, was incarcerated and died six years later. The rest of the group was carted off to Naples. There, the aunt was set free and Beatrice, the younger sister, was imprisoned in the Castel dell'Ovo for 18 years. Frederick's grandsons, however, were taken back to Apulia and locked up in the Castel del Monte for 33 years. In 1299 they were moved again to the Neapolitan Castel dell'Ovo, from where Beatrice had since been released. Unfortunately, the three occupants did not leave us any details of their 12,000 days in custody. We do know, however, that, like all the Hohenstaufens, they sang in the mornings and cried in the evenings.

In 1552 the Castel del Monte became the property of a noble dynasty. In 1656 dozens of noble families sought refuge here from the plague. In the 19th century the building fell into disrepair, and only after the turn of the 20th century was it restored and given its present appearance. The mysterious building has still not divulged its secrets, however.

*Frederick II on the Throne,*
from: *The Art of Hunting
with Birds*
Miniature
Ms. Pal. Lat. 1071
Biblioteca Apostolica
Vaticana, The Vatican

Frederick II so
anthropomorphized falcons
that he punished them as if
they were people when they
showed disobedience.

## Frederick II, the Eagle King

Frederick II was a great ornithologist. His descriptions and his observations about birds and the physical adaptations that enable them to fly are still of great scientific interest today. According to Frederick's thinking the world of birds was far more rooted in reality than that of humans. In fact, he regarded the world of humans as merely a pale reflection of the world of birds. Therefore, Frederick as emperor in the reflected world was a mirror of the eagle, king of birds, in the real world. In accordance with his ideal, he tried to shape his earthly kingdom in such a way that it resembled the birds' realm of the sky. This is why he named the town he founded in the Abruzzi region L'Aquila, "The Eagle."

### The gyrfalcon

One day while out hunting Frederick II released his favorite falcon and sent it chasing after a heron that had just flown by. It pounced on a young eagle which also happened to be flying past, seized it and laid it at the emperor's feet. This event, which he had never encountered before either as an ornithologist or as a hunter, concerned him deeply. After much deliberation he assembled the dignitaries of his kingdom in the Piazza del Mercato in Naples, where the death penalty was usually enforced. The royal falcon was tried in their presence. It was condemned to death and beheaded. A simple falcon, said the court, had dared to attack a young eagle, and thus the representative of imperial power. This lesson on the hierarchy of the bird world was to serve as a warning to the barons of the kingdom.

Frederick was not only an ornithologist; he was also a great friend of philology. Like that of 13th-century Florence, his court in Palermo was a cradle of the modern Italian language. Having grown up in a multilingual environment, Frederick was not content with merely founding a school for rhetoric and poetry, however. He was also fascinated by the question of how language develops and how it is communicated between individual members of a single species. Is it innate or acquired from the mother and other members of the same species? Frederick searched for the answer in the natural world by taking birds out of the nest as soon as they had hatched and ensuring that they were reared without hearing the song of other birds, or in fact any sound whatsoever. He discovered that a captive blackbird that had reached mating age

sang in exactly the same way as a wild blackbird; a captive goldfinch sang exactly like a wild goldfinch. Frederick wanted to repeat the experiment with people. In Naples he used the fortified Castel dell'Ovo as a place to raise "abandoned" children, as the foundlings mostly left in front of the church were called. He raised them isolated from every sound. These children, however, remained mute even when they reached the age at which children generally start to speak; not only that, but they refused to eat and died prematurely. The outcome of this experiment persuaded the emperor that humans were distinctly inferior to birds.

Left: A mosaic of the eagle, Frederick II's favorite bird, from the Norman palace in Palermo.

Below: Miniature with bird decorations, from: *The Art of Hunting with Birds* Cod. Pal. Lat. 1071, fols. 42v–43r Biblioteca Apostolica Vaticana, The Vatican

For Frederick II, the world of humans was merely a pale reflection of the real world of birds. The book is his tract on the diverse characteristics of birds. This page is about "the art of hunting with birds." It is thought that the illustrations around the edges were drawn by Frederick himself.

SWITZERLAND

Lausanne

Geneva

FRANCE

A **L** P S

AUSTRIA

Graz

Székesfehérvár

HUNGAR

Lake Balaton

Pécs

Meran
Etsch
Brixen
Bozen
Alba

South Tyrol/Trentino

Trento **14**
Calavino
**Castello del Buonconsiglio**
Belluno

Friuli Venezia Giulia

Udine

Ljubljana

SLOVENIA

Trieste

Zagreb

Maribor

Drava

CROATIA

Osijek

Aosta
Valle d'Aosta

Lago Maggiore

Como
Lake Como

Bergamo

Lombardy

Salò

Lake Garda
Verona

Veneto

Padua

Venice

45° n.Br

Novara

Vercelli

Turin

Piedmont

Milan **8** **Castello Sforzesco**
Lodi
Pavia
Cremona

Rijeka

Banja Luca

BOSNIA-HERCEGOVINA

Asti
Alessandria
Novi Ligure
Monferrato

Piacenza

Sala
Colorno

Mantova

Po

Comacchio

Ravenna

Tuzla

Alba

**12** **Gavi Ligure**

Genoa **15**

Fornovo
Parma

Fontanellato **11**

Reggio nell'E.
Modena

Bologna

**10** **Castello Estense**
Ferrara

Faenza
Forlì

Emilia Romagna

Cervia

Rimini

Sarajevo

MONACO
Nice
Ventimiglia

Liguria
Savona
Finale Ligure

Riviera di Ponente

Ligurian Sea

La Spezia
Sarzana

Carrara
Massa

**17** **6**

Lucca

**Castello Malaspina**

Pisa

**Vicopisano**

Livorno

**7**

Empoli

Florence

Prato

Castello di Romena

Ravaldino

Cesena

S. MARINO

**9** Imola

A P E

Poppi
**3**

Anghiari

**Castello dei Conti Guidi**

San Leo

**2**

Urbino

**16** **Gradara**

Pesaro

Ancona

Split

Mostar

Dalmatia

Adriatic Sea

Riviera di Levante

Monteriggioni

**4**

Siena
Montaperti

Montalcino **5**

L. d. Trasimeno

Anghiari

Perugia

Assisi

The Marches

Corsica

Ajaccio

Elba

Tuscany

Piombino

Grosseto

Umbria

Spoleto

Norcia

Ascoli Piceno

San Benedetto del Tronto

L. d. Bolsena

Orvieto

Terni

L'Aquila

Morrone 1328m

Pescara

Sardinia

San Pietro
Carbonia

Sassari

Olbia

Oristano

Barbária

**19** **Barumini**

**18** **Cagliari**

Tarquinia

Viterbo
Soriano

**13**

Bracciano

Trevignano
Anguillara

La Storta

**ROME** **1**

**Castel Sant'Angelo**

Anagni

Lazio

Frosinone

Abruzzi

Sulmona

Molise

Campobasso

Peschici

Gargano

Tavoliere

Foggia

Barletta

Benevento

Campania

Vesuvius 1277m

Castel Nuovo **20**

NAPLES

Castel dell'Ovo

Ischia

Nocera

Sorrento

Amalfi

Salerno

Capri

Trani

Bari

**23** **Castel del Monte**

Apulia

Alberobello

Brindisi

Castel Lagopesole

Potenza

Matera

Basilicata

Taranto

Lecce

Gulf of Taranto

Tyrrhenian

Sea

M e d i t e r r a n e a n

Calabria

Cosenza

Ionian Sea

Catanzaro

39°

42°

Trapani

Marsala

Calatafimi

Corleone

Caccamo

**21** **Palazzo dei Normanni**

Palermo

Madonie

Nebrodi

Sperlinga **22**

Etna 3340m

Straits of Messina

Messina

Reggio di C.

Taormina

Sicilian Channel

Caltanissetta

Catania

Sicily

**125 miles**

**(200 km)**

Tunis

Pantelleria

TUNISIA

Ragusa

Syracuse

9° ö.L.

12°

15°

18°

# Glossary

**Aedicule**. Frame of a window or door, consisting of two columns surmounted by a pediment.

**Albigensians or Albigenses.** Heretical sect centered in southern France in the 12th and 13th centuries. A branch of Catharism, the heresy of the **Cathars**.

**Antipope**. A person set up as pope without being lawfully elected, usually in opposition to someone already holding that post.

**Assisi, St. Francis of** (c. 1181–1226). Originally named Giovanni di Bernadone, St. Francis started life in a wealthy family, but later renounced his wealth and became devoted to a life of poverty. He founded the **Franciscan** order in 1209, basing its rule on his belief in poverty.

**Aurelian** (c. 215–275 A.D.). Roman emperor from 270–275. Originally a soldier, he rose through the ranks and was elected emperor by the army. He was responsible for building new defensive walls around Rome. Aurelian was assassinated by his own officers.

**Bailey**. External wall surrounding the **keep** of a castle; also the area between the inner and outer walls.

**Barbarossa, Frederick I** (c. 1123–1190). King of Germany and Holy Roman Emperor from 1152 to 1190. A member of the house of **Hohenstaufen**, Barbarossa (the nickname means "red beard") waged war on Italy and the papacy, but was ultimately beaten at the Battle of Legnano in 1176. He died *en route* to the Third Crusade.

**Baroque.** European art movement extending roughly from the end of Mannerism (c. 1590) to the beginning of the Rococo (c. 1725) with a characteristic tendency to the extravagant, elaborate and florid. Along with religious and mythological themes, Baroque art saw the appearance of allegory (the depiction of abstract concepts and themes), genre painting and landscapes. In painting, a classical and idealizing strand coexisted

*Miniature from the Luttrell Psalter* (detail), England, c. 1325. Ms. Add. 42130, fol. 207v, British Library, London

with realism; representational techniques were similarly diverse and ranged from the depiction of completely artificial worlds, including the use of optical illusions, through to an exaggerated Naturalism. The term was originally used in goldsmithing, where a *barocco* was an irregularly shaped pearl. The style is associated particularly with the **Counter-Reformation**, and is perhaps most strongly evident in those territories that were particularly affected by this movement.

**Basilica.** Term derived from the official building of a Greek magistrate, the Archon Basileus. In antiquity it denoted a roofed building with a double colonnade used for law courts, assemblies and markets. In the Christian era it meant a characteristic type of church building with a high nave and either two or four lower aisles, with a ground plan oriented towards the east. In addition, basilicas had windows on the

elevated walls (clerestory) where the roof of the aisle joined the nave wall. In general, the basilica has determined the shape of large churches in the West since the 4th century. In the late Gothic era the basilica was momentarily displaced by the hall church and in the Baroque period by the centrally planned church.

**Bastion.** Projection from a defensive structure, usually with walls constructed at an angle, designed to permit fire to facing flanks.

**Battlement.** A *parapet* with alternating high and low parts, sometimes known as crenellations. These are sometimes extremely ornate, as in the swallowtail or V-shaped battlements found in some examples of Italian medieval architecture.

**Benedictines.** Oldest order of Western monks, founded in Monte Cassino c. 529 A.D. by St. Benedict of Nursia (c. 480–547). The Benedictine rules formed the basis of Western monasticism. The main task of the order was to cultivate liturgy and prayer, and this was supplemented by scholarly, artistic and physical labor. Prayer and work became fundamental aspects of life, bound together in the expression *ora et labora*.

**Berm.** In defensive architecture, a horizontal surface extending from a moat to the slope of a *rampart*.

**Boccaccio, Giovanni** (1313–1375). *Humanist* Italian writer and poet. His most famous work is the *Decameron*, a collection of tales told by a group of young people trying to hide away to escape the plague. The young Boccaccio spent some time at the Neapolitan court, where he is said to have fallen in love with the daughter of King Robert, a woman immortalized as Fiammetta in his later writings.

**Borgia.** Italian dynasty prominent in Church and political affairs in the 1400s and 1500s. The family produced several popes and other leaders, but also achieved notoriety because of its reputation for treachery and double-dealing. Prominent members included Alfonso Borgia (1378–1458), who became Pope Calixtus III in 1455 and was responsible for bringing the family to prominence. Rodrigo Borgia also became pope, as Alexander VI, his daughter Lucrezia (1480–1519) became legendary for her skill at manipulation and intrigue.

**Bull** (papal). A written order from the pope concerning an important matter. The word derives from the Latin *bulla*, meaning "seal," because the document would be kept in a sealed box or sealed with the papal signet on wax.

**Byzantine (architecture).** Relating to the style of architecture that developed in the Byzantine or Eastern Roman Empire, characterized by very large domes, rounded arches, spires and minarets, and much use of mosaic.

**Campanile.** The bell tower of an Italian church, usually freestanding. Its isolated position was retained in Renaissance architecture but it rarely appears north of the Alps.

**Carolingians.** Frankish dynasty descended from Peppin the Short, which ruled over much of France and Germany from 751 until the 10th century.

**Castellum.** Roman fort or permanent camp, from which the modern word "castle" derives.

**Cateau-Cambrésis, Treaty of** (1559). There were actually two treaties of Cambrésis; one between England and France and one between France and Spain, ending the war the countries had fought from 1557 to 1559. Under the terms of the treaties France retained the disputed port of Calais, but it had to renounce its territorial ambitions in Italy.

**Cathars.** Followers of the heresy of Catharism, or the belief that Satan rules in this world, and that all material things are evil. The Cathars, who were based in Provence in the 12th and 13th centuries, rejected Catholic baptism in favor of Christ's spiritual baptism. They were ruthlessly crushed by the established Church.

**Charlemagne** (742–814). King of the Franks who subjugated surrounding peoples including the Saxons and **Lombards**, and became the first Holy Roman Emperor (as Charles I) in 800.

**Cinquecento** (Shortened form of *mille-cinquecento*, meaning 1500.) The 16th century. Used particularly in the context of Italian literature and visual arts from this period.

**Cistercians.** Monastic order. The Cistercian order had its origins in the reformed Benedictine monastery of Citeaux founded in 1098 by Robert von Molesmes (1027–1111). The new order set out to achieve fully the monastic ideal encapsulated in the rules of the **Benedictines**; the Cistercians therefore considered themselves a reforming movement within the Benedictine order.

**Comunero uprising** (Spain). Revolt in 1520–1521 in the kingdom of Castile, over taxes levied by Charles V, newly elected as

*Battle between Pyrrhus and Penthesilea, Queen of the Amazons* (detail), *c.* 1286, Ms 17, Add. 15268, fol. 128r, British Library, London

Holy Roman Emperor, and other transgressions by the monarch. The *comunero* forces were defeated at Villalar on April 23, 1521.

**Conclave.** The closed apartment in which the college of cardinals is confined during the process of electing a new pope. The gathering itself is also known as the conclave.

**Condottiere.** The leader of a troop of mercenaries, especially in post-medieval Italy.

**Consistory** (Roman). The assembly of cardinals called by the pope, and meeting in his presence.

**Counter-Reformation.** Movement aimed at the revival of the Roman Catholic Church,

dating from about the middle of the 16th century to the early 1700s. This was partly in response to the threat posed to the Church by the Protestant **Reformation**, which had its origins in Germany in 1517 and challenged traditional Catholic hegemony in northern Europe in particular. The Counter-Reformation can also, however, be seen as a continuation of reform attempts that had taken place as early as the Middle Ages.

**Curia.** The papal court and its officials.

**Dante** (Dante Alighieri; 1265–1321). Foremost Italian poet of the 13th century and founding father of Italian literature. His early work, *Vita nuova*, is a collection of poems about his love for Beatrice, generally accepted to have been Beatrice Portinari, a woman he seems to have loved all his life even thought they were both married to other people and she died young. His most famous work, the *Divine Comedy*, is an epic poem about a spiritual journey he makes, in the form of a visit to Hell and Purgatory with the ancient Roman poet Virgil as his guide. He finally journeys to Paradise as well, this time with the spirit of the departed Beatrice as his guide, and attains inner peace.

**Dominicans.** Mendicant order established in 1216 by St. Dominic (1170–1221) in Toulouse, and dedicated to the dissemination and defense of the faith through education and preaching. The Dominicans were especially involved in combating unsanctioned, "heretical" movements that operated outside the ambit of the Church during the Middle Ages. For this reason in 1232 the Dominicans were permanently charged by the Holy See with leading the Inquisition, the ecclesiastical courts which tried those accused of apostasy.

**Donjon.** Most heavily fortified, usually central, part of a medieval castle. It usually comprised a tower or **keep** with bedrooms and living rooms, and could be defended even if the outer parts of the castle were overrun. The word is sometimes used to denote only the lowest floor in a keep.

**d'Este.** Italian family that ruled Ferrara from the 13th to the 16th centuries. The dynasty was originally founded by Alberto Azzo II (996–1097).

**Exarchate** (Byzantine). After the Italian lands under the rule of the Ostrogoths had been reconquered (Rome was retaken in 536), the Byzantine or Eastern Roman Empire set up a government or exarchate in the Italian town of Ravenna to administer the central and southern Italian lands of the Empire. This exarchate lasted from 552 to 751, when the **Lombards** captured the region.

**Fuggers.** Wealthy dynasty that rose to prominence when one of its number was appointed banker to Sigismund of Tyrol in 1487. The Fugger family acted as financiers to both the popes and the **Habsburgs.**

**Gens.** One of a group of noble families in ancient Rome descended from a common ancestor in the male line, and sharing the same name.

**Ghibellines.** Faction in medieval Italy that originally supported the authority of the German emperor, especially against that of the pope. The conflict between the Ghibellines and the **Guelphs** was a major factor in Italian politics for many years.

**Giudicati.** Administrative units in Sardinia, established by the Byzantines when they ruled over the island from the 6th century until its conquest by the Islamic Arabs.

**Glacis.** A slope or incline in front of a fortification.

**Gonzaga.** Italian dynasty that ruled the city of Mantua from the 14th century. The Gonzaga were originally *condottieri* in the pay of the Venetians, employed to retain the balance of power against Venice's old enemy, Milan. They occasionally sold their services to the Milanese, as well, however. Under Lodovico Gonzaga (1414–1478) Mantua flourished, and with it the fortunes of the Gonzaga. Lodovico's grandson Francesco married the redoubtable Isabella d'Este, a noted patron of music and fine art, and under the couple the Mantuan court became one of the major centers of Renaissance culture in Italy.

**Gothic** (It. gotico, "barbaric, not antique"). Epoch of European art and architecture which existed in Italy from approximately 1230 to 1420. The term was initially disparaging (Goths = barbarians) and was used originally for an architecture in which pointed arches (which meet at a point at the keystone), the rib vault (formed by the intersection at right angles of two vaults of the same size with pointed arches) and flying buttresses appear as new architectural forms. Typical for this style is the cathedral with its emphasis on vertical elements and with its glazed walls and upper stories which flooded the interior with light.

**Guelphs.** Also known as Guelfs. Faction in medieval Italy that supported the papacy against the German emperors. Enemies of the **Ghibellines**. The conflict between the two groups was a major factor in Italian politics for many years.

**Guiscard, Robert** (*c.* 1016–1085). Norman adventurer, Duke of Apulia and Calabria, and founder of the Norman state of the Two Sicilies. Guiscard conquered much of southern Italy, expelling the Byzantines and the Arabs from their possessions there, and protected Pope Gregory VII from the invading army of the Holy Roman Empire.

**Habsburgs.** Royal family, originally from Switzerland, that virtually monopolized the title of Holy Roman Emperor from 1438 to 1806.

**Hadrian** (76–138 A.D.). Emperor of Rome 117–138. Successor to Trajan and builder of the wall that bears his name in Britain. The Castel Sant' Angelo in Rome is built on the site of Hadrian's mausoleum.

**Heresiarch.** The instigator of a religious heresy, or the founder of a heretical group.

**Hohenstaufen.** German princely family that provided rulers of Germany, Sicily and the **Holy Roman Empire** in the 12th and 13th centuries.

*Tiara of Constance of Aragon*, Palermo Cathedral

**Holy Roman Empire.** Political institution founded by Emperor Charlemagne in the year 800. He claimed for the emperor a similar status in secular matters to that held by the pope in spiritual matters. The empire was for most of its duration more of a loose federation of German principalities than a successor to the original Roman Empire, as Charlemagne had intended.

**Humanism.** Cultural movement that arose in Renaissance Italy, based on the study of classical texts, especially Greek and Roman, and the application of the values found in them to contemporary literature and morals.

**Index** (of prohibited books). List commissioned by the Council of Trent of books that had been condemned by the Church and could not be published.

**Indulgences.** Remission by the Roman Catholic Church of penalty for sin, through the merits of Jesus Christ and the saints. The concept of granting indulgences was not common until the 12th century, when it became widespread. Limited indulgences granted remission for particular days and years, whereas a plenary indulgence remitted the whole of a person's temporal punishment for his sins. They were first issued by Pope Urban II to Crusaders who made full confession of their sins.

**Inquisition.** Procedure authorized by the Roman Catholic Church with the aim of investigating suspected cases of heresy. The name is also applied to the institution established for this purpose. The Spanish Inquisition was given papal authority in 1478, and the Roman Inquisition in 1542.

**Interdict** (papal). Ecclesiastical instrument issued by the Roman Catholic Church partially excluding members from participation in the activities of the Church and from certain sacraments, but not from taking Communion. An interdict can be applied against individuals or against whole populations.

**Jubilee year.** Year in which the pope declared that pilgrims visiting Rome could earn **indulgences.** Jubilee years occurred every 100 years, and sometimes more frequently.

**Justification.** Process whereby God acquits man of punishment for his sins. In the early years of the Reformation there was disagreement between Catholics and Protestants (and for that matter between Lutherans and those of the Reformed persuasion) about whether justification was granted through faith alone, or whether it was obtained through good works, or by a combination of the two.

**Keep.** Inner portion of a medieval castle and residence of the incumbent lord. It was the most heavily fortified part of the castle.

**Landsknecht** (plural *Landsknechte*). A mercenary footsoldier of German origin of the 15th to 17th centuries; refers particularly to a pikeman.

**Lateran Councils.** Set of councils held in *Lateran Palace*, Rome, between the 7th and 18th centuries. The Fourth Lateran Council in 1215 was particularly important from a doctrinal point of view as it elaborated on the concept of ***transubstantiation*** and established the tradition of confession.

**Lateran Palace,** or **Lateran.** Palace in Rome that was once the home of the popes. It was destroyed by fire in 1308.

**Latifundia** (singular *latifundium*). A large estate, especially one devoted to agriculture and worked by slaves, in ancient Rome. Many of the *latifundia* eventually found their way into the control of the Church.

**Loggia.** Roofed structure, usually open on one side and flanked with pillars, serving as a sheltered gallery.

**Lombards** (also known as Longobards). A Germanic people who settled in northern Italy after 568, making many conquests of Italian territories.

**Machiavelli, Niccolò** (1469–1527). Italian political philosopher. After holding high political office in Florence he was exiled by the ruling Medici dynasty on suspicion of conspiracy, but later recovered some measure of official favor. His most famous work is *The Prince*, a political treatise advising secular rulers on the acquisition and use of power. He maintained that effective wielding of this power might require the use of unethical methods, in other words that "the end justifies the means." Machiavelli's

pragmatic, blunt attitude to politics led to the coining of the adjective "Machiavellian" to denote a manipulative, amoral person – particularly a politician.

**Margravate.** The domain of a margrave, a German prince, especially in the ***Holy Roman Empire***.

**Medici.** Mercantile Italian dynasty prominent in the 15th, 16th and 17th centuries; they ruled over Florence and Tuscany but had an influence on European history that extended far beyond the boundaries of Italy. Among the prominent members of the clan were Catherine de' Medici (1519–1589, who became queen of France as wife to Henry II), Cosimo I (1519–1574, known as Cosimo the Great, duke of Florence and first grand duke of Tuscany), and Lorenzo de' Medici (1449–1492, who was known as Lorenzo the Magnificent, a noted Renaissance patron).

**Merovingians.** Frankish dynasty founded by Clovis I, which ruled Gaul and parts of western Germany from approximately 500 to 751.

**Minnesong.** Type of German lyric poetry popular in the 12th to 14th centuries. Its exponents were called minnesingers.

**Nicaea,** First Council of. First ecumenical council of the Church, convened by Emperor Constantine in 325.

*Breakfast in the Garden of Massimiliano Sforza, Castello Sforzesco, Milan*

**Octopartite.** Having eight parts. Used especially in architecture, e.g. in the context of an eight-sided vault.

**Ostrogoths.** Tribe of Eastern Goths that set up a kingdom in Italy from 493 to 552.

**Parapet.** Low wall at the edge of a balcony, ramp, terrace, roof, etc. In non-defensive structures they are sometimes quite ornate, but their primary function is to prevent people from falling over the edge of the structure.

**Parian.** Descriptive term for a fine white marble mined on the Greek island of Paros in ancient times, but sometimes used to refer to any particularly high-quality whitish marble used for statuary.

**Parthenopian Republic.** Short-lived local republic established in Naples in 1797 during the era of Napoleonic rule.

**Peasants' War** (1524–1525). Violent uprising that started among the peasantry in Bavaria and spread to other German lands. The peasants had a number of demands, social and political, drawn up in a list of "12 articles." The rebellion was ruthlessly crushed.

**Pediment.** Low-pitched gable, usually triangular.

**Penance.** One of the sacraments of the Roman Catholic Church. The general meaning of the word is a voluntary atonement or punishment undertaken by the sinner to atone for sin. According to Church doctrine repentant sinners are absolved on confession of their sins to a priest, and on completion of the penance prescribed.

**Pentangular.** Having five angles.

**Purgatory.** A place of punishment in the afterlife, a transitional realm between earth and heaven. Catholics believe that after death worthy souls undergo a period of purification in Purgatory before the Last Judgment, when they will ascend to heaven. Protestants reject the concept of Purgatory.

**Quadriga.** A two-wheeled chariot drawn by four horses harnessed abreast.

**Quattrocento.** Literally "four hundred": the 15th century. Used particularly in the context of Italian literature and visual arts from this period.

**Rampart.** In a defensive structure, a thick wall with a platform or ramp on top surrounded by a parapet.

**Ravelin.** An outwork with two angled embankments.

**Reconquista** (Reconquest). 700-year process by which the Muslim Arabs, or Moors, were ousted from the Iberian Peninsula, which they had conquered in the 8th century. The Muslim territories were slowly eroded until the last Moorish stronghold – Granada, in southern Spain – was captured in January 1492 by the forces of the kingdoms of Castile and Aragon.

**Reformation.** A major religious movement that started in Germany in 1517 at the instigation of Martin Luther, aimed at altering the practice and doctrines of the Roman Catholic Church. It ultimately led to the establishment of the Protestant Churches.

**Romanesque.** Term used to describe forms from Roman architecture (round arches, piers, columns, vaults) that were used in European building in the early Middle Ages. The adjective covers the period from around 1000 (in France; later elsewhere) until the mid-13th century. The Romanesque eventually gave way to the *Gothic*, and there were various different national inflections of style and approach. Romanesque architecture flourished particularly in Burgundy, Normandy, northern Italy and Tuscany. Characteristic of Romanesque architecture is its practice of structuring the whole through the addition of individual, plastically composed elements as well as the interplay of cylindrical and cuboid forms.

**Savonarola, Girolamo** (1452–1498). Reforming Dominican preacher who denounced the worldliness and corruption of the Florentines and the Church. He briefly gained power in the city but was ultimately hanged for heresy.

**Schism.** Division of a group into two opposing factions, specifically in the context of the Church. The term is used most commonly to refer to the break between the Western and Eastern churches in 1054, and also to the period from 1378 to 1417 during which the Western Roman Catholic Church was itself divided by the election of rival antipopes.

**Scriptorium.** Room in a monastery or other religious house set up for copying classical texts by hand. In the 15th century secular *scriptoria* were established as well, especially in university towns.

**Scudo.** An old Italian silver coin.

Cassioli Amos (1832–1891), *Lorenzo de' Medici*, Coll. Chigi Saracini, Siena

**Sforza.** Family that ruled Milan from 1450 to 1535. The Sforza dynasty was founded by Giacomuzzo Sforza, a *condottiere*.

**Shawm.** A kind of oboe originating in the Middle Ages.

**Swiss Guard.** Corps of soldiers who guard the papal palace. It was established by Pope Julius II (1503–1513) and its members are still recruited from Switzerland and wear their traditional costume.

**Templars** ("Knights Templar"). One of the two major chivalric orders of the Middle Ages. Founded in 1118 with the original aim of protecting pilgrims to the Holy Land, it was given its rule in 1128. The order became increasingly wealthy and influential, functioning much as a bank in its later years.

**Tercios.** A Spanish infantry regiment of 3,000 men: 1,500 pikemen, 1,000 swordsmen and 500 harquebusiers, or soldiers equipped with an old-fashioned long-barreled gun called an arquebus.

**Transubstantiation.** Roman Catholic belief that after being consecrated, the "substance" or inner reality of the Eucharist becomes sacramentally the body and blood of Christ. The "accidents," or physical characteristics thereof, remain unchanged.

**Travertine.** Porous rock used extensively in building.

**Trecentro.** Literally "three hundred": the 14th century. Used particularly in the context of Italian literature and visual arts from this period.

**Trent, Council of.** General council called by the pope to discuss disciplinary reform in the Church, as well as matters of dogma. It spearheaded the counter reformation by clarifying many points of doctrine and practice. It fell into three periods: 1545–1547, 1551–1552 and 1562–1563.

**Tridentine.** Referring to the *Council of Trent*.

**Usury.** In contemporary use, the practice of loaning money at an exorbitantly high rate of interest. In early times, it simply meant money lending in general.

**Veduta.** An accurately rendered landscape or cityscape, especially in Italian art.

**Via Emilia.** Famous Roman road leading from Rimini on the Adriatic Sea to Piacenza, through Forlí, Faenza, Imola, Bologna, Modena, Parma and many other major Italian towns. The road was constructed in about 187 B.C. under the supervision of the Roman consul M. Aemilius Lepidus, after whom it is named.

**Visconti.** The ruling family of Milan from 1277 to 1447.

**Visigoths.** Western Gothic tribe that sacked Rome in 410.

**Waldensians or Waldenses.** A 12th-century heretical sect that arose in northern Italy and the French Alps. Its members wanted to return to the pure state of the very early Church.

# Important popes

**A chronological selection**

## Leo I (the Great) (440–461)

Originally from Tuscany, Leo's name is associated with the legend narrated by the chronicler Paul the Deacon (c. 720– c. 800) of his mission to the Hun king Attila, to persuade him to abandon his takeover of the Po region. Following the encounter with Leo, Attila did indeed give up the idea of invading Italy and conquering Rome. In a time of anarchy and the collapse of the Roman Empire, the pontificate of Leo strengthened the supremacy of the Church, not only over the warlike transalpine peoples such as the Huns or Gaiseric's Vandals, but also the numerous Christian heresiarchs of the East. Leo was among those who initiated the Council of Chalcedon in 451, which was intended to confirm the statutes of the First Council of Nicaea.

## Pelagius II (579–590)

Rome was besieged by the Lombards during Pelagius's pontificate. Though he managed to arrange an armistice with the Lombard leader Authari (585–589), he was unable to prevent the destruction of the monastery of Monte Cassino by the Benevento Lombards. Pelagius fell victim to the plague epidemic that ravaged Rome in 589.

## Gregory I (the Great) (590–604)

Gregory came from a celebrated Roman patrician family, the gens Anicia, that had been converted to Christianity some generations earlier. Gregory first appeared as a prefect of Rome, but left this office c. 575, distributed his wealth among the poor and withdrew into a monastery. He later came to the fore by founding the monastery of Sant'Andrea and numerous monasteries in Sicily, where his family possessed extensive *latifundia*. From 579 to 585, he occupied the office of a papal representative at the imperial court in Constantinople. His election as pope in 590 is associated with the miraculous ending of the plague that raged in Rome and his vision of the Archangel Michael over Hadrian's mausoleum. He distinguished himself as a model administrator of Church property and a remarkable organizer of Church structures. He succeeded in stabilizing relations with the Frankish Merovingian dynasty, granted the Jews religious freedom, promoted the establishment of welfare institutions and founded the famous choir school named after him.

## Stephen II (752–757)

During Stephen's pontificate, the Roman Church finally split from Constantinople and allied itself with the Carolingian rulers. To achieve the latter, Stephen went personally to Pepin's court to crown him king of the Franks. During Stephen's term of office, the papal chancery forged a document known as the Donation of Constantine, which was intended to provide historical legitimacy for the papacy and the Frankish empire. It also divided up between them the Italian territories that were subject to the Lombards or Constantinople. The document enabled the Roman Church to gain formal powers for a time.

## Leo III (795–816)

Brought up in poverty, Leo III was the first pope following the collapse of the Lombard empire. He promised loyalty and obedience to Charlemagne, who in return offered the Church protection. In 799, Leo was wounded and taken prisoner following a conspiracy by the Roman nobility. After being liberated by the duke of Spoleto, he fled to the king of the Franks, who had him escorted back to Rome.

In 800, Leo crowned Charlemagne Holy Roman Emperor there. Leo was also notable for his grand design for the walls of the "Leonine City," though construction was actually carried out by Leo IV (see below).

## Leo IV (847–855)

Leo's term of office coincided with the Saracen campaigns of conquest, which constituted a grave threat to Rome. Leo IV looked to the defenses of his territory and had the Vatican and Castel Sant' Angelo enclosed in a defensive wall to form the Leonine City. To counter the Saracen threat, he set up an alliance with the coastal cities of Amalfi, Gaeta and Naples, which swore an oath of loyalty in the Lateran and in 849 defeated the pirates in Ostia. In addition, Leo devoted himself to the spread of Gregorian chant.

## Gregory VII (1073–1085)

Even before St. Hildebrand of Soana was elected pope as Gregory VII, he had played an important part in Church reform. The main thrust of his ecclesiastical policy was to insist on the superiority of the Church over every other power,

install a strict hierarchy of the clergy, including a stringent demarcation from the laity, and close control of priestly and episcopal celibacy. A notable feature of his rule was the famous conflict with the Saxon emperor Henry IV over the question of lay investiture. In 1084, Henry IV declared himself ruler of Rome and confined the pope in the Castel Sant' Angelo. The Norman adventurer Robert Guiscard freed him, but in consequence the pope had to follow him to Salerno, where he died shortly after. He was canonized in 1606.

## Anacletus II (1130–1138)

A member of the powerful Roman family of Corleoni, Anacletus became a target of hostility because of his Jewish origins. Even today he is ranked among the antipopes. Nevertheless, he had the support of the Normans in southern Italy and shortly after his accession crowned Roger II king of Sicily.

## Innocent III (1198–1216)

As the scion of the great family of the counts of Segni, young Lotario de' Conti studied theology in Paris and law in Bologna before being elected pope at the age of 38. His theocratic papal policy picked up where Gregory VII had left off, insisting on the right of the Church to interfere not just in religious matters but all political questions. After the death of the Hohenstaufen emperor Henry VI in 1197 and his wife Constance d'Hauteville, queen of Sicily, in 1198, Innocent III became tutor and protector of the young Frederick II and confirmed him in his right to the imperial throne. However, relations between the young Hohenstaufen emperor and the pope deteriorated rapidly into hideously bitter conflict. The pope's successors continued the quarrel until the death of the emperor in 1250.

## Martin IV (1281–1285)

Simon de Brion or de Brie was elected pope following the intervention of Charles of Anjou. In return, he was to give the secular ruler his unconditional support. As Charles was also a Roman senator, he had the pope on his side in 1282 at the start of the bloody uprising against the Angevins in Sicily, known as the Sicilian Vespers. Because he favored the Angevins, Martin IV always had to live outside Rome, in Orvieto or Montefiascone. In his *Purgatory*, Dante spread the story that this greedy pope died of indigestion after eating eels.

### Celestine V (1294)

Born Pietro da Morróne, Celestine was in office for just five months. He had previously lived in the seclusion of a hermitage, founding the monastic congregation of hermits of St. Damian on Monte Maiella near Sulmona. Its members were called Celestines after him. After a two-year conclave he was elected pope, but soon fell victim to political intrigue and conspiracies. Only five months into his pontificate the venerable but unworldly 80-year-old pope resigned, the only pope in history to do so. Dante accused him of cowardice, but Petrarch praised him as a true saint.

### Boniface VIII (1294–1303)

Benedetto Caetani came from a noble Roman family. He became pope on Christmas Eve 1294, in the teeth of opposition from the powerful Colonna family. As a noted expert on canonical law, his chief preoccupation was with relationships with the emerging national monarchies of Europe. His opponents were James II of Aragon, the German, English and Hungarian

kings and, most of all, Philip the Fair of France. Boniface issued two bulls against him in an attempt to assert the secular as well as spiritual supremacy of the papacy. Philip initially tried via his legal adviser, Guillaume de Nogaret, to get the pope to call a council. Then he forged an alliance with the Colonnas and had the pope captured at his residence in Anagni. Legend has it that during his days in captivity there Boniface was forced to endure all kinds of blows and humiliations. On returning to Rome he died without being capable of any further political action. His major act was to nominate 1300 a jubilee year, the first such year.

### Clement V (1305–1314)

Bertrand de Got had previously been Bishop of Bordeaux. He was the first in the long series of French popes that conceded the decisive power over the fate of the Church to the French monarchy. In order to keep the papacy under his control, Philip the Fair had induced Pope Clement V to move the seat of the Church to

Avignon. Announced in 1308, the decision was put into effect the following year.

### Gregory XI (1370–1378)

A French pope who was born Pierre-Roger de Beaufort and was a nephew of Clement VI, Gregory finally moved the papacy back to Rome for good. He crushed the revolt in the Papal States with military force, and placed an interdict on Florence despite vain attempts by St. Catherine of Florence to intercede. At the end of 1377 he returned to Rome, and died there before the rebellious papal territories could be pacified.

### Urban VI (1378–1389)

The Neapolitan Bartolomeo Prignano was elected pope a year after the return from Avignon, in response to pressure from the Roman populace, who demanded a Roman or at least an Italian pope. His accession marked the beginning of a grave and sustained crisis in the course of which an illegal conclave was called and an antipope elected. This led to the great schism that generated military conflict in the Church lands and in Rome itself.

### Sixtus IV (1471–1484)

As pope, the former Minorite monk Francesco della Rovere stubbornly pursued a policy of developing the papacy's secular power, while at the same time extending the power of his own family; creating new principalities and city governorships which he

awarded to members of his family. To attain these objectives he employed all means available to a political prince of the Renaissance. The key office of cardinal was conferred on his nephew Giuliano della Rovere, later Pope Julius II, and his son Pietro Riario. His other son, Girolamo Riario, was appointed commander-in-chief of the papal troops. Sixtus and Girolamo together instigated the conspiracy to murder Lorenzo and Guiliano de' Medici.

### Alexander VI (1492–1503)

Following the course set by Sixtus IV, the installation of the Spanish Rodrigo Borgia brought the scandal of papal lust for power to its peak, because only corruption was able to ease this

candidate into office. When the political balance of Italy and Europe fell into a state of grave crisis, Alexander used the power of the Church to establish independent political rule, which he transferred to his son Cesare Borgia. Unlike even the worst of his pre-decessors and successors among the Renaissance popes, he manifested not the least sign of piety or interest in the true spiritual affairs of the Church.

### Julius II (1503–1513)

The ecclesiastical career of Giuliano della Rovere began in the shadow of his uncle, Pope Sixtus IV. He was elected unanimously after the briefest of conclaves. His aim was to strengthen the Church after its position had been undermined by the Borgia pope Alexander VI. He was a

very energetic man who followed political developments attentively, and sought to weld all the territories of the Papal States into a single entity as the dominant power of the Italian peninsula. In pursuance of this objective, between 1506 and 1511 he recaptured the Marches and the Romagna, subdued Perugia and Bologna and occupied Modena and Mirandola. The pope himself fought personally at the head of his troops. He also dedicated himself to reorganizing the Church's finances and extending trade, which left maximum freedom of operation to Jewish merchants. It was Pope Julius II who launched the rebuilding of St. Peter's, commissioned the frescoes for the Sistine Chapel from Michelangelo and the paintings of the Stanze in the Vatican from Raphael. During his term of office, artists such as Bramante, Pinturicchio and Sansovino worked for him in Rome.

### Leo X (1513–1521)

As second son of Lorenzo the Magnificent, Giovanni de' Medici had been earmarked for an ecclesiastical career from early childhood. For powerful Florentine families, control over the office of pope was the only way to settle the longstanding conflicts with the Church. The

principal influences on the young man were the most famous Florentine representatives of the Neo-platonic philosophical movement. Only much later did he devote himself to his studies of theology and canonical law. After the turbulent years when the Medici were driven out of Florence and the Florentine republic, his appointment as pope contributed greatly to the consolidation of Medici rule over the city.

# Select bibliography

## Rome, the papacy, and the Church-state

**H. Fuhrmann:** *Von Petrus zu Johannes Paul II*, Munich 1980
**F. Gregorovius:** *Geschichte der Stadt Rom im Mittelalter*, Darmstadt 1957
**C. Hoeffler:** *Don Rodrigo Borja*, Vienna 1889
**G. Di Meglio:** *Carlo V e Clemente VII*, Milan 1970
**R. Morghen:** *Gregorio VII e la riforma della Chiesa nel secolo XI*, Rome 1974
**G. Müller:** *Die römische Kurie und die Reformation 1523–1534*, Gütersloh 1969
**P. Partner:** *The Lands of St. Peter*, London 1972
**B. Schimmelpfennig:** *Das Papsttum*, Darmstadt 1984

## Genoa, Pisa, Sardinia, and the Mediterranean

**E. Ashtor:** *The Levant Trade in the Later Middle Ages*, Princeton 1983
**R. Borchardt:** *Pisa*. Ein Versuch, Stuttgart 1960
**E.H. Byrne:** *Genoese Shipping*, New York 1930
**C. Casula:** 'Castelli e fortezze', in: *Atlante della Sardegna*, Rome 1980
**G. Francesco:** *Storici arabi delle Crociate*, Turin 1987
**A. Frugoni:** *Le repubbliche marinare*, Turin 1963
**D. Gioffre:** *Il mercato degli schiavi a Genova nel secolo XV*, Genoa 1971
**D. Herlihy:** *Pisa in the Early Renaissance*, Yale 1958
**J. La Roncière:** *La découverte de l'Afrique au Moyen-Age*, Cairo 1925
**B. Lewis:** *The Assassins*, London 1967
**R.S. Lopez:** *Storia delle colonie genovesi nel Mediterraneo*, Genoa 1998
**R.S. Lopez:** *Benedetto Zaccaria, ammiraglio e mercante nella Genova del Duecento*, Florence 1996
**A. Arribas Palau:** *La conquista de Cerdeña por Jaime II. de Aragón*, Barcelona 1952
**S. Petrucci:** *Re in Sardegna, a Pisa cittadini*, Bologna 1988
**S. Runciman:** *A History of the Crusades*, Cambridge 1951–1954
**M. Schwob:** *La croisade des enfants*, Paris 1895
**P. Tafur:** *Andanças é viajes por diversas partes del mundo avidos*, Madrid 1874
**M. Tangheroni:** *Politica, commercio, agricoltura a Pisa nel Trecento*, Pisa 1973

## Prehistoric buildings in Sardinia

**G. Lilliu:** *Il nuraghe di Barumini e la stratigrafia nuragica*, Cagliari 1955
**H. Müller-Karpe:** *Handbuch der Vorgeschichte*, Munich 1968

## The Tuscan hinterland: Lucca, Siena, and Florence

**R. von Albertini:** *Das florentinische Staatsbewusstsein im Übergang von der Republik zum Prinzipat*, Berne 1955
**C. Barbagallo:** *Dante Alighieri, i Bianco-Ghibellini esuli e i Romena*, Rome 1899
**P. Cammarosano:** *Monteriggioni*, Milan 1983
**R. Cantagalli:** *La guerra di Siena*, Siena 1962

**J. Cleugh:** *The Medici*, New York 1975
**R. Davidsohn:** *Geschichte von Florenz*, 4 vols., Berlin 1896–1927
**L. Douglas:** *Storia politica e sociale della Repubblica di Siena*, Rome 1969
**M. Ferrari:** *La congiura dei pazzi*, Rome 1945
**A. Mancini:** *Storia di Lucca*, Lucca 1981
**Y. Milo:** *Political Opportunism in Guidi Tuscan Policy*, Pisa 1981
**P. Miquel:** *Les guerres de religion*, Paris 1980
**B. de Monluc:** *Commentaires 1521–1576*, vol. III, Paris 1981
**R. Pauli:** *Das Regnum Italiae in ottonischer Zeit*, Tübingen 1982
**E. Pellegrini:** *La caduta della Repubblica di Siena*, Siena 1991
**C. De Seta and J. Le Goff:** *La città e le mura*, Bari 1989
**M. Viroli:** *Il sorriso di Niccolò*, Rome 1998
**E.E. Whipple:** *A Famous Corner of Italy*, London 1928

## The episcopal principality of Trento (Trent) and the Counter-Reformation

**H. Decker-Hauff:** *Gärten und Schicksale, historische Stätten und Gestalten in Italien*, Stuttgart 1992
**A. Gorfer:** *Guida dei castelli del Trentino*, Trento 1967
**J. Guenther:** 'Bernhard von Cles', in: *Contemporaries of Erasmus*, Toronto, Buffalo and London 1985
**H. Jedin:** *Geschichte des Konzils von Trient*, 5 vols., Freiburg, Basle and Vienna 1982
**G. von Pölnitz:** *Anton Jacob Fugger*, Tübingen 1958–1963
**A. Prosperi:** *Tribunali della coscienza*, Turin 1996

## Ferrara and the d'Este

**R. Bacchelli:** *La congiura di don Giulio d'Este*, Milan 1943
**G. Bertoni and E.P. Vicini:** *Il castello di Ferrara ai tempi di Niccolò III*, Bologna 1907
**T. Dean:** *Land and Power in Late Medieval Ferrara*, Cambridge 1988
**W.L. Gundersheimer:** *Ferrara. The Style of a Renaissance Despotism*, Princeton 1973
**G. Medri:** *Il volto di Ferrara nella cerchia antica*, Rovigo 1963
**F. Pezza:** *Il maestro Bartolino da Novara*, Mortara 1934

## Milan and the Sforza

**B. Belotti:** *Il dramma di Gerolamo Olgiati*, Milan 1929
**P. Blastenbrei:** *Die Sforza und ihr Heer*, Heidelberg 1987
**A. Colombo:** 'L'ingresso di Francesco Sforza in Milano e l'inizio di un nuovo principato', in: *Archivio storico lombardo*, vol. XXXII, 1905
**Ph. de Commynes:** *Mémoires*, Paris 1924
**H. Kühner:** *Caterina Sforza*, Zürich and Stuttgart 1957
**F. Malaguzzi Valeri:** *La corte di Ludovico il Moro*, Milan 1913–1923
**L.G. Pélissier:** *Louis XII et Ludovico Sforza*, Paris 1896

## Naples, Palermo, and the kingdom of Sicily

**D. Abulafia:** 'The end of Muslim Sicily', in: *Muslims under Latin Rule, 1100–1300*, Princeton 1990

**D. Abulafia:** *The Two Italies. Economic Relations between the Norman Kingdom of Sicily and the Northern Communes*, Cambridge 1977
**D. Abulafia:** *Frederick the Second. A Medieval Emperor*, London 1988
**D. Abulafia:** *The French Descent into Renaissance Italy, 1494–1495. Antecedents and Effects*, Aldershot 1995
**G. Agnello:** *L'architettura aragonese-catalana in Italia*, Palermo 1969
**M. Amari:** *La guerra del vespro siciliano*, vol. III, Florence 1872
**G. Bellafiore:** *Architettura in Sicilia nelle età islamica e normanna (827–1194)*, Palermo 1990
**K.J. Beloch:** *Campanien*, Berlin 1879
**K.J. Beloch:** *Bevölkerungsgeschichte Italiens*, 3 vols., Berlin and Leipzig 1937–1961
**T.N. Bisson:** *The Medieval Crown of Aragon. A Short History*, Oxford 1986
**L. Bruhns:** *Hohenstaufenschlösser*, Königstein im Taunus 1959
**B. Croce:** *Storia del Regno di Napoli*, Bari 1931
**L. Dufour and A. La Gumina:** *Imago Siciliae. Cartografia storica della Sicilia: 1420-1860*, Catania 1999
**N.F. Faraglia:** *Storia della regina Giovanna II d'Angiò*, Lanciano 1904; *Friderici Romanorum Imperatori Secundi (Frederick II, Holy Roman Emperor): De arte venandi cum avibus*, Graz 1969
**V. Gleijeses:** *La storia di Napoli*, Naples 1990
**H. Götze:** *Castel del Monte. Gestalt und Symbol der Architektur Friedrichs II.*, Munich 1984
**F. Gregorovius:** *Castel del Monte*, Leipzig 1880
**P. Herde:** *Karl I. von Anjou*, Stuttgart 1979
**H. Houben:** *Roger II. von Sizilien. Herrscher zwischen Orient und Okzident*, Darmstadt 1997
**E. Kantorowicz:** *Kaiser Friedrich der Zweite*, Berlin 1927
**Y. Labande-Maillfert:** *Charles VIII. La jeunesse au pouvoir (1470-1495)*, Paris 1975
**E.G. Léonard:** *Les Angevins de Naples*, Paris 1954
**F. Maurici:** *Castelli medievali in Sicilia. Dai bizantini ai normanni*, Palermo 1992
**J.C. Rovira:** *Humanistas y poetas en la corte napolitana de Alfonso el Magnánimo*, Alicante 1990
**S. Runciman:** *The Sicilian Vespers*, Cambridge 1958
**A. Ryder:** *The Kingdom of Naples under Alfonso the Magnanimous*, Oxford 1975
**F.W. Schirrmacher:** *Die letzten Hohenstaufen*, Göttingen 1871
**L. Sciascia:** *Le donne e i cavalieri, gli affanni e gli agi. Famiglia e potere in Sicilia tra XII. e XIV. secolo*, Messina 1993

## The *condottieri* in the Renaissance

**W. Block:** *Die Condottieri. Studien über die sogenannten unblutigen Schlachten*, Berlin 1913
**J.J. Deiss:** *Captains of Fortune: Profiles of Six Italian Condottieri*, Gollancz 1966
**E. Ricotti:** *Storia delle compagnie di ventura*, Turin 1844
**A. Semerau:** *Die Condottieri*, Jena 1909

## Military architecture

**A. Cassi Ramelli:** *Dalle caverne ai rifugi blindati. Trenta secoli di architettura militare*, Milan 1964
**B. Ebhardt:** *Die Burgen in Italien*, 6 vols., Berlin 1917–1927

# Index

**Page 332:** lh col., above
Solimena, Francesco (1657–1747) *The Meeting between Pope Leo and Attila* (detail) Leo I, oil on canvas, Pinacoteca di Brera, Milan

**Page 332:** lh col., below
Antonello da Messina (*c*. 1430–1479) *Polyptych* (detail) Gregory I (the Great), oil on canvas, Museo Nazionale, Messina

**Page 332:** center col., above
School of Raphael *Coronation of Charlemagne* (detail) Leo III, fresco, Stanze di Raffaello, Vatican, Rome

**Page 332:** center col., below
Anonymous *Gregory VII* (detail), wood engraving, *c*. 1880, from a drawing by Otto Knille

**Page 332:** rh col., center
Anonymous *Pope Innocent III Shows the Monastery the Foundation Bull* (detail), fresco, Sacro Speco, Subiaco

**Page 333:** lh col., above
Anonymous *Pope Boniface VIII Proclaims the Jubilee Year* (detail), post 1300, fresco, San Giovanni in Laterano, Rome

**Page 333:** lh col., below
Anonymous *Triumph of St. Thomas Aquinas* (detail) Clement V, fresco, Santa Maria Novella, Florence

**Page 333:** center col., center
Melozzo da Forlì (1438–1494) *Sixtus IV Appoints Bartolomeo Platina Prefect of the Biblioteca Vaticana* (detail) Sixtus IV, fresco, Pinacoteca, Musei Vaticani, Rome

**Page 333:** center col., below
Bernardino di Betto (Pinturicchio) *Resurrection* (detail) Alexander VI, fresco, Appartamento Borgia, Vatican, Rome

**Page 333:** rh. col., above
Raphael (1483–1520) *Bolsena Fair* (detail) Julius II, fresco, Stanze di Raffaello, Vatican, Rome

**Page 333:** rh. col., below
Bronzino (1503–1572) *Leo X* (detail), Museo Mediceo, Palazzo Medici Riccardi, Florence

## Picture and map credits

The publisher thanks museums, collectors, libraries and photographers for granting permission to reproduce copyright material and their support in helping us to produce this book. The editors and publishers have made every effort up to the close of production to discover all other owners of illustration copyright. Persons and institutions that may not have been contacted and claim rights in illustrations used are asked to contact the publishers.
All photographs © Könemann Verlagsgesellschaft mbH, Cologne/Photo: Markus Bollen, Bensberg
With the exception of:
A.P.T., Lucca (97); Architetta Elena Buonfrate, Turin (179); Archiv für Kunst und Geschichte, Berlin (33, 45 above, 219 above, 220, 221, 224, 225, 295, 305, 314, 334 center below); Archivi Alinari, Florence (14, 73, 121, 124 left, 289); Archivio Arnoldo Mondadori Editore, Milan (141); Archivio Fotografico della Soprintendenza per i Beni Artistici e Storici di Modena e Reggio Emilia (156); Archivio Fotografico della Soprintendenza ai Beni Culturali della Regione Autonoma Valle d'Aosta, Aosta (105); Archivio di Stato, Lucca, Fondo Stampe (91 above, 93); Archivio di Stato, Parma (161); Archivio di Stato di Siena (72, 88); Archivio Storico Odescalchi, Bracciano (185 above); Archivio Vasari, Rome – photo: E. Ghilardi, Lucca (96); Artothek, Peissenberg – photo: Hans Hinz (57); Nicolò Orsi Battaglini, Florence (41, 82, 137 above); Bayerische Staatsbibliothek, Munich (76, 92); Biblioteca Ambrosiana, Milan (127); Biblioteca Apostolica Vaticana, Vatican City (324, 325 below) – photo: E. Noack, Cologne (172 above, 173); Biblioteca Estense, Modena (261); Biblioteca Nazionale Vittorio Emanuele III, Naples – photo: Massimo Velo (191 above); Biblioteca Trivulziana, Milan (118 above); Bibliothèque Nationale de France, Paris (62, 99, 104, 191 below); Bildarchiv Foto Marburg (246 above right, 293); Bildarchiv Preussischer Kulturbesitz, Berlin (81) – photo: Jörg P. Anders (170); Bridgeman Art Library, London (113 below); British Library, London (78 above, 80 right, 139, 234, 245, 246 above left, 276 below, 280, 283, 327, 328); The British Museum, London (218 above); Castello Odescalchi, Bracciano (188, 189 above); Civica Raccolta delle Stampe Achille Bertarelli, Castello Sforzesco, Milan (120 left); Martin Classen (216 below, 226, 227); Collection Viollet, Paris (87); Comune di Foligno (108); Carlo Delfino Editore, Sassari (266, 272 above, 273); Editions Mengès, Paris – photo: Robert Polidori (130); Elemond, Milan (151, 154, 155); Fotogramma, Bari (319, 320 below, 322, 323); Galleria d'Arte Antica e Moderna, Florence (190); Galleria Nazionale, Parma (164 above); © Giraudon, Paris (80 left, 276 above); Ernesto Greci, Parma (164 below); Claus Hansmann, Munich (8/9); Istituto Terziarie Francescane Beata Angelina, Foligno (101); Andrea Jemolo, Rome (6/7); © Könemann Verlagsgesellschaft mbH, Cologne/map, diagram: Peter Frese, Munich (77 above and center, 268, 269 above, 285 below)/© Andromeda, Oxford Limited, 1983 (12)/from Herbert de Caboga-Stuber, Kleine Burgenkunde, Bonn: Schroeder, 1961 (78 below)/from Giovanni Lilliu, Raimondo Zucca, Su Nuraxi di Barumini, Sassari: Carlo Delfino Editore, no date. (269 below)/photo: Andrea Jemolo (8, 10, 11, 15, 22, 2431, 34)/map, diagram: Rolli Arts, Essen (66, 118 below, 176, 201 below, 310 below, 320 above)/Studio für Landkartentechnik, Norderstedt (326); Musée Condé, Chantilly (276); Kunsthistorisches Museum, Vienna (157); Lensini – Archivio di Opere d'Arte, Siena (84 below); Metropolitan Museum of Art, Elisha Whittelsey Collection, Elisha Whittelsey Fund, 1949 [49.95.1022] (74 right); Ministero dei Beni e le Attività Culturali, Firenze – photo: E. Noack, Cologne (67); Museo Civico Medievale, Bologna – photo: C.N.B. & C. (100); Museu de Arte de São Paulo – photo: Luiz Hosaka (217); Museum Allerheiligen, Schaffhausen, Peyersche Tobias Stimmer Stiftung-Stiftung (248); Eduard Noack, Cologne (32, 36, 56 center, 74 left); Oronoz, Madrid (114 above); Österreichische Nationalbibliothek, Vienna (103, 193); Parrocchia di San Sigismondo re e martire Cremona – photo: Paolo Quiresi (123); Luciano Pedicini/Archivio dell'Arte, Naples (47 above, 288, 304); Lothar M. Peter, Berlin (38/39, 48); Pierpont Morgan Library, New York – photo: Art Resource, New York (109); Jens Rademacher, Hamburg (77 below); Ragazzini, Rome (309, 310 above); Rheinisches Bildarchiv, Cologne (244); RMN, Paris – photo: Gérard Blot (292 left); Royal Collection Picture Library © HM Queen Elizabeth I (115); SCALA group S.p.A., Antella/Florence (13, 16, 17, 18, 20, 23, 35, 37, 46, 53, 66, 68, 69, 79, 86, 89, 98, 102, 107, 120 right, 122, 124 right, 125, 126, 128, 129, 131, 135, 136, 140, 142, 143, 144, 145, 146 below, 147, 150, 153 below, 160 above, 163, 165, 166/167, 168 below, 169, 172 below, 186/187, 192, 194, 195, 216 above, 218 below, 222, 232, 233 below, 241, 243, 246 below, 255 below, 263, 264, 274, 275, 281, 292 right, 298, 300, 312, 313, 316, 329, 330, 331, 334 except center below, 335); Servizio Beni Culturali Ufficio Castello del Buonconsiglio Monumenti e Collezioni Provinciali, Trento (198, 208); Società Siciliana per la Storia Patria, Palermo – photo: Publifoto (299); Staatliche Museen zu Berlin–Bildarchiv Preussischer Kulturbesitz, Berlin-photo: Dietmar Katz (19); Suermondt-Ludwig-Museum, Aachen – photo: Anne Gold (247); Prof. Domenico Taddei e Associati, Florence (50); Heribert Tenschert, Bibermühle (59, 61, 63 above, 277) – photo: E. Noack, Cologne (60); Universitätsbibliothek Heidelberg (146 above, 171); Victoria & Albert Museum, London, Picture Library (249); Württembergische Landesbibliothek, Stuttgart (199 above).

## Text sources

**Dante Alighieri**, *Divine Comedy*, Canto 5, Inferno, translated by Henry Wadsworth Longfellow, published by Houghton, Mifflin and Co., Boston 1895.

© 2000 Könemann Verlagsgesellschaft mbH
Bonner Straße 126, D-50968 Cologne

Publishing and art director: Peter Feierabend
Project manager: Ute Edda Hammer
Project assistants: Jutta Buness, Jeannette Fentross, Petra Stammen, Ulla Wöhrle
Layout: Birgit Hoffmann
Picture editors: Mitra Nadjafi, Achim Heinze
Production: Mark Voges
Reproduction: CDN Pressing, Caselle di Sommacampagna (VR)

Original title: *Burgen in Italien*

© 2001 for this English edition
Könemann Verlagsgesellschaft mbH

Translation from German: Paul Aston, Heather Campion-Bye and Ruth Chitty in association with Cambridge Publishing Management
Editing: Allison McKechnie in association with Cambridge Publishing Management
Typesetting: Cambridge Publishing Management
Project management: Jackie Dobbyne and Sheila Hardie for Cambridge Publishing Management
Project coordination: Nadja Bremse-Koob and Isobel Kerr
Production: Petra Grimm
Printing and Binding: Mladinska Knjiga, Ljubljana
Printed in Slovenija

ISBN 3-8290-1578-X

10 9 8 7 6 5 4 3 2 1